To Jim
With all good wishes
Marw

Many thanks for
your assistance with
this work.
Bob Schwartz
Feb, 1966

See page 57

DISORDERS OF CARBOHYDRATE METABOLISM IN INFANCY

By

Marvin Cornblath, M.D.
Professor of Pediatrics
The University of Illinois
College of Medicine, Chicago

and

Robert Schwartz, M.D.
Associate Professor of Pediatrics
Western Reserve University
School of Medicine;
Cleveland Metropolitan General Hospital

Volume III in the Series
MAJOR PROBLEMS IN CLINICAL PEDIATRICS

ALEXANDER J. SCHAFFER
Consulting Editor

W. B. Saunders Company, Philadelphia and London, 1966

Disorders of Carbohydrate Metabolism in Infancy

Affectionately dedicated to

Joan, Nancy, Polly, Ben
and
Joyce, Alan, Murphy, Nancy

Foreword

It gives me great pleasure to introduce the third volume in the Saunders series, Major Problems in Clinical Pediatrics. The subject of the hypoglycemias has assumed ever greater importance as advance has followed advance in our understanding of this symptom. The choice of authors came as naturally as did that of Avery for newborn lung disorders and Markowitz and Kuttner for rheumatic fever.

I have known Marvin Cornblath since he came to us in Baltimore in 1953 where he served at The Sinai Hospital and The Harriet Lane Home. He left us in 1959 to go to Chicago where he was associated at first with Northwestern University Medical School and more recently with that of the University of Illinois. He is an unusually gifted pediatric clinician and an astute research scientist. Since 1956 virtually all of his energies have been directed toward problems of carbohydrate metabolism, mostly in newborn infants, and he has learned much and taught us much in this until then a virtually unexplored field.

I had not known Robert Schwartz, unfortunately, until a few years ago. After his graduation from Yale Medical School in 1947 he served sequentially in New York, Boston and, most recently, at Western Reserve University and the Metropolitan General Hospital in Cleveland, Ohio. Many of his 30 contributions to pediatric literature have been based upon original and ingenious studies of carbohydrate and fat metabolism.

The output of these two authors represents a large fraction of the new knowledge which has accumulated in this field in the past fifteen years, knowledge which is not only of theoretical importance but is immediately applicable to many clinical disorders. I feel that pediatricians the world over are fortunate that their collaboration made this volume possible.

ALEXANDER J. SCHAFFER

vii

Preface

... our first encounters with Nature's own chemical error rarely lack an element of disbelief or even indignation. Only as the fantastic complexity of our genetic-metabolic make-up dawns on us do we begin to wonder that her slips are so few. And even more slowly do we realize that they are, in fact, not nearly so few as we had imagined.

Editorial, The Lancet, September 1963, p. 619.

The disorders of carbohydrate metabolism exemplify the intimate relationship between the clinical and basic sciences. The pathogenesis of these disturbances has been elucidated and effective therapy often introduced as a result of investigations initiated in the laboratory and extended to the bedside. Unsuspected and puzzling clinical manifestations likewise have stimulated investigators to clarify and reinterpret metabolic pathways and physiological observations.

In the past three decades, this relationship has resulted in a better understanding of the genetics, biochemistry, physiology, and clinical findings of a number of diseases. New disorders have been discovered and have provided a stimulus for further research.

In this monograph, we have attempted to present our own current concepts of the normal and abnormal physiology of carbohydrate metabolism in the fetus, the pregnant mother, the neonate, and the infant. In citing references to the literature we have tried to be selective rather than comprehensive. We have tried to emphasize known facts and to relate them to the management of clinical problems of the infant as they present to the physician. Certain prejudices will be apparent in both interpretation and treatment; we hope these will serve as a stimulus to research into the many unsolved problems that yet remain.

Since each of us has followed a different path in training, we hope that the combination of our backgrounds has resulted in a comprehensive approach to the problems of carbohydrate metabolism in the newborn and infant. One of us (M. C.) became interested in these problems under the tutelage and stimulation of Alexis F. Hartmann, Carl F. Cori, Harry H. Gordon, Victor A. Najjar, and C. R. Park. The other (R. S.) was guided by Daniel C. Darrow, L. Emmett Holt, James L. Gamble, William M. Wallace, Charles S. Davidson and Charles A. Janeway; the M. D. Seminar luncheons of A. Baird Hastings were also a major stimulus. Any advance or success which results from the merging of these two pathways of training and inspiration can be attributed to the excellence of our teachers.

The pioneering investigations of Professor S. Van Creveld have been the model for all further studies and continue to stimulate research in every phase of carbohydrate metabolism. His contributions to this field over four decades have been monumental.

The authors are grateful to many for permission to use published and unpublished data. Any error in interpretation is solely our responsibility.

We wish, first, to thank Dr. Irving Schulman and Dr. Frederick C. Robbins, our department chairmen, whose encouragement and forbearance enabled us to take the time and devote the effort necessary to complete this task. Several conferences with Doctors Robert A. Ulstrom and Henry S. Sauls were invaluable in our attempt to unravel the mysteries of hypoglycemia in infancy and to present a rational approach to diagnosis and therapy. Grateful appreciation is expressed to Professors Andrea Prader and Niilo Hallman and to Doctors E. R. Froesch, S. Auricchio, R. Gitzelmann, and Robert E. Greenberg for use of their manuscripts. Thanks are also due to Doctors Sydney Segal, Giorgio Semenza, and Ira M. Rosenthal for reviewing selected chapters and to Doctors L. Stanley James, Melvin M. Grumbach, James W. Farquhar, Lula O. Lubchenco, John W. Gerrard, and W. A. Cochrane; Professors J. H. Hutchison and R. Zetterström; and Dr. M. G. Hardinge for allowing us to reproduce data and pictures and charts of their patients, some of which have not been published before.

Much of our own work that is reported in this book has been made possible through the collaboration of a number of research associates, trainees, and fellows. For their loyalty and effort we wish to thank Doctors Ephraim Y. Levin, Dimitrios Nicolopoulos, Gloria S. Baens, Susan H. Wybregt, Salomon H. Reisner, Audrey E. Forbes, Russell Snow, Paula B. Mulligan, Malcolm Bowie, Harold Gamsu, Chiung H. Chen, Michael L. McCann and Peter A. J. Adam. Their interest, stimulation, penetrating questions and enthusiasm were always important.

We gratefully acknowledge the expert secretarial assistance and devotion of Mrs. De Lores Stratten and Mrs. Marian Perez. Our thanks are expressed to Mrs. Jane Squires and Miss Gretchen Kruissink of the department of medical illustration at the University of Illinois for preparing the charts and tables. Miss Bernita A. Youngs provided the therapeutic diets in the appendix, and Miss Barbara Millar verified each reference in the bibliography. Finally, we thank Dr. Alexander Schaffer and the Saunders Company for inviting us to participate in this series of monographs.

The research studies of M. C. reported in the monograph were supported in part by a research grant (HD 00235-04) and a training grant (HD 88-02) from the National Institute of Child Health and Human Development and a research grant (6015-04) from the National Institute of Arthritis and Metabolic Disease, National Institutes of Health, United States Public Health Service, as well as by research grants from The National Foundation and the Psychiatric Training and Research Fund of the Illinois Department of Mental Health. The research of R. S. was supported by a research grant (AM 06795-02) and a training grant (TI-AM 5356-03) from the National Institute of Arthritis and Metabolic Diseases, by a Public Health Service Research Career Program Award (K3HD 1488-02) of the National Institute of Child Health and Human Development, and by grants from the Association for Aid to Crippled Children and the Cleveland Diabetes Fund.

MARVIN CORNBLATH

ROBERT SCHWARTZ

Contents

PART

I

Introduction

Chapter One

THE METABOLISM OF CARBOHYDRATE

The primary function of carbohydrate in man is to provide energy for cellular metabolism. Specific organs and tissues vary in their glucose requirement, depending upon their energy requirement and their ability to utilize other substrates as sources of energy. A variety of controlling mechanisms, including the circulation, the specific properties of the cell membrane, hormonal interrelationships and intracellular metabolism, also determine the need of specific organs for glucose. The liver is unique in its ability both to store glucose as glycogen and to provide free glucose, depending upon the availability of carbohydrate and the needs of the peripheral tissues. In contrast, the brain requires a constant supply of glucose as such. The level of glucose in the blood reflects a dynamic equilibrium between the glucose *input* from dietary sources, plus that released from the liver and kidney, and the glucose *uptake* that occurs primarily in brain, muscle and adipose tissue.

In the fetus, neonate and young infant, the rapid rate of differentiation, maturation and growth, along with the increased basal energy requirement and variable physical activity contribute to the greater caloric requirements during this dynamic period of life. In order to better explain the carbohydrate disorders of infancy, a brief discussion of the general aspects of carbohydrate metabolism is presented.

Exogenous Carbohydrate

The fetus receives glucose by continuous infusion from the mother; this glucose is his major source of energy and probably his only source of

3

carbohydrate. After birth and a period of starvation, the infant is presented with complex sugars. The breast-fed infant ingests the disaccharide lactose, whereas the formula-fed infant may be offered the disaccharides maltose and sucrose and the polysaccharide dextrin as well. With the addition of solid foods, another polysaccharide, starch, is introduced, and this ultimately becomes the major source of dietary carbohydrate.

Digestion

Although the fetus at three months has well developed digestive enzymes and continuously swallows and absorbs amniotic fluid, the relative importance of gastrointestinal absorption *in utero* as a source of energy is undetermined, but probably is not significant. After birth, lactose is hydrolyzed to glucose and galactose in the brush border of the small intestine. Similarly, sucrose is split to glucose and fructose, and maltose to two molecules of glucose. The more complex oligo- and polysaccharides are hydrolyzed to maltose and isomaltose by salivary and pancreatic amylases before final digestion by disaccharidases. If administered alone, galactose is absorbed at a faster rate than glucose, which is, in turn, more rapidly absorbed than fructose. However, if glucose and galactose are given simultaneously, the rate of galactose absorption is reduced, implying competition for a common active transport mechanism. The hydrolytic enzymes are localized in the brush border of the epithelium of the small intestine. Thus, the polysaccharides are digested in the lumen to disaccharides, which are absorbed into the brush border where they are further hydrolyzed to monosaccharides and then transported across the cell to the portal circulation.

Distribution

Of the monosaccharides that are absorbed intact into the portal circulation, almost all the galactose and a major portion of fructose are removed by the liver. The extent of uptake of glucose by the liver varies greatly and depends upon the nutritional status of the individual, the quantity of glucose and a variety of hormonal factors. Disaccharides, as such, may be absorbed in trace quantities in young infants and appear in the urine.

The distribution of glucose, whether derived from the diet or from the liver through gluconeogenesis (net synthesis of glucose from amino acids and other precursors) or glycogenolysis, is circulation-dependent. Organs which are rapidly and continuously perfused at high blood flow rates include the liver, brain, kidney and heart. Glucose diffuses into these tissues in proportion to the plasma-to-cell-concentration ratio. Insulin does not appear to control movement of glucose into the liver and brain cells.

In contrast to these rapidly perfused organs, two important controlling tissues, muscle and adipose tissue, are perfused at slower and variable rates. These tissues extract glucose from the blood at varying rates, depending also upon membrane permeability as influenced by insulin. Other slowly perfused tissues and organs, such as bone and connective tissue, do not appear to be quantitatively important to glucose metabolism. The over-all distribution of glucose is through a volume somewhat greater than that of the plasma and interstitial fluid, but much less than that of the total body water.

The major determinants of the level of glucose in the blood are the intake from the diet and the output from the liver, balanced against the uptake of the major organs: brain, heart, muscle, adipose tissue and liver. When the source of dietary carbohydrate is limited, as in starvation, the rate of uptake of glucose by muscle, adipose tissue and the heart is essentially nil, so that the major recipient of the hepatic output is the brain.

Intracellular Metabolism

In all tissues, glucose is phosphorylated to glucose-6-phosphate, which is a key intermediate for a variety of metabolic pathways. Intracellular controlling mechanisms, such as energy requirements of the cell, availability of other substrates, oxygen and hormones, determine the directions of glucose metabolism. Therefore, glucose-6-phosphate can be (1) converted to glycogen for storage; (2) metabolized by way of the glycolytic pathway to provide glycerol for fat synthesis and high energy phosphates (ATP); and (3) oxidized by way of the pentose phosphate cycle to provide reduced cofactors (TPNH) for fatty acid synthesis and pentose. In the absence of oxygen, glycolysis results mainly in lactic acid production as occurs with strenuous muscular activity. Otherwise, aerobic metabolism of pyruvate and lactate derived from glycolysis occurs with the formation of acetyl CoA, which may be synthesized into fatty acids or oxidized for energy via the Krebs citric acid cycle.

In the liver cell, in addition to the above, other pathways for glucose-6-phosphate include glucuronide formation for conjugation and the formation of free glucose through the mediation of the specific enzyme, glucose-6-phosphatase. Within these cells other unique metabolic pathways are present. Gluconeogenesis from certain amino acids and glycerol can be a significant source of glucose formation.

Hormonal Control

Many of the hormones have as one of their effects the control of glucose homeostasis, but insulin is the only hormone whose major action results in hypoglycemia. A primary effect of this hormone appears to be an increase in the permeability of muscle and fat cell membranes. Other effects include inhibition of hepatic glucose output and lipolysis, and stimulation of glycogen synthesis, lipogenesis and protein synthesis.

In contrast to insulin, the other hormones important in carbohydrate metabolism are noteworthy for their ability to increase the blood glucose. Thus, both glucagon and epinephrine activate the phosphorylase system in the liver, resulting in glycogenolysis and increased hepatic glucose output. Epinephrine, in addition, activates phosphorylase in muscle, inhibits insulin secretion and diminishes peripheral uptake of glucose. Glucocorticoids have a major effect in the liver by stimulation of gluconeogenesis. The activities of glucose-6-phosphatase, fructose-1,6-diphosphatase and phosphoenolpyruvate carboxykinase have been found to be increased after administration of these steroids. Although the specific mechanism of action of growth hormone in man is less clear, acute administration of this hormone results in elevation of the plasma free fatty acids, while prolonged administration can result in hyperglycemia.

Relationship Between Free Fatty Acids and Glucose

A close relationship exists between the metabolism of glucose and the free fatty acids. Free fatty acids may be synthesized from glucose in adipose tissue and liver and esterified with glycerol to form depot fat. In the presence of an excessive glucose supply and insulin, lipogenesis is stimulated. If intracellular glucose is limited, lipolysis occurs with the release of free fatty acids, which are bound to plasma albumin and transported for utilization in a variety of tissues, including liver, heart and muscle. Essentially, the hormones which tend to maintain the blood glucose level also increase lipolysis. It has been postulated that in the presence of elevated free fatty acids, there may be an inhibition of muscle glucose uptake and diversion of glucose from peripheral tissue to the brain. Thus, an increase in glucose production in the liver and a reduction in glucose utilization in muscle are synergistic in maintaining the substrate supply to the brain.

With the ingestion of food, the blood glucose rises, insulin is released, the hepatic output of glucose is inhibited and glycogen is stored in liver, muscle and adipose tissue. Fat synthesis occurs simultaneously. Under these conditions, the secretion of growth hormone, glucocorticoids, epinephrine and glucagon is suppressed.

On the other hand, in starvation, blood glucose slowly decreases, insulin release is suppressed and growth hormone, glucocorticoid and perhaps glucagon are secreted. Lipolysis, gluconeogenesis and glycogenolysis also occur. Clearly, the type of diet, the number of calories ingested, the amount of activity and the over-all metabolic requirements of the individual are factors which influence the level of sugar in the blood.

The purpose of this review has been to indicate the complex inter-relationships of the metabolic factors that the physician should consider in the management of disorders of carbohydrate metabolism. Details of specific biochemical events are discussed in the subsequent chapters. The reader is referred to standard texts of biochemistry for further discussion of carbohydrate metabolism.

Chapter Two

METABOLIC ADJUSTMENTS (HOMEOSTASIS) IN PREGNANCY

While the effects of labor and delivery are known to influence the immediate adjustment of the newborn infant, less well defined is the influence of maternal metabolism during pregnancy prior to labor on the infant's metabolism after birth. This chapter presents some of the current knowledge of carbohydrate metabolism during pregnancy and delivery as it affects the adaptive changes which occur in the fetus and newborn infant. The metabolism of the mother, the placenta and the fetus are reviewed separately.

There are three major ways in which the metabolism of the pregnant woman may be considered unique: (1) the metabolic changes associated with the hormonal alterations of pregnancy; (2) the effects of placental metabolism and (3) the effects of fetal metabolism. There is some question whether these phenomena can or should be sharply separated, partly because physiological studies of the pregnant woman do not permit adequate differentiation of the relative effects of these areas.

Maternal hormonal adjustment may be of major influence in early pregnancy because of the relatively small mass of the conceptus (placenta and fetus), whereas the latter assumes greater relative importance toward the end of pregnancy.

MATERNAL METABOLISM

Oral Glucose Tolerance Tests

Early studies indicated that postabsorptive blood sugar levels remained normal through pregnancy.[1] Hyperglycemia associated with

Table 1.   Glucose Tolerance Test

		Fasting	One hour	Two hours	Three hours
Mean blood sugar (mg./100 ml.)		69.3	103.6	91.7	79.4
Standard deviation		±10.4	±30.8	±25.8	±24.0
First test (2nd trimester)	Mean	69.3	94.9	85.3	73.9
Second test (3rd trimester)	Mean	69.8	111.5	93.3	82.5

meals (alimentary hyperglycemia) was both high and prolonged and was associated with glycosuria. In addition, renal glycosuria was found to be more common during pregnancy. These early studies were interpreted to suggest that the utilization of glucose was decreased in the pregnant woman, although not to the degree found in individuals with diabetes mellitus. Alternative current interpretations of the same results have emphasized the necessity for a standardized technique in performing any glucose tolerance test, including an adequate diet high in carbohydrate for 3 to 5 days preceding the test. Variably delayed gastric emptying and altered intestinal absorption also have been considered important modifying factors affecting blood sugar levels in pregnancy.

With a standardized procedure used throughout their series, Wilkerson and O'Sullivan[2, 3] re-evaluated the oral glucose tolerance test in 752 unselected pregnant women. The Somogyi-Nelson analysis of venous blood was made after each woman had been given 100 gm. of oral glucose. The results are shown in Table 1.

Since only 2.8 per cent of the sample was obtained prior to 14 weeks' gestation, the data for the first trimester are inadequate. However, repeat tests were obtained in 215 pregnant women during the second and third trimesters (Table 1). These data demonstrate the behavior of the glucose tolerance test in this phase of pregnancy. Although there is no difference in the fasting blood sugars in these patients, a progressive rise with advancing pregnancy is evident in postglucose values. Values from an individual patient, however, may show either a rise or fall with advancing pregnancy, which makes interpretation in the individual difficult.

Most studies of carbohydrate metabolism during pregnancy are confined to the second and third trimesters and do not permit adequate assessment of the influence of early pregnancy on tolerance to an oral load of glucose.

Intravenous Glucose Tolerance

In contrast to these observations on oral glucose tolerance are the studies of Burt[4] and Silverstone and associates,[5] during each trimester and also post partum, utilizing the intravenous glucose tolerance test. This test offers the advantage of eliminating gastrointestinal factors and may permit a more definitive analysis of glucose tolerance. This technique may be less physiologic than an oral glucose load; however, the advantages appear to be sufficiently great to warrant use of the test for future investigation. The studies of Silverstone et al.[5] in a larger series of pregnant women permit a more definitive interpretation of glucose metabolism during pregnancy. The tolerance tests were performed in a standardized manner by injection into an antecubital vein of 50 ml. of 50 per cent glucose within 2 minutes. Frequent, carefully timed blood samples were obtained for 60 minutes and the results used to calculate a disappearance constant (k).* The k value derived from the total glucose concentration is k_t.

Table 2.

	No.	Fasting Blood Sugar mg./100 ml.		k_t (disappearance rates) %/min.	
		Mean	S.E.	Mean	S.E.
Nonpregnant	30	65.9 $\pm$	1.2	1.67 $\pm$	0.08
First trimester	21	61.3 $\pm$	1.5	2.42 $\pm$	0.14
Second trimester	20	59.1 $\pm$	1.6	1.92 $\pm$	0.09
Third trimester	20	59.6 $\pm$	1.9	1.91 $\pm$	0.10
One week post partum	25	56.1 $\pm$	2.0	1.58 $\pm$	0.08

In an alternative method of analysis of the data from the rapid intravenous glucose tolerance tests, y may be the increment in blood glucose above the fasting level. The k value derived in this manner is referred to as k_i. In nonpregnant adults, this method of analysis is considered to be independent of the body size or the dose of glucose administered.[6] The increment rate, k_i, is numerically larger than the value k_t.

The mean data of the intravenous tolerance tests for normal pregnant women are summarized in Table 2 and should be compared with the data

* The data from 10 to 60 minutes after injection of glucose were analyzed according to the first order equation: $\log_e y = \log_e A - kt$, where y is blood glucose concentration in mg./100 ml., A is the intercept with the vertical axis and t is the lapsed time in minutes. The index of tolerance (k) may be determined from the visually fitted slope of a graph of the log of the glucose concentration against them. If two concentrations, c_1 and c_2 are obtained at times t_1 and t_2, then:

$$\frac{\log_e c_1 - \log_e c_2}{t_2 - t_1} = k$$

$$\text{or} \quad \frac{2.303 \, (\log c_1 - \log c_2)}{t_2 - t_1} = k$$

$$\text{if } c_2 = \tfrac{1}{2} c_1, \text{ then } \frac{0.693}{t_\frac{1}{2}} = k$$

$t_\frac{1}{2}$ = time interval for concentration to fall by 50 per cent
$k \times 100$ = per cent/min. rate

obtained from oral tolerance tests (Table 1). In contrast with the higher
blood sugar values observed with the oral studies, the rates of glucose
disappearance observed after intravenous injection are increased and more
rapid. In particular, the rate found in the first trimester is significantly
more rapid than that found in non-pregnant women or later in pregnancy.
These data from early pregnancy have been interpreted as consistent with
a state of physiologic hyperinsulinism. However, they have not been
adequately correlated with plasma insulin measurements.

Bleicher, O'Sullivan and Freinkel[7] studied the fasting blood sugar
level and k_t (disappearance rate) in 10 normal pregnant women carefully
selected to exclude diabetics and prediabetics. They compared third trimester tests with those done in the same patients one week post partum.
Fasting blood sugars in this small series were significantly lower in the
antepartum group (mean ± S.E.: 75.2 ± 2.77 vs. 92.5 ± 2.73 mg./100
ml.); however, the fractional rates of glucose disappearance were not
significantly altered (k_t = 1.41 ± 0.09 vs. 1.29 ± 0.12 per cent min.) (Fig.
1). The rates differ from those of Silverstone because of the different time

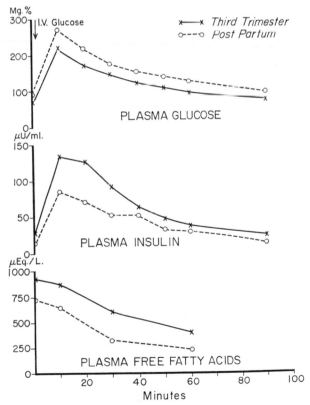

Figure 1. A comparison of intravenous glucose tolerance tests in women during
the third trimester of pregnancy and post partum. (Adapted from Bleicher, O'Sullivan
and Freinkel, New England J. Med., 271:866, 1964.)

periods used for analysis. These authors omitted 5- and 10-minute values in order to allow for more complete initial mixing.

Burt[13] studied 20 pregnant women beyond 20 weeks' gestation by use of a standardized intravenous dose of 25 gm. of 50 per cent glucose given rapidly, with serial blood sugar being determined frequently over the subsequent 1 to 2 hours.[4] Fasting blood sugar levels were statistically lower in the pregnant subjects, but he observed no differences when increments of blood sugar greater than the fasting levels were compared in pregnant and postpartum women. He also measured the levels of inorganic phosphorus in plasma, which were lower with fasting in the pregnant than in the postpartum woman; moreover, the decrease in phosphorus during the glucose tolerance test was attenuated in the pregnant women. Burt suggested that the diversion of glucose from the peripheral tissues to the liver was a possible explanation for the changes in plasma inorganic phosphorus. This phenomenon requires verification and clarification.

The intravenous tolerance tests cited[4, 5, 7] do not, in themselves, support the concept of pregnancy as a diabetogenic state, because no impairment in glucose disposal is evident in the normal pregnant woman.

Comparison of Oral and Intravenous Glucose Tolerance Tests

The question of abnormal glucose metabolism in pregnancy was studied by Welsh,[8] who compared oral with intravenous tolerance tests in pregnant women selected for potential diabetes mellitus. His patients were not grossly obese, had no evidence of intercurrent or chronic disease and showed one or more of the following: (1) glucosuria in current or past pregnancies, (2) family history of diabetes mellitus, (3) past history of abortions, stillbirths, fetal abnormalities or maternal complications, (4) past history of excessively large infants at birth (> 4000 gm.) or (5) symptoms of hypoglycemia 3 to 5 hours postprandially. Thus, these patients were selected because of a higher expected incidence of glucose intolerance. The oral test was performed with a standardized dose of 100 gm. dextrose; venous blood samples were obtained for Somogyi sugar analyses. Using the criteria of Wilkerson and Remeir,[2] he considered an abnormal oral glucose tolerance test as one characterized by two or more values equal to, or exceeding, a fasting blood sugar value of 100 mg./100 ml., a 60 minute value of 170; a 120 minute value of 120 and a 180 minute value of 110 mg./100 ml. Sixty-two of 128 women had abnormal oral tolerance tests.* When 27 of these 62 women were re-evaluated by the intravenous technique, 19 had normal rates of glucose removal ($k_i > 3$

---

* The recently revised recommendations of O'Sullivan[3] for an abnormal oral glucose tolerance test in pregnancy are two or more of the following: fasting blood sugar over 90 mg./100 ml.; 1 hour value over 165 mg./100 ml., 2 hours over 145 mg./100 ml. and 3 hours over 125 mg./100 ml.

per cent/min.). It is apparent that there are significant discrepancies between these two methods of evaluating glucose tolerance in pregnancy.

Insulin

Endogenous Response to Glucose

The recent development of techniques to assay insulin and insulin-like materials has permitted further interpretation of the metabolic adjustments during pregnancy. It is beyond the scope of this review to discuss the significance and interrelationships of the three most frequently used assay systems: radioimmunoassay, rat epididymal fat pad bioassay and rat diaphragm bioassay.[11]

Spellacy and Goetz,[12] using a radioimmunoassay, evaluated plasma insulin changes during intravenous glucose tolerance tests in women in the third trimester and post partum (40 days or more). Although values for fasting blood sugar were lower during pregnancy compared with those post partum, fasting plasma insulin levels were higher (mean 108.7 vs. 61.7 microunits/ml., respectively). Fifteen minutes after the intravenous administration of glucose, the mean plasma insulin level for pregnant women was three times that in the postpartum state. Throughout the first hour after the dose of glucose, plasma insulin values were significantly higher in the women tested during the third trimester. Although glucose values are not given, glucose tolerance apparently was not altered. Bleicher et al.[7] reported similar studies in which plasma free fatty acids as well as plasma insulin and glucose were measured sequentially in response to an intravenous load of glucose (Fig. 1). The previously reported elevation of free fatty acids in plasma of fasting pregnant women was confirmed.[13, 14]

Figure 1 shows the changes in plasma insulin, glucose and free fatty acids in women in the third trimester as compared with those in the postpartum period. Although lower concentrations of blood glucose are achieved during pregnancy, higher plasma insulin concentrations are found. The rate of glucose disposal was unchanged in this study, and the increment decrease in plasma free fatty acids was similar in both groups. In pregnancy, serum insulin-like activity has also been found to be elevated twofold when the rat epididymal fat pad bioassay system was used.[15]

Studies to date agree that for a given level of plasma glucose elevation, a higher associated plasma "insulin" level is found in pregnant women in the third trimester as compared with that in nonpregnant women.* This is the current basis for the concept that pregnancy is a diabetic-like state.

---

* Spellacy and associates[81] recently compared first trimester women with postpartum women and observed a slight elevation of plasma insulin response to an intravenous glucose load in the first trimester group.

Metabolism of Insulin

The rate of turnover of insulin in man was first studied by Berson and associates[16] by the single injection of radioactive iodinated (I^{131}) bovine insulin. From the time curve of protein precipitable radioactivity, a biologic half-life of 35 minutes was obtained for insulin in nonpregnant women. In a recent report by Gitlin,[17] a half-life of approximately 20 minutes was obtained for 9 pregnant women given radioiodinated human insulin immediately prior to cesarean section. During studies of placental transfer of I^{131} insulin (bovine) in pregnant rhesus monkeys, Josimovich and Knobil[18] noted a slightly shortened half-life of insulin as compared with that in nonpregnant controls. Goodner and Freinkel[19] observed the fractional rate of I^{131} insulin to be decreased from a half-life of 20.8 to 15.4 minutes in control versus pregnant rats, respectively. The faster turnover of insulin during pregnancy could be due to increased maternal, placental or fetal uptake or degradation of insulin. Regarding the first hypothesis, an increase in insulin proteolysis has been found in the liver of pregnant rats over that of nonpregnant controls.[20]

Sensitivity to Exogenous Insulin

Although the response to a glucose load results in an elevated *endogenous* level of plasma insulin, the response of the pregnant woman in the third trimester to *exogenous* insulin is attenuated.[21] Regular insulin (0.1 unit/kg. I.V.) produced less of a fall in the level of blood glucose in pregnant than that in postpartum women. However, the rate of recovery from hypoglycemia was no different. Furthermore, the response to an immediately repeated dose of insulin did not differ from the initial response.[22]

Insulin Release Mechanisms

When administered late in pregnancy, tolbutamide, a sulfonylurea compound that stimulates insulin release from the pancreas, does not produce so great a fall in the concentration of blood glucose as it does in the nonpregnant subject.[23] When a dose of 20 mg./kg. body weight was given intravenously, the nonpregnant woman had a decrease in blood glucose concentration of 40.3 mg./100 ml. at 30 minutes, whereas the pregnant woman had a decrease of only 23.9 mg./100 ml., which was delayed until 60 minutes. The percentage fall in blood glucose from the fasting level was not determined. Kalkhoff and associates[24] have found similar responses to intravenous tolbutamide associated with a fourfold greater secretion of insulin in normal pregnant women.

In contrast, L-leucine, which stimulates insulin release under special circumstances, has had no effect on the blood glucose in pregnancy.[7] Fasting women in the third trimester given 150 mg. L-leucine per kg. body weight by mouth showed a decline in the mean plasma glucose level from 80.7 to 74.8 mg./100 ml. without a demonstrable rise in plasma insulin.

Counterregulatory Mechanisms (Contrainsulin Effects)

Glucagon

Glucagon is one of the hormonal factors that operates to elevate blood glucose. The status of endogenous glucagon in pregnancy is currently under investigation and should be made clear in the future because of the availability of radioimmunoassay techniques. Studies of the response to exogenous glucagon have revealed definite differences in the response of pregnant women and nonpregnant controls.[25] In doses of 20 μg./kg. given intravenously, glucagon resulted in (1) a higher increment response over the fasting level, (2) a more prolonged curve without the hypoglycemic rebound seen in 60 minutes and (3) a smaller decrease in serum inorganic phosphate at 20 to 40 minutes. These studies suggest that hepatic stores of glycogen can be mobilized during pregnancy; however, "insulin resistance" prevented the normally rapid regulation of blood sugar concentration. Since plasma insulin levels were not measured during the test, further interpretation must be limited.

Adrenomedullary Hormones

Endogenous catecholamine levels as well as the response to infused epinephrine and norepinephrine during late pregnancy have been studied by Zuspan and associates.[26] Plasma levels of epinephrine and norepinephrine were similar in patients in early spontaneous labor or at term just before labor was induced with oxytocin. These observations agree with those of Hochuli, who, in addition, reported increased levels of epinephrine in plasma during prolonged labor.[27, 28]

The effects of norepinephrine and epinephrine infusions were studied in normal pregnant women at term.[20] Unfortunately, the observations were limited to measurements of uterine contractility and the cardiovascular response. Epinephrine was infused in both normal and toxemic women and levels of free fatty acids (FFA) estimated.[29] A prompt increase occurred in the levels of FFA in both groups, but no measurements of glucose were made.

The role of the catecholamines in carbohydrate regulation in pregnancy requires further study.

Thyroid

The increase in the basal metabolic rate in the latter half of pregnancy may be due to the great energy demands of the fetus. Protein-bound iodine concentration is also elevated in pregnancy. However, this is related to an increase in specific thyroxine-binding protein (TBP) in the plasma[30] and is not necessarily a measure of increased metabolism. Since TBP remains high during the puerperium when rapid changes in carbohydrate metabolism occur, it is unlikely that the increased thyroxine activity is significant in regulating over-all sugar metabolism in pregnancy.

Adrenocortical Hormone

Increased plasma levels of 17-hydroxycorticosteroids found in the third trimester are further elevated during labor and vaginal delivery. There is less rise associated with elective cesarean section. ACTH produces a normal increase in the levels of plasma steroids. Using C^{14} steroid, Migeon et al.[31] found that the half-life of "free" radioactivity in plasma was twice that in nonpregnant controls.[32] Since urinary steroid C^{14} was diminished, a slower rate of catabolism of cortisol rather than a more rapid rate of production was postulated to explain the elevated plasma values. More recently, transcortin, a plasma protein fraction that binds corticoid, has been found to be elevated in pregnancy.[33] Whether elevated levels of adrenocortical hormones exist at critical cellular sites in the liver and muscle as well is unknown.

Growth Hormones

Proteins with specific growth-promoting effects and related physiologic actions have recently been recognized in pregnancy.[24, 34, 35] An endogenous protein with an immunologic similarity to human growth hormone of pituitary origin has been identified in extracts of placenta and in maternal plasma and urine during pregnancy. This substance, variously known as growth hormone-like substance (GHLS), growth hormone-prolactin (GHP) and placental lactogen (PL), disappears promptly upon delivery of the fetus and placenta. The evidence suggests that it is of placental rather than fetal or maternal (nonplacental) pituitary origin. The purified placental hormone was clearly distinguishable from human growth hormone by physiochemical and immunochemical properties. Until sufficient human placental growth hormone-prolactin has been isolated for clinical physiological studies, knowledge of its role in pregnancy will be limited.

Kalkhoff and associates[24] have studied diabetogenic factors associated with pregnancy. In 42 normal pregnant women, plasma GHLS was elevated by the tenth week of gestation and persisted at elevated levels throughout pregnancy. No values at all fell within the normal limits that had been found in a large population of nonpregnant, nonobese women. Following delivery, plasma GHLS levels fell abruptly to normal by 6 to

8 hours post partum. The presence or absence of lactation did not influence this pattern.

The mechanism for the secretion of immunologic growth hormone in man is sensitive to (a) obvious deprivation of intracellular glucose, produced by either hypoglycemia or administration of 2-deoxy-D glucose, (b) rapidly falling blood glucose concentration, (c) fasting and (d) muscular exercise.[36] Furthermore, glucose administration abruptly suppresses release of the hormone. Raben has shown that human growth hormone administration results in rapid release of free fatty acids from adipose tissue.[37] The extent to which these mechanisms are operative in carbohydrate homeostasis during pregnancy awaits clarification.

Renal Glycosuria

Renal glycosuria, which is more common during pregnancy, was found in 39 of 66 pregnant women with normal oral glucose tolerance tests.[9] Glucosuria was observed to occur at blood sugar levels below 140 mg./100 ml. Except for this random glucosuria (it was random in 34 of 39 patients), these patients could not be distinguished clinically from those pregnant women without glucosuria. Lactosuria must be distinguished from glucosuria by use of specific analytical techniques (glucose oxidase or chromatography) in late pregnancy.

The mechanisms of renal glucosuria in pregnancy were studied by Welch and Sims[9] in normal women without evidence of impaired carbohydrate metabolism, renal disease or complications of pregnancy. Using discrete renal function techniques, these investigators observed that the glomerular filtration rate was increased from mean values of 124 ml./min. in nonpregnant women to 151 ml./min. during pregnancy, an observation which confirmed previous studies. Pregnant women with and without renal glycosuria had the same mean glomerular filtration rate of 151 ml./min. In contrast, tubular maximal reabsorption of glucose (Tm_G) in the pregnant glucosuric women was distinctly lower than that in either the normal control or aglucosuric pregnant women ($Tm_G = 310$ vs. 366 and 378 mg./min./1.73 sq.m. respectively). Thus, both glomerular filtration rate and tubular reabsorption contribute to the increased urinary loss of glucose. Since the increased filtration rate may be counterbalanced in part by the lower fasting blood sugar concentration in these women, the increase in the filtered load of glucose presented to the renal tubule may be minimized. Under these conditions, the more important factor would appear to be the decreased tubular reabsorptive capacity. Whether this latter phenomenon is a peculiarity of pregnancy per se or intrinsic to the individual in the nonpregnant state awaits more definitive serial studies. Titration studies of glucose are needed to further define the spectrum of change in terms of homogenous or heterogenous populations of nephrons as described by Reubi.[10] The significance of glycosuria during pregnancy also awaits long-term follow-up studies. Whether it presages diabetes mellitus is unknown. Although the outcome of pregnancy in these women does not appear to be adversely affected, the possibility of subtle physiologic alterations in the newborn infant has not been considered.

Metabolic Adjustments to Pregnancy: Postulates

Two recent hypotheses to explain the changes in glucose metabolism during pregnancy place emphasis, respectively, on the excessive growth hormone-like activity and on maternal "glucose starvation." Daughaday and his associates[24] have interpreted the elevated fasting plasma insulin levels, hyperresponse of plasma insulin to glucose loads, hyperresponse to the insulinogenic stimulus tolbutamide, diminished responsiveness to exogenous insulin and elevated fasting plasma free fatty acids to suggest significant peripheral antagonism to insulin. They suggest that the placental lactogen may be the major factor producing insulin antagonism in pregnancy. This may be due either to its own intrinsic growth hormone-like activity or its synergistic effect with pituitary growth hormone.

Freinkel,[7] on the other hand, has suggested that the metabolic adjustments of pregnancy may be explained in terms of "accelerated starvation." He suggests that the products of conception, i.e., the placenta and fetus, utilize glucose and other nutrients preferentially, and thus are an additional burden upon the mother for glucose. The increasing demands of the fetus during pregnancy pre-empt glucose and gluconeogenetic precursors from the mother with a resulting "adaptive state of starvation." The increased plasma free fatty acids and diminished fasting blood glucose are manifestations of this sequence of events. He postulates that several lipolytic hormones, including growth hormone, glucagon, etc., may be released as a response to this "starvation state." The insulin effects are considered secondary and any contrainsulin factors, from whatever source, may be adaptive responses to stabilize maternal glucose metabolism.

Additional studies throughout pregnancy and immediately post partum will be needed before these differences in interpretation of available data can be resolved. Furthermore, the role of GHLS or placental lactogen must be clarified before definitive conclusions will be justified.

THE PLACENTA

The study of the mechanisms whereby the metabolism, development and growth of the fetus are supported by the placenta has received renewed impetus with recent technological advances. Recently several symposia and reviews have focused on this general area.[38-40] The following discussion is restricted to the area of carbohydrate metabolism in the placenta.

Glucose Transfer Across the Placenta

Earlier studies of respiratory quotients before birth and of the blood glucose concentration in fetal blood suggest that carbohydrate is a major source of fetal energy and that glucose is freely diffused across the placenta. Simple diffusion is defined as a transfer down a chemical potential gradient in which the kinetics follow Fick's law; the rates are in accordance with predictions based on the physicochemical properties of the substance.[41] But since fructose, which has the same molecular weight as glucose, does not cross the placenta as rapidly as glucose[42-44] the mechanism is almost surely more complicated than simple diffusion. Furthermore, stereospecificity of the transport process has been defined.[45] Either active transport or facilitated diffusion may explain the transfer process.

In active transport, transfer of molecules across membranes involves expenditure of metabolic energy, and the molecular species may be transferred against an electrochemical gradient. Facilitated diffusion is characterized by: (1) a faster rate of transfer than would be predicted on physicochemical grounds, (2) kinetics which deviate from Fick's law and usually show saturation at high concentrations, (3) competition for the transfer mechanism by related compounds and (4) possibly specific inhibitors which are competitive. The transfer is usually down a chemical potential gradient.

Widdas favors facilitated diffusion as the mechanism for glucose transfer across the placenta,[41] noting that a concentration gradient from mother to fetus is always present for glucose, unless the latter has been infused experimentally into the fetal circulation. Chinard and associates[43] infused glucose into women and monkeys prior to and at cesarean section. They observed parallel responses in the blood sugar of the fetus and of the mother in the third month of intrauterine life as well as at term. A significant maternal-fetal gradient of glucose was observed. Battaglia et al.[46] have re-examined glucose concentration gradients across the monkey placenta at known periods of gestation. They analyzed maternal arterial, maternal uterine venous, and fetal umbilical artery blood for glucose concentrations. The plasma arteriovenous differences for glucose across the uterus (maternal surface of placenta) averaged 14.9 mg./100 ml., while the concentration gradient across the whole placenta averaged 26.6 mg./100 ml. The latter, or transplacental gradient, was derived as $\frac{1}{2} (M_a + M_v) - F_a$, where M_a, M_v and F_a are maternal arterial, maternal uterine vein and fetal arterial glucose concentrations, respectively. These investigators review the complexity of the system in which amniotic and fetal pools are superimposed on maternal pools during pregnancy. They emphasize the importance of simultaneous analysis of fetal and maternal arterial concentrations. Until good methods of determining flow rates across the uterus, across the placenta and in the fetus are developed it will be impossible to describe fully the physiologic events.

Fructose Transfer Across the Placenta

In the pregnant human female, fructose is undetectable in the fasting state, but rises to a discernible level after the ingestion of sucrose- or fructose-containing foods. The infusion of fructose in a variety of pregnant species, including guinea pigs,[44] monkeys and man,[43] has resulted in high maternal fructose levels with very large maternal-fetal or transplacental gradients. Sustained infusions of fructose to the mother result in a slow transfer of fructose to the fetus, with a gradually rising level. This behavior of fructose is in marked contrast to the rapid transfer of glucose given similarly. In studies by McCann and associates,[48] fructose infusions to normal women during labor resulted in large maternal-fetal concentration differences at the time of delivery: maternal levels of 60 to 80 mg./100 ml. vs. 10 to 15 mg./100 ml. in blood from the umbilical vein. Levels in blood from the umbilical artery were always slightly lower than those from the vein. Although detailed studies of fructose injections into fetal monkey or man have not been made to evaluate the reverse transfer across the placenta,[42] the studies *in situ* with the isolated guinea pig placenta do indicate a very slow transfer rate of fructose compared to either α or β glucose.[45]

Fructose Metabolism in Fructogenic Species

Fructose has assumed importance in placental metabolism in recent years since the demonstration that certain species, especially ungulates, are fructogenic, i.e., the fetus has levels of fructose in blood greater than 10 mg./100 ml.[49] While the original studies were made in sheep, they have been extended to a variety of species, including goat, horse, ox and pig, to name a few. Of equal importance is the observation that rat, guinea pig, rabbit, monkey and man are not fructogenic, and only small amounts of fructose have been found in the plasma. In sheep, the fetal or newborn lamb was found to have high plasma fructose levels which disappeared slowly after birth. Maternal fructose levels were very low. The origin of fructose was shown clearly to be the placenta. This hexose was formed from maternal glucose as demonstrated by the incorporation of isotopically labeled glucose into fructose. The fructose level in the fetus correlated better with glucose concentrations in the umbilical vein than with maternal glucose levels. That a competition in fetal tissues between fetal glucose and fructose also occurred was evident from the higher fetal fructose levels when blood glucose was raised, i.e., a decrease in fructose uptake occurred. The importance of fetal fructose in these species is unknown; however, Huggett has correlated this with placental stores and has suggested that this may be an important source as a reserve of nutrient for these species.[49]

Glycogen

Although maternal glucose appears to be the major source of nutrient energy for the fetus, significant amounts of glycogen have been found in the placenta. Glycogen stores in this organ were first described by Claude Bernard. Villee[50] has found that glycogen content of the human placenta is highest at about the eighth week of gestation and declines thereafter until 18 to 20 weeks, after which time, a level of 15 to 20 mg./100 gm. dry weight is maintained until term. Thus, the total amount of glycogen in the placenta at term is still appreciable because of the increased size of the placenta (Fig. 2). In addition, the distribution of glycogen may be important, as shown by Huggett in studies of the rabbit placenta.[49] A clear correlation between energy requirements of the rapidly growing fetus and placental glycogen availability has not yet been determined.

Enzymes

The observations that glycogen is present in significant quantities and that isolated placental slices produce lactate, imply the presence of the enzymes of the glycolytic pathway, as well as the phosphorylated intermediates.[47, 51] Hagerman and Villee have determined enzyme activities of hexokinase, isomerase and glucose-6-phosphatase, as well as nonspecific phosphatase in placenta.

Studies of slices of human placenta *in vitro* have indicated net production of glucose by dilution of C-14 glucose.[50] Even before 15 weeks' gestation, the human placenta was capable of gluconeogenesis from labeled pyruvate. Glucose-6-phosphatase activity necessary for final conversion to free glucose declined throughout gestation in parallel with the decreasing placental glycogen concentration. The significance of this enzyme in transplacental glucose movement is not known. A complete review of uterine and placental enzymes has recently been published by Hafez.[52]

The rate of oxygen consumption of the human placenta has been found to decrease from the tenth week to term.[53] The energy metabolism of the placenta has been poorly defined. The divergent views of respiratory metabolism in this organ may stem from differences in methodology in the individual studies.

A

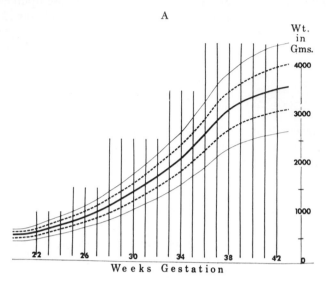

Weeks Gestation

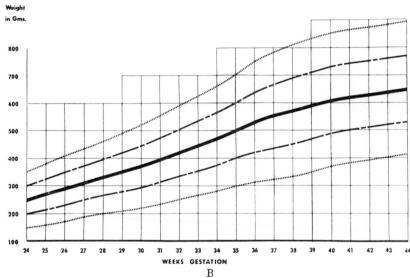

B

Figure 2.   Fetal and placental growth in the second half of pregnancy. *A,* Fetal growth by weeks of gestation. Heavy solid line indicates mean; dashed line, ±1 standard deviation; solid light line, ±2 standard deviations. *B,* Placental growth by weeks of gestation. Solid line indicates mean; dashed line, ±1 standard deviation; and dotted line, ±2 standard deviations. Since glycogen concentration remains constant during this phase (see text), an increased glycogen content parallels weight gain. Observe the differences between fetal and placental growth. (From Hendricks, Obst. & Gynec., *24:*357, 1964.)

Insulin

The question of placental permeability to insulin is not yet clearly defined. Buse, Roberts and Buse[54] injected radioiodinated crystalline beef insulin into pregnant women prior to delivery. They could find only minute amounts of labeled trichloroacetic-precipitable material (presumed protein) in fetal plasma, while significant amounts of labeled material were found in the placenta. They concluded that the placenta was relatively impermeable to insulin, but degraded significant quantities of this hormone. Freinkel and Goodner[55] had previously studied placentas from human and other species and had found an active "insulinase system" for proteolytic inactivation of insulin. Spellacy and associates[56] have measured plasma insulin by radioimmunoassay technique in both maternal venous and umbilical venous blood at the time of delivery. In 30 women they could detect no correlation between the two values and concluded that human insulin does not freely pass the placental barrier.

In contrast to these observations are the studies of Josimovich and Knobil,[18] utilizing iodinated bovine insulin injected into either the maternal or fetal circulation of the rhesus monkey. Insulin, separated chromatographically from other iodinated compounds, was found to traverse the primate placenta. More recently, Gitlin, Kumate and Morales[17] studied the fate of radioiodinated human insulin injected intravenously into women before delivery. From a kinetic analysis of their data, they concluded that insulin does pass the placental barrier in both directions equally. While their observations of radioactive human insulin transfer in the fetus at term are valid, analysis and interpretation of these data depended upon values for levels of plasma insulin in newborn infants and these values were obtained from the literature and not reconfirmed experimentally. The latter remain to be determined precisely and may alter the magnitude of the calculated placental exchange.

A direct physiological effect of insulin on placental permeability or metabolism in man is yet to be demonstrated *in vivo*. However, utilizing human placental slices, Villee demonstrated an increase in glucose utilization and glycogen synthesis in the presence of insulin without an effect on oxygen consumption or lactate production.[53]

Other Hormones

The placenta has assumed greater importance in recent studies, which have defined the biochemical mechanisms of protein gonadotropin and steroid hormone production.[54] Whether these have any direct influence on carbohydrate metabolism is not known. It has been suggested that adrenal steroid hormones are derived from the placenta during pregnancy; however, Ryan[57] considers the evidence insufficient for this view. More important are the recent studies of Josimovich and Atwood,[34] Kaplan and Grumbach[35] and Kalkhoff et al.,[24] which have identified a growth hormone-like substance of placental origin.* The latter presumably is an important contrainsulin factor. Further studies of this material may clarify the alterations of glucose and fatty acid metabolism which occur during pregnancy.

Amniotic Fluid

Amniotic fluid has not been considered an important source of nutrient for the fetus or placenta, even though water diffuses freely and rapidly across the membranes. Little information on sugar diffusion is available. The concentration of glucose in amniotic fluid is low. Pedersen originally observed a delay in equilibrium between maternal sugar levels and amniotic fluid concentrations.[58] Whether this is related to differential permeability at the membranes or to absorption by the fetus after rapid ingestion via the gastrointestinal tract is unknown. Wood and associates[59] found mean maternal venous blood sugars (Folin-Wu) of 71.9 mg./100 ml., while simultaneously obtained amniotic fluid had a sugar level of only 13.2 mg./100 ml. In patients with prolonged pregnancy the glucose levels in amniotic fluid were lower. Lactic acid levels were consistently higher in amniotic fluid than in peripheral venous blood and there was no correlation with the blood sugar level. Fetal distress or delay in onset of respiration was more common when the lactic acid level was above 40 mg./100 ml. These data were considered to be influenced primarily by fetal rather than by placental metabolism. Previously, Hendricks[60] had found a high concentration of lactate, averaging 77.9 mg./100 ml. in amniotic fluid obtained at term. More recently, Räihä[61] analyzed organic acids in amniotic fluid obtained from normal pregnant women at term but prior to onset of uterine contractions. His mean data indicated that amniotic fluid contained the following concentrations (mg./100 ml.): lactate–75.96, pyruvate–0.82, citrate–5.55, α-ketoglutarate–0.74 and total acetone bodies–0.87. He also determined acid-base balance, which indicated a mixed acidosis of amniotic fluid (pH–7.12, pCO_2–50.6, standard bicarbonate 16.35 mEq./L.). Although α-ketoglutarate and citrate were higher in amniotic fluid than in cord blood, the major organic acid increase was due to lactate as noted previously. Again, this was considered to be derived from *fetal* excretion, although a contribution from intra-amniotic glycolysis must be considered as well. Further studies in this area should provide important information about the intrauterine status of the fetus.

THE FETUS

While the process of delivery produces an alteration in the continuum of development, the adjustments of the newborn, and of the young infant

* See section on Maternal Metabolism, p. 16.

in particular, must be considered in the light of previous experiences *in utero*.

Glycogen and Enzymes of Carbohydrate Metabolism

The acquisition of specific biosynthetic systems with respect to carbohydrate occurs fairly early in fetal development. In mammalian primate tissues, including man, Villee[62, 63] found significant glycogen in liver, kidney, lung, brain and diaphragm by 9 to 10 weeks of gestation. While there is a paucity of data for human fetuses beyond 20 weeks' gestation, a variety of mammalian species have been shown to have an increased content of glycogen in liver and muscle toward the end of gestation.[64] Since these trends are evident in monkey fetuses as well, similar changes presumably occur in the human. At term, the fetal liver contains a higher concentration of glycogen than ever occurs later in life; levels exceeding those in livers of well fed adult mammals and in the range observed in glycogen storage disease are found (above 8 gm./100 gm. wet tissue and as high as 18 gm./100 gm.). The presence of glycogen in these tissues inferentially indicates the presence of the synthesizing enzymes of the glycogen cycle. Whether the enzymes involved in *degradation* of glycogen are absent or are simply inactive cannot be inferred. Few studies have been made of specific enzyme activities in human tissues after 28 weeks' gestation. In the fetuses of other mammalian species (guinea pig, rat) there is no activity of glucose-6-phosphatase in the liver, but it rapidly develops to very high levels in the newborn.[65, 66] In contrast, preliminary studies in human fetal liver have demonstrated glucose-6-phosphatase activity as early as the fourth or fifth month of gestation.[67] Similar high values have been observed for fetal glucose-6-phosphatase in the monkey prior to delivery.[68] Auricchio and Rigillo[69] have analyzed glucose-6-phosphatase activity of the human fetal liver from 5 to 9 months of gestation. Enzyme activity at pH 6.8 was appreciable, but was lower than that in the adult.

Recent studies of Jacquot and Kretchmer,[70] Dawkins[68] and Kornfeld[72] have been directed toward the interrelationship between the enzymes of the glycogen cycle and perinatal glucose homeostasis. In the rat, enzymes concerned with glycogen synthesis, including phosphoglucomutase and glycogen synthetase, increased rapidly toward the end of gestation when glycogen accumulation was maximal.[70] Hepatic phosphorylase increased more slowly, however, while in this species glucose-6-phosphatase increased abruptly before delivery. But this phenomenon was prevented in the rabbit by decapitation *in utero* at a critical stage before rapid accumulation of liver glycogen occurred.[73] In the rat, a similar phenomenon occurs in which glycogen deposition can be prevented by adrenalectomy in the mother and restored by glucocorticoid therapy or ACTH to the fetus. Decapitation of the fetal rat is associated with a lower level of glycogen synthetase and glucose-6-phosphatase.[70] Other hormones have been implicated in fetal glycogen metabolism as well. The role of insulin and placental hormones remains to be defined.

Of some interest are the observations of Grillo et al.[74] on the chick embryo. Glycogen synthetase activity has been demonstrated at the time of appearance of glycogen and this has been correlated with the onset of insulin formation. Since insulin stimulates synthetase activity and glycogen synthesis, the interrelationship of the development of these factors is noteworthy. Thirteen enzymes concerned with carbohydrate metabolism have been studied in rat fetal liver by Burch and associates.[75] Hexokinase was high in the fetus, but declined to adult levels, while phosphorylase increased during fetal life, but declined after birth. Other enzymes had variable patterns of development. Walker[76] examined hepatic specific fructokinase activities in fetal, newborn and adult rats, rabbits and guinea pigs. He found this enzyme to be absent in the fetal livers, but to develop postnatally, reaching adult levels by 7 to 10 days. He correlated physiology with biochemistry, by demonstrating a diminished fructose tolerance in newborn rabbits prior to hepatic fructokinase development.

Intermediate Metabolism

Aerobic Metabolism

The metabolism of specific human fetal tissues has been studied *in vitro* extensively by Villee and associates.[62, 63, 77] The early studies were on fetuses of 6 to 22 weeks' gestation, available because of therapeutic interruption of pregnancy. Oxygen consumption of fetal liver slices incubated with glucose and pyruvate was highest at 7.5 to 10 weeks' gestation and then declined toward term. In contrast, lactate production under these conditions tended to remain constant. There were variations among different tissues; however, the heart produced the largest amounts of lactate. Glucose production was observed in fetal liver at the tenth week, in lung at about the eleventh week, and in kidney at about the fifteenth week of development. However, heart, skeletal muscle, and brain did not produce free glucose. Pyruvate production was similar to that of lactate and was constant in liver from 7.5 to 40 weeks. Respiratory carbon dioxide from various substrates was measured for different tissues of varying age. For liver, approximately 30 per cent of carbon dioxide production derived from pyruvate, while only 3 to 6 per cent was derived from glucose when the incubating media contained approximately equal amounts of these substrates. Later studies[77] showed that the respiratory quotient for fetal liver was 1.31 compared to 0.91 for adult liver. The former was interpreted to indicate a rapid rate of fatty acid synthesis. The patterns of metabolism varied for other tissues, but indicated that as early as 8 weeks of development, the several tissues of the human fetus are well differentiated biochemically.

Anaerobic Metabolism

Because of the ability of the newborn mammal to withstand severe hypoxia compared to the adult, Villee and associates also studied the effects of anoxia (incubation of tissues in nitrogen) on metabolism.[77] Fetal liver had a high rate of lactic acid production under anaerobic conditions, a threefold increase compared with twofold for adult liver. The rate of glycolysis was two to four times greater anaerobically than aerobically. Lipogenesis from a variety of substrates was markedly reduced under anaerobic conditions. Acetate and pyruvate were the most effective precursors for fat synthesis in the fetal liver aerobically.

Brain. A sequential analysis of brain tissue indicated a higher metabolic activity in the brain stem early, with an increase in that of the cortex during development. Thus, 13 cm. fetuses had *higher* rates of consumption of oxygen and of production of lactate in the brain stem, while equivalent tissues from fetuses 3 to 4 weeks older had *similar* rates in the brain stem and the cortex. The brain had little glycogen and depended upon exogenous glucose for its source of energy. Of interest was the observation that substrates other than glucose were also metabolized, including acetate and pyruvate.

Cardiac and Skeletal Muscle. In contrast to other tissues, cardiac muscle, which also had a high content of glycogen, utilized large amounts of glucose both aerobically and anaerobically; furthermore, lactate production was high in both conditions. The heart was less affected by an anaerobic environment than other tissues. Incubation with insulin aerobically increased glucose utilization.

Skeletal muscle differed from heart muscle in that incubation in nitrogen increased glycogen utilization and lactate production. Furthermore, this tissue, aerobically, increases the percentage of pyruvate metabolized to carbon dioxide with increasing development. Diaphragm slices taken at as early as 10 weeks' gestation showed increased glucose utilization with aerobic incubation in the presence of insulin.

The studies of anaerobic metabolism of diverse fetal tissues *in vitro* indicated that lipogenesis is depressed under these conditions, whereas glycolysis is increased and of major significance. To what extent physiological adjustments *in utero* reflect a hypoxic state in which enzyme activities and metabolic pathways compensate to protect the fetus and maintain metabolism is unknown.

Blood Glucose in the Fetus

While there have been a moderate number of studies of glucose concentration in the fetal circulation *at the moment of delivery* (see section on Placental Metabolism, p. 19), there is little information about glucose concentration in fetal blood *prior to birth*, in man or other primates. Karvonen and associates[78] obtained umbilical cord vein samples from the human fetus at vaginal hysterotomy prior to a therapeutic interruption of pregnancy. They found blood glucose values as low as 20 mg./100 ml. in a 22 week old fetus. Infusions of glucose or fructose to the mother resulted in transfer to the fetus, with higher transfer rates for glucose compared to fructose.

Shelley[79] and Dawes and associates[80] have studied fetal monkeys (term gestation—168 days) from 53 to 10 days before term and 8 to 15 days after birth. The level of blood glucose was constant during fetal life and ranged from 20 to 36 mg./100 ml. The maternal levels of blood glucose were about twice the fetal values, with similar variations. The fetal values were also definitely lower than in the postpartum newborn, in whom levels above 40 mg./100 ml. were attained by 8 to 10 days of age. No fructose was observed in fetal blood, confirming the earlier observations of Chinard and associates.[43]

Effects of Intrauterine Anoxia

In observations on fetal monkeys, Dawes et al.[80] compared arterial oxygen saturation, blood lactate and blood glucose. Oxygen saturation varied from 54 to 77 per cent, while blood lactate was less than 20 mg./100 ml. and glucose averaged 29 mg./100 ml. Asphyxia in a monkey of 141 days' gestation resulted in a fall in oxygen saturation to 2 per cent and a rise in blood lactate to 78 mg./100 ml. Initially, a rise in blood pressure occurred, followed by a later fall, while heart rate fell rapidly after onset of asphyxia. In contrast to these observations, one asphyxiated monkey 9 days old had a very transient rise in blood pressure followed by a profound fall, bradycardia and defecation. He tolerated asphyxia for a much shorter period and had a fall in blood glucose, although lactate rose. Survival tended to parallel cardiac glycogen level, which was highest in fetal life and lowest after birth.

SUMMARY

In recent years, the biosynthetic mechanisms of the developing fetus and placenta have received new attention. The acquisition of enzymatic processes has been further defined. The complex enzyme systems necessary for glycogen synthesis and metabolism are well developed in the fetus. Hormonal control, especially by the pituitary-adrenal system, is critical to the development of these systems. Glycolysis and anaerobic metabolism appear to be efficient as well. Although tracer techniques have permitted a dynamic analysis in some species, there is insufficient information to correlate adequately the physiological adjustments of the pregnant woman with the fetus.

REFERENCES

1. Peters, J. P., and Van Slyke, D. D.: Quantitative Clinical Chemistry. Baltimore, The Williams and Wilkins Company, 1946, Vol. I. Interpretations, pp. 196, 197.
2. Wilkerson, H. L., and O'Sullivan, J. B.: A study of glucose tolerance and screening criteria in 752 unselected pregnancies. Diabetes 12:313, 1963.
3. O'Sullivan, J. B., and Mahan, C. M.: Criteria for the oral glucose tolerance test in pregnancy. Diabetes 13:278, 1964.
4. Burt, R. L.: Peripheral utilization of glucose in pregnancy and the puerperium. Obstet. Gynec. 4:58, 1954.
5. Silverstone, F. A., Solomons, E., and Rubricius, J.: The rapid intravenous glucose tolerance test in pregnancy. J. Clin. Invest. 40:2180, 1961.
6. Amatuzio, D. S., Stutzman, F. L., Vanderbilt, M. J., and Nesbitt, S.: Interpretation of the rapid intravenous glucose tolerance test in normal individuals and in mild diabetes mellitus. J. Clin. Invest. 32:428, 1953.
7. Bleicher, S. J., O'Sullivan, J. B., and Freinkel, N.: Carbohydrate metabolism in pregnancy. V. Interrelations of glucose, insulin, and free fatty acids in late pregnancy and post partum. New England J. Med. 271:866, 1964.
8. Welsh, G. W., III: Studies of abnormal glucose metabolism in pregnancy. Diabetes 9:466, 1960.
9. Welsh, G. W., III, and Sims, E. A.: The mechanisms of renal glucosuria in pregnancy. Diabetes 9:363, 1960.
10. Reubi, F.: Quelques aspects de diabète rénal. Helvet. med. acta 17:493, 1950.
11. Levine, R., and Mahler, R.: Production, secretion and availability of insulin. Ann. Rev. Med. 15:413, 1964.
12. Spellacy, W. N., and Goetz, F. C.: Plasma insulin in normal late pregnancy. New England J. Med. 268:988, 1963.
13. Burt, R. L.: Plasma nonesterified fatty acids in normal pregnancy and puerperium. Obstet. Gynec. 15:460, 1960.
14. Burt, R. L.: Plasma nonesterified fatty acids in pregnancy. II. Experimental modification. Amer. J. Obstet. Gynec. 80:905, 1960.
15. Leake, N. H., and Burt, R. L.: Insulin-like activity in serum during pregnancy. Diabetes 11:419, 1962.
16. Berson, S. A., Yalow, R. S., Bauman, A., Rothschild, M. A., and Newerly, K.: Insulin-I[131] metabolism in human subjects: demonstration of insulin binding globulin in circulation of insulin treated subjects. J. Clin. Invest. 35:170, 1956.
17. Gitlin, D., Kumate, J., and Morales, C.: On the transport of insulin across the human placenta. Pediatrics 35:65, 1965.
18. Josimovich, J. B., and Knobil, E.: Placental transfer of I[131]-insulin in the rhesus monkey. Am. J. Physiol. 200:471, 1961.
19. Goodner, C. J., and Freinkel, N.: Carbohydrate metabolism in pregnancy: the turnover of I[131]-insulin in the pregnant rat. Endocrinology 67:862, 1960.
20. Goodner, C. J., and Freinkel, N.: Carbohydrate metabolism in pregnancy: the degradation of insulin by extracts of maternal and fetal structures in the pregnant rat. Endocrinology 65:957, 1959.
21. Burt, R. L.: Peripheral utilization of glucose in pregnancy. III. Insulin tolerance. Obstet. Gynec. 7:658, 1956.
22. Burt, R. L.: Insulin sensitivity in pregnancy. Insulin-primed insulin tolerance. Obstet. Gynec. 21:412, 1963.

23. Burt, R. L.: Reactivity to tolbutamide in normal pregnancy. Obstet. Gynec. *12*: 447, 1958.

24. Kalkhoff, R., Schalch, D. S., Walker, J. L., Beck, P., Kipnis, D. M., and Daughaday, W. H.: Diabetogenic factors associated with pregnancy. Trans. Ass. Am. Physicians 77:270, 1964.

25. Burt, R. L., and Julian, N.: Carbohydrate metabolism in pregnancy. Amer. J. Obstet. Gynec. *74*:551, 1957.

26. Zuspan, F. P., Cibils, L. A., and Pose, S. V.: Myometrial and cardiovascular responses to alterations in plasma epinephrine and norepinephrine. Amer. J. Obstet. Gynec. *84*:841, 1962.

27. Hochuli, E., Kaeser, O., and Burger, M.: Adrenalin- und Noradrenalinbestimmungen in Blutplasma unter der Geburt. Experientia *12*:356, 1956.

28. Hochuli, E.: Adrenalin- und Noradrenalinbestimmungen in Blutplasma in der Schwangerschaft, unter der Geburt und bei Schwangerschaftstoxikose. Geburtsch. u. Frauenh. *20*:835, 1960.

29. Zuspan, F. P., Nelson, G. H., and Ahlquist, R. P.: Epinephrine infusions in normal and toxemic pregnancy. I. Nonesterified fatty acids and cardiovascular alterations. Am. J. Obstet. Gynec. *90*:88, 1964.

30. Dowling, J. T., Freinkel, N., and Ingbar, S. H.: Thyroxine-binding by sera of pregnant women, newborn infants, and women with spontaneous abortion. J. Clin. Invest. *35*:1263, 1956.

31. Migeon, C. J., Prystowsky, H., Grumbach, M. M., and Byron, M. C.: Placental passage of 17-hydroxycorticosteroids: comparison of the levels in maternal and fetal plasma and effect of ACTH and hydrocortisone administration. J. Clin. Invest. *35*:488, 1956.

32. Migeon, C. J., Bertrand, J., and Wall, P. E.: Physiological disposition of 4-C14-cortisol during late pregnancy. J. Clin. Invest. *36*:1350, 1957.

33. Slaunwhite, W. R., Jr., and Sandberg, A. A.: Transcortin: a corticosteroid-binding protein of plasma. J. Clin. Invest. *38*:384, 1959.

34. Josimovich, J. B., and Atwood, B. L.: Human placental lactogen (HPL), a trophoblastic hormone synergizing with chorionic gonadotropin and potentiating anabolic effects of pituitary growth hormone. Am. J. Obstet. Gynec. *88*:867, 1964.

35. Kaplan, S. L., and Grumbach, M. M.: Studies of a human and simian placental hormone with growth hormone-like and prolactin-like activities. J. Clin. Endocrinol. *24*:80, 1964.

36. Daughaday, W. H., and Parker, M. L.: Human pituitary growth hormone. Ann. Rev. Med. *16*:47, 1965.

37. Raben, M. S.: Growth hormone. I. Physiologic aspects. New England J. Med. *266*:31, 1962.

38. Hagerman, D. D., and Villee, C. A.: Transport functions of the placenta. Physiol. Rev. *40*:313, 1960.

39. Plentl, A. A. (ed.): Symposium on the Placenta. Am. J. Obstet. Gynec. *84*:1541, 1962.

40. Cross, K. W. (ed.): Foetal and neonatal physiology. Brit. Med. Bull. *17*:79, 1961.

41. Widdas, W. F.: Transport mechanisms in the foetus. Brit. Med. Bull. *17*:107, 1961.

42. Karvonen, M. J., and Räihä, N.: Permeability of placenta of the guinea pig to glucose and fructose. Acta physiol. scandinav. *31*:194, 1954.

43. Chinard, F. P., Danesino, V., Hartmann, W. L., Huggett, A. St.G., Paul, W., and Reynolds, S. R. M.: The transmission of hexoses across the placenta in the human and the rhesus monkey (*Macaca mulatta*). J. Physiol. *132*:289, 1956.

44. Davies, J.: The permeability of the rabbit placenta to glucose and fructose. Am. J. Physiol. *181*:532, 1955.

45. Folkart, G. R., Dancis, J., and Money, W. L.: Transfer of carbohydrates across guinea pig placenta. Am. J. Obstet. Gynec. *80*:221, 1960.

46. Battaglia, F. C., Hellegers, A. E., Heller, C. J., and Behrman, R.: Glucose concentration gradients across the maternal surface, the placenta, and the

amnion of the rhesus monkey (*Macaca mulatta*). Am. J. Obstet. Gynec. 88:32, 1964.

47. Hagerman, D. D., and Villee, C. A.: The transport of fructose by the human placenta. J. Clin. Invest. 31:911, 1952.

48. McCann, M. L., Kotchen, J., Katigbak, E. B., Likly, B., and Schwartz, R.: The prevention of hypoglycemia in infants of diabetic mothers. Presented at the proceedings, Soc. for Ped. Res., May 5, 1965 (35th meeting).

49. Huggett, A. St.G.: Carbohydrate metabolism in the placenta and foetus. Brit. Med. Bull. 17:122, 1961.

50. Villee, C. A.: Regulation of blood glucose in the human fetus. J. Appl. Physiol. 5:437, 1952–53.

51. Hagerman, D. D., Roux, J., and Villee, C. A.: Studies of the mechanism of fructose production by human placenta. J. Physiol. 146:98, 1959.

52. Hafez, E. S. E.: Uterine and placental enzymes. Acta endocrinol. 46:217, 1964.

53. Villee, C. A.: The metabolism of the human placenta *in vitro*. J. Biol. Chem. 205:113, 1953.

54. Buse, M. G., Roberts, W. J., and Buse, J.: The role of the human placenta in the transfer and metabolism of insulin. J. Clin. Invest. 41:29, 1962.

55. Freinkel, N., and Goodner, C. J.: Carbohydrate metabolism in pregnancy. I. The metabolism of insulin by human placental tissue. J. Clin. Invest. 39:116, 1960.

56. Spellacy, W. N., Goetz, F. C., Greenberg, B. Z., and Ells, J.: The human placental gradient for plasma insulin and blood glucose. Am. J. Obstet. Gynec. 90:753, 1964.

57. Ryan, K. J.: Hormones of the placenta. Am. J. Obstet. Gynec. 84:1695, 1962.

58. Pedersen, J.: Glucose content of the amniotic fluid in diabetic pregnancies. Acta endocrinol. 15:342, 1954.

59. Wood, C., Acharya, P. T., Cornwell, E., and Pinkerton, J. H. M.: The significance of glucose and lactic acid concentration in the amniotic fluid. J. Obstet. Gynaec. Brit. Commonwealth 70:274, 1963.

60. Hendricks, C. H.: Studies on lactic acid metabolism in pregnancy and labor. Am. J. Obstet. Gynec. 73:492, 1957.

61. Räihä, N. C. R.: Organic acids in fetal blood and amniotic fluid. Pediatrics 32:1025, 1963.

62. Villee, C. A.: The intermediary metabolism of human fetal tissues. Cold Spring Harbor Symposia on Quantitative Biology 19:186, 1954.

63. Villee, C. A., and Kimmelstiel, R.: Effects of anoxia on intermediary metabolism in fetal tissues. Neonatal Studies IV:3, 1955. (International Children's Centre.)

64. Shelley, H. J.: Glycogen reserves and their changes at birth and in anoxia. Brit. Med. Bull. 17:137, 1961.

65. Nemeth, A. M.: Glucose-6-phosphatase in the liver of the fetal guinea pig. J. Biol. Chem. 208:773, 1954.

66. Kretchmer, N.: Enzymatic patterns during development. Pediatrics 23:606, 1959.

67. Ashmore, J., and Weber, G.: The role of hepatic glucose-6-phosphatase in the regulation of carbohydrate metabolism. Vitamins and Hormones 17:91, 1959.

68. Dawkins, M. J. R.: Glycogen synthesis and breakdown in fetal and newborn rat liver. Ann. N. Y. Acad. Sc. 111:203, 1963.

69. Auricchio, S., and Rigillo, N.: Glucose-6-phosphatase activity of human foetal liver. Biol. Neonat. 2:146, 1960.

70. Jacquot, R., and Kretchmer, N.: Effect of fetal decapitation on enzymes of glycogen metabolism. J. Biol. Chem. 239:1301, 1964.

71. Nemeth, A. M., Insull, W., Jr., and Flexner, L. B.: Glycogenosis in the liver of the fetal guinea pig. J. Biol. Chem. 208:765, 1954.

72. Kornfeld, R., and Brown, D. H.: The activity of some enzymes of glycogen metabolism in fetal and neonatal guinea pig liver. J. Biol. Chem. 238:1604, 1962.

73. Jost, A., and Hatey, J.: Influence de la décapitation sur la teneur en glycogène du foie du foetus de lapin. C. R. Soc. Biol. (Paris) 143:146, 1949.

74. Grillo, T. A. I., Okuno, G., Price, S., and Foá, P. P.: The activity of uridine diphosphate glucose-glycogen synthetase in some embryonic tissues. J. Histochem. *12*:275, 1964.

75. Burch, H. B., Lowry, O. H., Kuhlman, A. M., Skerjance, J., Diamant, E. J., Lowry, S. R., and Von Dippe, P.: Changes in patterns of enzymes of carbohydrate metabolism in the developing rat liver. J. Biol. Chem. *238*:2267, 1963.

76. Walker, D. G.: The post-natal development of hepatic fructokinase. Biochem. J. *87*:576, 1963.

77. Villee, C. A., Hagerman, D. D., Holmberg, N., Lind, J., and Villee, D. B.: The effects of anoxia on the metabolism of human fetal tissues. Pediatrics *22*:953, 1958.

78. Holmberg, N. G., Kaplan, B., Karvonen, M. J., Lind, J., and Malm, M.: Permeability of human placenta to glucose, fructose and xylose. Acta physiol. scandinav. *36*:291, 1956.

79. Shelley, H. J.: Blood sugars and tissue carbohydrate in foetal and infant lambs and rhesus monkeys. J. Physiol. *153*:527, 1960.

80. Dawes, G. S., Jacobson, H. N., Mott, J. C., and Shelley, H. J.: Some observations on foetal and new-born rhesus monkeys. J. Physiol. *152*:271, 1960.

81. Spellacy, W. N., Goetz, F. C., Greenberg, B. Z., and Ells, J.: Plasma insulin in normal and "early" pregnancy. Obstet. Gynec. *25*:862, 1965.

82. Hendricks, C. H.: Patterns of fetal and placental growth: The second half of normal pregnancy. Obstet. Gynec. *24*:357, 1964.

Chapter Three

CARBOHYDRATE HOMEOSTASIS IN THE NEONATE (FULL TERM AND LOW BIRTH WEIGHT)*

Dramatic physiologic, biochemical and anatomic alterations occur at birth and during the first hours, days and weeks of extrauterine life, and changes in the over-all metabolic requirements and sources of energy are among the most striking of these. *In utero,* the fetus is supplied with a constant infusion of glucose, essential fatty acids, amino acids, vitamins, minerals, water and oxygen. In addition, he is maintained at a controlled temperature and provided with an efficient excretory system via the placenta (see Chapter Two). But at birth, all of this stops abruptly. The lungs expand and with the changing circulation take over the function of providing oxygen to the tissues and removing carbon dioxide and water vapor. Concurrently, the circulation gradually changes from the fetal to the adult type. The kidneys must perform their vital function without the assistance of the placenta. The brain is subjected to multiple new stimuli; the rate of myelination increases; new synapses and pathways are established. The central nervous system assumes control of respiration and circulation. At the same time, the liver must initiate and then further develop many complex activities, including the conjugation (by glucuronide) and excretion of many toxins, the esterification of fatty acids and the production, while the child is fasting, of glucose for the large, glucose-dependent brain.

* The designation *low birth weight* has been used instead of premature to describe infants with a birth weight of less than 2500 grams, usually of unknown period of gestation, as suggested by the Committee on the Fetus and Newborn of the American Academy of Pediatrics (1964).

Immediately after birth, the respiratory quotient (RQ) falls from 1.0, a level which indicates that carbohydrates are the major source of energy, to 0.8 to 0.9, suggesting that fatty acids have become an important sugar substitute during the first hours of life. Changes in blood sugar levels reflect these many alterations in carbohydrate metabolism that occur normally in the infant after delivery.

Although levels of total reducing substance (TRS), true sugar (TS) and glucose have been measured in the blood of newborns since 1911 (see reviews by Norval[1, 2]), there is still disagreement as to the normal range of blood sugar values in the neonate, and as to the precise limits of significantly low or high concentrations. Much of this confusion is a result of differences in techniques in collecting, precipitating and analyzing the blood for true sugar. Apparent differences in results may be attributed to failure of precise reporting of the age of the infant, the time of initiation and composition of feedings and the duration of fasting before sampling. Most authors agree that the blood sugar concentrations in full term infants decrease during the first hours of life,[3, 4] and reach levels within the range of the normal adult (60 to 90 mg./100 ml.) by 4 to 10 days of age.[1, 5, 6] In infants younger than this, it is not unusual to find levels considered to be hypoglycemic by adult standards. The blood glucose levels tend to be even lower in infants of low birth weight[7, 8] and in infants of diabetic mothers.[9-11] As indicated above, however, the absolute values reported vary a great deal, according to the method of analysis used, and a critical reappraisal of differences in reported results is indicated. Values for glucose or true sugar in the blood for normal full term and low birth weight infants during the first hours, days and weeks of life are important reference standards and must be clearly defined.

FACTORS INFLUENCING THE RELIABILITY OF DETERMINATION OF TRUE BLOOD SUGAR OR GLUCOSE

Physiological Influences

At birth, the glucose level in the infant is proportional to that in the mother but fluctuates over a wide range during the first 6 to 24 hours of life. Therefore, the age of the infant in hours, during the first 48 hours after birth, and then in days, must be known if recorded values are to have any significance. The duration of fasting of the infant is also important, particularly in the low birth weight group. Baens et al.[8] and Cornblath et al.[12] have demonstrated irregular and unpredictable variations in glucose levels after a 4 to 5 hour fast in infants weighing less than 2200 grams at birth. As a matter of fact, the repeated sampling of capillary blood can of itself produce changes in blood sugar in the full term infant during the first hours of life.[13]

There does not appear to be a significant diurnal variation in levels of glucose in either full term[1] or low birth weight[8] infants.

Although no correlation was found between changes in blood sugar and a fall in rectal temperatures during the first hour of life in 13 healthy, vaginally delivered term infants who were kept at 25°C. in the nude,[14] our own recent studies have shown that the initial chilling experienced by the newborn infant, if the temperature is not carefully controlled, may be associated with a significant fall in blood glucose levels at 4 to 6 hours

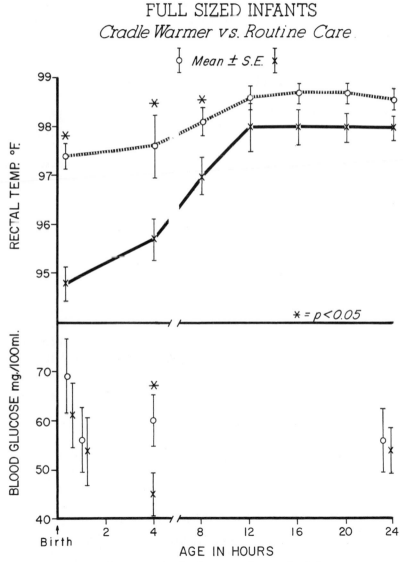

Figure 3. Ten infants were randomly assigned to each of the two groups.

of age. The mean rectal temperatures of 10 full-sized infants were maintained above 97°F. from within 15 minutes after birth by placing the infants in a *cradle-warmer** which provided radiant heat in amounts controlled by a sensitive thermistor placed on the infant's skin. Infants treated in the routine fashion (which consisted of being wrapped in blankets and then given a bath with a hexachlorophene detergent on admission to the nursery) had rectal temperature below 95°F. to 96°F. for as long as 4 hours (Fig. 3). The routinely handled babies had significantly lower levels of blood glucose at 4 to 6 hours of age than those of the infants kept warm. No differences in mean blood sugar values were noted at ½, 1 or 24 hours of age. Our results, as well as those of others, emphasize the need for more data correlating body temperature, oxygen consumption and glucose utilization[15] in both full-sized and low birth weight infants.[16]

Handling the Blood Specimen

Care must be exercised in handling the blood sample. The increased rate of *in vitro* glycolysis in the red blood cells of the newborn infant has been demonstrated by a number of authors.[8, 17, 18] Twenty-eight blood samples from low birth weight infants less than 3 days of age, were found to have a mean (±S.D.) glucose level of 57 ±12.5 mg./100 ml. After standing at room temperature for 3 hours, 13 of the samples had glucose levels of less than 20 mg./100 ml. and in 7 there was no detectable glucose. If whole blood is permitted to stand, erroneously low values for blood sugar may be recorded. Glycolysis in shed blood can be prevented by keeping the sample on ice; by separating the cells immediately and analyzing the plasma for glucose; by adding sodium fluoride (2 mg./ml. of blood) to the anticoagulant; or by precipitating the blood at once. If sodium fluoride is added the blood may be kept, if refrigerated, for as long as 48 hours without loss of sugar; however, this concentration of fluoride may affect the accuracy of some methods that use glucose oxidase for the glucose analysis.[8] Fluoride does not affect the test if the blood is precipitated with barium or sodium hydroxide and zinc sulfate.

Methodology

The proteins in blood interfere with the accurate analysis of glucose in all chemical methods and must be removed either by dialysis or precipitation.[19] The precipitating reagents used for this purpose include tungstic acid (Folin-Wu and modifications), trichloroacetic acid (TCA[20]), perchloric acid (Boehringer) and the alkaline salts of zinc (Somogyi[21]).

---

* The cradle-warmer was described in a letter to the editor by Drs. Rodaway and Oliver (Lancet *1*:1220, 1965).

The latter precipitate glycolytic intermediates, glutathione, sodium fluoride and other nonsugar reducing substances as well as protein. The analysis of the Somogyi protein-free filtrates indicates true sugar (TS) values if proper chemical techniques are used,[22] or glucose if a specific glucose oxidase is used. Chemical methods which depend upon the ability of a sugar to be oxidized or complexed include copper,[23] ferricyanide,[22] O-aminobiphenyl[24] and anthrone reagents of correct pH and salt concentration.[22] True sugar values include glucose, fructose and galactose, although the latter has a reducing power only four-fifths that of glucose. Tungstic, perchloric and trichloroacetic acid do not remove noncarbohydrate reducing substances and, therefore, total reducing substance (TRS) is estimated by the chemical methods. The TRS value, which includes all sugars, glycolytic intermediates, glutathione, ascorbic acid, uric acid and creatine, can vary between —3 and +60 mg./100 ml. (mean 24.3 mg./100 ml.) from a true sugar value in the newborn.[25] This great variability and nonspecificity make values of TRS virtually impossible to interpret in the neonate. On the other hand, if a specific enzymatic method is used to analyze either the trichloroacetic, the perchloric or the tungstic acid filtrate of blood from a newborn, the reduced glutathione present in high concentrations in the red blood cells of the neonate inhibits the color development in the glucose-oxidase system, resulting in erroneously low levels of glucose.[20, 21] This may be avoided by the use of $Ba(OH)_2$ and $ZnSO_4$ (Somogyi) as the precipitating reagents which remove glutathione. Glucose is stable in all of the protein-free filtrates of blood for at least 48 hours with refrigeration.

In addition to specificity, the reliability and reproducibility of the method used for the blood glucose determination must be known. Errors in pipetting small samples of blood (0.05 to 0.2 ml.) must be determined by analyzing repeated aliquots of the same blood. The variability of the sugar analysis may be as little as ±2.0 mg./100 ml., using 0.5 ml. blood and the Somogyi true sugar method (less than 5 per cent),[26] or as great as ±6 to ±10.0 mg./100 ml. (10 to 40 per cent) with smaller blood samples obtained by inexperienced personnel. The variability of results due to technical errors was reported to be less than ±5.0 mg./100 ml. in the majority of the data presented for the normal neonate (Tables 3, 4, 5).

Since the levels of galactose and fructose are usually minimal (less than 5 mg./100 ml.) in the normal infant, true sugar methods[21] can be used as a reliable estimate of blood glucose. Sixty-nine blood samples from low birth weight infants were analyzed for true sugar and glucose with a mean difference of 3.5 mg./100 ml. (range —7 to +18 mg./100 ml.).[8] Furthermore, the true sugar (Somogyi) levels obtained by Ward[7] during the first 48 hours of life in the blood of low birth weight infants were essentially identical with the glucose levels (glucose-oxidase) reported during the same time of life by Baens, et al.[8] (Table 5).

Table 3. Levels of Sugar in Whole Blood in Normal Full-Term Infants

Group	No.		Prior to Milk Feedings at Delivery			Age (hours)											Reference
			Mat.	Umbilical Vein	Umbilical Artery	1/2	1	1-1/2	2	2-1/2	3	4	6	9	12	24	
I Blood sugar mg./100 ml.	46	Mean	108	80	68	60	51	50	52	56	56		56	52	52		Creery & Parkinson[3], 1953
		S.E.	4.2	2.6	4.3	2.5	2.4	2.0	1.8	1.8	2.0		1.6	1.4	1.8		
		Range	68–154	49–126	40–118	27–110	21–87	19–79	30–77	34–90	30–90		32–82	30–73 Normal vaginal	10–75 vaginal		
II Blood sugar mg./100 ml.	32	Mean	Birth	76		77	71		64			63	63	Normal vaginal			Farquhar, 1954[5]
		S.E.		2.6		3.5	3.7		2.4			2.0	2.0				
		Range		43–105		44–128	39–121		39–102			31–87	38–90				
IIIa True blood sugar mg./100 ml.	13	Mean	Vaginal, no fluid to mother 85			55	55		48			55	47	Normal			Cornblath et al.[4], 1961
		S.E.	4.6			5.8	5.2		3.5			3.5	3.9				
		Range	63–121			34–90	35–89		22–73			30–71	27–78				
IVb	7	Mean	Cesarean section, saline I.V. to mother 85	64		75	76		70			60	57			54	
		S.E.	11.2	6.0		6.6	11.8		8.5			9.7	5.3			5.0	
		Range	46–131	38–90		58–107	34–136		45–108			47–101	35–76			43–76	
Vc	23	Mean	Cesarean section, glucose, I.V. to mother 149	107		72	67		57			60	53			67	
		S.E.	17.3	12.6		8.0	8.5		6.1			4.3	3.7			5.7	
		Range	77–354	61–204		31–125	28–117		35–115			27–90	32–77			35–109	
IIId	8	Mean	Vaginal, glucose I.V. to mother 127	89		54	47		41			50	51				
		S.E.	20.1	12.9		8.4	8.3		5.8			4.8	7.0				
		Range	80–250	54–163		27–98	16–82		19–71			34–80	29–81				

Table 4. Levels of Sugar in Whole Blood in Normal Full Term Infants after Initiation of Feeding

Group	No.	Period of Fasting	Method		Age (days)									Reference
					1	2	3	4	5	6	7-13	14-20	21-27	
I True blood sugar mg./100 ml.	51	4 hr.	Somogyi	Mean	55	57	62	68	67					Norval et al., 1949[1]
				S.E.	1.4	1.2	1.5	1.7	1.2					
				Range			15 to 120							
II Blood sugar mg./100 ml.		8 hr.	Ramsey	Mean	66	65	69	73	74	78	81			Farquhar, 1954[5]
				S.E.	2.1	2.0	2.0	2.0	1.8	1.8	1.3			
				Range	43-102	46-91	42-89	49-96	51-94	55-105	54-114			
III Blood glucose mg./100 ml.	10-35	4-1/2 hr.	Glucose Oxidase	Mean	57	57	70	69	68	70	71	69	72	Cornblath and Reisner, 1965[6]
				S.E.	1.8	2.9	3.4	2.3	4.7	2.9	3.3	4.5	2.2	
				Range	21-85	46-77	49-88	58-81	36-90	55-82	58-88	46-104	62-82	

Table 5. Levels of Sugar in Whole Blood in Low Birth Weight Infants

Age (hours) — Groups I and IIa

Group		At Birth Cord	0-3	4-6	12	18	24	30	36	42	48	References
I True blood sugar mg./100 ml.	Mean	71	47	⎰	45	43	43	44	41	46	50	Ward, 1953[7]
	S.E.	6.0										
	Range	24-140	26-72		18-107	15-62	16-60	18-90	25-60	18-78	19-80	
	No. determinations	21	20		23	23	14	15	10	14	14	Somogyi
IIa Blood glucose mg./100 ml.	Mean		41	47	48	43	45		44				Baens et al., 1963[8]
	S.E.		2.6	2.5	3.1		2.5		1.7				
	Range		24-72	21-70	25-89		23-84		18-73				
	No. determinations		20	26	22		37		49				Glucose oxidase

Age (days) — Groups III and IIb

Group		0	1	2	3	4	5	6	7	8	9	10	11	12	13	14-20	21-27	28-55	References
III True blood sugar mg./100 ml.	Mean	45	53	55	60	60	58	63	63	66	65	71	65	63	64				Fast: 2-3 hr. Norval[2], 1950
	S.E.	1.8	1.6	2.0	1.9	2.0	1.4	1.7	1.9	2.1	2.1	2.9	1.7	2.3	2.0				
	Range	18-73					15 to 115 mg./100 ml. →												
	No. determinations	33 ———							28	25	24	23	23	23	22				Somogyi
IIb Blood glucose mg./100 ml.	Mean	44		39	40	42	43	43	45							56	52	48	Fast: 3-1/2 - 4 hrs. Baens et al., 1963[8]
	S.E.	1.7		1.9	1.9	2.1	2.1	2.2	1.6							2.8	2.9	2.5	
	Range	18-73		15-73	20-64	21-79	18-78	22-83	28-61							23-98	18-77	22-83	
	No. determinations	45		43	32	33	33	40	33							26	43		Glucose oxidase

(7-13 day)

Since glucose has been shown to be distributed equally throughout the plasma and intracellular water,[27] the *concentration* of glucose in plasma is somewhat higher than that in whole blood. Capillary blood, being a variable mixture of arterial and venous blood, may have levels of sugar greater than that in peripheral venous blood in the presence of a higher hematocrit.[26] Recently, Stur[28] followed the changes in the hematocrit and true sugar content of plasma, whole blood and red cells in 10 normal infants from birth (mixed cord blood) to 48 hours of age. Significant changes in hematocrit occurred and the relation of true sugar between the plasma and red cell remained constant (1.5 to 1.7:1). In 12 other infants, the mean sugar content of blood supposedly drawn from the inferior vena cava was 14 mg./100 ml. higher than that of heel capillary blood obtained 5 minutes before an exchange transfusion was initiated. Unfortunately, the method for determining the position of the umbilical catheter was not stated. These differences in levels of sugar varied from 4 to 39 mg./100 ml. and did not correlate with the variations in hematocrit of 8 to 24 per cent. The length of time between samplings, the stimulus of introducing an umbilical catheter and the fact that blood from the inferior vena cava also contains blood from the hepatic vein (which should have a high glucose content) could all contribute to the differences in the levels of sugar observed. Furthermore, the finding of both high and very low levels of true sugar in capillary blood from the warmed heel would invalidate Stur's conclusion that the low values reflect local conditions caused by poor circulation to the skin. However, since the samples were not obtained simultaneously from the umbilical catheter and heel and blood flows were not measured, these data, like those reported for capillary-venous differences in the lower limb,[26] are not amenable to precise analysis.

Although many of the early studies of total reducing substances in blood in newborns resulted in valid conclusions,[17, 29–31] these will not be discussed here. Only those studies which include enough details to insure the validity and specificity of the methods will be analyzed in defining the normal, or expected, levels of glucose in the blood of the full-sized and low birth weight neonate.

NORMAL FULL TERM INFANTS

The First Hours of Life

At birth, the sugar level in the blood from the umbilical vein is related to that in the mother (70 to 80 per cent of her level) and is usually higher than that from the umbilical artery. The absolute values vary depending upon the time of the last meal, the duration and nature of the labor and whether parenteral glucose was given to the mother before delivery. Thus, the blood sugar levels in the umbilical vein can vary between 40 and 90 mg./100 ml. after a normal vaginal delivery during which the mother was given no intravenous glucose. On the other hand, levels of sugar as high as 160 to 200 mg./100 ml. have been reported in umbilical vein blood if the mother has been given parenteral glucose prior to and during delivery (Table 3) (Fig. 4). Following birth, there is usually a fall in the infant's level of glucose, the rate being dependent on the starting values, with stabilization at mean blood sugar levels of 45 to 60 mg./100 ml. between 4 and 6 hours of age.[3, 4, 30] Creery and Parkinson[3] followed 23 male and 23 female normal full term infants delivered vaginally at ½- and then at 3-hour intervals during the first 12 hours of life, using a method of glucose analysis which measures some nonsugar reducing substances. Of the 412 sugar determinations done between ½ hour and 12 hours of age, only 9 values (2.2 per cent) were less than 30 mg./100 ml., and the range of sugar levels was between 10 and 110 mg./100 ml. The mean sugar values were between 50 and 60 mg./100 ml., with little change after the first hour of life (Table 3). After following 51 infants for 6 hours after birth, Cornblath et al.[4] reported that 8 of 350 determina-

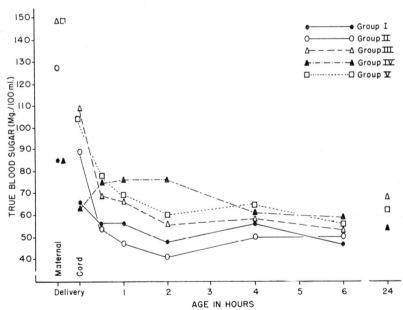

MEAN CONTROL BLOOD SUGAR CURVES

Figure 4. Blood sugar determinations were obtained on 50 full-sized infants between birth and 24 hours of age. (From Cornblath et al., Pediatrics 27:378, 1961.)

	Labor	*Vaginal*	*I.V. Glucose*
Group I	+	+	0
II	+	+	+
III	0	0	+
IV	0	0	0
V	+	0	+

tions (2.3 per cent) of true sugar were below 30 mg./100 ml. in 7 infants during the first 6 hours of life. The mean levels of sugar ranged between 47 to 60 mg./100 ml. by 6 hours of age. If the blood sugar levels were low at birth, an increase, rather than a fall, occurred (see Group IIIb, Table 3 and Fig. 4). **Thus, during the first 6 to 12 hours of life before feedings have been initiated, values for blood sugar vary between 30 and 125 mg./100 ml. in normal infants, with mean values of 50 to 60 mg./100 ml.**[3, 4, 5]

With Feedings

Once feedings are begun, and regardless of whether the infant has been fasting for 4 or even 8 hours before the blood is obtained for sugar analysis, the mean levels of sugar tend to rise (Table 4), but wide fluctuations in individual values persist. The range is from 40 to 120 mg./100 ml. in infants between 1 and 28 days of age. After 24 hours of age, fewer low concentrations were found, and yet the mean fasting levels during the first 72 hours of life were lower than those of the older child or adult. The mean levels in the first week of life were 55 to 70 mg./100 ml. with true sugar or specific glucose methods and 65 to 78 mg./100 ml. with a method measuring some nonglucose reducing substances[5, 32] (Table 4). The effect of breast versus formula feeding or of early feeding versus prolonged fasting on the levels of glucose in the full-sized neonate is unknown. After 72 hours of age, the majority of infants maintain levels of glucose over 50 mg./100 ml. The infants with sugar levels between 30 and 50 mg./100 ml. have been asymptomatic and are not considered to be at risk. Most investigators regard levels of true sugar or glucose in the blood below 30 mg./100 ml. as hypoglycemic in the full term infant during the first 72 hours of life; and thereafter values below 40 mg./100 ml. as hypoglycemic. This definition is a statistical one based on the observation that less than 3 per cent of the blood sugar levels measured in the first 12 hours of life were below 30 mg./100 ml. and no concentrations below this level were found after 48 hours of life in normal full term babies (Tables 3 and 4). No adequate studies have been reported which permit a correlation between low levels of blood glucose and subsequent neurologic or mental growth and development in the full-sized term infant.

LOW BIRTH WEIGHT INFANTS

Before Feeding

In contrast with the considerable body of knowledge about blood glucose levels in full term infants in the first hours of life, there is relatively little information about low birth weight infants. The most complete study was that done by Ward.[7] One hundred fifty-four true sugar determinations (Somogyi) were made at 6-hour intervals between birth and 48 hours of age on 21 infants; 10 weighed between 1.8 and 2.5 kg.; 5, between 1.46 and 1.79 kg.; and 6, less than 1.46 kg. Four infants were fed small amounts of 5 per cent glucose water during the time of study. The mean sugar value from mixed cord blood was 66 mg./100 ml. with a range of 40 to 140 mg./100 ml. Subsequently, a fall to a mean of 47 mg./100 ml. occurred at 0 to 6 hours and to a mean of 41 mg./100 ml. at 36 hours. The mean true sugar then rose to 46 and 50 mg./100 ml. at 42 and 48 hours of age in the 14 survivors. The range of blood sugar values during this time was from 15 to 107 mg./100 ml. (Table 5). At least 6 (4.5 per cent) of the blood sugar levels were between 15 and 19 mg./100 ml. In this study, there was no correlation between the levels of blood sugar and birth weight, clinical distress or survival. Of particular interest, the range and mean of 154 blood glucose (glucose-oxidase) values obtained in the first 48 hours of life by Baens et al.[8] were essentially identical with those reported by Ward (Table 5). In both surveys, between 15 and 20 per cent of the sugar determinations were less than 30 mg./100 ml. In an extensive experience from our laboratories, only an occasional blood glucose value (1.2 per cent) has been less than 20 mg./100 ml. In contrast with the term infant, the low birth weight infant is often starved for a longer period of time and, if fed, is often given relatively small quantities of fluid or calories.

In the low birth weight infant, blood sugar values tend to be lower than those in the full term infant (Fig. 5) and vary between 20 and 100 mg./100 ml. during the first 48 hours after birth.

After Feeding

In studies that began with the infant's second day, Norval found that in 33 well low birth weight infants of 1430 to 2280 grams birth weight, daily mean true sugar levels ranged between 55 and 63 mg./100 ml. in the first week of life and between 63 and 71 mg./100 ml. in the second week.[2] Blood samples were obtained 2 to 3 hours after feedings; all infants were on a 2- to 3-hour feeding schedule. None received any feedings during the initial 24 hours; the majority were fed at 24 hours, but a few were starved until 48 hours of age. She found that there was no correlation between blood sugar values and birth weight or temperature. However, higher mean blood sugars were observed between days 5 and 8 in infants fed every 2 hours as compared with those in infants fed every 3 hours. Four of the 9 infants who died had blood sugar levels below 20 mg./100 ml.

In contrast, Baens et al.,[8] measuring blood glucose levels between birth and 2 months of age in low birth weight infants, found in 109 cases, mean levels significantly lower than those reported by Norval (Table 5). However, 32 per cent of the babies weighed under 1500 grams and 56 per cent between 1500 and 2000 grams at birth; all were fed at 3- to 4-hour intervals and rather slowly initially. Infants weighing over 1250 grams at birth received glucose water in the first 24 hours of age in small amounts. Thereafter, they received between 7 and 40 calories/kg. between 48 and 72 hours of age, depending on birth weight and ability to tolerate feedings and then never more than 110 calories/kg. at full feeding. In addition, 54 of the 109 infants evidenced clinical distress, including respiratory distress, sclerema, apathy and cyanotic or apneic spells. Only four infants in this series died, indicating that very sick low birth weight babies have not been included. Thus, in a large number of low birth weight babies from extramural as well as intramural sources, the mean blood glucose was 39 mg./100 ml. (range 15 to 73) on day 2 and gradually increased to 45 mg./100 ml. (range 28 to 61) during the second week of life, with means of 56 and 52 mg./100 ml. in the third and fourth weeks, respectively (Table 5, Fig. 5). A wide range of values between 15 and 98 mg./100 ml. was found throughout this entire period of observation.

During the first week of life, lower blood glucose levels could be correlated with a birth weight under 2.0 kg., with Caucasian race and with

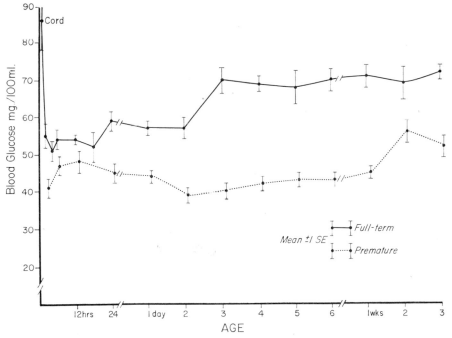

Figure 5. A total of 206 determinations of blood glucose levels were obtained in 179 full-sized infants (> 2.5 kg.) and a total of 442 determinations, in 104 low birth weight infants (< 2.5 kg.) throughout the neonatal period. (From Cornblath and Reisner, New England J. Med. 273:378, 1965.

male sex. There were no statistical correlations between mean glucose values and illness, gestational age or bilirubin levels. The studies did not include the relationship between blood glucose levels and the time of initiating feedings, nor were breast-milk feedings utilized. Statistically, 98.8 per cent of the glucose values were over 20 mg./100 ml. in these infants; thus, levels of glucose less than 20 mg./100 ml. were considered as being significantly hypoglycemic (see Chapter Five).

In surveying the levels of blood glucose during the first 4 days of life in all admissions to a premature nursery during 1963 and 1964, the mean levels of glucose were correlated with the age at which feedings were initiated. The results are tabulated in Table 6. Infants who had a mean birth weight of 1.83 kg. and were given their first feeding before 24 hours of age had a significantly higher mean blood glucose on day 2 and day 3 than did infants with a mean birth weight of 1.75 kg. and a 32-hour period of fasting. On day 3, the infants who had been starved for 32 hours had a mean glucose level lower than that of infants fed between 24 and 32 hours of age (Table 6). Smallpeice and Davies[55] have advocated the initiation of breast milk feedings "shortly after delivery" in amounts of 60 ml./kg. during the first 24 hours of life, of 90 ml./kg. during the second, and of 120–150

Table 6.   The Correlation of Blood Glucose Levels with
Age of First Feeding

Age First Fed (hours)	Birth Wt. Mean (range)	Mean ± S.E. Whole Blood Glucose mg./100 ml. Age (hours)				
		0–24	24–48	48–72	72–96	96–120
< 16	1.93 kg. (1.43–2.15)	51 ± 4.2 (7)+	48 ± 2.7 (14)	48 ± 3.6 (14)	47 ± 4.5 (11)	59 ± 2.9 (4)
16–24	1.83 kg. (1.15–2.42)	53 ± 5.1 (15)	52 ± 2.3 (38)	52 ± 2.5 (35)	53 ± 2.4 (33)	54 ± 3.7 (22)
24–32	1.87 kg. (1.25–2.41)	47 ± 3.4 (19)	46 ± 1.9 (53)	49 ± 2.1 (54)	52 ± 1.8 (49)	53 ± 2.5 (31)
32–40	1.75 kg. (1.36–2.4)	51 (3)	48 ± 4.0 (13)	44 ± 2.7 (13)	45 ± 2.2 (13)	53 (2)

Groups	Days 0	1	2	3	4
16–24 vs. 24–32		t = 2.01*			
16–24 vs. 32–40			t = 2.17*	t = 2.46*	
24–32 vs. 32–40				t = 2.47*	

*p = <.05
+Figures in parentheses refer to number of infants in each group.

ml./kg. during the third and fourth 24 hours of age by the use of indwelling polyvinyl nasogastric tubes. Early-fed infants of between 1.0 and 2.0 kg. birth weight passed meconium sooner, regained their birth weight more quickly and had lower bilirubin levels than another group of infants of similar weight cared for in another nursery and fed smaller amounts at a later age (between 4 and 32 hours after delivery). However, the early initiation of breast milk feedings appeared to have little influence on the blood glucose levels since the mean value of the lowest glucose determined for 50 infants during the first 80 hours of age was 43 mg./100 ml., which was almost identical with the results reported by Baens et al.[8] and Ward.[7] Eight of the 50 early-fed infants had a blood sugar level at or below 20 mg./100 ml. Unfortunately, the study was not a controlled one and all of the results must be verified in a properly randomized controlled investigation before any recommendations are justified.

After 24 hours of age and throughout the first month of life, the low birth weight infant has significantly lower blood glucose levels than the full term infant (Fig. 5). The blood sugar is rarely less than 30 mg./100 ml. in the full term infant and rarely less than 20 mg./100 ml. in the low birth weight infant. The upper limit of a normal blood sugar level is 125 mg./100 ml. based on the data presented (Tables 3, 4, 5).

Glucose Levels in Cerebrospinal Fluid

The sugar content of the *cerebrospinal fluid* (CSF) is usually only 60 to 70 per cent that of a simultaneously obtained *blood* glucose determination in children and adults. A number of studies of CSF and blood total reducing substances have been done in the neonate, both full term and low birth weight (see Otila[33] for review). In the young infant, CSF sugar concentrations have been reported which are higher than those in blood (Liebe, 8 of 111[34]; Otila, 13 of 26 infants[33]). Unfortunately, it is impossible to determine from these studies the reliability of the values for blood total reducing substances because no description was given of precautions to prevent glycolysis in this blood. However, since the total reducing substance in CSF is essentially glucose, whereas other nonglucose substances are present in blood filtrates (*vide supra*), one may speculate that the sugar concentration in the CSF in the neonate can exceed values of glucose in blood. Concentrations of glucose over 300 mg./100 ml. in the CSF have been reported in the syndrome of transient diabetes mellitus in the neonate (see Chapter Six), suggesting an increased permeability and penetration of glucose into the CSF in these young babies. In contrast, in diabetic adults with blood sugars of 600 mg./100 ml., the CSF glucose concentration usually will not exceed 250 mg./100 ml.[35]

A careful study of simultaneous blood and CSF glucose determinations under conditions of hypo- and hyperglycemia is needed before normal values for CSF sugar concentrations or their relationship to blood levels can be made in the neonate.

PHYSIOLOGIC CONTROL OF BLOOD GLUCOSE LEVELS IN NEONATE

Although many theories have been offered in the past to explain the relatively low blood sugar levels, and their marked fluctuations, in the neonate, only recently have studies been done in an attempt to elucidate the physiologic mechanisms involved.

The mechanisms accounting for the low levels of sugar during the first hours of life in the newborn, when compared to a minimum normal of 50 mg./100 ml. in the adult, have been explored extensively. Insufficient production of glucose by the liver and excessive peripheral utilization of sugar have been proposed as possible causes. The theory of increased utilization is shaken by these recent findings: normal levels of immunologic insulin[36] and insulin-like material[37] in the plasma; slow disappearance of glucose administered intravenously[37, 38]; absence of an elevation in plasma insulin activity following a rapid infusion of glucose; and prolonged hyperglycemia after administration of glucagon with or without epinephrine. Actually, then, peripheral utilization of glucose in the neonate is low, possibly as a result of the elevated concentrations of growth hormone observed at and after birth[39] and of the rise in the level of free fatty acids (FFA) as the blood sugar values fall.[40]

The role of the liver is less clear. Until feedings are begun, the major source of glucose is glycogenolysis and gluconeogenesis in the liver. The enzymatic capability to perform both functions has been demonstrated in the fetus[41] (see Chapter Two), but its physiologic and endogenous hormonal control have not been elucidated in the newborn. Indirect studies of the known metabolic pathways of carbohydrate metabolism in the liver have been initiated. For example, galactose, administered intravenously, results in a prompt elevation of the level of glucose, although the over-all rate of utilization of galactose is slow in the first hours of life.[13] A rapid infusion of fructose produces a transient hypoglucosemia within the first 6 hours of life, a reaction more prolonged than that which occurs after 24 to 36 hours of age,[42] suggesting a limit in the capacity of some of the metabolic pathways, cofactors or enzymes in the newborn liver. However, a marked hyperglucosemia occurs after the initial phase. Although the rates of disappearance from the blood of all three hexoses (glucose, galactose and fructose) are diminished in the newborn infant, conversion of galactose and fructose to glucose does occur promptly.

Information about the endogenous neural, hormonal and enzymatic responses to low levels of glucose in blood during the first days of life is limited. Indirect evidence would suggest that the quantity of transplacental corticosteroid may be important as measured by the hyperglycemic response to glucagon in the first 2 hours of life.[4, 43] If the baby is delivered without labor and the level of 17 OH-corticosteroid in plasma is low in the newborn, the blood sugar response to glucagon is minimal compared to that following administration of compound F (cortisol). Yet, the neonate appears capable of producing steroids in quantities consistent with his body surface.[44] The stimuli necessary to provoke the adrenal cortex in the first hours after birth, and the degree of its responsiveness, require further study. Certain stresses (hypoglycemia has not yet been identified as one of them) can provoke increased production of epinephrine and norepinephrine in premature infants in the first 24 hours of life.[45] In the full term infant between 2 and 7 days of age, insulin-induced hypoglycemia did result in a significant increase in epinephrine excreted in the urine,[46] similar studies of glucagon levels and production are also necessary. Levels of growth hormone have been found to be high immediately after birth and to rise rapidly with insulin-induced hypoglycemia in the first hours of life.[39] Whether the epinephrine and steroid response are similar is not known. Studies of free fatty acids during induced and spontaneous hypoglycemia are also needed. Although a prompt secretion of growth hormone occurs in the newborn infant, he is exquisitely sensitive to insulin which, in doses of 0.1 u/kg. intravenously, or of 0.25 u/kg. subcutaneously, can produce a prolonged and severe hypoglycemia.[46, 47] The reason for this prolonged low level of sugar is not apparent. More data and knowledge of the hormonal interrelationships and control in the metabolism of glucose, and in gluconeogenesis and glycogen synthesis and breakdown during the first hours and days of life are needed.

In the low birth weight infant, the relatively low levels of glucose persist for a much longer period, and few studies have been done to elucidate the mechanisms. In 1929, Van Creveld[17] studied 60 well low birth weight infants by means of oral glucose tolerance tests, measurements of glycolysis in the blood, hematocrits and changes in total reducing substance (TRS) levels with age. He concluded that the low levels of TRS were not due to excess insulin, increased glycolysis or lack of glycogen stores in the liver, but rather to faulty hepatic regulation of glucose output. From then until 1963 few reports exploring the variability of glucose levels in the low birth weight infant were published.[12] At this time, an indirect approach was used to estimate over-all carbohydrate metabolism in low birth weight infants between 1 and 62 days of life. This was done by measuring the rate of glucose disappearance, the blood glucose response to tolbutamide, to leucine, to glucagon and to epinephrine, and the rate of disappearance of fructose or galactose and their conversion to glucose. A total of 148 tolerance tests was done on 114 infants who weighed between 1.02 kg. and 2.26 kg. at birth. The reduced rate of either utilization or removal of an intravenous glucose load, as well as the minimal hypoglycemic response to tolbutamide and to leucine would not support the hypothesis that an excess of or hypersensitivity to endogenous insulin is responsible for the low levels of glucose found in these low birth weight infants. On the other hand, the hypoglycemia after exogenous insulin was striking during the first days of life, indicating that the insulin-sensitive peripheral tissues were capable of response.

Estimates of glycogen stores in the liver of the premature infant were made by measuring the hyperglycemic response to glucagon with or without epinephrine. It would appear that the stores of glycogen in the liver are high during the first 6 hours of life[4, 48] and are reduced between 3 and 7 days of age (as shown by lack of increment in the hyperglycemia after increasing the glucagon tenfold (30 to 300 µg./kg.) in the latter group.)[12] After 7 days glycogen stores are increased and appear adequate as suggested by the prolonged hyperglycemia observed after administration of glucagon plus epinephrine.

Both an ample reserve of glycogen and the dynamic process of gluconeogenesis are important in maintaining an adequate level of blood glucose in the absence of a sufficient exogenous supply (as occur with fasting) or in the presence of excess peripheral utilization. But before gluconeogenesis can occur, amino acids must be deaminated. The conversion of fructose to glucose is another indirect measure of a portion of the metabolic pathway involved in gluconeogenesis. Although the rate of fructose disappearance increases with age, hyperglucosemia follows the intravenous administration of fructose even in the 1 day old low birth weight infant.

Galactose in milk is one of the major sugars ingested by the low birth weight infant and has been reported to produce hypoglucosemia in some infants who did not have galactose intolerance.[49] Both oral[50] and intravenous[12] galactose result in a prompt rise in blood glucose in low birth weight infants.

Although indirect, the data obtained in studies of the premature infant do suggest that insulin secretion is diminished during the first days of life and that no major metabolic block is demonstrable in the liver of the early-born. Furthermore, low birth weight infants are able to produce corticosteroids[44] and epinephrine[45] during the first days of life and to increase the levels of the latter in respiratory distress. The premature infant also has high plasma levels of growth hormone during the first 8 weeks of life and can respond to insulin-induced hypoglycemia with a significant increase in growth hormone secretion on his very first day.[39] Until direct measurements of hepatic glucose production, of peripheral utilization in muscle and brain, and of endocrine secretions and responses to changes in blood glucose can be made, the relative importance of the liver and peripheral utilization in determining levels of blood glucose cannot be appreciated. However, with the evidence available, it is possible to postulate that the low glucose values may be related to the insulin-insensitive, glucose-dependent brain and to inadequate liver function. The brain in the low birth weight infant is more than 6 times its proportional size in the adult[51] and is undergoing rapid myelination, proliferation and growth in the neonatal period.[52] Therefore, the brain may be utilizing the glucose at a rate exceeding the maximal glucose-producing capacity of the liver.[12] This hypothesis is susceptible to experimental verification by measuring blood flow and oxygen and glucose consumption across the brain and glucose production by the liver. This must be done before any conclusions are justified.

Further studies in small, low birth weight infants are indicated utilizing the best available analytical techniques. These investigations should consider the effects on blood glucose levels of the infant's condition at birth, of his body and skin temperatures, of his oxygen consumption, of his respiratory quotient, and of whether feedings begin early or late. One such study has been interpreted to show no effect on the blood glucose levels from repeated glucagon administration or early feeding.[53] However, between 24 and 48 hours of age, the starved group had mean blood sugar (±S.D.) levels of 27.5 ±12 to 34.8 ±14.0 mg./100 ml., whereas the early-fed group had levels of 37.5 ±8.6 to 54 ±18.8 mg./100 ml. Thereafter, the levels in all groups were similar. Verification of this finding under carefully controlled conditions seems indicated.

SUMMARY

The blood sugar level in the normal full term infant at birth is 70 to 80 per cent that of his mother. In the first hours of life the range of values varies between 30 and 100 mg./100 ml., with mean levels of about 50 mg./100 ml. After 72 hours of age the levels following a 4- to 8-hour fast soon reach mean values of 65 to 80 mg./100 ml.

In the low birth weight infants, blood glucose values may range between 20 and 100 mg./100 ml. during the first 2 months of life. Values are significantly lower than those in the full term infant throughout this period.

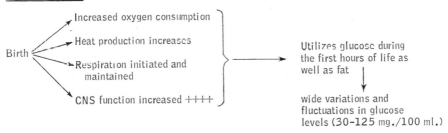

Full-sized Term:

Birth →
- Increased oxygen consumption
- Heat production increases
- Respiration initiated and maintained
- CNS function increased ++++

Utilizes glucose during the first hours of life as well as fat ↓

wide variations and fluctuations in glucose levels (30–125 mg./100 ml.)

The balance between hepatic production and peripheral utilization results in equilibration of the blood sugar level at a mean of 50 mg./100 ml. until feedings are begun. Thereafter, between 48 and 72 hours of age, the balance shifts to mean glucose levels of 60 to 70 mg./100 ml. with adequate feedings and regulation of glycogen metabolism, gluconeogenesis and glucose production.

Figure 6. Schematic summary of the control of blood glucose levels in the full-sized term infant.

Low Birth Weight:

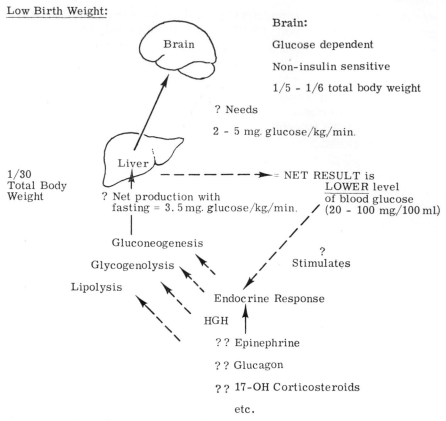

Brain:

Glucose dependent

Non-insulin sensitive

1/5 - 1/6 total body weight

? Needs

2 - 5 mg. glucose/kg./min.

1/30 Total Body Weight

? Net production with fasting = 3.5 mg. glucose/kg./min.

= NET RESULT is LOWER level of blood glucose (20 - 100 mg./100 ml)

Gluconeogenesis

Glycogenolysis

Lipolysis

?
Stimulates

Endocrine Response

HGH

?? Epinephrine

?? Glucagon

?? 17-OH Corticosteroids

etc.

Figure 7. Schematic summary of the control of blood glucose levels in the low birth weight infant.

REFERENCES

1. Norval, M. A., Kennedy, R. L. J., and Berkson, J.: Blood sugar in newborn infants. J. Pediat. *34*:342, 1949.
2. Norval, M. A.: Blood sugar values in premature infants. J. Pediat. *36*:177, 1950.
3. Creery, R. D. G., and Parkinson, T. J.: Blood glucose changes in the newborn. I. The blood glucose pattern of normal infants in the first 12 hours of life. Arch. Dis. Child. 28:134, 1953.
4. Cornblath, M., Ganzon, A. F., Nicolopoulos, D., Baens, G. S., Hollander, R. J., Gordon, M. H., and Gordon, H. H.: Studies of carbohydrate metabolism in the newborn infant. III. Some factors influencing the capillary blood sugar and the response to glucagon during the first hours of life. Pediatrics 27:378 1961.
5. Farquhar, J. W.: Control of the blood sugar level in the neonatal period. Arch. Dis. Child. *29*:519, 1954.
6. Cornblath, M., and Reisner, S. H.: Blood glucose in the neonate, clinical significance. New England J. Med. 273:378, 1965.
7. Ward, O. C.: Blood sugar studies on premature babies. Arch. Dis. Child. 28:194, 1953.

8. Baens, G. S., Lundeen, E., and Cornblath, M.: Studies of carbohydrate metabolism in the newborn infant. VI. Levels of glucose in blood in premature infants. Pediatrics 31:580, 1963.

9. Reis, R. A., DeCosta, E. J., and Allweiss, M. D.: The management of the pregnant diabetic woman and her newborn infant. Am. J. Obstet. Gynec. 60:1023, 1950.

10. Pennoyer, M. M., and Hartmann, A. F., Sr.: Management of infants born of diabetic mothers. Postgrad. Med. 18:199, 1955.

11. Farquhar, J. W.: The significance of hypoglycaemia in the newborn infant of the diabetic woman. Arch. Dis. Child. 31:203, 1956.

12. Cornblath, M., Wybregt, S. H., and Baens, G. S.: Studies of carbohydrate metabolism in the newborn infant. VII. Tests of carbohydrate tolerance in premature infants. Pediatrics 32:1007, 1963.

13. Mulligan, P. B., and Schwartz, R.: Hepatic carbohydrate metabolism in the genesis of neonatal hypoglycemia. Effects of the administration of epinephrine, glucagon, and galactose. Pediatrics 30:125, 1962.

14. James, L. S.: Personal communication.

15. Gandy, G. M., Adamsons, K., Jr., Cunningham, N., Silverman, W. A., and James, L. S.: Thermal environment and acid-base homeostasis in human infants during the first few hours of life. J. Clin. Invest. 43:751, 1964.

16. Sinclair, J. C., and Silverman, W. A.: Relative hypermetabolism in undergrown, human neonates. Lancet 2:49, 1964. (Letter to the Editor.)

17. Van Creveld, S.: Carbohydrate metabolism of premature infants; blood sugar during fasting. Am. J. Dis. Child. 38:912, 1929.

18. Zinkham, W. H.: An in-vitro abnormality of glutathione metabolism in erythrocytes from normal newborns. Pediatrics 23:18, 1959.

19. Sunderman, W. F., Copeland, B. E., MacFate, R. P., Martens, V. E., Nauman, H. N., and Stevenson, G. F.: Manual of American Society of Clinical Pathologists Workshop on Glucose. Am. J. Clin. Path. 26:1355, 1956.

20. Relander, A., and Räihä, C. E.: Differences between the enzymatic and O-toluidine methods of blood glucose determinations. Scand. J. Clin. Lab. Invest. 15:221, 1963.

21. Somogyi, M.: Determination of blood sugar. J. Biol. Chem. 160:69, 1945.

22. Fales, F. W., Russell, J. A., and Fain, J. N.: Some applications and limitations of the enzymic, reducing (Somogyi), and anthrone methods for estimating sugar. Clin. Chem. 7:389, 1961.

23. Somogyi, M.: Notes on sugar determinations. J. Biol. Chem. 195:19, 1952.

24. Athanail, G., and Cabaud, P. G.: Simplified colorimetric method for true blood glucose. J. Lab. & Clin. Med. 51:321, 1958.

25. Hallman, N.: Studies on the blood sugar of newborn children and of the children of diabetic mothers. Bibl. Paediat. 4:535, 1959. (Modern Problems in Pediatrics.)

26. Cornblath, M., Levin, E. Y., and Gordon, H. H.: Studies of carbohydrate metabolism in the newborn. I. Capillary-venous differences in blood sugar in normal newborn infants. Pediatrics 18:167, 1956.

27. MacKay, E. M.: The distribution of glucose in human blood. J. Biol. Chem. 97:685, 1932.

28. Stur, O.: Studies on the physiologic hypoglycemia of newborns. Biol. Neonat. 6:38, 1963.

29. Morriss, W. H.: The obstetrical significance of the blood-sugar with special reference to the placental interchange. Bull. Johns Hopkins Hosp. 28:140, 1917.

30. Ketteringham, R. C., and Austin, B. R.: Blood sugar during labor, at delivery and postpartum, with observations on newborns. Am. J. Med. Sci. 195:318, 1938.

31. Ketteringham, R. C., and Austin, B. R.: Induced hyperglycemia at delivery; its effect and clinical application. Am. J. Obstet. Gynec. 37:1000, 1939.

32. Ramsay, W. N. H.: Determination of reducing sugar in blood. Biochem. J. 47:xli, xlii, 1950.

33. Otila, E.: Studies on the cerebrospinal fluid in premature infants. Acta Paediat. 35:(suppl. 8) 3, 1948 (see p. 65).

34. Liebe, S.: Zur Diagnose und Prognose geburtstraumatischer intrakranieller Blutungen. Mschr. Kinderheilk. *83*:1, 1940.
35. Fishman, R. A.: Studies of the transport of sugars between blood and cerebrospinal fluid in normal states and in meningeal carcinomatosis. Trans. Am. Neurolog. Assoc. *88*:114, 1963.
36. Spellacy, W. N., Goetz, F. C., Greenberg, B. Z., and Ells, J.: The human placental gradient for plasma insulin and blood glucose. Am. J. Obstet. Gynec. *90*:753, 1964.
37. Baird, J. D., and Farquhar, J. W.: Insulin-secreting capacity in newborn infants of normal and diabetic women. Lancet *1*:71, 1962.
38. Bowie, M. D., Mulligan, P. B., and Schwartz, R.: Intravenous glucose tolerance in the normal newborn infant: the effects of a double dose of glucose and insulin. Pediatrics *31*:590, 1963.
39. Cornblath, M., Parker, M. L., Reisner, S. H., Forbes, A. E., and Daughaday, W. H.: Secretion and metabolism of growth hormone in premature and full term infants. J. Clin. Endocr. *25*:209, 1965.
40. Novak, M., Melichar, V., Hahn, P., and Koldovsky, O.: Levels of lipids in the blood of newborn infants and the effect of glucose administration. Physiol. Bohemoslov. *10*:488, 1961.
41. Villee, C. A.: Regulation of blood glucose in the human fetus. J. Appl. Physiol. *5*:437, 1953.
42. Schwartz, R., Gamsu, H., Mulligan, P. B., Reisner, S. H., Wybregt, S. H., and Cornblath, M.: Transient intolerance to exogenous fructose in the newborn. J. Clin. Invest. *43*:333, 1964.
43. Oh, W., Baens, G. S., Migeon, C. J., Wybregt, S. H., and Cornblath, M.: Studies of carbohydrate metabolism in the newborn infant. V. The effect of cortisol on the hyperglycemic response to glucagon. Pediatrics *30*:769, 1962.
44. Kenny, F. M., Malvaux, P., and Migeon, C. J.: Cortisol production rate in newborn babies, older infants, and children. Pediatrics *31*:360, 1963.
45. Cheek, D. B., Malinek, M., and Fraillon, J. M.: Plasma adrenaline and noradrenaline in the neonatal period, and infants with respiratory distress syndrome and placental insufficiency. Pediatrics *31*:374, 1963.
46. Greenberg, R. E., Lind, J., and von Euler, U. S.: Effect of posture and insulin hypoglycemia on catecholamine excretion in the newborn. Acta Paediat. *49*:780, 1960.
47. Hartmann, A. F., and Jaudon, J. C.: Hypoglycemia. J. Pediat. *11*:1, 1937.
48. Hartmann, A. F.: Pathologic physiology in some disturbances of carbohydrate metabolism. J. Pediat. *47*:537, 1955.
49. Cornblath, M., Levin, E. Y., and Marquetti, E.: Studies of carbohydrate metabolism in the newborn. II. The effect of glucagon on the concentration of sugar in capillary blood of the newborn infant. Pediatrics *21*:885, 1958.
50. Hartmann, A. F., Grunwaldt, E., and James, D. H.: Blood galactose in infants and children. J. Pediat. *43*:1, 1953.
51. Haworth, J. C., and Ford, J. D.: Blood-sugar in infants after lactose feedings. Lancet *2*:794, 1960.
52. Richter, D.: The stability of the nervous system during development. *In* Wolstenholme, G. E. W., and O'Connor, M. (eds.): Ciba Foundation Symposium on Somatic Stability in the Newly Born. Boston, Little, Brown, 1961, 296.
53. Kennedy, C.: Physiologic characteristics of growth of the human brain. J. Pediat. *59*:928, 1961.
54. Haworth, J. C., and Ford, J. D.: The effect of early and late feeding and glucagon upon blood sugar and serum bilirubin levels of premature babies. Arch. Dis. Child. *38*:328, 1963.
55. Smallpeice, V., and Davies, P. A.: Immediate feeding of premature infants with undiluted breast-milk. Lancet *2*:1349, 1964.

PART II

Problems of the Newborn and Neonate

Chapter Four

INFANT OF THE
DIABETIC MOTHER

"These infants are remarkable not only because like foetal versions of Shadrach, Meshach and Abednego, they emerge at least alive from within the fiery metabolic furnace of diabetes mellitus, but because they resemble one another so closely that they might well be related. They are plump, sleek, liberally coated with vernix caseosa, full-faced and plethoric. The umbilical cord and the placenta share in the gigantism. During their first 24 or more extra-uterine hours they lie on their backs, bloated and flushed, their legs flexed and abducted, their lightly closed hands on each side of the head, the abdomen prominent and their respiration sighing. They convey a distinct impression of having had such a surfeit of both food and fluid pressed upon them by an insistent hostess that they desire only peace so that they may recover from their excesses. And on the second day their resentment of the slightest noise improves the analogy while their trembling anxiety seems to speak of intra-uterine indiscretions of which we know nothing" (Farquhar). (Fig. 8)

The infant of the diabetic mother, so exquisitely described by Farquhar[1] has survived an unusual genetic and environmental ordeal. While the ability to conceive does not apparently differ between diabetic and nondiabetic women, fetal wastage, neonatal mortality and morbidity in the offspring of diabetic mothers are significantly higher. Dekaban and Baird[2] studied 245 pregnancies of 48 diabetic mothers against comparable nondiabetic controls in a retrospective survey. In addition to a high abortion and stillbirth rate, a high neonatal death rate and morbidity rate were found (Table 7).

If the mother was in the prediabetic phase, neonatal mortality was

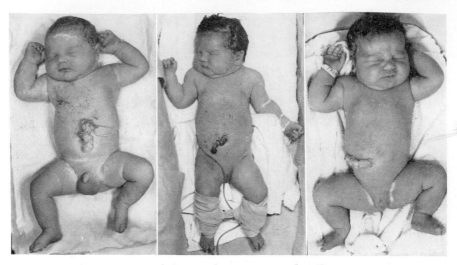

*. . . for some of us are out of breath
And all of us are fat.* (Lewis Carroll)

Figure 8. Unrelated infants of diabetic mothers observed by J. W. Farquhar. (From Arch. Dis. Childhood 34:76, 1959, with the kind permission and cooperation of Dr. Farquhar.)

not abnormal, but total fetal wastage was increased significantly. In contrast to these data, Kyle's[3] recent summary indicates that the incidence of spontaneous abortion in diabetic pregnancies (10 per cent) is not increased over that in nondiabetics; however, a higher rate has been reported by White[4] for women with longstanding diabetes and vascular complications. All authorities agree that if gestation goes beyond 28 weeks, survival is diminished for the infant from a diabetic pregnancy. The improvement in over-all survival rates in recent years—from 60 to over 80 per cent—appears to be the result of combined careful medical, obstetric and pediatric management.

Table 7.   Fetal and Neonatal Wastage in Diabetes Mellitus

	Total No.	Abortions		Stillbirths		Neonatal Deaths		Abnormal Survivors	
		No.	%	No.	%	No.	%	No.	%
Diabetes	157	47	29.9	18	11.5	13	8.3	6	3.8
Prediabetes	78	16	20.5	4	5.1	1	1.3	2	2.6
Controls	249	31	12.4	3	1.2	9	3.0	1	0.4

*Data obtained from Dekaban and Baird[2] in a retrospective study. Prediabetes was defined as the period preceding the diagnosis of diabetes. In this study, prediabetes would have included undiagnosed gestational diabetes as well as prediabetes as defined in this text.

THE MOTHER AND HER DISEASE

The analysis of the diverse problems presented by maternal diabetes has been difficult because of the complexity of the metabolic disturbance. White[5] has suggested a classification based on severity of the disease, which would permit comparison of data reported by different clinics. Table 8 presents a classification modified so as to include less manifest and more subtle forms of the derangement. Class A, which has received recent emphasis from Miller,[6] Carrington[7] and Dolger et al.,[8] appears to represent a heterogenous group which can be subdivided into three groups: (1) gestational diabetes, (2) prediabetes and (3) infants of diabetic fathers. *Gestational diabetes* is defined as an abnormality of glucose tolerance (oral or intravenous), demonstrable during pregnancy, with reversion to normal within 6 weeks after delivery. This type of diabetes is particularly common in obese women (over 200 lb. body weight). *Prediabetes* as defined here includes pregnant women with a genetic liability to the disease, but who have normal glucose tolerance. The genetic predisposition is evidenced by a strong family history of diabetes, a history of previous overweight infants (> 4 kg. or 9 lbs.) or of unexplained stillbirths beyond 28 weeks' gestation. Previously, gestational diabetes had been included in the prediabetic classification. Thus, a woman might have prediabetes without an abnormality of glucose metabolism, but might later evidence gestational diabetes and might finally develop overt diabetes. Miller[9] and Kriss[10] have emphasized the importance of excessive birth weight in infants in predicting the possible occurrence of overt diabetes mellitus in the mother. The final subgroup represents situations in which the father is diabetic: there are conflicting

Table 8. Modified White Classification of Diabetes and Pregnancy[5]

Class A	— High fetal survival, no insulin, minimal dietary regulation.
	1. Gestational diabetes — abnormal glucose tolerance test during pregnancy which reverts to normal within a few weeks after delivery.
	2. Prediabetes — normal glucose tolerance test, but family history of diabetes, previous large infants or unexplained stillbirths.
	3. Infants of diabetic fathers (?).
Class B	— Onset of diabetes in adult life after age 20 years, duration less than 10 years, no vascular disease.
Class C	— Diabetes of long duration (10–19 years) with onset during adolescence (over 10 years) with minimal vascular disease.
Class D	— Diabetes of 20 years or more duration, onset before age 10 years, evidence of vascular disease (i.e., retinitis, albuminuria, hypertension).
Class E	— Patients with D plus demonstrable calcification of pelvic vessels.
Class F	— Patients with D plus nephritis.

reports concerning the paternal genetic effects of diabetes on the infant.[11] (Classes B through F are summarized in Table 8.)

Until recently, clinical and investigational emphasis has been given to infants of *insulin-dependent* diabetics. For example, in the extensive selected series from the Joslin Clinic reported by Gellis and Hsia,[12] only 11 out of 767 pregnancies occurred in women from the Class A group (glucose tolerance abnormality only). However, the importance of the Class A group is evident in the recent experience of Dolger,[8] who reported 137 Class A patients in a total of 253 diabetic pregnancies in a general hospital population. Moreover, the neonatal mortality was 4.4 per cent in this group, significantly greater than that in a nondiabetic population. The prevalence of diabetes in pregnancy is reported to be 1 in 116 (0.86 per cent) for gestational diabetes and 1 in 500 to 1 in 1000 for overt diabetes.[13]

Perinatal mortality has been related to the mother's diabetes, to the pregnancy and to the delivery. Neither the degree of insulin dependence, the age of onset nor the duration of diabetes influences fetal survival; the *severity* of the derangement, as judged by vascular complications (Classes E–F), determines the rate of fetal loss. In the Gellis series, fetal mortality was 70 of 481, or 14.5 per cent for combined classes B and C, but 79 of 275, or 28.7 per cent for combined classes D through F. While ketoacidosis and coma also have a detrimental effect on the fetus, maternal hypoglycemia apparently does not have an important relationship to survival.

Factors related to *pregnancy* which may affect the outcome are toxemia and hydramnios. The incidence of toxemia is not greater in diabetics unless vascular disease is also present. With toxemia, fetal loss *in utero* has been higher, but neonatal loss is not increased.[14] Although there *appears* to be a greater perinatal loss when the diabetic mother has toxemia, the data are conflicting. Hydramnios, an associated complication, may have an adverse affect upon the fetus. Pedersen and Jørgensen[15] estimated amniotic fluid in diabetic pregnancies and observed that in 50 per cent there were volumes greater than 1000 ml. and in 20 per cent there were volumes greater than 1500 ml. but they found no correlation with diabetic retinitis, toxemia, fetal mortality or birth weight. In contrast, Stevenson[16] has reported an increased incidence, associated with hydramnios, of stillbirths, of congenital malformations, and of early deaths in infants who did not have congenital malformations.

Importance of Prenatal Care

Control of Maternal Diabetes

Improvement in mortality rate has been attributed to a variety of factors of which intensive care by a medical team appears to be the most significant. Brandstrup, Osler and Pedersen[17] have also observed a difference in mortality depending upon the duration of hospitalization prior to delivery. In a series of 486 babies, the perinatal mortality was 12 per cent when the mother had been hospitalized for longer than 70 days before delivery; 18 per cent for those observed for 53 to 69 days; and 29 per cent when predelivery observations were only 0 to 52 days. This last group did not always benefit from preterm delivery, and this factor may represent a significant variable. In or out of the hospital, primary attention is directed toward metabolic stability and homeostasis in the mother (and hence in the fetus), including good nutrition and the avoidance of keto-acidosis, of excessive glycosuria and of irregular or marked fluctuations in the blood glucose concentration. While hypoglycemia has not been directly correlated with fetal morbidity and mortality, its effect on fetal metabolism has not yet been adequately defined in humans. It is known that fetal heart rate irregularities have been recorded in a high percentage of cases in which the mother had hypoglycemia.[18] Therefore, further studies correlating hypoglycemia and its effects on the fetus are indicated and, until such data are available, hypoglycemia should be prevented insofar as is possible. In many clinics, long term hospitalization of the pregnant diabetic has been used to achieve close dietary and insulin control.

Gestational diabetes with obesity poses additional dietary problems, since caloric restriction in such patients may result in ketonuria secondary to starvation. Four or five small meals equally spaced may be necessary under these circumstances.

Hormone Therapy of the Mother

The controversial program of adjunct therapy with estrogen and progesterone was first proposed by Smith and Smith,[19] who noted in the pregnant diabetic an increased level of serum and urinary chorionic gonadotropin which was apparently related to the fetal death rate. White et al.[20] have vigorously advocated such therapy and have attributed their good results in the outcome of diabetic pregnancies to this. A study in England[21] failed to support this observation, nor is there a definitive report which clearly shows hormone therapy to be beneficial. In fact, intensive medical care without hormone therapy by Brandstrup, Osler and Pedersen[17] has resulted in equally good results.

Early Interruption of Pregnancy

There is general agreement that insulin-dependent diabetics (Classes B through F) benefit from interruption of pregnancy between 35 and 37 weeks' gestation provided the fetus is of reasonable size. Delivery prior to 35 weeks is associated with an excessive neonatal mortality, while postponement of delivery until after 37 weeks has resulted in a higher still-birth rate. There appears to be less agreement as to whether Class A gestational diabetics, in whom perinatal mortality is low, should be delivered preterm. Carrington and associates[22] have suggested that the gestational diabetic and the prediabetic may require as intensive an obstetric-medical-pediatric management as the more overt diabetic; certainly, in studying the problem, neonatal morbidity (i.e., respiratory distress syndrome, hyperbilirubinemia, hypoglycemia and hypocalcemia) must be considered along with mortality rates. In a preliminary study, Dolger[8] has observed an improvement in perinatal survival associated with early delivery in Class A patients. (This was not, however, a controlled study; he simply compared results for patients delivered at term in the years before 1962 with those delivered at 38 weeks since 1962.)

Hospitalization before Delivery

Prior to the time of delivery, determined by obstetrician, internist and pediatrician, the patient should be hospitalized and brought to a stable metabolic state, normoglycemic and without ketonuria. Obstetricians dissent as to the relative advantages of elective cesarean section and vaginal delivery with elective pitocin induction. All agree that early delivery is much more important than mode of delivery. In many clinics induction is attempted on 3 successive days provided there are not obstetric contraindications. If induction is unsuccessful, delivery is effected by cesarean section. During induced labor and delivery, or during cesarean section, intravenous administration of fluids with glucose and regular insulin may be necessary to avoid marked hyperglycemia and ketonuria. Blood sugar and ketone (serum acetone) determinations should be made during this phase. Possible obstetric complications may be premature rupture of the membranes, uterine inertia with prolonged labor and shoulder dystocia. Maternal and umbilical cord vein and artery blood sugar values taken at delivery are useful baselines for future management of the infant. The same blood samples may also be used for determination of bilirubin and of calcium and other electrolytes.

THE NEWBORN INFANT AND HIS PROBLEMS

The infant of the diabetic mother has survived diverse metabolic alterations which have affected profoundly his intrauterine growth and development. These infants have obvious physical stigmata and multiple metabolic alterations, and some have a prolonged stormy course, but a significant number (40 to 60 per cent) have an uneventful neonatal period: the over-all survival rate is 80 to 90 per cent. While survival is the ultimate goal, morbidity, and especially morbidity with permanent sequelae, cannot be disregarded. The consequences of congenital anomalies, respiratory distress syndrome, hypoglycemia, hypocalcemia, electrolyte abnormalities, hyperbilirubinemia, heart failure, renal vein thrombosis and hypoparathyroidism must be considered in the management and ultimate evaluation of success of a therapeutic regimen.

Size, Weight and Water

These infants often have, in addition to their obese, plethoric and cushingoid appearance, visceromegaly involving heart, liver, spleen, and hypertrophy of the umbilical cord. Not only are they overweight for gestational age, they have increased length as well. At 260 days of gestation, the infant of the diabetic mother is comparable to a normal infant at term with respect to weight and length. Interruption of pregnancy and careful obstetric-medical management tend to minimize the excess weight gain. It must be noted, however, that some investigators have suggested that there may be a more favorable outcome in the larger obese infants. Brandstrup[17] has reported that the prognosis is best when the fetal age is between 252 and 266 days and the fetal weight between 3500 and 3950 gm.

These infants formerly were thought to be edematous at birth; however, pitting is not noted until after the first day of life. More recent data indicate that the excessive body weight is a result of increased body fat, rather than fluid.[23-25] When starved and deprived of water during the initial days after delivery, they lose more weight over a longer period than do normal infants.[26] The reason for this unexpectedly high weight loss with starvation is not known. In the first 48 hours, urine volumes are larger than those from more mature infants of nondiabetic mothers. Renal sodium excretion is also higher when compared with infants of similar weight[27]; however, when compared with infants of comparable gestation, this difference is insignificant.[28] Early feeding minimizes the weight loss and abolishes the difference when compared with nondiabetic controls.[26]

Ventilation and Acid-Base Balance

Recently, Prod'hom and associates[29] reported the adjustment of ventilation and acid-base balance in 20 asymptomatic white infants of diabetic mothers (Classes B to F) and of 35 to 39 weeks' gestational age, delivered by elective cesarean section under spinal anesthesia. Apgar scores were greater than 4 at 1 minute, and above 8 at 5 minutes. Sixteen infants had normal x-rays of the chest; in 4, there were varying degrees of hyperinflation and minimal infiltrates, while in 1, diffuse nodularity occurred at 1 hour, but subsided by 24 hours. Adjustment of ventilation was found to be complete within 4 hours after delivery. A right-to-left shunt of 20 to 25 per cent persisted throughout the first day of life. While a slight respiratory acidosis was present for 1 to 4 hours, acid-base control was similar to that in infants of nondiabetic mothers. A low arterial P_{CO_2} was noted at 24 hours both in infants of diabetic mothers and control infants. A respiratory rate above 60 was observed in 6 of 17 infants at 4 hours of age, all of whom had small tidal volumes, high physiologic dead-space to tidal volume ratios and relatively little increase in minute volume. These infants did not have other evidence of respiratory distress and were otherwise well. These authors concluded that asymptomatic infants of diabetic mothers have as good ventilatory and acid-base control as normal infants.

The Respiratory Distress Syndrome

One of the most serious neonatal complications is the respiratory distress syndrome.* The clinical criteria for diagnosis include an expiratory grunt initially, followed shortly by a pattern of difficult inspiratory breathing with retraction of the sternum and intercostal spaces while the abdomen is protruded. Later, flaring of the alae nasi and cyanosis may be present. The infant is irritable, with a "complaining cry" and hoarseness. The inspiratory effort is brief, while expiration is prolonged. Fine crackling rales may be heard. In infants whose course is unfavorable, an ashen color is associated with a fall in body temperature, declining respiratory rate and apneic episodes.

The presence of respiratory difficulty in the initial hours after delivery may be related to intracranial anomalies or hemorrhage, cardiac failure, aspiration, pneumothorax, diaphragmatic hernia, etc. In addition to careful physical examination, roentgen studies are necessary to clarify the diagnosis. The presence of a fine, diffuse bilateral reticulogranular appearance in the x-ray of the chest is consistent with the diagnosis of respiratory distress syndrome associated with hyaline membrane disease.

Both a respiratory and metabolic acidosis (increased lactic acid and carbon dioxide tension, reduced buffer base and decreased pH) are usually observed in the severe respiratory distress syndrome. Reardon[30] has studied these relationships with reference to hypoglycemia in infants of diabetic mothers. In sick infants, she noted a decreased plasma pH and an elevated P_{CO_2} at delivery by cesarean section. Blood glucose, which was elevated at birth, fell during the initial hours of life, while respiratory acidosis persisted beyond 4 hours of age. In surviving infants, treated with intravenous 5 per cent glucose in 0.45 per cent sodium chloride (30 ml./

---

* This subject has been treated extensively by Mary Ellen Avery in *The Lung and Its Disorders in the Newborn Infant.*[70] The reader is referred to this source for a discussion of pulmonary physiology, diagnosis and management.

lb./day), arterial P_{CO_2} was normal by 24 hours, although plasma pH remained low. Electrolyte abnormalities, including azotemia, hyperkalemia and hyperphosphatemia, may occasionally be noted in these infants if the prenatal course has been difficult. These may be similar to the findings in "distressed" infants noted earlier by McCance and Widdowson.[31]

Carbohydrate Metabolism

Following delivery, glucose concentrations in offspring of diabetic mothers decline rapidly to values below those observed in normals. Thus, approximately 50 per cent of these babies have glucose concentrations below 30 mg. per 100 ml. in the first 6 hours of life.[32, 33]

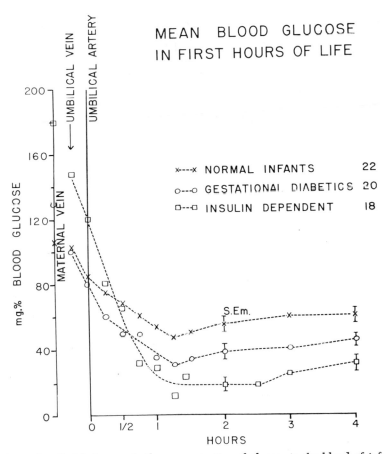

Figure 9. Serial changes in the concentration of glucose in the blood of infants immediately following delivery. The group from mothers with gestational diabetes had abnormal intravenous glucose tolerance tests during pregnancy but received no insulin therapy. (Adapted from McCann et al., Proc. Soc. Ped. Res., May, 1965.)

Recent observations by McCann et al.[34] have indicated that infants of diabetic mothers may be subdivided into those from mothers with gestational diabetes and those born of mothers with insulin-dependent diabetes. The infants from mothers with gestational diabetes had, on the average, lower blood sugars at 2 hours of age than did normal infants; however, the values were higher than those found in infants of insulin-dependent mothers. Furthermore, the rate of fall in blood sugar immediately after delivery was slowest in the normal infants, intermediate in the infants of mothers with gestational diabetes and most rapid in those of insulin-dependent diabetics (Figs. 9, 10).

The initial rate of fall in glucose concentration varies directly with the concentration in maternal blood at the time of delivery, with very high levels resulting in an initial precipitous decline. The level at which the blood sugar stabilizes between 2 and 6 hours of age does not correlate with the initial concentrations at delivery. In many infants, blood sugar rises spontaneously after 4 to 6 hours to values not unlike those found in infants of nondiabetics (Chapter Three).

The course of changes in the blood sugar level in the hypoglycemic infants usually follows one of three patterns. The majority have a tran-

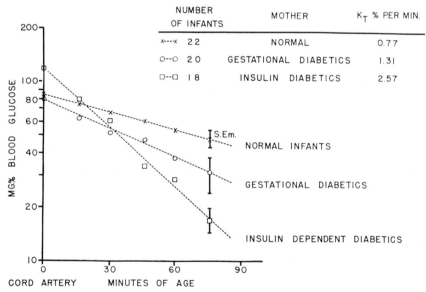

THE RATE OF GLUCOSE DISAPPEARANCE IMMEDIATELY AFTER BIRTH

	NUMBER OF INFANTS	MOTHER	K_T % PER MIN.
x---x	22	NORMAL	0.77
o--o	20	GESTATIONAL DIABETICS	1.31
□--□	18	INSULIN DIABETICS	2.57

Figure 10.   Blood glucose concentrations from the three groups of infants whose data are shown in Figure 9. Data plotted semilogarithmically in the first 90 minutes after delivery. Observe the differences in the rate of disappearance: slow for normal infants, very rapid for infants whose mothers were insulin dependent and intermediate for infants of gestational diabetic mothers who received no exogenous insulin. Compare with Figure 12, p. 73. (Adapted from McCann et al., Proc. Soc. Ped. Res., May, 1965.)

sient, asymptomatic phase soon after birth, lasting between 1 and 4 hours, following which a spontaneous rise occurs. Some have a prolonged initial phase of hypoglycemia (often severe, below 15 mg./100 ml.), which may persist for several hours and be associated with symptoms. Others, after an apparently benign initial phase, develop symptomatic hypoglycemia

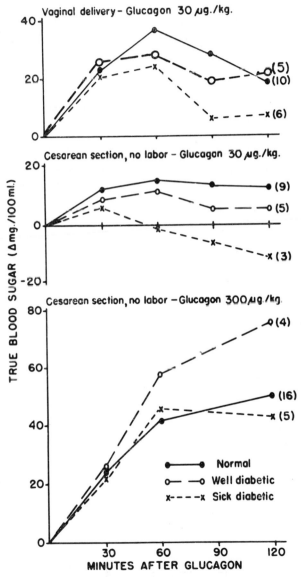

Figure 11. Relation of labor in the mother and condition of the infant to the concentration of blood sugar following small and large doses of glucagon. All infants were 2 hours of age or younger. (From Cornblath et al., Pediatrics 28:592, 1961.)

after 12 to 24 hours. Pennoyer and Hartmann[32] found that only 16 babies had symptoms among 38 with blood sugar values under 30 mg./100 ml. Of these, only 5 did not have associated problems which could have contributed to the clinical manifestations. Symptoms such as apnea, cyanosis, limpness, failure to suck, absent Moro reflex, listlessness, convulsions and coma may be related to hypoglycemia alone (Chapter Five).

Treatment

When symptoms and hypoglycemia coexist at any age, therapy directed at elevating the concentration of glucose in the blood should be initiated. A prompt response to therapy is evidence that hypoglycemia was indeed the cause of the symptoms. However, if the hypoglycemia has been of long duration or if the symptoms are due to other causes, either a partial or delayed response to therapy may occur. During the first hours of life, glucagon in high dosage (300 μgm. per kg. I.V. or I.M.) can elevate the blood sugar level for 2 to 3 hours in most infants[33] (Fig. 11). However, if the infant is severely ill, glucose administered intravenously is the treatment of choice. Unless blood sugar levels can be measured at 2- to 6-hour intervals, either form of therapy may be inadequate to keep the blood sugar at a proper level. Hutchison et al.[35] have advocated fructose solutions instead of glucose in the management of respiratory distress syndrome. They have reported that glucose levels are stabilized with this therapy in nondiabetic infants. McCann et al.[34] have administered a combination of glucose and fructose or fructose alone to well infants of mothers with gestational diabetes as a single injection soon after delivery and produced an elevated level of glucose for 2 to 3 hours. Furthermore, when fructose was infused in women with gestational diabetes during labor and delivery, the hypoglucosemia usually observed in the infant during the first hours of life was corrected or delayed. Preliminary observations with intravenous fructose administration to symptomatic infants of diabetic mothers suggest that this may be preferable to intravenous glucose, but since the significance of hypoglycemia without symptoms remains unknown, no specific recommendations for therapy seem justified. However, in those infants with *excessively* low blood sugar values (under 20 mg./100 ml.), conservative management would consist of supporting the blood glucose level.

Calcium Metabolism

In addition to the electrolyte and acid-base derangement associated with the respiratory distress syndrome, occasional sick infants have other alterations related to calcium metabolism. Hypocalcemia with tetany is now recognized as a significant complication in the infant of the diabetic mother.[36-38] Chvostek's sign, carpopedal spasm, and Trousseau's sign are unreliable indicators of tetany in any newborn infant. Neuromuscular and behavioral alterations have been described, but many of the symptoms and signs are nonspecific and similar to those described for hypoglycemia and hypoxia. Hyperexcitability seems to be a common observation. Gittleman et al.[38] observed that 6 of 22 infants of diabetic mothers had serum calcium levels below 8.0 mg. per 100 ml., which was considered abnormal on the first day of life. In another group of infants of prediabetic mothers, who had either gestational or noninsulin dependent diabetes, 7 of 36 infants had similarly low levels. Since most of these infants were delivered preterm, their calcium levels should be compared with those of infants of like gestation and mode of delivery. Previously, Gittleman et al.[39] had shown that many low birth weight infants may have low serum calcium values without symptoms and related to a variety of factors, e.g., complications of pregnancy, of labor or of the immediate postnatal period. In infants delivered by elective cesarean section for cephalopelvic disproportion or for repeat cesarean section, hypocalcemia was noted in 13.7 per cent. A similar incidence, 11.8 per cent, was found for infants delivered by elective cesarean section in well controlled diabetics.

The mechanism of the hypocalcemia in these infants is unknown. The decrease in serum protein concentrations and calcium binding does not explain the findings. Similarly, serum phosphorus levels are slightly elevated, but not to the extent observed in older infants with the neonatal tetany associated with high solute milk feedings. Nor are the acid-base disturbances adequate as etiologic explanations. A physicochemical internal derangement related to parathyroid function and bone metabolism appears to be the most likely explanation, since renal and gastrointestinal factors cannot account for hypocalcemia occurring a few hours after birth. It is of some interest that the low levels of calcium may persist, as in the 2 infants of diabetic mothers who were found to have idiopathic hypoparathyroidism.[40]

Clinical Management

The diagnosis of symptomatic hypocalcemia depends upon obtaining a serum calcium determination and must be differentiated from manifestations of central nervous system disease, hypoglycemia, hypoxia, etc. An electrocardiogram may be helpful in the infant with hypocalcemia since prolongation of the QT interval may be present. Once the diagnosis of hypocalcemic tetany is suspected and blood obtained, intravenous calcium gluconate (5 to 10 cc. as a 10 per cent solution) should be given slowly and immediately, with EKG monitoring to avoid heart block. Thereafter, either calcium lactate, in a total dosage of 1 to 2 grams daily, may be given orally or calcium chloride, in a total daily dosage not to exceed 50 ml. of a 2 per cent solution given by mouth; the latter may be irritating to the gastric mucosa if given in a more concentrated form and may produce acidosis if given for prolonged periods. Therapy may be continued by mouth for 1 week, with repeated determinations of serum calcium concentrations. Therapy should also include feedings of a low solute milk.

Bilirubin Metabolism

Hyperbilirubinemia occurs more commonly in infants of diabetic mothers than in controls of comparable weight or gestation.[41-43] Recently, Taylor et al.[43] reported that the serum bilirubin values in umbilical cord blood from infants of diabetic mothers were similar to values from controls; but significant differences in bilirubin concentrations between the groups were apparent at 48 hours of age. The 48-hour value for serum bilirubin did not correlate with the value for umbilical cord blood, with the degree of hepatomegaly or splenomegaly or with the presence of edema. The direct Coombs test was negative in 27 infants whose major blood type was compatible with that of the mother; the direct and indirect Coombs were both negative in 2, with a possible O-A incompatibility. Although the number of nucleated red blood cells was high initially, a sharp drop was found on the second and third day of life. Hematologic studies did not suggest an explanation of the mechanism of the phenomenon. In particular, there was no evidence for increased hemolysis. Olsen et al.[42] drew similar conclusions from 94 surviving infants. Of 87 infants without evidence of hemolytic disease, 23 (26 per cent) had serum bilirubin values greater than 20 mg./100 ml., an incidence greater than that in a series of infants of nondiabetic mothers. The curves for infants of diabetic mothers were similar to those for normal infants with birth weights below 2000 gm. and with gestational ages of less than 257 days. Vaginal delivery was associated with a higher incidence of serum bilirubin, above 20 mg./100 ml., than was cesarean section. It is known that complicated vaginal delivery predisposes to hyperbilirubinemia. The observations of Zetterström et al.,[41] who first emphasized the problem of hyperbilirubinemia in the infant of the diabetic mother, have not been confirmed with respect to the high incidence of ABO isoimmunization.

The Effects of Early Feeding

In a study of the effects of early and late feeding of infants of diabetic mothers in the management of the respiratory distress syndrome, Hubbell et al.[44] found that infants fed as early as 4 hours after delivery had lower serum bilirubin levels at 72 hours of age than did the paired infants who had been fasted for 48 hours. Of 48 pairs of infants, 5 of the early-fed group versus 16 in the fasted group had serum bilirubin values above 20 mg./100 ml. The mechanism for this difference is unknown, although a relationship to glucose metabolism and glucuronide conjugation has been suggested. Volume changes associated with weight loss alone cannot account for these differences.

Other Clinical Complications

The sick infant of the diabetic mother may have a variety of other clinical problems, including intracranial, adrenal or renal hemorrhage, congenital anomalies, renal vein thrombosis or congestive heart failure. One often finds a large heart on roentgen examination in asymptomatic infants: this alone is not an indication for digitalization. In the presence of a rapidly enlarging liver, tachypnea and tachycardia, however, such therapy is suggested. Urinalyses are essential in all these infants to confirm or to detect overt or silent abnormalities of the genitourinary system.

Renal Vein Thrombosis

Maternal diabetes was first recognized as a predisposing factor to renal vein thrombosis in the infant by Avery, Oppenheimer and Gordon in 1957.[45] Since then Takeuchi and Bernirschke[46] have reported a series of 16 cases, 5 from mothers with diabetes, 7 from prediabetics (presumptive), and 4 from women with improved diabetic status. The incidence in the diabetic population is unknown. The presence of a mass in the flank or abdomen associated with proteinuria and hematuria suggests the diagnosis. Unilateral thrombosis may be treated by nephrectomy.[47] The pathogenesis of this complication is speculative at best; local stasis of blood in renal veins possibly secondary to an osmotic diuresis due to hyperglycemia has been suggested by most authors, but this is inadequate to explain the occurrence of thrombosis in infants born to mothers with prediabetes. The mechanism remains obscure.

Congenital Anomalies

The infants of diabetic mothers have an increased incidence of congenital malformations.[2, 12, 48] Recently, Pedersen et al.[49] reported an incidence of congenital anomalies of 6.4 per cent in offspring of diabetic mothers as compared with 2.1 per cent in a control group. They suggested that the incidence was correlated with the severity of vascular complications in the mother. Insulin reactions and hypoglycemia did not appear to affect the incidence of congenital malformations. In recent years, the improvement in the management of the diabetic mother and her infant has been responsible for increasing the number of survivors. Thus, the importance of diagnosing and treating correctable anomalies in these infants is apparent.

PATHOLOGY

The placenta of the diabetic mother is not remarkable: the fine structure of the chorionic villi is normal and the capillary and epithelial basement membranes are not increased in width. Arteriolar narrowing of the placental bed is not a feature of this condition unless pre-eclamptic toxemia is present. Often there is excess amniotic fluid,[15] the explanation of which is not apparent.

The infant shows characteristic pathologic alterations which explain, in part, his clinical condition. First, the large size observed at term is the result of increased body fat, rather than edema. Total body water is decreased;[24] fat determined by direct whole body tissue analysis is increased.[25] In infants delivered preterm, gigantism and splanchnomegaly are less evident. The striking pathologic feature is the hypertrophy and hyperplasia of the beta cells in the islets of Langerhans.[50–52] In addition, the pancreas has an unusual infiltrate of eosinophils. A similar eosinophilic infiltration has been observed in guinea pigs following the injection of large amounts of antibody to guinea pig insulin. While the liver has not always been found to be enlarged and glycogen laden, increased hematopoiesis has been a consistent observation. The heart is often overweight and enlarged. The brain is small for both body weight and gestation. The lungs frequently have features of hyaline membrane disease and hemorrhage (see Avery[70]). The kidneys show varying degrees of immaturity as evidenced by fetal glomeruli, which supports the concept that the infants are immature relative to their size. Hemorrhages have been reported in the adrenal gland and kidneys. Renal vein thrombosis also seems to occur more frequently in these infants. The pituitary and adrenal gland often do not have any demonstrable abnormalities.

PATHOPHYSIOLOGY

No single hypothesis has been proposed which satisfactorily accounts for the diverse metabolic abnormalities of the infant of the diabetic or prediabetic mother. Attention has been focused primarily on the beta cell hyperplasia and glucose homeostasis. While such infants have a rapid fall in the concentration of blood sugar in the period immediately following delivery,[32, 53] the mechanism for this has only recently been demonstrated to differ from that observed in normal infants (Figs. 9, 10).[34] The admin-

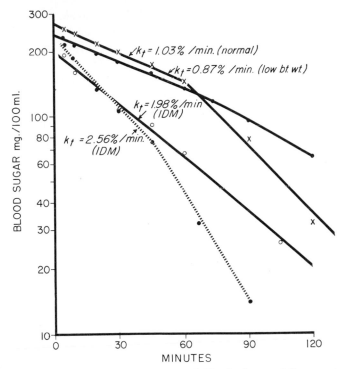

Figure 12. A semilogarithmic graph of blood glucose following intravenous injection of 1 gm. of glucose per kilogram of body weight. The rates of glucose disappearance (k_t) for normal[73] and low birth weight[74] infants are given for comparison. The two infants of diabetic mothers with fast k_t's were studied by Dr. Beverly F. Likly and provided data similar to those obtained by Baird and Farquhar.[54]

istration of intravenous glucose (as in a tolerance test) results in a prompt, rapid disposal of glucose from the blood when compared with similar observations in infants of nondiabetic mothers[54] (Fig. 12). Understanding of the interrelationship between carbohydrate and fat metabolism has been extended recently with the elucidation of the role of plasma free fatty acids (FFA) (a fraction of long chain C_{12}–C_{18} fatty acids which exist in low concentrations in plasma bound to albumin), which have a very rapid turnover and are an important source of energy to a variety of tissues.[55] Previously, FFA have been shown to be elevated in starvation, diabetes, and following administration of epinephrine, growth hormone or corticosteroid. Conversely, plasma FFA levels have been depressed by administration of glucose, glucagon or insulin. Glucose uptake by adipose tissue inhibits FFA release, while glucose deprivation or unavailability stimulates FFA release. This concept has been extended recently by the suggestion that a glucose-fatty acid cycle exists between adipose tissue, plasma and muscle FFA in which the control of these factors with reference to insulin sensitivity is critical.[56]

In a preliminary communication, Melichar, Novak, Hahn and Koldovský[57] have reported low values of plasma FFA and glucose in infants of diabetic mothers. Chen and associates[58] have studied levels of FFA in plasma of infants of gestational diabetics (Figs. 13, 14). At delivery, maternal plasma FFA levels were higher than those of control women some of whom were and some of whom were not given glucose intravenously during labor and delivery. Plasma levels of FFA, both from the umbilical artery and vein, were low in all infants. In the infants of diabetic mothers, plasma free fatty acids rose to low normal levels by 120 minutes after birth, whereas values in control infants were significantly higher. Plasma total lipids in venous blood from the umbilical cord are low in infants from both diabetic and nondiabetic mothers;[59, 60] however, plasma cholesterol and phospholipid values tend to be slightly higher in the infants of diabetic mothers, even though maternal plasma contains much higher concentrations of the lipid fractions at delivery.

These physiologic observations of levels of glucose and free fatty acids suggest a state of *functional hyperinsulinism* in the infant of the diabetic mother. Baird and Farquhar[54] measured insulin-like activity in plasma using the rat diaphragm technique. Fasting values in 6 infants of diabetic mothers were similar to values in normal infants; however, following intravenous glucose, a greater rise in insulin-like activity was found in the former. More recently, Stimmler et al.,[61]* using an immunoassay, found plasma insulin levels elevated in umbilical vein samples from 5 infants of diabetic mothers. In 1 infant, elevated levels persisted even though hypoglucosemia was present throughout the initial 23 hours of life. The persistent elevated levels suggest either a reduced clearance of insulin in the newborn or a lack of intrinsic control of insulin secretion by glucose. These observations support the hypothesis advocated by Pedersen[53] that maternal hyperglycemia may be an important factor responsible for the metabolic abnormalities in such infants. Accordingly, fetal hyperglycemia may stimulate fetal islet cell insulin release with persistent fetal hyperinsulinism. The latter promotes glucose uptake in a variety of organs and tissues, including adipose tissue. The surfeit of glucose in the presence of excess insulin results in the characteristic obesity. This attractive hypothesis is consistent with the observations in manifest diabetes; however, there is no evidence that latent or prediabetes is associated with fluctuations in the level of blood glucose in the pregnant woman, and yet some infants from these women have the same embryopathy as infants of overtly diabetic mothers.

Other hypotheses have even less evidence to support them. A genetic influence was suggested from the observations of Jackson[11] that infants of diabetic fathers have features similar to those whose mothers are diabetic. This report has remained controversial. The adrenocortical theory

* O'Brien, Stimmler, and Brazie have subsequently indicated that the assay used was not specific for insulin and that these values require revision.[62]

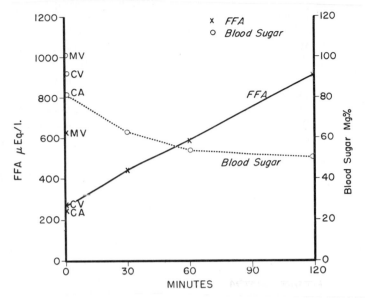

Figure 13. Data obtained from a vaginally delivered infant whose mother received glucose intravenously during labor. MV, CV and CA refer to maternal vein, umbilical cord vein, and cord artery. Observe the rapid rise in free fatty acid (FFA) in the normal infant at 2 hours of age.

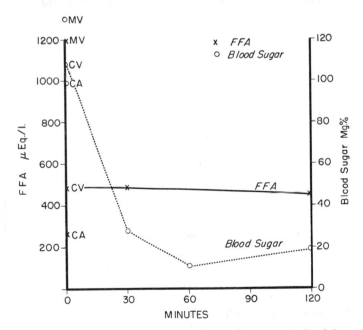

Figure 14. Data similar to Figure 13, obtained in a vaginally delivered infant of a diabetic mother. In this patient, glucose fell to values below 30 mg. per 100 ml. while plasma free fatty acids remained suppressed. These data suggest physiologic hyperinsulinism in the infant of the diabetic mother.

suggested that hyperadrenocorticism was a major factor,[63] but the levels of plasma 17-hydroxycorticosteroids are similar in diabetic and control mothers at delivery; furthermore, the values in cord plasma are low (below 10 μg./100 ml.) and no different from those in control infants.[64] Hypercorticism prior to delivery remains unproved. It is true that urinary excretion of adrenal corticoids appears to be increased during the first days of life,[65] but these data are inadequately controlled for mode of delivery and their significance remains to be clarified. Similarly, the growth hormone–pituitary hypothesis is based on the large size and excessive growth of these infants. The recent data of Kalkhoff et al.[66] indicate that levels of growth hormone-like substances in cord plasma are elevated, but less so in infants of diabetic mothers than in controls. Another possible mechanism is based on the observations of Vallance-Owen and Lilley,[67] who have demonstrated plasma insulin antagonists in diabetes. These oppose the action of insulin in muscle but do not interfere with its lipogenic function. An excess of insulin antagonists transplacentally acquired may explain some of the metabolic effects observed in infants of diabetic mothers.

The final analysis of this complex problem will require techniques which would permit the study of the fetus *in utero*. The influence of the maternal environment is evident in overt diabetes: maintenance of normoglycemia in the pregnant diabetic prevents excessive fetal growth. On the other hand, pathologic manifestations are present in some instances which suggest that factors intrinsic to the fetus may also be important. Peel[68] has reported an example of biovulvar twins, one of whom weighed 9 lbs. 2 oz. at 37 weeks and was a typical "cushingoid" infant while the other was 4 lbs. 12 oz. and appeared normal. The placentas weighed 2 lbs. 10 oz. and 14 oz., respectively. No data on blood sugars were available for these infants.

MANAGEMENT

While there remains diversity of opinion regarding many aspects of the management of the infant of the diabetic mother, it is clear that the only way to attain the best survival rates is by a collaborative effort on the part of the internist, the obstetrician and the pediatrician. The pregnant diabetic requires careful supervision with close follow-up throughout pregnancy.[69] Control of diet, activity and insulin are necessary to achieve a stable maternal environment for the fetus. Prolonged and early hospitalization may be necessary to achieve this. At delivery, meticulous attention to glucose and insulin administration is necessary to control maternal blood glucose within the normoglycemic range. Ketosis must be avoided throughout pregnancy and delivery. Delivery for the permanent diabetic is best achieved at 35 to 37 weeks for maximal infant survival. The gestational diabetic and prediabetic may benefit from induced, elective delivery at 37 to 38 weeks, although this is not yet proved.

At delivery the initial management of the infant should be the responsibility of a pediatrician adept at resuscitation of the newborn. Apgar scores at 5 minutes after delivery are important and of prognostic value. After respirations are established, gastric emptying to obtain the volume of the stomach's contents is indicated as a diagnostic measure for intestinal obstruction; the relationship of gastric aspiration to the subsequent development of the respiratory distress syndrome is not established. Ideally, the precise state of control of the mother's diabetes at delivery should be known to the pediatrician. Maternal and cord venous and cord arterial blood sugar values should be obtained at delivery. Blood sugar determinations from serial heel punctures at 1, 2, and 4 hours will define the degree of hypoglycemia. Irrespective of their size, these infants should be cared for in an intensive-care nursery, i.e., premature or neonatal unit. Temperature, humidity and oxygen should be monitored carefully and regulated according to the infant's response. Routine utilization of high oxygen and humidity is not indicated. Early (before 12 hours) oral feedings with glucose or fructose water are recommended unless serious complications are present. Antibiotics are given only for known or suspected infections and not prophylactically.

A large proportion (40 to 60 per cent) of infants will have a relatively uneventful course and require nothing more than careful observation and a routine urinalysis before discharge. Even these infants, however, may be poor feeders, regain weight slowly and require longer hospitalization than the infant of a nondiabetic mother.

These complications suggest the following management procedures subject, of course, to evaluation of the individual infant:

Therapy for the *respiratory distress syndrome* includes oxygen (high concentrations may be necessary) and parenteral fluids including buffers and sugar. (For details see Avery,[70] Stahlman,[71] Hutchison,[35] and Chu et al.[72]) Therapy in the respiratory distress syndrome is rapidly changing as a result of new information on pathogenesis and etiology. Therefore, specific recommendations at this time are inappropriate.

The *transient asymptomatic hypoglycemia* (levels < 20 mg./100 ml.) during the first hours of life will respond to intravenous glucagon (300 μg./kg. body weight) (Fig. 11). *Sick* infants with hypoglycemia should be given intravenous glucose. In our experience, an initial single intravenous injection of 0.5 to 1.0 gm. glucose per kg. body weight as 25 per cent glucose, followed by a continuous infusion of 60 to 70 cc./kg./day of 10 to 15 per cent glucose in water should maintain the blood glucose level within normal limits. If, on repeated assay, the concentration of glucose remains low (< 30 mg./100 ml.), steroids or ACTH may be necessary (see Chapter Five). Careful and frequent observation of the infant is essential to avoid overhydration, heart failure and pulmonary edema. After the blood sugar has remained stabilized for 12 hours, the amount of parenteral glucose should be reduced gradually by giving 10 and then 5 per cent glucose over a 6- to 12-hour period to avoid reactive hypoglycemia.

Neither glucagon nor subcutaneous fluids has been found effective in treating the infant who has *symptomatic* hypoglycemia.

Hypocalcemic tetany may be treated with 5 to 10 cc. of 10 per cent calcium gluconate administered slowly intravenously with constant monitoring of the heart rate. Therapy should be continued for several days with oral calcium salts and a low solute formula.

The relationship between kernicterus, *serum levels of bilirubin*, marked hypoglycemia and severe derangements in acid-base balance and oxygen saturation in the respiratory distress syndrome requires clarification before definite recommendations for the management of any specific bilirubin level are justified. Early feedings have been shown to be effective in preventing the rise in bilirubin.[44]

A high index of suspicion for both hypoglycemia and hypocalcemia will result in appropriate diagnosis and early therapy and may prevent late sequelae.

SUMMARY

Diabetes during pregnancy not only affects maternal metabolism, but also has diverse effects on the fetus and newborn. Congenital anomalies of the fetus are more common. Anatomic alterations include increased body fat, increased islet cells with beta cell hyperplasia, organomegaly and increased hemopoiesis. Hyperinsulinism and hypoglycemia occur but do not often produce serious symptomatic effects. Respiratory distress syndrome is the most serious complication. Hyperbilirubinemia and hypocalcemia are also important complications. The infant of the diabetic or prediabetic mother, whether delivered early (37 weeks' gestation) or at term is a high-risk infant who requires more intensive nursing care than a normal infant of comparable weight or gestation.

REFERENCES

1. Farquhar, J. W.: The child of the diabetic woman. Arch. Dis. Child. 34:76, 1959.
2. Dekaban, A., and Baird, R.: The outcome of pregnancy in diabetic women. 1. Fetal wastage, mortality, and morbidity in the offspring of diabetic and normal control mothers. J. Pediat. 55:563, 1959.

3. Kyle, G. C.: Diabetes and pregnancy. Ann. Int. Med. 59:No. 1, pt. 2 (Suppl. 3), 1963.

4. White, P., Koshy, P., and Duckers, J.: The management of pregnancy complicating diabetes and of children of diabetic mothers. Med. Clin. North America 37:1481, 1953.

5. White, P.: Symposium on diabetes mellitus; pregnancy complicating diabetes. Am. J. Med. 7:609, 1949.

6. Miller, H. C.: Offspring of diabetic and prediabetic mothers. Advances Pediatrics 8:137, 1956.

7. Carrington, E. R.: Pregnancy and diabetes. Diabetes 13:91, 1964 (Editorial).

8. Dolger, H., Bookman, J. J., and Nechemias, C.: The management of diabetes in pregnancy. J. Mount Sinai Hosp. N. Y. 30:479, 1963.

9. Miller, H. C.: The effect of diabetic and prediabetic pregnancies on the fetus and newborn infant. J. Pediat. 29:455, 1946.

10. Kriss, J. P., and Futcher, P. H.: The relation between infant birth weight and subsequent development of maternal diabetes mellitus. J. Clin. Endocrinol. 8:380, 1948.

11. Jackson, W. P. U.: Prediabetes: a survey. South African J. Lab. Clin. Med. 6:127, 1960.

12. Gellis, S. S., and Hsia, D. Y.-Y.: The infant of the diabetic mother. A.M.A. J. Dis. Child. 97:1, 1959.

13. O'Sullivan, J. B.: Gestational diabetes. Unsuspected, asymptomatic diabetes in pregnancy. New England J. Med. 264:1082, 1961.

14. Hagbard, L.: Pregnancy and diabetes mellitus. Springfield, Ill. Charles C Thomas, 1961. American Lecture Series No. 449 (Chapter 5).

15. Pedersen, J., and Jørgensen, G.: Hydramnios in diabetics. Amount of amniotic fluid in relation to treatment. Acta Endocrinol. 15:333, 1954.

16. Stevenson, A. C.: The association of hydramnios with congenital malformations. In Wolstenholme, G. E. W., and O'Connor, C. M. (eds.): Ciba Foundation Symposium on Congenital Malformations. Boston, Little, Brown and Co., 1960, p. 241.

17. Brandstrup, E., Osler, M., and Pedersen, J.: Perinatal mortality in diabetic pregnancy. Acta Endocrinol. 37:434, 1961.

18. Roszkowski, I., and Janczewska, E.: The daily glycemia profile in pregnancy. Am. J. Obstet. Gynec. 88:204, 1964.

19. Smith, G. V., and Smith, O. W.: Internal secretions and toxemia of late pregnancy. Physiol. Rev. 28:1, 1948.

20. White, P., Gillespie, L., and Sexton, L.: Use of female sex hormone therapy in pregnant diabetic patients. Am. J. Obstet. Gynec. 71:57, 1956.

21. Medical Research Council: The use of hormones in the management of pregnancy in diabetics. Lancet 2:833, 1955.

22. Carrington, E. R., Shuman, C. R., and Reardon, H. S.: Evaluation of the prediabetic state during pregnancy. Obstet. Gynec. 9:664, 1957.

23. Garn, S. M.: Fat, body size and growth in the newborn. Human Biol. 30:265, 1958.

24. Osler, M., and Pedersen, J.: The body composition of newborn infants of diabetic mothers. Pediatrics 26:985, 1960.

25. Fee, B. A., and Weil, W. B., Jr.: Body composition of infants of diabetic mothers by direct analysis. Ann. New York Acad. Sc. 110:869, 1963.

26. Farquhar, J. W., and Sklaroff, S. A.: The post-natal weight loss of babies born to diabetic and non-diabetic women. Arch. Dis. Child. 33:323, 1958.

27. Cook, C. D., O'Brien, D., Hansen, J. D. L., Beem, M., and Smith, C. A.: Water and electrolyte economy in newborn infants of diabetic mothers. Acta Paediat. 49:121, 1960.

28. Osler, M.: Renal function in newborn infants of diabetic mothers. Acta Endocrinol. 34:287, 1960.

29. Prod'hom, L. S., Levison, H., Cherry, R. B., Drorbaugh, J. E., Hubbell, J. P., Jr., and Smith, C. A.: Adjustment of ventilation, intrapulmonary gas exchange,

and acid-base balance during the first day of life: normal values in well infants of diabetic mothers. Pediatrics 33:682, 1964.

30. Reardon, H. S.: Infants of diabetic mothers. Biochemical studies and management of infants of diabetic mothers. In Report of Thirty-first Ross Conference on Pediatric Research, Adaptation to Extra-uterine Life. Columbus, Ohio, Ross Laboratories, 1959, p. 72.

31. McCance, R. A., and Widdowson, E. M.: Metabolism and renal function in the first two days of life. Cold Spring Harbor Symposia on Quantitative Biology 19:161, 1954.

32. Pennoyer, M. M., and Hartmann, A. F., Sr.: Management of infants born of diabetic mothers. Postgrad. Med. 18:199, 1955.

33. Cornblath, M., Nicolopoulos, D., Ganzon, A. F., Levin, E. Y., Gordon, M. H., and Gordon, H. H.: Studies of carbohydrate metabolism in the newborn infant. IV. The effect of glucagon on the capillary blood sugar in infants of diabetic mothers. Pediatrics 28:592, 1961.

34. McCann, M. L., Katigbak, E. B., Kotchen, J., Likly, B., and Schwartz, R.: The prevention of hypoglycemia in infants of diabetic mothers. Presented at the proceedings, Soc. for Ped. Res., May 5, 1965 (35th meeting).

35. Hutchison, J. H., Kerr, M. M., Douglas, T. A., Inall, J. A., and Crosbie, J. C.: A therapeutic approach in 100 cases of the respiratory distress syndrome of the newborn infant. Pediatrics 33:956, 1964.

36. Zetterström, R., and Arnhold, R. G.: Impaired calcium-phosphate homeostasis in newborn infants of diabetic mothers. Acta Paediat. 47:107, 1958.

37. Craig, W. S.: Clinical signs of neonatal tetany: with especial reference to their occurrence in newborn babies of diabetic mothers. Pediatrics 22:297, 1958.

38. Gittleman, I. F., Pincus, J. B., Schmerzler, E., and Annecchiarico, F.: Diabetes mellitus or the prediabetic state in the mother and the neonate. A.M.A. J. Dis. Child. 98:342, 1959.

39. Gittleman, I. F., Pincus, J. B., Schmerzler, E., and Saito, M.: Hypocalcemia occurring on the first day of life in mature and premature infants. Pediatrics 18:721, 1956.

40. Kunstadter, R. H., Oh, W., Tanman, F., and Cornblath, M.: Idiopathic hypoparathyroidism in the newborn. Am. J. Dis. Child. 105:499, 1963.

41. Zetterström, R., Strindberg, B., and Arnhold, R. G.: Hyperbilirubinemia and ABO hemolytic disease in newborn infants of diabetic mothers. Acta Paediat. 47:238, 1958.

42. Olsen, B. R., Osler, M., and Pedersen, J.: Neonatal jaundice in infants born to diabetic mothers. Danish Med. Bull. 10:18, 1963.

43. Taylor, P. M., Wolfson, J. H., Bright, N. H., Birchard, E. L., Derinoz, M. N., and Watson, D. W.: Hyperbilirubinemia in infants of diabetic mothers. Biol. Neonat. 5:289, 1963.

44. Hubbell, J. P., Drorbaugh, J. E., Rudolph, A. J., Auld, P. A., Cherry, R. B., and Smith, C. A.: "Early" versus "late" feeding of infants of diabetic mothers. New England J. Med. 265:835, 1961.

45. Avery, M. E., Oppenheimer, E. H., and Gordon, H. H.: Renal-vein thrombosis in newborn infants of diabetic mothers. New England J. Med. 265:1134, 1957.

46. Takeuchi, A., and Benirschke, K.: Renal venous thrombosis of the newborn and its relation to maternal diabetes. Biol. Neonat. 3:237, 1961.

47. Tveterås, E., and Rudstrom, P.: Renal thrombosis of the newborn; Report of a primary case successfully treated by surgery. Acta Paediat. 45:545, 1956.

48. Hagbard, L.: Diabetes and prediabetes. Mod. Probl. Pediat. 8:221, 1963. (Bibliotheca Paediatrica, fasc. 81.)

49. Pedersen, L. M., Tygstrup, I., and Pedersen, J.: Congenital malformations in newborn infants of diabetic women. Correlation with maternal diabetic vascular complications. Lancet 1:1124, 1964.

50. Cardell, B. S.: Hypertrophy and hyperplasia of the pancreatic islets in new-born infants. J. Path. Bact. 66:335, 1953.

51. Potter, E. L.: Pathology of the Fetus and the Newborn. 2nd ed. Chicago, Year Book Medical Publishers, Inc., 1961, p. 335.

52. McKay, D. G., Benirschke, K., and Curtis, G. W.: Infants of diabetic mothers:

histologic and histochemical observations of the pancreas. Obstet. Gynec. 2:133, 1953.

53. Pedersen, J., Bojsen-Møller, B., and Poulsen, H.: Blood sugar in newborn infants of diabetic mothers. Acta Endocrinol. 15:33, 1954.

54. Baird, J. D., and Farquhar, J. W.: Insulin-secreting capacity in newborn infants of normal and diabetic women. Lancet 1:71, 1962.

55. Dole, V. P.: The significance of nonesterified fatty acids in plasma. A.M.A. Arch. Intern. Med. 101:1005, 1958.

56. Randle, P. J., Garland, P. B., Hales, C. N., and Newsholme, E. A.: The glucose fatty acid cycle, its role in insulin sensitivity and the metabolic disturbances of diabetes mellitus. Lancet 1:785, 1963.

57. Melichar, V., Novak, M., Hahn, P., and Koldovský, O.: Free fatty acids and glucose in the blood of various groups of newborns. Preliminary report. Acta Paediat. 53:343, 1964.

58. Chen, C. H., Adam, P. A. J., Laskowski, D. E., McCann, M. L., and Schwartz, R.: The plasma free fatty acid composition and blood glucose of normal and diabetic pregnant women and of their newborns. Pediatrics (In press).

59. Pantelakis, S. N., Cameron, A. H., Davidson, S., Dunn, P. M., Fosbrooke, A. S., Lloyd, J. K., Malins, J. M., and Wolff, O H.: The diabetic pregnancy; a study of serum lipids in maternal and umbilical cord blood and of the uterine placental vasculature. Arch. Dis. Child. 39:334 1964.

60. Mortimer, J. G.: Cord blood lipids of normal infants and infants of diabetic mothers. Arch. Dis. Child. 39:342, 1964.

61. Stimmler, L., Brazie, J. V., and O'Brien, D.: Plasma-insulin levels in the newborn infants of normal and diabetic mothers. Lancet 1:137, 1964.

62. O'Brien, D., Stimmler, L., and Brazie, J. V.: Plasma-insulin levels in the newborn infants of normal and diabetic mothers. Lancet 2:366, 1964 (Letter to the Editor).

63. Farquhar, J. W.: The possible influence of hyperadrenocorticism on the foetus of the diabetic woman. Arch. Dis. Child. 31:483, 1956.

64. Migeon, C. J., Nicolopoulos, D., and Cornblath, M.: Concentrations of 17-hydroxycorticosteroids in the blood of diabetic mothers and in blood from umbilical cords of their offspring at the time of delivery. Pediatrics 25:605, 1960.

65. Smith, E. K., Reardon, H. S., and Field, S. H.: Urinary constituents of infants of diabetic and non-diabetic mothers. I. 17-hydroxycorticosteroid excretion in premature infants. J. Pediat. 64:652, 1964.

66. Kalkhoff, R., Schalch, D. S., Walker, J. L., Beck, P., Kipnis, D. M., and Daughaday, W. H.: Diabetogenic factors associated with pregnancy. Tr. A. Am. Physicians 77:270, 1964.

67. a. Vallance-Owen, J., and Lilley, M. D.: An insulin antagonist associated with plasma-albumin. Lancet 1:804, 1961.

    b. Vallance-Owen, J., and Lilley, M. D.: Insulin antagonism in the plasma of obese diabetics and prediabetics. Lancet 1:806, 1961.

    c. Editorial: A new concept of diabetes. Lancet 1:809, 1961.

68. Peel, Sir John: Diabetes in pregnancy. Proc. Roy. Soc. Med. 56:1009, 1963.

69. Gordon, H. H.: The infants of diabetic mothers. Am. J. Med. Sc. 244:129, 1962.

70. Avery, M.: The Lung and Its Disorders in the Newborn Infant. Philadelphia, W. B. Saunders Co., 1964. Major Problems in Clinical Pediatrics, Vol. I.

71. Stahlman, M.: Treatment of cardiovascular disorders of the newborn. Pediat. Clin. North America 11:363, 1964.

72. Chu, J., Clements, J. A., Cotton, E., Klaus, M. H., Sweet, A. Y., Thomas, M. A., and Tooley, W. H.: The pulmonary hypoperfusion syndrome; preliminary report. Pediatrics 35:733, 1965.

73. Bowie, M. D., Mulligan, P. B., and Schwartz, R.: Intravenous glucose tolerance in the normal newborn infant: the effects of a double dose of glucose and insulin. Pediatrics 31:590, 1963.

74. Cornblath, M., Wybregt, S. H., and Baens, G. S.: Studies of carbohydrate metabolism in the newborn infant. VII. Tests of carbohydrate tolerance in premature infants. Pediatrics 32:1007, 1963.

Chapter Five

TRANSIENT SYMPTOMATIC HYPOGLYCEMIA IN THE NEONATE

The relatively low levels of glucose (30-60 mg./100 ml.) observed in some full-sized and many low birth weight infants during the first week of life have led some observers to consider that even the total absence of glucose in the blood of the neonate may be a physiological occurrence. However, careful evaluations of blood sugar values in the newborn, with proper attention to technique and analytical methods, have shown that extremely low to absent values of sugar in blood do not occur in normal infants and are, therefore, not normal (Chapter Three). Hypoglycemia in the neonate during the first week of life can be defined as persistent blood glucose concentrations under 20 mg./100 ml. in the premature or low birth weight infant, and under 30 mg./100 ml. from birth to 72 hours of age and under 40 mg./100 ml. thereafter in the full-sized or term infant. This definition of hypoglycemia is based on the considerations that 97 to 98 per cent of blood glucose determinations are higher than these values in normal infants and that symptomatic hypoglycemia may occur in the presence of glucose levels less than these concentrations. Symptomatic neonatal hypoglycemia is characterized by episodes of tremors or "jitteriness," cyanosis, apathy, convulsions, apnea or respiratory distress, a weak or high-pitched cry, limpness, difficulty in feeding, and eye rolling.[1, 2] The clinical manifestations subside in response to intravenous glucose.

Before 1959, only isolated cases of symptomatic hypoglycemia[3, 4] had been reported in infants during the first days of life. At that time, 8 neonates with transient symptomatic hypoglycemia were described.[1] Subsequently, more than 100 newborn infants with this syndrome have been either reported in detail[1, 2, 5, 6] or alluded to in the literature.[7-11] It is now clear that abnormally low levels of blood glucose with symptoms occur predominantly in the male infant who is of low birth weight for his period of gestation. In a significant number of cases, the affected infant was the smaller member of a twinship. Some of the infants also had polycythemia and/or primary central nervous system abnormalities. The symptoms as well as the hypoglycemia are usually transient in nature. Although this characteristic is also observed in infants of diabetic mothers (see Chapter Four), it distinguishes this group of infants from those who have other known forms of hypoglycemia that may become apparent in the newborn period but that tend to be persistent or to recur (see Table 14). Examples of the latter include recurrent idiopathic spontaneous hypoglycemia,[12] hereditary galactose intolerance (galactosemia), lack of epinephrine secretion after induced hypoglycemia,[13] glycogen storage diseases,[14] and nesidioblastoma,[15] adenoma,[16] or hyperplasia of the islet cells of the pancreas.[3] (See Chapters Seven, Eight and Eleven.)

Incidence

The incidence of transient neonatal symptomatic hypoglycemia has been found to vary between 1.3 per thousand full term births[9] and 1.7[17] to 2.9 per thousand live births (Table 9). In a survey of levels of glucose in blood during the first 5 days of life in infants admitted to a premature nursery during 1963 and 1964, two or more blood samples were obtained from 244 of 322 infants. Of the 244, 14 infants had blood glucose levels under 20 mg./100 ml. and had symptoms of hypoglycemia, an incidence of 5.7 per cent[18] (Table 9).

Table 9. Incidence of Neonatal Symptomatic Hypoglycemia

Nursery Population	No. Births or Admissions	No. with Hypoglycemia	Rate/1000	Reference
Full-term births	9,000	12	1.3	Zetterström et al., 1963
Total births	3,000	5	1.7	Gruenwald, 1964
Total births	6,000	12	2.0	Neligan et al., 1963
Total births (1963)	2,775	8	2.9	Cornblath, 1964
Premature admissions (1963 and 1964)*	322	14	43.4	Wybregt et al., 1964

*This high incidence probably approaches the true incidence of hypoglycemia. It is the result of a survey of blood sugar levels in 244 of 322 infants admitted during a two-year period.

CLINICAL FEATURES

The pertinent data from our experience with 40 infants[1, 2, 18] have been grouped with those in the literature[5, 6] in order to characterize transient symptomatic hypoglycemia in the neonate. This summary includes information about the mothers, their parity, pregnancy and delivery; and about the infants, their gestation, sex, condition at birth, weight, clinical course, therapy and outcome (Tables 10 and 11).

Mothers

In the mothers there were no characteristic factors of age, race or parity. Of those mothers of known parity 21 were multigravida and 24 primigravida. None of the mothers had diabetes mellitus or other apparent metabolic illnesses. During the current pregnancy, half of the mothers had toxemia of pregnancy as defined by hypertension, edema and albuminuria. Except for pre-eclampsia, no other complications of pregnancy, labor or delivery tended to recur in the histories, yet one-third of the deliveries could be classified as complicated because of a prolonged or abrupt second stage, bleeding, or compromise of the fetus. Only rarely was an infant delivered by cesarean section, the majority being delivered vaginally from a cephalic presentation. There was no relationship between the hypoglycemic problem in these infants and premature rupture of the membranes, the duration of labor, or the analgesic or anesthetic agents used.

Twin pregnancies occurred in a significantly increased incidence, accounting for 18 per cent of the hypoglycemic infants.

Table 10. Neonatal Symptomatic Hypoglycemia in 56 Infants[1, 2, 5, 6, 18]

MOTHERS:	Age	15–41 years[1, 2]			
	Race	19 Negro, 21 White[1, 2]			
	Parity	21 Multigravida[1, 2, 5], 24 Primigravida[1, 2]			
	Pregnancy	24 Uneventful, 28 Toxemia			
	Twins	10 (6 first born, 4 second)			
	Delivery	22 Uneventful, 13 Complicated			
	Vaginal	52			
	Cesarean section	4			
INFANTS:	Condition at birth:	Good 36			
		Fair 12 ⎫ required assisted ventilation			
		Poor 8 ⎭			
	Sex:	38 males; 18 females			
	Birth weight (kg):	<1.0 1–1.5 1.5–2.5 2.5–3.5 >3.5			
		5 14 26 10 1			
	Percentile for gestational age*	<10th	10–25th	25–50th	>50th
	Birth weight	36	10	4	5
	Birth length	17	8	5	1

*After Lubchenco et al.[19]

Infants

At birth, two-thirds of the infants breathed and cried spontaneously; the remainder required assisted ventilation. The infants presented no unique appearance at delivery except that they were small for the period of gestation. Several infants were polycythemic and plethoric at birth. Male infants predominated (male:female = 2.1:1). The majority of the infants weighed less than 2500 grams at birth, 18 per cent were between 2500 and 3500 grams, and the heaviest weighed 5150 grams. The latter, a female, had an unusual clinical course in that her symptoms persisted for 26 days even though she had a low normal level of sugar on day 9 (Case 3, Haworth et al.).[5] The most consistent observations were that the hypoglycemic infants were of low birth weight for their period of

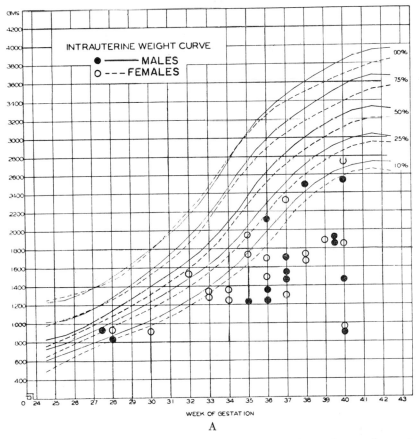

A

Figure 15. Weights (A) and lengths (B) at birth of 34 infants with transient neonatal symptomatic hypoglycemia plotted against weeks of gestation. (From Lubchenco et al.: Pediatrics 32:793, 1963, and personal communication.)

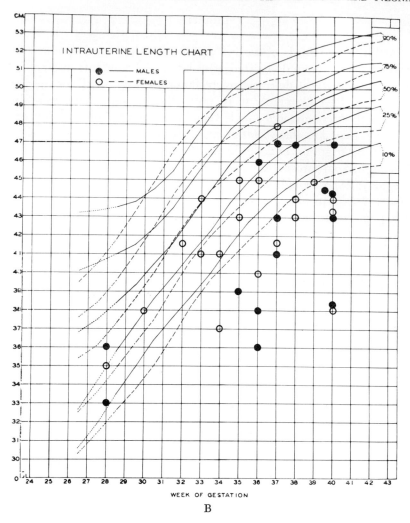

Figure 15. Continued.

gestation, were not of prolonged gestation, and did not have the appearance of the infant with the postmature placental insufficiency syndrome described by Clifford.[20] When compared to the intrauterine growth curves of Lubchenco et al.,[19] the birth weights of 90 per cent of the babies were below the 50th percentile for gestation while those of 65 per cent were below the 10th percentile (Table 10). The association of low birth weight for the period of gestation and hypoglycemia was further supported by the finding that in 10 sets of twins in whom hypoglycemia occurred, the smaller infant of the two always had hypoglycemia.[21] Hypoglycemia was not related to birth order or sex in the twins. None showed evidence of the parabiotic syndrome described in twins.

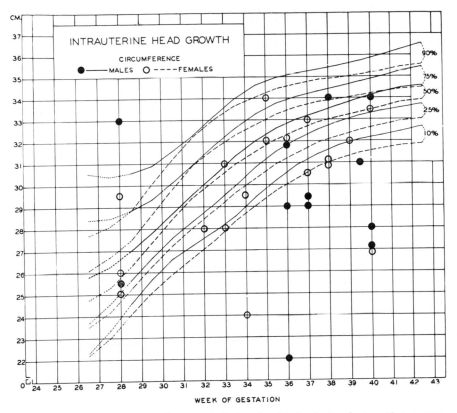

Figure 16. The circumference of the head at birth of 80 infants with transient symptomatic hypoglycemia has been plotted against weeks of gestation. (From Lubchenco et al.,[19] personal communication.)

Size for Gestation

In 34 hypoglycemic infants, both weight and length were determined at birth. In 30 of these, head circumference was noted as well. According to the percentile charts of Lubchenco et al.,[19] all the infants were below the 50th percentile for weight, and 26 (76 per cent) were below the 10th percentile (Fig. 15, *A*). All the infants were at or below the 50th percentile for length as well, but only 17 (50 per cent) were less than the 10th percentile (Fig. 15, *B*). In sharp contrast, the head circumferences of 10 infants were greater than the 50th percentile and those of only 10 (30 per cent) were below the 10th percentile (Fig. 16). It would appear that the hypoglycemic infants are both underweight and small in stature for their period of gestation, but that, as a group, their head size is less affected. The infants are somewhat more underweight than underlength.

Table 11. Neonatal Symptomatic
Hypoglycemia in 56 Infants[1, 2, 5, 6, 18]

Clinical Manifestations	No.	Presenting Sign
Tremors ("jitteriness")	42	20
Cyanosis	43	19
Convulsions	29	9
Apnea, irreg. resp.	23	6
Apathy	16	2
Cry, high pitched or weak	10	1
Limpness	13	4
Refusal to feed	5	1
Eye rolling	2	2

Age of Onset (Hours)

<6	6–24	24–48	48–72	>72
8	6	18	18	6

Table 12. Neonatal Symptomatic Hypoglycemic
Hypoglycemia in 56 Infants[1, 2, 5, 6, 18]

Laboratory — Blood glucose < 25 mg./100 ml. in all

Polycythemia 7/37
Hypocalcemia (<8.0 mg./100 ml.) 5/25, 3 < 7 mg./100 ml.
Cerebrospinal fluid — abnormal 2/25
Urine normal in 41 infants

Outcome	40[1, 2, 18]	6[5]	10[6]
Normal	17	4	4
Abnormal	5	2	4
Died	3	0	2

Clinical Course

The infants were often well at birth and then, after a symptom-free period, had episodes of tremors, "jitteriness," cyanosis, convulsions, apnea, limpness or apathy associated with a weak or high-pitched cry, refusal to feed, eye rolling, and labored, irregular respirations (Table 11). Although none of these signs or symptoms could be said to be specific for hypoglycemia, the clustering of manifestations is highly suggestive, especially when convulsions, tremors or "jitteriness" are present. Most often, clinical manifestations appeared between 24 and 72 hours of life. In some, these occurred during the first 24 hours after birth and as early as 2½ to 6 hours of age; in others, as late as 7 days of age. Signs and symptoms were transient, but tended to recur over a long period of time.

Diagnosis

A variety of disturbances (Table 13) may cause the clinical manifestations described. Furthermore, the analysis of blood glucose (as does every laboratory determination) has a degree of variability—especially at low values. Therefore, the diagnosis of symptomatic hypoglycemia depends upon the finding of sequential levels of blood sugar below 20 mg./100 ml. in the low birth weight infant and a prompt (minutes to hours) response to intravenous glucose. However, if the hypoglycemia has persisted undiagnosed for more than 24 to 36 hours or is secondary to intracranial pathology, the alleviation of symptoms following glucose administered intravenously may be delayed for 12 to 24 hours or may be incomplete.

Table 13. Differential Diagnosis in Neonate with Episodes of Tremors, Cyanosis, Convulsions, Apnea, Irregular Respiration, Apathy, High Pitched or Weak Cry, Limpness, Refusal to Feed, Eye Rolling

1. Central nervous system
   a. congenital defect
   b. birth injury, anoxia
   c. infection
   d. kernicterus

2. Sepsis

3. Heart disease
   a. congenital
   b. acquired
   c. arrhythmias

4. Iatrogenic
   a. drugs to mother
   b. overheating

5. Adrenal hemorrhage

6. Polycythemia

7. Metabolic
   a. hypocalcemia
   b. hyponatremia
   c. hypernatremia
   d. pyridoxine dependency
   e. magnesium deficiency
   f. uremia
   g. NEONATAL SYMPTOMATIC HYPOGLYCEMIA

Differential Diagnosis of Clinical Manifestations

The differential diagnosis in the neonate with the manifestations noted above has been outlined in Table 13.

Central nervous system abnormalities, including anoxemia or hemorrhagic injury, congenital anomalies or infections, can produce similar signs and symptoms with or without hypoglycemia. In addition to culture and microscopic examination of the cerebrospinal fluid, the bedside five tube test for spinal fluid sugar or Dextrostix (Ames) should be used as a rapid diagnostic procedure in any symptomatic baby. Lumbar punctures were performed on 25 hypoglycemic infants; in 23, the only abnormality in the cerebrospinal fluid was a low or zero level of sugar, often the first suggestion that hypoglycemia existed. The only other abnormalities noted were an isolated elevation of the spinal fluid protein concentration in one infant and blood from a cerebral hemorrhage in another (Table 12). On the other hand, 2 infants with congenital cerebral anomalies which were lethal in early infancy,[2] and 2 with microcephaly[6] also had symptomatic hypoglycemia. None of the infants manifested the neurological signs clinically associated with kernicterus. In 13 infants, in whom measurements were made, the levels of bilirubin did not exceed 18 mg./100 ml.

There was no evidence that *sepsis, heart disease, iatrogenic factors* or *adrenal hemorrhage* were responsible for the clinical features present in these hypoglycemic infants.

Although 7 affected infants had *polycythemia* as defined by a level of hemoglobin higher than 25 gm./100 ml. during the first week of life, none had permanent polycythemia or subsequently developed cyanotic heart disease. This relatively high incidence of polycythemia (12 per cent) is of particular interest because convulsions in the neonate have been reported with and attributed to polycythemia. However, metabolic measurements, including glucose levels, were not reported as part of these studies.[22]

Neonatal tetany has a number of features in common with symptomatic neonatal hypoglycemia.[23, 24] The predominence of males, prematurity and complications of labor or delivery may occur in both syndromes. Indeed, levels of calcium below 8 mg./100 ml. were found in 5 of 25 hypoglycemic infants, but only 3 infants had values below 7 mg./100 ml. Many hypoglycemic infants were given calcium gluconate as initial therapy. However, maternal diabetes mellitus, complicated labors, frequent cesarean section, manifestation of symptoms during the first 24 to 36 hours of life, vomiting, gastrointestinal bleeding and edema were all common in the infant with hypocalcemic tetany.[23] In addition, the hypoglycemic infants responded dramatically to parenteral glucose alone.

Although *hypo-* and *hypernatremia, uremia, pyridoxine dependency* and *magnesium deficiency* may all present with similar clinical manifestations, these could not be implicated in the hypoglycemic infants in this report.

Differential Diagnosis of the Hypoglycemia

Once the diagnosis of hypoglycemia has been established, it is necessary to consider the various causes of low blood sugar in the newborn infant (Table 14). The characteristic history, physical and laboratory findings in the majority of conditions listed are discussed elsewhere in the monograph (see index). Only that group of infants with persistent or intractable hypoglycemia variously described as "infant giants" (Ulstrom) or infants resembling foetopathia diabetica will be briefly presented here.

Familial neonatal hypoglycemia resembling foetopathia diabetica has been described in 2 infants by Hansson and Redin.[25] These infants were huge, resembled infants of diabetic mothers, and had intractable, prolonged, and fatal hypoglycemia. The infants showed hyperplasia of the beta cells of the pancreas at postmortem. A similar infant (who also had a normal sibling and a nondiabetic mother) was seen in Baltimore in 1955 (M.C.). This female infant weighed 4418 gm. at birth and developed symptomatic hypoglycemia at 36 hours of age with a blood sugar level of less than 10 mg./100 ml. Over the next 40 days of life, repeated convulsive episodes recurred in spite of parenteral glucose and large doses of cortisone and ACTH. Eight days before death, with serum corticoid levels of 230 μg./100 ml. (normal is 10–20 μg./100 ml.), the levels of blood glucose were 12 mg./100 ml. and rose to only 28 mg./100 ml. after administration of glucagon (100 μg.). At postmortem, bilateral pneumonia, fatty changes in the liver, aberrant pancreatic tissue without islets in the jejunum and small islet cells of the pancreas were described. Glycogen concentration in the liver postmortem was 0.8 per cent; in muscle, 0.23 per cent. The glucose-6-phosphatase activity in liver was normal, 592 μg. P liberated/ 100 mg. tissue/hr.* Subsequently, another sibling died of intractable hypoglycemia within hours of birth. An example of a nonfatal case of this syndrome may be the third patient reported by Haworth et al.[5]

A number of infants with persistent severe hypoglycemia beginning within hours after birth have been described.[3, 12, 26-28] Except for 2 patients with adenomas of the islet cells of the pancreas discussed by Crigler,[27] the prognosis in these infants has been poor in respect to subsequent mental and neurological development. In some infants it was not possible to control the hypoglycemia even with massive doses of ACTH, steroids and parenteral glucose, and subtotal pancreatectomy was necessary. In these infants, very low to zero blood sugar levels were found in the absence of symptoms. Therefore, it was essential that blood sugar profiles be done throughout the 24 hours before medical therapy was considered effective. The marked retardation in development and the difficulty in maintaining normoglycemia in infants with persistent, intractable hypoglycemia has prompted Crigler to suggest that "if an adequate explanation for the initial hypoglycemia is not available and the hypoglycemia persists into the third month of life, surgical exploration of the pancreas is indicated, with subtotal pancreatectomy if no specific lesion is found."[27] This

---

* Dr. G. F. Cori performed the postmortem glycogen and enzyme analyses.

recommendation emphasizes the importance of establishing the etiology of the low blood sugar as well as the urgency of instituting therapy to maintain normoglycemia.

Table 14. Differential Diagnosis of Neonatal Hypoglycemia

Persistent
　　　Intractable "infant giants"
　　　　　Familial neonatal
　　　Idiopathic spontaneous recurrent
　　　　　Leucine sensitive
　　　　　? Lack of epinephrine response
　　　Hereditary defects in metabolism
　　　　　Glycogen storage disease (types I, III)
　　　　　Glycogen synthetase deficiency
　　　　　Fructose intolerance
　　　　　Galactose intolerance (galactosemia)
　　　Islet cell adenoma

Transient
　　　Infants of diabetic mothers
　　　Central nervous system
　　　　　Hemorrhage, infection
　　　　　Congenital malformation
　　　Adrenal hemorrhage
　　　Cold injury
　　　NEONATAL SYMPTOMATIC HYPOGLYCEMIA

Therapy

Once the diagnosis of symptomatic hypoglycemia has been established by observation of the symptom complex described and by a reliable determination of glucose in blood under 20 mg./100 ml., it is important that therapy be initiated immediately.* First 1 to 2 cc./kg. of 50 per cent glucose in water is given intravenously in a peripheral vein, followed by a continuous infusion of 75 to 100 cc./kg./day of 15 per cent glucose in water for the first 24 to 48 hours of life. After 48 hours of age, the parenteral glucose can be increased in volume to 100 to 110 cc./kg./day and should contain 40 mEq./liter of NaCl (quarter strength saline) in order to prevent iatrogenic hyponatremia (Case 9, Wallis and Brown[6]). Oral feedings should be introduced as soon as possible after clinical manifestations subside. If symptoms recur or persist and the levels of glucose in blood remain below 30 mg./100 ml. after 6 to 12 hours of intravenous

* Once a hypoglycemic level of blood glucose has been reported in a symptomatic infant, another blood sample should be obtained for a repeat glucose determination at the time that the intravenous administration of glucose is started. If the glucose level in this sample is also significantly low, a diagnosis of symptomatic hypoglycemia is made.

glucose, hydrocortisone (5 mg./kg./day orally every 12 hours) or ACTH (4 u./kg./day intramuscularly every 12 hours) should be added to the regimen. It is important to maintain the parenteral glucose and steroids until symptoms have cleared and the levels of glucose in blood have been stabilized for a period of at least 48 hours. The concentration of the intravenous glucose should then be decreased to 5 per cent and slowly discontinued over 4 to 6 hours as oral feedings, adequate in calories and amount, are taken. *If the intravenous glucose infiltrates or is stopped abruptly, a reactive hypoglycemia may ensue and symptoms recur.* The ACTH and steroids should be discontinued slowly over several days, using the levels of glucose as a guide (Table 15).

Table 15.   Therapy in Neonatal Symptomatic Hypoglycemia

Initial: 1–2 cc./kg. 50% glucose I.V.

Continue with
      75–100 cc./kg. 15% glucose/water until 48 hours
        of age; thereafter
      100–110 cc./kg./24 hours 10% glucose/0.25 N saline

If symptoms persist or recur, or glucose is
      <30 mg./100 ml.
      Hydrocortisone 5 mg. twice daily or
      ACTH 4 units twice daily

If the serum calcium is below 8 mg./100 ml., calcium chloride (0.5 to 2.0 gm. daily as a 2 per cent solution) may be given orally for 2 to 3 days only and then calcium lactate should be substituted and added to the low solute feeding until calcium levels are normal.

Clinical Course and Follow-up

The majority of infants respond promptly. Symptoms subside within minutes to hours after therapy, and glucose levels become stabilized within 2 to 4 days. But others have required therapy for as long as 10 to 14 days before blood glucose levels stabilize in the normal range.

Some infants have had a recurrence of hypoglycemia when glucose was discontinued too abruptly. Two had recurrences of hypoglycemia with infections at 18 and at 51 days and one, spontaneously, at 8 months of age. The latter patient has had recurrent episodes of hypoglycemia and, at age 3 years, she has ketotic hypoglycemia (see page 234). Seven infants, followed for 3 years, have not had additional episodes of hypoglycemia. Some of the infants, who were either untreated or, in retrospect, treated inadequately, have subsequently had convulsions in the absence of hypoglycemia.

Since experience with this syndrome has been limited, the ultimate neurological status and mental and emotional development of these infants are unknown. Unfortunately, to date, 20 per cent have shown obvious mental and neurological defects and another 10 per cent have died. Death has usually resulted from complicating infections or associated congenital anomalies. Unfortunately, deaths as a result of unrecognized hypoglycemia alone are also known to the authors. In a personal communication, Zetterström reported that epilepsy developed in half the infants whose hypoglycemia was diagnosed at the time of convulsions in the newborn period. Some infants have primary central nervous system defects such as arrested hydrocephalus, microcephaly and cerebral palsy. On the other hand, many of the hypoglycemic newborns who were treated promptly and vigorously are developing normally. The survey of levels of blood glucose in the nursery population cited on p. 83 will permit a prospective analysis of the role of hypoglycemia in subsequent development. In this study, infants with hypoglycemia are matched with those who had normal levels of glucose and both are being followed with annual neurological, psychological, and psychometric evaluation of their growth and development.

Pathogenesis

The association of transient neonatal symptomatic hypoglycemia with a low birth weight for the period of gestation suggests intrauterine malnutrition as an important factor in this syndrome. While these infants are both underweight and understature for their period of gestation (Fig. 15), they have disproportionately large heads (Fig. 16). In twins, of 11 smaller members with hypoglycemia, 10 weighed 250 to 1700 gm. less than the larger twin.[21] Six of the larger twins had normal levels of blood sugar while the remaining 4, in whom no sugar levels were done, had an uneventful clinical course. In 13 sets of twins who were discordant in birth weight by over 25 per cent, 11 of the smaller members, who weighed under 2 kg. at birth, were hypoglycemic (Fig. 17). Thus, it is the malnourished small infant who is susceptible and develops significantly low levels of glucose in blood. Dawkins[29] reported that the ratio of the weight of the brain to that of the liver remains essentially constant between 30 and 40 weeks gestation in fully grown infants. However, in the infants who were of low birth weight for the period of gestation, the ratio increased significantly, indicating that the brain is disproportionately larger than the liver in intrauterine malnutrition. In addition, Shelley[30] found reduced levels of total carbohydrate at postmortem (often < 1 mg./gm.) in liver, heart and skeletal muscle of infants who were "rather small for dates." Furthermore, Sinclair and Silverman[31] reported a relatively increased oxygen need in undergrown human neonates. All this evidence would suggest that the susceptible infant may have markedly reduced

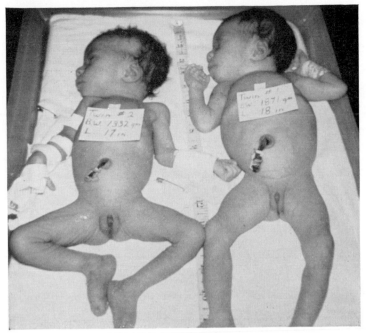

Figure 17. Discordant twins, 1332 gm. and 1871 gm. birth weight. The smaller twin had symptomatic hypoglycemia on the second day of life.

glycogen stores at birth and a liver inadequate to maintain the glucose needs of the relatively oversized glucose-dependent brain and of the body's relative hypermetabolism. These speculations require experimental verification in hypoglycemic infants and comparable controls.

Carbohydrate Tolerance Tests

In an attempt to elucidate the pathogenesis of the low sugar levels, a variety of carbohydrate tolerance tests have been performed in these babies to estimate their peripheral utilization of glucose, release of insulin, and available glycogen reserves in the liver.[2] Intravenous glucose tolerance tests were done in 8 hypoglycemic infants and a disappearance constant (k_t) calculated (see Chapter Two). In 7 of the 8 infants, the k_t was within normal limits, ranging between 1.1 and 1.57 per cent per minute.[32] The one infant in whom the disappearance rate was significantly elevated was just 3 years of age, and had ketotic hypoglycemia. However, many of the other infants were either being treated or had received therapy before the intravenous glucose tolerance test was done. Eleven hypoglycemic infants responded to tolbutamide (10 to 20 mg./kg. I.V.) with a significantly greater and more prolonged hypoglycemia than did control infants pretreated with ACTH (Fig. 18). Leucine (150 mg./kg. orally)

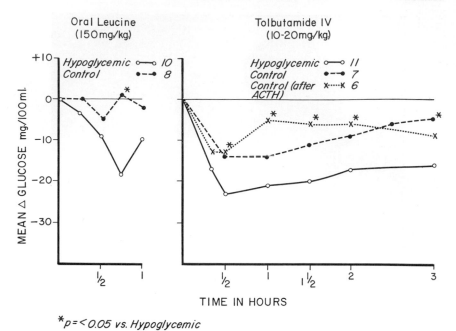

Figure 18.   Leucine and tolbutamide tolerance tests in infants with symptomatic neonatal hypoglycemia as compared with levels in control infants of low birth weight and comparable age. (Adapted from Cornblath et al., Pediatrics 33:388, 1964.)

produced a fall in the blood sugar in the hypoglycemic infants but not in controls (Fig. 18). It would appear that both leucine and tolbutamide may result in an excessive stimulus to insulin release, whereas acute hyperglucosemia does not since the disappearance rates after intravenous glucose are normal.

Glucagon and glucagon-plus-epinephrine tolerance tests indicated a reduced hyperglycemic response in hypoglycemic infants when compared to that found in control infants of the same age. Moreover, several of the hypoglycemic infants showed either no response or an actual fall in blood sugar after administration of epinephrine and glucagon at the onset of their illness. After therapy was initiated, a marked increase in the hyperglycemic response to glucagon with epinephrine occurred in a number of infants tested, suggesting that glycogen stores can easily be replenished in these babies or gluconeogenesis stimulated (Fig. 19).

In our hospitals, whenever possible, the investigation of any neonate with symptomatic hypoglycemia includes the assay of plasma for levels of insulin, growth hormone (HGH) and free fatty acids (FFA) and of urine for catecholamines. To date, 6 infants have been studied and one (L.M.) is presented in detail (see Case Report 2, page 100, and Figures

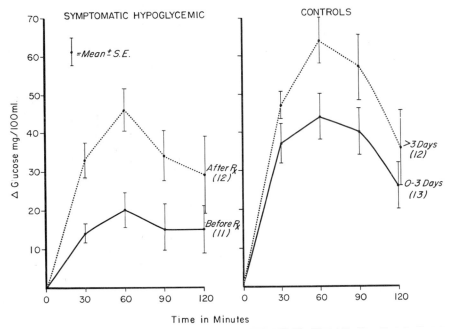

Figure 19. Glucagon-epinephrine tolerance test in low birth weight infants. Epinephrine (5 µg./kg.) was administered intramuscularly followed by glucagon (300 µg./kg.) intravenously in hypoglycemic neonates before and after therapy with glucose or steroids. A significant increase in the hyperglycemic response occurred after therapy. The controls represent the hyperglycemic response of low birth weight infants of two different age groups.

21 and 22). In L. M., prior to therapy, glucagon and epinephrine produced essentially no change in the blood glucose level, but a rise in FFA from 440 µEq./L. to over 1200 µEq./L., and yet the moderately elevated insulin levels of 18 and 22 mµ/ml. fluctuated very little (Figure 21). In contrast, after therapy and about 2 weeks later, glucagon-plus-epinephrine produced a striking hyperglycemia and elevation in FFA; HGH values remained unchanged, but plasma insulin levels fell throughout 90 of the 120 minutes (Fig. 22). After tolbutamide, glucose levels diminished from 70 to 35 mg./100 ml. and HGH from 25 to less than 10 mµg./ml., whereas FFA rose from 750 to 1400 µEq./L. and insulin from 10 to 18 µu./ml. Norepinephrine, epinephrine, and VMA excretion increased significantly during tolbutamide-induced hypoglycemia (Fig. 23). Although preliminary, these data are compatible with the hypothesis that the hypoglycemia results from reduced glycogen stores in the liver and a sensitive aberrant insulin release mechanism complicated by a failure of HGH secretion following induced hypoglycemia. Additional studies are necessary before any conclusions are justified.

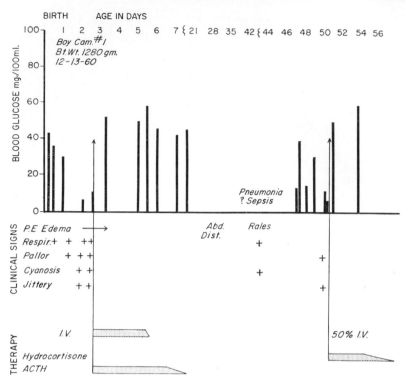

Figure 20. Symptomatic hypoglycemia in the neonate. The levels of glucose in blood, clinical manifestations and therapy are shown for Boy CAM No. 1 (see text for details).

Case Reports

Case 1. (Fig. 20.) CAM No. I (M. R. H. No. H901), a 1.28 kg. white male infant, first of twins, was born at home on December 13, 1960. The mother was a 19 year old primigravida. The pregnancy had been uneventful until the precipitous delivery of twins. There was a time lapse of half an hour between the birth of the two infants. The weight of the second twin was 1.64 kg. Blood sugar values obtained from the unaffected infant at 5½, 11, and 36 hours of age were 68, 25, and 41 mg./100 ml. This infant developed respiratory distress and died at 40 hours of age.

The first twin breathed and cried spontaneously after birth and was in fair condition when transferred to Michael Reese Premature Station at 4 hours of age. The physical examination was within normal limits. Blood sugar values obtained at 5½ and 12½ hours of age were 43 and 84 mg./100 ml. After 24 hours he began to moan and grunt and had subcostal retractions as well as periods of pallor and apnea. These symptoms were more pronounced at 50 hours of age, and cyanosis, jitteriness, and jaundice were also observed. At that time, the level of glucose in blood was 6 mg./100 ml. At 57 hours the blood glucose was 11 mg./100 ml. Therapy was initiated and included intravenous glucose and ACTH. The symptoms subsided shortly thereafter, but at 62 hours of age the infant was still tremulous following stimulation. This reaction subsided in the next 10 hours, at which time the blood sugar was 52 mg./100 ml. Repeated determinations of blood glucose were within the normal range. At 80 hours of age intravenous glucose was discontinued. An intravenous glucagon tolerance test (30 μg./kg.) was done on the fifth day with the following results: fasting blood glucose, 58 mg./100 ml.; at 30 minutes, 90 mg./100 ml.; at 60 minutes, 67 mg./100 ml.; at 90 minutes, 61 mg./100 ml.; and at 120 minutes, 58 mg./100 ml. A fasting blood sugar value on the sixth day showed a level of 45 mg./100 ml. On the seventh day an oral leucine tolerance test was done with an initial blood sugar of 42 mg./100 ml. and no change in subsequent values. Throughout his hospitalization fasting blood sugar values were obtained at regular intervals and were normal. His favorable clinical course was interrupted by pneumonitis on the 43rd day, which responded well to antibiotics and supportive measures. On the 43rd day a fasting blood sugar level of 13 mg./100 ml. was noted and similarly low levels persisted during the next 3 days. Because he had no symptoms, treatment was withheld. A combined glucagon and epinephrine tolerance test was done at 50 days of age. Two fasting levels of glucose were 6 and 11 mg./100 ml., and 30 minutes after glucagon and epinephrine, the level of glucose was 27 mg./100 ml.; at 120 minutes 9 mg./100 ml.; and at 180 minutes 15 mg./100 ml. The test was discontinued because the infant became very "jittery." An injection of 5 cc. of 50 per cent dextrose in water was given intravenously and hydrocortisone started, with immediate relief of symptoms. Twelve hours later, the blood glucose was 59 mg./100 ml. On the 51st day he received 20 cc. of whole blood because the hemoglobin had fallen to 7 gm./100 ml. The glucose levels remained within the normal range and hydrocortisone was discontinued at 59 days of age. On the 72nd day a right herniorrhaphy was done and tolerated well. Four days later the baby was discharged in good condition.

At 13 months, CAM No. I weighed 8.75 kg. and was 74 cm. tall. He could crawl, climb out of his playpen, babble, play "pat-a-cake" and walk with support. He seemed to understand his mother's commands. A 3-hour fasting blood sugar was 94 mg./100 ml. When seen at 2 years he weighed 11.4 kg. and was 85 cm. tall. He was a very active, normal boy. He could run, climb, say single and paired words, and was sufficiently well co-ordinated to push his tricycle around the house. He had had no episodes of fainting, convulsions, or any other abnormal behavior. The blood sugar level at this time was 88 mg./100 ml. When last seen at 4 years of age, he could recognize block letters, knew his own address and telephone number, and talked about his pet puppy. Physical examination was within normal limits. Neurological examination revealed hyperactive deep tendon reflexes bilaterally, suggesting mild spasticity. This did not interfere with his normal activity.

Case 2. (L. M. No. 57-91-38.) This 1.5 kg. Negro male infant was born at home on August 12, 1964 at 12:45 a.m. after 32 weeks gestation (25th percentile for gestational age) to a 14 year old primigravida. The mother had fever 2 days before delivery and received aspirin. The infant was delivered by the Chicago Maternity Center. The onset of labor was spontaneous and presentation was cephalic. The baby breathed and cried spontaneously.

He was transferred to the neonatal nursery of the Research and Educational Hospitals at 2 hours of age. On admission, his color was very red, with cyanosis, yet he was active. No respiratory distress was present. He was placed in an incubator at 89°F. and in 28 per cent oxygen. Physical examination revealed a small, deeply red infant with minimal subcutaneous tissue. The head circumference was 28 cm.; chest circumference, 24 cm.; total length, 41 cm.;

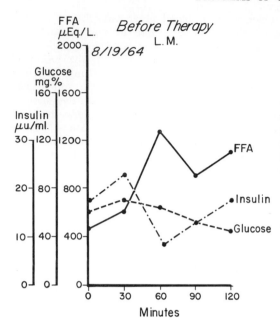

Figure 21. Glucagon-epinephrine tolerance test in an infant with transient neonatal hypoglycemia (Case 2, L. M.). Levels of free fatty acids (FFA), insulin and glucose were measured prior to and during the tolerance test.

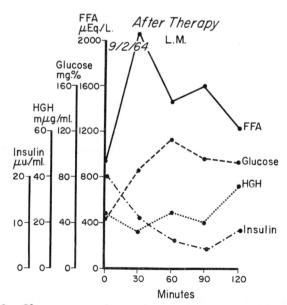

Figure 22. Glucagon-epinephrine tolerance test in a neonate with symptomatic hypoglycemia treated with intravenous glucose. Levels of insulin, growth hormone (HGH), free fatty acids (FFA) and glucose were obtained before and during the tolerance test.

and the weight to length ratio was 1.5. The remainder of the physical examination was within normal limits.

During the first 24 hours he became edematous, jaundiced, and had mild acrocyanosis and a shrill cry. He was jittery with handling, and took dextrose water feedings. Blood sugar values obtained at 8 hours and 32 hours of age were 48 and 35 mg./100 ml., respectively. The hemoglobin was 14.2 gm. per cent, reticulocytes, 14.6 per cent, and WBC, 6700/mm³. Total bilirubin was 7.6 mg./100 ml. at 32 hours of age. Because of the maternal history of fever, blood and throat cultures were obtained from the baby. Penicillin (50,000/kg./day) and Kantrex (7.5 mg./kg./day) were given. Blood sugar values obtained on days 2, 3, and 4 were 36, 29, and 25 mg./100 ml., respectively.

On the 5th day of life, the infant was lethargic and had episodes of twitching but was less jaundiced. A blood sugar determination taken that morning was 6 mg./100 ml. A repeat in the afternoon showed that the blood sugar level was 19 mg./100 ml. A glucagon-epinephrine tolerance test was done at that time with the following results: fasting blood glucose, 60 mg./100 ml.; at 30 minutes, 70 mg./100 ml.; at 60 minutes, 61 mg./100 ml.; at 90 minutes, 52 mg./100 ml.; and at 120 minutes, 45 mg./100 ml. (Fig. 21).

At the end of the test he was started on therapy consisting of 50 per cent glucose (2 cc./kg. of body weight I.V.), followed by 15 per cent glucose (75 cc./kg. of body weight) for 24 hours. Subsequent blood sugar determinations made daily were within the normal range (> 30 mg./100 ml.). Intravenous fluids (5 per cent dextrose in quarter strength saline), penicillin and kanamycin were continued.

The baby continued to be apathetic and lethargic, with intermittent episodes of vomiting on days 6, 7 and 8. He was reported to be jittery only if handled. A lumbar puncture was done at 8 days of age. The cerebrospinal fluid was clear and contained 274 mg./100 ml. protein. Urinalysis was negative except for a trace of albumin. The total bilirubin was 7.5 mg./100 ml. with 0.6 mg./100 ml. of conjugated bilirubin.

The blood culture obtained on the first day of life was reported to contain Staphylococcus aureus, coagulase-positive. Therefore, this infant had septicemia as well as hypoglycemia. This may account for the delay in improvement of his symptoms. Antibiotics were changed to methicillin (100 mg./kg./day) and chloramphenicol (25 mg./kg./day). On days 9 and 10 the jaundice was more intense. He still vomited occasionally and had intermittent abdominal distention. He was given nothing by mouth and continuous intravenous fluids. Total bilirubin at this time was 9.2 mg./100 ml. with 0.7 mg./100 ml. conjugated. Hemoglobin was 9.4 gm. per cent, WBC was 7900/mm.³ with 1 metamyelocyte, 2 stab neutrophils, 36 segmented neutrophils, 3 eosinophils, 43 lymphocytes and 16 monocytes. Oral thrush was first noted at 11 days of age and the child was treated with mycostatin and methicillin.

On the twelfth and thirteenth days of life the infant began to improve. There was no further emesis or abdominal distention. He was less jaundiced and more active. Oral feedings were started again and were retained. Intravenous fluids were discontinued on the thirteenth day of life. On the fifteenth day the infant was clinically well. All antibiotics were discontinued, and the glucagon epinephrine tolerance test was repeated with the following results: The fasting blood glucose was 42 mg./100 ml.; 30 minutes, 86 mg./100 ml.; 60 minutes 113 mg./100 ml.; 90 minutes, 95 mg./100 ml.; 120 minutes, 93 mg./100 ml. (Fig. 22). On September 17, 1964 at 40 days of age a tolbutamide tolerance test (20 mg./kg. I.V.) was done; the fasting blood glucose was 65 mg./100 ml.; 30 minutes, 37 mg./100 ml.; 60 minutes, 30 mg./100 ml.; at 120 minutes, 38

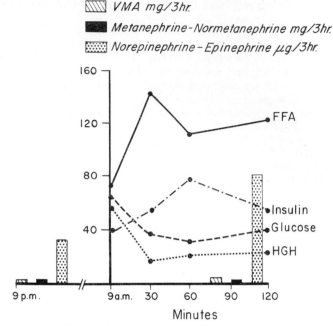

Figure 23. Tolbutamide (20 mg./kg. I.V.) tolerance test was done on L. M. (Case 2), a neonate with symptomatic hypoglycemia, after recovery. Free fatty acids (FFA) are μEq./L. $\times$ 10; insulin is μu./4 ml.; growth hormone (HGH), mμg./ml.; and glucose, mg./100 ml.

mg./100 ml. Urine catecholamines were collected 12 hours prior to the tolerance test during and following the test. An increase in the norepinephrine-epinephrine fractions was observed (Fig. 23).

The remainder of his hospital course was uneventful and he was discharged at 2 months of age, weighing 2565 gm. His general condition was good. At his first well baby follow-up visit at 2½ months of age, the infant was taking cereal, fruits and vitamins. He was active, alert, would follow light, smile and raise his head from the prone position. Physical examination was normal. Head circumference was 36.5 cm., chest circumference 31 cm., and total length 50 cm. His weight was 3232 gm. and he was doing well.

SUMMARY

Transient symptomatic neonatal hypoglycemia has been found in infants who are of low birth weight for their period of gestation and especially males and the smaller of twins. A prompt clinical response to hypertonic parenteral glucose is usual. The pathogenesis of this syndrome may be linked to intrauterine undernutrition as evidenced by diminished glycogen stores in the liver at the time symptomatic hypoglycemia occurs. The growth and development, both physical and mental, of these infants remains to be studied.

TRANSIENT NEONATAL SYMPTOMATIC HYPOGLYCEMIA

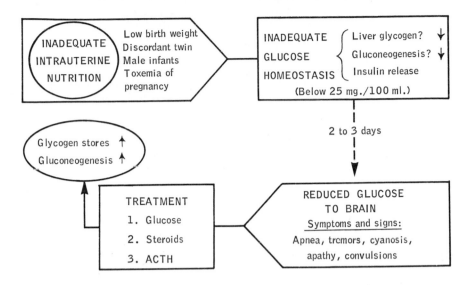

REFERENCES

1. Cornblath, M., Odell, G. B., and Levin, E. Y.: Symptomatic neonatal hypoglycemia associated with toxemia of pregnancy. J. Pediat. 55:545, 1959.
2. Cornblath, M., Wybregt, S. H., Baens, G. S., and Klein, R. I.: Symptomatic neonatal hypoglycemia: studies of carbohydrate metabolism in the newborn infant, VIII. Pediatrics 33:388, 1964.
3. Hartman, A. F., and Jaudon, J. C.: Hypoglycemia. J. Pediat. 11:1, 1937.
4. Wilkins, L.: The Diagnosis and Treatment of Endocrine Disorders in Childhood and Adolescence, Springfield, Ill., Charles C Thomas, 1957, p. 464.
5. Haworth, J. C., Coodin, F. J., Finkel, K. C., and Weidman, M. L.: Hypoglycemia associated with symptoms in the newborn period. Canad. Med. Ass. J. 88:23, 1963.
6. Brown, R. J., and Wallis, P. G.: Hypoglycemia in the newborn infant. Lancet 1:1278, 1963.
7. Harris, R., and Tizard, J. P.: The electroencephalogram in neonatal convulsions. J. Pediat. 57:501, 1960.
8. Neligan, G. A., Robson, E., and Watson, J.: Hypoglycaemia in the newborn. A sequel of intrauterine malnutrition. Lancet 1:1282, 1963.
9. Zetterström, R., [Eeg-Olofson, O., and Nilsson, L.] Neonatal chemistry. (Discussion workshop.) Ann. New York Acad. 111:537, 1963.
10. Tynan, M. J., and Haas, L.: Hypoglycaemia in the newborn. Lancet 2:90, 1963 (Letter to the Editor).
11. Creery, R. D. G.: Hypoglycaemia in the newborn. Lancet 1:1423, 1963 (Letter to the Editor).
12. McQuarrie, I.: Idiopathic spontaneously occurring hypoglycemia in infants. A.M.A. Am. J. Dis. Child. 87:399, 1954.
13. Broberger, O., and Zetterström, R.: Hypoglycemia with an inability to increase the epinephrine secretion in insulin-induced hypoglycemia. J. Pediat. 59:215, 1961.
14. Mason, H. H., and Andersen, D. H.: Glycogen disease. A.M.A. Am. J. Dis. Child. 61:795, 1941.

15. Sherman, H.: Islet-cell tumor of pancreas in a newborn infant (nesidioblastoma). A.M.A. Am. J. Dis. Child. 74:58, 1947.
16. François, R., Pradon, M., Sherrer, M., and Ugliengo, A. R.: Hypoglycemia due to pancreatic islet cell adenoma. J. Pediat. 60:721, 1962.
17. Gruenwald, P.: Chronic fetal distress. Clin. Pediat. 3:141, 1964.
18. Wybregt, S. H., Reisner, S. H., Patel, R. K., Nellhaus, G., and Cornblath, M.: The incidence of neonatal hypoglycemia in a nursery for premature infants. J. Pediat. 64:796, 1964 and unpublished observations.
19. Lubchenco, L. O., Hansman, C., Dressler, M., and Boyd, E.: Intrauterine growth as estimated from liveborn birth-weight data at 24 to 42 weeks of gestation. Pediatrics 32:793, 1963 and personal communication.
20. Clifford, S. H.: Postmaturity—with placental dysfunction. J. Pediat. 44:1, 1954.
21. Reisner, S. H., Forbes, A. E., and Cornblath, M.: The smaller of twins and hypoglycaemia. Lancet 1:524, 1965.
22. Wood, J. L.: Plethora in the newborn infant associated with cyanosis and convulsions. J. Pediat. 54:143, 1959.
23. Saville, P. D., and Kretchmer, N.: Neonatal tetany: a report of 125 cases and review of the literature. Biol. Neonat. 2:1, 1960.
24. Craig, W. S., and Buchanan, M. F. G.: Hypocalcaemic tetany developing within 36 hours of birth. Arch. Dis. Child. 33:505, 1958.
25. Hansson, G., and Redin, B.: Familial neonatal hypoglycemia. A syndrome resembling foetopathia diabetica. Acta Paediat. 52:145, 1963.
26. Schwartz, O., Goldner, M. G., Rosenblum, J., and Avin, J.: Neonatal hypoglycemia; report of a case of unusual duration. Pediatrics 16:658, 1955.
27. Crigler, J. F.: Idiopathic hypoglycemia, clinicopathological exercise. Discussion of a case. New England J. Med. 266:1269, 1962.
28. Sauls, H. S., Jr., and Ulstrom, R. A.: Hypoglycemia. In Kelley, V. C. (ed.): Brennemann's Practice of Pediatrics. Hagerstown, Md., W. F. Prior, 1965.
29. Dawkins, M. J. R.: Hypoglycaemia in childhood. Proc. Roy. Soc. Med. 57:1063, 1964.
30. Shelley, H. J.: Carbohydrate reserves in the newborn infant. Brit. Med. J. 1:273, 1964.
31. Sinclair, J. C., and Silverman, W. A.: Relative hypermetabolism in undergrown human neonates. Lancet 2:49, 1964 (Letter to the Editor).
32. Cornblath, M., Wybregt, S. H., and Baens, G. S.: Studies of carbohydrate metabolism in the newborn infant. VII. Tests of carbohydrate tolerance in premature infants. Pediatrics 32:1007. 1963.

Chapter Six

TRANSIENT DIABETES
MELLITUS IN EARLY INFANCY

Permanent juvenile diabetes mellitus, which ultimately is associated with a deficiency in insulin, occurs only rarely in infants under 6 months of age. However, a discrete clinical entity that simulates diabetes mellitus has been described in the first 6 weeks of life. Characteristically, in this temporary or transient diabetes mellitus, ketonuria is absent but hyperglycemia, glycosuria and dehydration may be severe.

Hyperglycemia in the neonate may be defined as a state in which the blood glucose or true sugar level is over 125 mg./100 ml. after a 4-hour fast (see Chapter Three). However, in the clinical syndromes associated with hyperglycemia, the blood sugar levels usually exceed 250 mg./100 ml. and may be as high as 1300 mg./100 ml. Some of these infants have permanent juvenile diabetes mellitus, with acidosis and ketosis, requiring the lifelong use of insulin,[1, 2] but the majority have a type of temporary diabetes from which they recover. The latter is insulin-sensitive and is usually not associated with ketosis. Only this syndrome of temporary diabetes mellitus in infancy, also referred to as congenital neonatal pseudo-diabetes, or congenital temporary diabetes, will be discussed here.[3-5]

Probably the first patient identified as having this syndrome was the son of a physician who presented with "honeyed napkins," polyuria, polydipsia, polyphagia, dry skin and emaciation a few days after birth. Glycosuria was identified at 14 days of age, and the infant died of a urinary tract infection after 6 months (Kitselle, 1852, described by Lawrence and McCance[6]). Ramsey[7] reported the first unequivocal case of this syndrome in a neonate whose hyperglycemia and glycosuria were well documented. After a 25-year follow-up, the patient remained healthy and was accepted

Table 16.　Summary of Data—Fifteen Cases of Transient Diabetes Mellitus in Early Infancy

Author	Case No.	Sex	Birth Weight (kg.)	Gestation	Clinical Manifestations	Age Detection	Highest Blood Sugar (mg./100 ml.)	Acetonuria	Duration Glycosuria or Rx	Rx-Insulin (units/day)	Comment	Follow-up
Ramsey, 1926	1*	M	2.20	F.T.	Fever, URI, polyuria, rapid wasting polyphagia	31 days	263	not tested	13 weeks 18 days insulin	4	Urine sugar-free in 4 days. Recurrence if insulin stopped Five normal sibs	25 years—O.K. for military service
Lawrence and McCance, 1931	2	F	3.57	F.T.	Gangrene, wasting dehydration, fever	18 days	600	neg.	9 days 5 days insulin	6 3	Albuminuria, WBC, casts. Gangrene healed 11 weeks ? insulin reactions	3 months
Strandqvist, 1932	3	M	2.20	F.T.	Abscess, wasting, dehydration	6 weeks	420 TRS	neg.	14 days insulin	2		9 months
Nawrocka-Kanska, 1952	4	M	2.70	F.T.	Vomiting, (12 days), dehydration	18 days	268	positive	12 days	none	CSF xanthochromic Sugar 92 mg./100 ml.	1 year
Arey, 1953	5	M	2.20	F.T.	Sudden weight loss, dehydration	13 days	555	trace	6 weeks	2-1/2 to 8	BUN 56 mg. % Hb 16 gm.%	5 months Normal G.T.T. 7 months
Keidan, 1955	6	F	2.78	F.T.	Dehydration, pale, wasted, boil on thigh	4 weeks	245	trace	17 days normal electrolytes	none	Convulsions, 'bloody CSF CSF sugar 212 mg./100 ml.	10 months 140 mg./100 ml. — 1/2 hour p.c.
Engleson and Zetterqvist 1957	7	M L = 49.0 cm.	2.78	F.T.	Wasted—postmature, vomiting	5 days	720	neg. (positive Ix)	3 months	4 to 8	CSF sugar 380 mg./100 ml. Relapse at 9 weeks Insulin started at 3 weeks of age	3 years normal G.T.T.
	8	F L = 47 cm.	2.02	F.T.	Wasted, grayish pallor, poor suck	11 days	560	neg.	186 days	6 to 8	One insulin reaction	1 year—normal G.T.T. normal in development
Jeune and Riedweg, 1960	9	M L = 48.5 cm.	2.93	F.T.	Dehydration, enteritis, acidosis	5 days	434	neg.	3 days	4 to 6	E. coli-0111B4 Two convulsions with insulin Normal plasma and urinary 17 OHCS	6-1/2 months, normal development

Table 16. Summary of Data—Fifteen Cases of Transient Diabetes Mellitus in Early Infancy (Continued)

Author	Case No.	Sex	Birth Weight (kg.)	Gestation	Clinical Manifestations	Age Detection	Highest Blood Sugar (mg./100 ml.)	Acetonuria	Duration Glycosuria or Rx	Rx - Insulin (units/day)	Comment	Follow-up
Gerrard and Chin, 1962	10*	M L = 46 cm.	2.26	F.T.	Wasted at birth, routine hernia	4 weeks	160	neg.	4 months	none	Diabetic G.T.I. Uneventful herniorrhaphy	17 months→normal G.T.I.
Hutchison, Keay, and Kerr, 1962†	11	F	2.41	F.T.	Weight loss, pallor, alert, dehydrated	17 days	666	neg.	18 months	60	Frequent hypoglycemia. Normal male sib. Normal G.T.I. (2-1/2 years)	8-1/2 years—mental defective
	12	F	1.93	F.T.	Wasted, dehydrated, vomiting, polyuria	10 days	1292	neg.	4-1/2 months	35	Frequent hypoglycemia. Recurrence insulin withdrawal. Two normal sibs	2-3/4 yrs.—convulsion 5 yrs.—defective hemiplegia
	13	F	2.13	36 weeks	Weight loss, sudden collapse, fever, dehydration	34 days	800	neg.	28 days 17 days insulin	4 to 7	CSF = sugar 253 mg./100 ml. (Prot. = 80 mg./100 ml.) Two normal sibs	3-1/2 yrs.—defective
	14	F	1.84	43 weeks	Weight loss, postmature	12 days	750	neg.	8 weeks	24	Tolbutamide—21 days. Relapse in 48 hours	6 months
Burland, 1964	15	F	1.85	F.T.	Dysmature, wasted, dehydrated, weight loss	13 days	870	neg.	23 days	?		11 weeks→normal G.T.I.

F.T. = Full term
G.T.T. = Glucose tolerance test
CSF = Cerebrospinal fluid

*Positive F.H. for diabetes
†All had normal G.T.I. at follow-up

for military service.[3] Subsequently, reports on at least 15 patients with variations of the condition have been published[3-14] and others are known to the authors.

Transient neonatal diabetes mellitus is rare; the exact incidence is unknown. Hutchison et al.[5] reported 4 patients seen between 1952 and 1961 and suggested "that a lack of awareness has led to mistaken diagnoses and to the preventable deaths of some affected infants."

CLINICAL MANIFESTATIONS

The infants were characteristically of low birth weight yet were full term. Ten of the 15 infants reported weighed less than 2500 grams at birth and 4 weighed between 2.5 and 3.0 kg. (Table 16). The sexes were almost equally represented. There was a positive family history of dia-

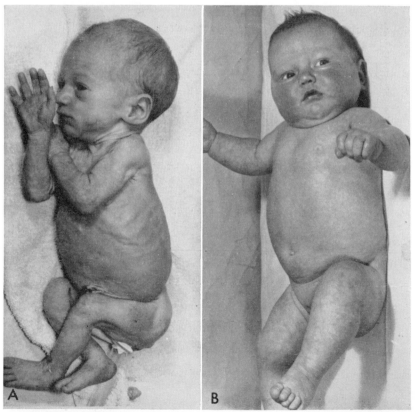

Figure 24. A, Patient was 14 days old and emaciated yet alert after 48 hours of therapy. B, Picture taken at 3½ months of age. (From Hutchinson et al., Brit. M. J. 2:436, 1962.)

betes mellitus in two instances. The most striking presenting signs and symptoms were marked dehydration and wasting, often in the presence of an adequate food intake and in the absence of vomiting or diarrhea. These infants had a "peculiar pallor and lined, aged appearance which was associated with remarkably 'open-eyed' alert facies" according to Hutchison et al.[5] (Fig. 24). Subcutaneous fat was minimal. Rarely, there was evidence of infection and vomiting. Sudden weight loss, polyuria, and occasionally fever were also recorded. The diagnosis was made as early as 5 days or as late as 6 weeks, but usually before 3 weeks of age. All the clinical manifestations *can* be present at birth.

The diagnosis is based on glycosuria, present in all, and hyperglycemia, ranging between 160 to 1292 mg./100 ml. Glucose tolerance tests should not be necessary for diagnosis. Ketosis does not occur. Acetonuria is almost never present and has been reported definitely as a transient phenomenon in only 2 instances (Table 16, Cases 4 and 7). Lumbar punctures were performed in several infants, and the cerebrospinal fluid sugar was elevated to levels as high as 380 mg./100 ml. Thus, the sugar content of the CSF can be diagnostic in both transient diabetes and transient neonatal hypoglycemia (page 88).

Only limited laboratory data are available for the patients reported and the information given does not permit an evaluation of the acid-base derangement. In a few instances, the serum sodium concentration and CO_2 content were decreased, while serum chloride concentration was normal. These data, although inadequate and incomplete, suggest that the acidosis results from a depletion of extracellular buffer unrelated to ketone production. Urinary 17-keto and 17-hydroxy (OH) steroid excretion measurements were made in 4 infants and were normal in 3. In 1 infant (Table 16, Case 13), the 17-OH corticosteroid excretions were elevated before recovery as well as 1½ years later.

CLINICAL COURSE

A few infants did not require insulin, but those who did responded dramatically. In view of the repeated hypoglycemic episodes reported in two cases in whom there was daily use of a total of 30 to 60 units of regular insulin in divided doses, it would appear that a dosage in the order of 2 to 8 units (1 to 3 u./kg. body weight/day) used by a number of other authors is more appropriate. In many cases, the infants were maintained on oral feedings and did not require intravenous fluids. Dehydration is rapidly corrected, weight gain ensues, and the clinical manifestations are quickly reversed (Fig. 24). Glycosuria may persist for as long as 18 months (Case 10) or subside in 3 to 14 days (Cases 2, 3, 4 and 9). The duration of the hyperglycemia is also variable. Once the hyperglycemia and glycosuria disappear, the results of the glucose tolerance test frequently return to normal. Five patients have been followed for periods ranging from 3 to 25 years with no evidence of recurrence.

The diagnostician must differentiate between the transient type and true diabetes mellitus, which may be severe and lead to a rapidly fatal outcome in the young infant.[4] In permanent diabetes, ketosis and acetonuria are common and the age of onset is usually later, although the disease has been diagnosed as early as 9 days of age.[2] Certainly, the prognosis for cure and for prolonged therapy differ markedly in these two forms of diabetes.

One infant was erroneously diagnosed as having congenital adrenal hyperplasia. The salt-losing variety of the adrenogenital syndrome can produce a similar picture of acute onset of weight loss, vomiting, and dehydration. Hereditary galactose intolerance can also present a similar picture and be misdiagnosed as diabetes because of the presence of reducing substance in the urine. Testing the urine specifically for glucose (glucose oxidase: Testape, Clinistix, Combistick) and determining the blood *glucose* level, which is very high in transient diabetes mellitus, are essential in making an accurate diagnosis. The work-up of any underweight term or post-term infant who is doing poorly, losing weight, or rapidly becoming dehydrated should include a complete urinalysis, including total and specific reducing substances, and a blood glucose determination.

THERAPY

The treatment of these infants should be directed toward control of the hyperglycemia and its associated hypertonicity and dehydration. Insulin therapy must be individualized; small, intermittent doses with frequent measurements of blood sugar to avoid hypoglycemia are essential. Total doses varying between 1 and 3 units of insulin per kilogram of body weight per day have been found to be effective.

In the presence of marked hyperglycemia (blood sugar values over 400 mg./100 ml.) and dehydration, parenteral fluids may be necessary. Physiologic management can be achieved provided repeated microblood sugar analyses are available and are used. Under these circumstances, the hypertonicity and the osmotic diuresis which are responsible for the dehydration are best corrected by the use, initially, of non-glucose containing fluids. Solutions of hypotonic electrolytes (120 mEq./L. sodium, e.g., ⅘ Ringers, ⅕ water) in quantities of 60 to 80 ml. per kg. are given in the first 12 hours or until the blood glucose concentration has fallen to 300 mg./100 ml. Thereafter, additional fluids containing 40 mEq./L. sodium (as ¼ Ringer's solution) and *2.5 or 5 per cent glucose* in quantities up to 150 to 200 ml. per kg. per day are recommended. In view of the varying sensitivity to insulin and the dangers of hypoglycemic reactions, glucose (2.5 to 5 per cent) should be included in the initial fluids if careful monitoring of the blood sugar is not possible.

ETIOLOGY AND PATHOGENESIS

A variety of etiologic factors have been suggested in this syndrome, including a transient hypothalamic imbalance, infection, adrenocortical disturbance and hypoinsulinism secondary to hypoplasia of the beta cells. Apropos of the last hypothesis, Gerrard and Chin[13] found a flat oral glucose tolerance curve in the mother of their patient and postulated that she always maintained a relatively stable low glucose concentration in her blood. Since the glucose level in the fetus is proportional to that in the mother, the infant would have a low level of glucose *in utero*, with a failure of insulin production due to lack of stimulation. The failure of Case 14 (Table 16) to respond to tolbutamide would support this thesis, as does the lack of subcutaneous fat and the wasting seen in most of these babies. Postnatally, the continued stimulation of the beta cells finally results in the production of enough insulin to compensate for the diabetic state, which would thus be only temporary. It is puzzling, however, that the mother of Case 10, who continued to have a flat oral glucose tolerance curve, subsequently had an infant who was normal (Gerrard, personal communication). The only other mother who was tested during the pregnancy of her affected infant was said to have a normal glucose tolerance test (Case 14).

Some authors have suggested that infections may be the cause of the transient diabetes; however, only a few of the infants had infections prior to the onset of symptoms. Adrenal hyperfunction alone is unlikely as an etiologic factor in view of the insulin-sensitivity of these babies. Further studies of plasma levels of insulin, 17-OH corticosteroids, growth hormone, and free fatty acids, as well as tolerance tests with tolbutamide and leucine and R.Q. determinations might elucidate the pathogenesis of transient diabetes mellitus.

SUMMARY

The syndrome of transient diabetes mellitus in the neonate occurs in underweight term infants who are wasted, look alert and become quickly dehydrated—all in the absence of vomiting, diarrhea or infection. Glycosuria is marked and ketonuria is rare. The hyperglycemia is striking, often exceeding values of 300 to 500 mg./100 ml. The infants are insulin sensitive and have responded to 4 to 8 units of insulin daily. The hyperglycemia and glycosuria are transient, as is the need for insulin. Thus far, permanent diabetes has not been reported in these infants.

REFERENCES

1. Schwartzman, J., Crusius, M. E., and Beirne, D. P.: Diabetes mellitus in infants under one year of age. A.M.A. J. Dis. Child. 74:587, 1947.
2. Guest, G. M.: Infantile diabetes mellitus: 3 cases in successive siblings, 2 with onset at 3 months of age and 1 at 9 days of age. A.M.A. J. Dis. Child. 75:461, 1948 (Abstract).
3. Arey, S. L.: Transient diabetes in infancy. Pediatrics 11:140, 1953.
4. Engleson, G., and Zetterqvist, P.: Congenital diabetes mellitus and neonatal pseudodiabetes mellitus. Arch. Dis. Child. 32:193, 1957.
5. Hutchison, J. H., Keay, A. J., and Kerr, M. M.: Congenital temporary diabetes mellitus. Brit. Med. J. 2:436, 1962.
6. Lawrence, R. D., and McCance, R. A.: Gangrene in an infant associated with temporary diabetes. Arch. Dis. Child. 6:343, 1931.
7. Ramsey, W. R.: Glycosuria in the new-born treated with insulin. Tr. Am. Pediat. Soc. 38:100, 1926.
8. Strandqvist, B.: Infantile glucosuria simulating diabetes. Acta Paediat. 13:421, 1932.
9. Nawrocka-Kanska, B.: Diabetic syndrome in intracranial haemorrhage in newborn. Pediat. Pol. 27:1067, 1952.
10. Wylie, M. E. S.: A case of congenital diabetes. Arch. Dis. Child. 28:297, 1953.
11. Keidan, S. E.: Transient diabetes in infancy. Arch. Dis. Child. 30:291, 1955.
12. Jeune, M., and Riedweg, M.: Syndrome diabètique transitoire chez un nouveau-né. Pédiatrie 15:63, 1960.
13. Gerrard, J. W., and Chin, W.: The syndrome of transient diabetes. J. Pediat. 61:89, 1962.
14. Burland, W. L.: Diabetes mellitus syndrome in the newborn infant. J. Pediat. 65:122, 1964.

PART III

Hereditary Metabolic Disorders

Chapter Seven

DISORDERS OF
GLYCOGEN METABOLISM

A variety of types of disturbance of glycogen metabolism have been described over the past 37 years. The first patient was recognized and reported by Snapper and van Creveld in 1928,[1] at which time they proposed a defect in glycogen mobilization to explain hepatomegaly, hypoglycemia and ketonuria in a young boy. The nature of this hepatic form of glycogen storage disease was further elucidated by the pathological studies of von Gierke[2] and by the biochemical studies of Schönheimer[3] in the following year. Von Gierke's case was also noted to have renal involvement, hence the designation "hepatonephromegalia glycogenica." Van Creveld[4] reviewed the glycogen storage syndromes in detail in 1939 and emphasized the variations in the clinical and pathological observations. Mason and Andersen[5] in 1941 reported extensively a patient with hepatomegaly, hypoglycemia and acidosis in the newborn period who was studied carefully prior to death from infection at 2 months of age. In their classification they also included other hepatic diseases such as galactose intolerance, excessive insulin therapy in diabetes mellitus, and infantile cirrhosis. The cases of hepatic involvement with glycogen accumulation were recognized to have variable metabolic disturbances, but no definitive subclassification was possible. The accumulation of excessive fat in the livers of these patients was emphasized by Debré.[6]

Shortly after the original report of van Creveld, an apparently unrelated syndrome of glycogen accumulation in the heart of a young infant (7 months) was noted by Pompe in 1932.[7] Subsequently, van Creveld[4, 8] analyzed tissues from a similar case and found excessive glycogen in skeletal as well as cardiac muscles. Scattered reports of isolated cardio-

115

megaly in infancy and of a generalized muscular disorder were reviewed and summarized in 1950 by Di Sant'Agnese, Andersen and Mason.[9, 10]

Thus, initially, two categories of disease entities were apparent, the hepatorenal group and the cardiomuscular group. Two other distinct syndromes have emerged in more recent years. Andersen[11] first described a storage disease with an abnormal concentration of glycogen in the liver and with progressive hepatic and reticuloendothelial involvement which terminated in cirrhosis with hepatic failure. This appears to be the rarest of the glycogen disorders. The other recently described syndrome is one of skeletal muscle involvement with an onset in childhood but not usually diagnosed until adulthood. McArdle[12] first reported this in 1951 when he called attention to the combination of weakness and cramping pain with persistent muscle stiffness after activity or exercise. Thus, a classification was established from the clinical manifestations of hepatorenal, cardiomuscular, hepatic cirrhotic, or muscular types of glycogen storage disease.

NORMAL GLYCOGEN AND GLUCOSE METABOLISM

Biochemical classification was not possible until the details of the pathways of glycogen metabolism were elucidated by the major contributions of the Coris, Leloir, Kalckar, Colowick, the Stettens, Sutherland, Larner, Illingworth and Hers (as reviewed in[13, 14, 80]). The biochemical basis for the classification of the glycogen storage diseases was presented by G. T. Cori[15] in her Harvey Lecture in 1954. This schema recently has been extended by Hers[16] and now includes six or seven distinct biochemical types. A brief review of glycogen metabolism is presented here as a basis for understanding the biochemical classification of the glycogen disorders (Fig. 25). Although additional enzyme systems have been reported to be involved in glycogen metabolism, the nature and significance of these remains to be clarified.[80]

Under normal environmental circumstances, dietary glucose is removed from the portal circulation by the liver. After diffusion through the hepatic cell membrane, glucose is phosphorylated to glucose-6-phosphate by glucokinase and/or hexokinase, with transfer of a high energy bond from ATP to the glucose molecule. Glucose-6-phosphate occupies a central position in cell metabolism of carbohydrate since at least four direct pathways for its metabolism exist. These include (1) glycolysis, (2) pentose cycle, (3) synthesis to glycogen or (4) release as free glucose in liver, kidney or intestine. Glucose-6-phosphate may be degraded via the Emden-Meyerhof glycolytic pathway either to lactic acid or, through acetyl Co-A and the Krebs cycle, ultimately to yield CO_2, H_2O, and energy. A portion of the glucose-6-phosphate may be metabolized via the pentose cycle with the production of reduced triphosphopyridine nucleotide (TPNH) and CO_2.

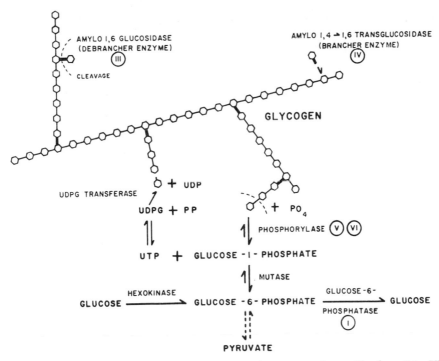

Figure 25. Schematic representation of glycogen synthesis. Numbers I to VI refer to sites of enzymatic defect in the various types of glycogen storage disease. Type II (alpha acid maltase) and type VII (synthetase or UDPG transferase) are not indicated specifically.

Glycogen Synthesis

One pathway for glucose-6-phosphate is for the synthesis of glycogen. Glucose-6-phosphate is converted to glucose-1-phosphate through an intermediate diphosphate stage. This reversible reaction is mediated by the enzyme phosphoglucomutase. Thus, glucose-1-phosphate is both the precursor and a product of the glycogen cycle.

Glycogen synthesis and degradation, formerly considered to be mediated by a common enzyme, have now been established to be independent pathways. Synthesis occurs when glucose-1-phosphate is converted to uridine diphosphoglucose (UDPG) by a specific pyrophosphorylase and uridine triphosphate. This step is reversible *in vitro*. Then the UDPG is reacted with a "glycogen primer" to lengthen the chain in α-1,4 linkages. This reaction is catalyzed by a specific UDPG-glycogen glucosyl transferase or glycogen synthetase, is unidirectional, and is stimulated by glucose-6-phosphate. (Insulin is known to increase glycogen synthetase activity in experimental animals.) When chains of variable length have been produced, further increase in molecular size depends on producing α-1,6 branch points with the aid of a specific branching enzyme, amylo-1,4 → 1,6 transglucosidase. Further lengthening of both chains can then occur by the action of glycogen synthetase. Continuous sequential action of the two enzymes in the presence of adequate substrate results in formation of large molecules of multitiered, branched glycogen. The size of the molecule and number of branch points is highly variable, so that it is impossible to define a single crystalline structure for glycogen. In general, the inner tiers of glycogen have more branch points than the outer tiers.

Glycogen Degradation

Glycogen degradation is mediated through at least two known enzyme systems: (1) phosphorylase and (2) debrancher (amylo 1,6 glucosidase). The activation and inactivation of the phosphorylase enzyme are complex activities and depend upon a number of reactions, including

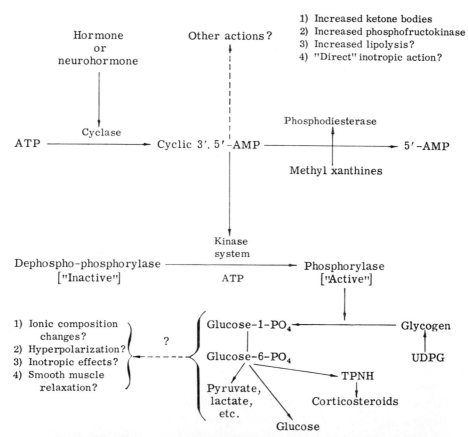

Figure 26. The cyclase-phosphorylase enzyme systems that are important in glycogen degradation. (From Sutherland, The Harvey Lect. 57:17, 1962.)

the formation of cyclic 3′,5′ adenosine monophosphate (Fig. 26). Two hormones, glucagon and epinephrine, are activators of the cyclase and thus the phosphorylase systems. Phosphorylase in the presence of inorganic phosphate removes a glucose molecule from the α-1,4 glucosidic linkage to produce glucose-1-phosphate, the original precursor in glycogen synthesis, thus completing the cycle. Phosphorylase is inactive at the 1,6 branch points and stops along the straight chain of terminal α-1,4 linkages at some distance from the branch point. The debrancher removes a molecule of glucose at the 1,6 position hydrolytically, producing free glucose which is not phosphorylated. Thus, sequential degradation of glycogen results in production of approximately 90 per cent glucose-1-phosphate and 8 to 12 per cent free glucose. The latter then may be a limited source of blood glucose from the liver as well as muscle, fat, and other tissues which contain the enzymes of the glycogen cycle.

Liver Glucose Output

The hepatic release of glucose is mediated through the action of a specific enzyme, glucose-6-phosphatase. While this enzyme is normally found in liver, kidney and intestinal mucosa, it is absent from muscle, adipose tissue and erythrocytes which therefore cannot release significant quantities of glucose. Glucose-6-phosphatase is unidirectional and appears to be active when the blood sugar levels fall postprandially or with fasting. The activity of this enzyme in animal liver is further increased by starvation, cortisone and alloxan diabetes. Glucose output from the liver is dependent upon adequate glucose-6-phosphatase activity, whether the source of substrate, glucose-6-phosphate, be derived from glycogen degradation or from gluconeogenesis from amino acids.

CLASSIFICATION OF DISORDERS OF GLYCOGEN METABOLISM

Defects in glycogen metabolism could appear at any of the enzymatic steps described above. No deficiencies have been reported for phosphoglucomutase, which appears to be present in tissue in excessive concentrations, but specific defects in each of the synthetic and degradative steps in glycogen formation have been described. The absence of glucose-6-phosphatase in liver was the first proven enzyme defect in the glycogen diseases.[17] The most intensely studied defects involve glucose-6-phosphatase, phosphorylase and debrancher enzymes. Very recently, Hers[18] has described a lysosomal system which hydrolyses glycogen at an acid pH (acid alpha glucosidase) and may be important in regulating cytoplasmic

Table 17. Classification of Glycogen Diseases

Type	Organs Involved	Glycogen content (gm./100 gm.)	Glycogen structure	Enzyme activity decreased	Blood sugar	Blood lactate	Others
I (von Gierke)	Liver	> 8.0	N	Glucose-6-phosphatase	Very low	High	Pyruvate↑
	Kidney	Increased	N	Glucose-6-phosphatase			Urate↑
	Intestine	Increased		Glucose-6-phosphatase			FFA↑
	RBC	Normal		None			Lipids↑
	WBC	Normal		?			
III (Cori)	Generalized	Increased	Abnormal	Amylo 1,6 glucosidase	Very low or low	Normal	Lipids↑ sl.
	Esp. liver	Increased	Abnormal				
	RBC	?	Abnormal				
	WBC		Abnormal	Amylo 1,6 glucosidase		Normal–high	Lipids↑
VI (Hers)	Liver	Increased	N?	Phosphorylase	Low		
	Kidney	?	N				
	RBC	N or H	N	Phosphorylase			
	WBC	?		Normal			
				Normal			
V (McArdle)	Muscle	Increased	N	Phosphorylase	Normal	Low	Myopathy
	RBC	?					
	WBC						
	Liver						
II (Pompe)	Generalized	Increased	Normal	Acid maltase	Normal	Normal	Cardiomegaly
	Liver	Increased					Myopathy
	Heart	Increased					CNS
	Muscle	Increased		Acid maltase			
	RBC	N					
	WBC	?					
IV (Andersen)	Generalized	Increased?	Abnormal	Amylo 1,4,6 transglucosylase	Normal	Normal	Cirrhosis
	Liver						
	R–E system	Normal	Abnormal				
	RBC						
VII (Lewis)	Liver	Decreased	Normal (?)	Glycogen synthetase	Very low	?	Fatty liver
	Kidney			?			
	RBC			Normal			

N = normal   H = high

glycogen accumulation. He has reported the absence of this enzyme in the cardiac form of glycogen diseases.

G. T. Cori and Hers have classified the diseases of glycogen metabolism into 6 types, according to the deficient enzymes. Another classification, based on the organs involved, has been found previously to be useful both clinically and physiologically in these inborn errors of metabolism. The two schemata will be combined here, with the broad categories of hepatic, muscular, and cardiac disease and the specific enzymatic defects, as described by Cori and Hers, included within each group (Table 17).

The hepatorenal glycogen diseases may result from deficiencies of three different enzymes: glucose-6-phosphatase (type I), amylo 1,6 glucosidase (type III), and phosphorylase (type VI). The other, rarer hepatic type (IV) may involve the deficiency or absence of amylo 1,4 → 1,6 transglucosidase. The muscular types include the cardiomuscular, with a deficiency of acid maltase or α-glucosidase (type II), and the skeletomuscular with absence of phosphorylase (type V). Most recently, a defect in hepatic glycogen synthetase (type VII) has been reported.[19]

HEPATIC (RENAL) SYNDROMES

Glucose-6-Phosphatase Defect (Type I)

The classical disease is manifested early in infancy by hepatomegaly without splenomegaly, with or without symptoms associated with hypoglycemia.[20] The liver is firm, smooth and may extend to the iliac crest, filling a major portion of the protuberant abdomen. There are no signs of cirrhosis or portal hypertension. Although the kidneys are often enlarged, they may not be palpable because of the massive hepatomegaly. Cardiomegaly does not occur. The infant or child is short in stature but appears well nourished. The cheeks and extremities have excessive adipose tissue ("doll-like facies") (Fig. 27), but the musculature is diminished and flabby. The face appears plethoric and may be moist with perspiration. If the patient is starved, agitated or ill, respirations may be rapid and deep due to acidosis. Easy bruising and a hemorrhagic tendency are common. Nose bleeds occur frequently. Some patients have xanthomata which appear as orange colored papules over the upper and lower extremities (Fig. 28). Lipemia retinalis may be noted. The neurological examination is unremarkable. Mental development varies: some children are mentally retarded, others are normal.

Variations of this general clinical description occur. In the most severe form, the syndrome may manifest itself in the first days of life with profound hypoglycemia and acidosis with rapid progression to death, if un-

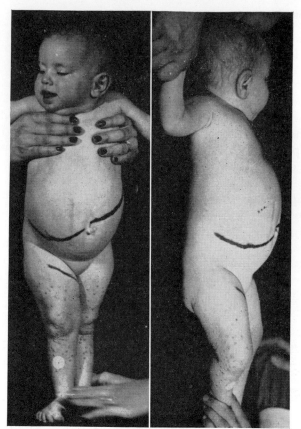

Figure 27. Infant with proved glycogen storage disease, glucose-6-phosphatase deficiency, showing the doll-like facies, hepatomegaly and xanthomata on the lower extremities.

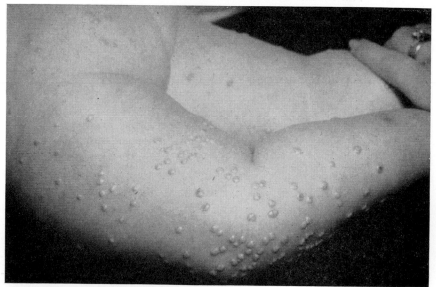

Figure 28. Xanthomata in glycogen storage disease with an absence of glucose-6-phosphatase.

diagnosed.[5, 21] On the other hand, the infant may be asymptomatic and only later in infancy or early childhood show a protuberant abdomen due to hepatomegaly and fail to thrive or grow.

Laboratory Tests

Although the routine urine and blood studies are usually within normal limits, ketonuria is often present after a brief fast. Thrombocytemia has been observed. Others may have a prolonged bleeding time in the absence of thrombocytemia. Chemical analyses usually reveal the fasting blood sugar (glucose) concentration to be low or absent, depending on the duration of the fast, and the carbon dioxide content to be low. Serum concentrations of Na, K, Cl and urea are normal; serum bilirubin and other liver function tests (thymol flocculation and turbidity, cephalin cholesterol flocculation, alkaline phosphatase, prothrombin time, bromosulfonphthalein retention) are normal; serum proteins may be slightly elevated, with a normal electrophoretic pattern. The levels of serum enzymes glutamic oxalacetic transaminase (GOT), glutamic pyruvic transaminase

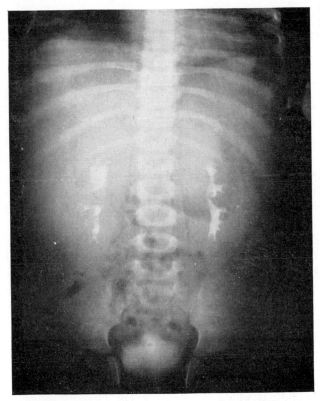

Figure 29. Intravenous pyelogram from an infant with hepatorenal glycogen storage disease, showing enlarged kidneys.

(SGPT), fructose 1,6 diphosphate aldolase (ALD) and ornithine car-
bamoyl transferase (OCT) may be elevated, but lactic dehydrogenase is
normal.[22] The blood pH may be either low or normal, depending upon
whether a metabolic acidosis is present. Concentrations of lactate and
pyruvate in blood are elevated, as may be those of urate and free fatty
acids in plasma.[23] The plasma may be lactescent as a result of a generalized
increase in lipids, including triglycerides, phospholipids and cholesterol.
Serum ketones may also be elevated.

A glucose tolerance test, either oral or intravenous, gives no specific
diagnostic information, although a diabetic-type delayed response or a
diphasic curve may be found. Plasma free fatty acid elevation, often noted
with hypoglycemia, returns to normal levels (as does blood lactate) when
normoglycemia is maintained by frequent glucose feedings.

Roentgen studies reveal generalized growth retardation. The heart is
not enlarged. The abdomen is filled with a large liver mass. The spleen is
obscured. Intravenous pyelography indicates bilateral symmetrical enlargement (Fig. 29) of the kidneys, which extend into the lower abdomen.
The pelvis and calyces are thin and elongated, but dye is excreted
promptly.

Special Studies

The glycogen content and structure in erythrocytes as described by
Sidbury et al.[24] are normal. Leukocytes analyzed by Williams and Field
have been found to contain normal phosphorylase and debrancher enzymes.[25, 26]

The diagnosis may be inferred from the results of tolerance tests
which measure the breakdown of glycogen to glucose or lactate, and the
conversion of other hexoses to glucose. Glucagon or epinephrine can be
used to stimulate glycogenolysis and release of glucose from the liver:[27, 28]
glucagon is preferred since it is more specific for liver phosphorylase activation, whereas epinephrine has also a skeletal muscle effect. Ideally, both
blood glucose and lactate should be assayed simultaneously. Following a
short fast of 4 to 6 hours, 30 to 100 micrograms of glucagon per kilogram
of body weight is given intravenously or intramuscularly in a single injection. Serial blood samples are obtained at 15-minute intervals for 2 hours.
An epinephrine test is similarly performed using 30 micrograms (0.03 ml.
1/1000 dilution) of synthetic epinephrine per kilogram, subcutaneously.
The responses are shown in Figure 30. Blood glucose may either decline
to unmeasurable levels, or remain unchanged at fasting level, or increase
slightly, but does not usually increase promptly or exceed a value 50 per
cent greater than the fasting level within 30 minutes.* In contrast, blood

---

* Rarely, patients with undetectable hepatic glucose-6-phosphatase have responded to glucagon with a prompt, significant hyperglycemia. The explanation for
this unusual reaction remains obscure.

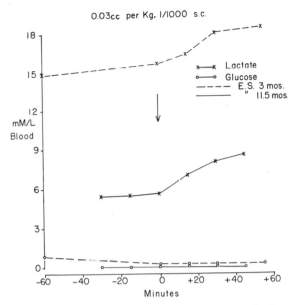

Figure 30. Epinephrine tolerance tests in a patient with absence of glucose-6-phosphatase: type I, glycogen storage disease. The patient had high levels of lactate in the blood and low levels of glucose. Epinephrine resulted in further elevation of the lactate without a rise in glucose. (From Schwartz et al., Pediatrics, *19*:585, 1957.)

lactate increases rapidly and markedly (occasionally to values over 150 mg./100 ml.) within 30 to 60 minutes: in the normal individual, glucagon does not produce a significant rise in lactate (Figs. 37, 38). Such elevations of lactate are associated with reciprocal effects on buffer bicarbonate so that the pH and the CO_2 contents are decreased. If the patient is tachypneic and hyperpneic (acidotic) at the conclusion of the test, the feeding is supplemented with sodium bicarbonate in a dose of 2 milliequivalents per kilogram body weight. The failure of rise in blood glucose and in lactate could also be caused by a defect in amylo 1,6 glucosidase, phosphorylase or deficient liver glycogen. Thus, the glucagon and epinephrine tests are not specific.

In order to evaluate glucose-6-phosphatase activity more directly and to bypass glycogenolysis, the intravenous galactose tolerance test described by Schwartz et al.[29] or the intravenous fructose tolerance test (Hers et al.[30]) may be used. In both tests, after a short fast of no more than *4 to 6 hours*, the galactose (1 gm./kg. body weight) or fructose (0.5 gm./kg. body weight) is given rapidly within 2 to 3 minutes intravenously as a 25 per cent solution. Blood samples are taken to determine total hexose, glucose (glucose oxidase technique) and/or fructose (resorcinol method) as well as lactate at 10-minute intervals for 1 hour. The injected hexose disappears rapidly from the circulation. The absence of a rise in blood glucose (glucose oxidase) concentration while lactate in the blood increases, is presumptive evidence of a defect in glucose-6-phosphatase (Figs. 31, 32, 39 and 40). The fructose test may result in a greater degree of lactic acidosis than the galactose test[31] and may require sodium bicarbonate therapy at the conclusion.

Biochemical Diagnosis. The diagnosis is established by biochemical analysis of material obtained from liver biopsy. Hers[16] has developed a technique for analysis of micro quantities of tissue, as much as can safely be obtained from an infant by punch biopsy. Open biopsy at laparotomy carries the advantage of availability of larger tissue samples for multiple analyses as well as control of bleeding. The patient must be carefully evaluated for bleeding disorders and for the ability to withstand anesthesia. Ketosis, lactic acidosis, hypoglycemia and infection must be corrected prior to surgery. The child is given a continuous infusion of glucose on the night before surgery and during exploration. An adequate biopsy sample must be immediately frozen on solid carbon dioxide or in liquid nitrogen for biochemical analysis. If biochemical enzymatic analyses are to be meaningful, *the specimen must not be frozen in either alcohol or acetone with dry ice, or placed in fixatives.* Additional specimens should be placed in alcohol for glycogen staining and in Zenker's acetic acid and in formalin for routine histologic examination. Special fixation is necessary for electron microscopy. A sterile specimen should be frozen for possible viral or bacteriological cultures at a later date. At the time of laparotomy, *muscle samples* should also be obtained for biochemical and histologic examination as described for the liver.

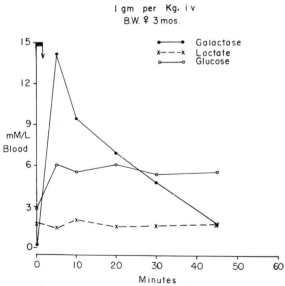

Figure 31. Intravenous galactose tolerance test in a normal child. Galactose disappeared rapidly, glucose rose, while lactate remained low. (From Schwartz et al., Pediatrics 19:585, 1957.)

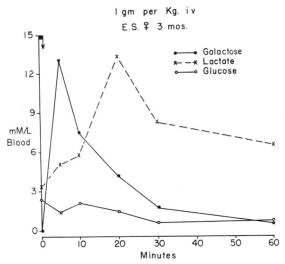

Figure 32. Intravenous galactose tolerance test in an infant with absence of glucose-6-phosphatase. Galactose disappeared rapidly, glucose decreased, while lactate rose markedly. (From Schwartz et al., Pediatrics 19:858, 1957.)

Glycogen Analyses. The frozen biopsy material should be analyzed for glycogen and for activities of the enzymes of the glycogen cycle.[16, 32] Chemical analysis of the liver specimen shows a high glycogen content, greater than 5 per cent of wet tissue. Fat content, including subfractions of lipids, is elevated to values greater than 4 to 8 per cent of wet weight. Proper analysis includes a nitrogen, protein or RNA determination which is a more correct reference base than weight for both lipid and glycogen concentration. The presence of excessive fat results in a falsely low glycogen content per unit total tissue. The glycogen should also be isolated by successive precipitations in 55 per cent ethyl alcohol. A spectral analysis of an iodine-polysaccharide complex can more specifically characterize the glycogens. Short polymers with straight chains of 4 to 6 glucose units give no iodine color. Those of 8 to 12 units give a red color with a peak at 520 μ, followed by transitional colors until a length of 30 to 35 units is reached, when the iodine color becomes blue, with a peak of 600 μ. Sequential degradation of the isolated glycogen by crystalline phosphorylase and amylo 1,6 glucosidase may be used to characterize its structure and number of branch points.

Enzyme Assays. An homogenate prepared from fresh or quick-frozen tissue (liver or kidney) is used to assay enzyme activities. Glucose-6-phosphatase is assayed by measuring the liberation of inorganic phosphate from glucose-6-phosphate in acetate buffer (pH 6.5). Lack of activity is evidence for the diagnosis of type I glycogen storage disease. Levels of 10 per cent or less of normal glucose-6-phosphatase activity have been reported and may represent nonspecific "alkaline" phosphatases or

incomplete defects. Other enzyme activities, including those of phosphorylase, amylo 1,6 glucosidase, phosphoglucomutase and phosphofructokinase,
are usually found to be normal if the tissue has been properly prepared
and analyzed. Recently, the enzymes of glycogen synthesis (UDPG pyrophosphorylase and UDPG transglucosylase or synthetase) have been found
to be normal in these patients.[33] Biopsy of the small intestine by use of an
orally passed tube has been used for enzyme studies. Glucose-6-phospha-
tase activity has been found to be deficient in this tissue, as well as in liver
and kidney.[34, 35]

In Vitro Studies.   Further data may be obtained from the study of
the intact liver slice. Incubation with radioactive carbon-14 labeled glucose may demonstrate synthesis by incorporation of label into glycogen.
Addition of glucagon or epinephrine to the medium to demonstrate
glycogenolysis may result in insufficient unlabeled glucose release to dilute
the radioglucose concentration, so that the specific activity of glucose is
unchanged. However, hexose-phosphate glycolytic intermediates may
accumulate or lactate may rise. Thus, with the tissue slice, a similar response to that in the intact individual is possible, i.e., a failure to release
glucose from the liver slice in the presence of an increased production of
lactate.

Pathology

At laparotomy, the liver is large and smooth with a gleaming capsule.
It has a definite yellow, fatty appearance. There is no nodularity or irregu-
larity in its surface. Microscopically, the hepatic cells are large and swollen,
with centrally placed nuclei (Fig. 33). Staining with a standard hema-
toxylin and eosin preparation indicates normal preservation of lobular
architecture without any inflammation, cirrhosis or tumor. There are many
vacuolated areas, both within and apparently outside the hepatic cells.
Examination of the alcohol-fixed specimens with Best's stain or with the
Schiff's periodic acid (PAS) technique indicates numerous red- or purple-
staining granules of carbohydrate in the hepatic cells. Vacuoles often
persist, however, and are identified as fat by Sudan stain on Zenker's or
formalin fixed material. In some instances, the amount of fat exceeds that
of glycogen. The glycogen is further characterized histochemically by
subjecting sections to diastase action prior to staining (Fig. 34). By comparison with appropriate controls, it is possible to demonstrate digestion of
the PAS positive material, indicating the presence of glycogen rather than
a mucopolysaccharide. Iodine stains have been also used to characterize
abnormal glycogen structure.

Examination of skeletal muscle in type I disease shows no particular
abnormalities. The kidney is grossly enlarged and has normal architecture:
microscopic examination indicates glycogen-laden proximal tubular cells.
Without a quantitative biochemical analysis for glycogen and enzymes of
the tissue, histologic diagnosis can be only presumptive.

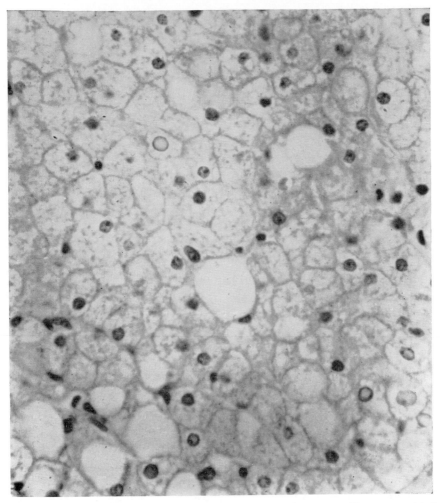

Figure 33. Photomicrograph of the liver in glycogen storage disease associated with an absence of glucose-6-phosphatase. The cells are swollen and the nuclei are centrally placed. The large clear areas reflect loss of fat.

Pathophysiology

The pathophysiology of this type I defect is best considered developmentally beginning *in utero*. Unlike other mammalian species (rat, guinea pig), in which there is no activity of the enzyme glucose-6-phosphatase before birth, the human fetus has been shown to have such activity as early as at 10 weeks' gestation.[36] Hence, the concept proposed by Nemeth[37] of the persistence of a fetal state, with failure of enzyme induction at birth, is untenable. The defect is a genetic one and implies a primary failure of development. The presence of inhibitors or the absence of glucose-6-phosphatase activators has not been demonstrated in this disease. *In utero,*

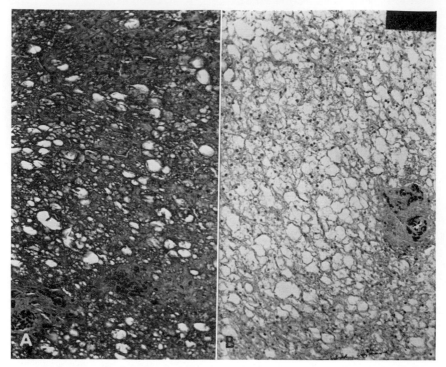

Figure 34. Low power view of a liver biopsy specimen from a patient with type I glycogen storage disease. The clear areas represent fat removed in processing. *A,* Darkly stained glycogen in the hepatic cells. *B,* After digestion with diastase, showing loss of dark staining glycogen; the central nuclei are now evident.

since the primary energy source is glucose which is derived transplacentally from the mother, the fetal liver has a minor role as regards glucose homeostasis. Furthermore, the fetal circulation uniquely provides for a bypass of the liver via the ductus venosus so that only a fraction of the glucose supplied by the mother passes through the liver. The variable manifestations of type I disease in the newborn period may be related to differences in intrauterine hepatic blood flow. Since the infant receives a constant infusion of glucose from the mother, peripheral glucose metabolism is maintained intact, hypoglycemia and its consequences do not occur, and relatively normal intrauterine growth results.

Following delivery, the infant with complete absence of glucose-6-phosphatase is unable to sustain a normal blood glucose level, and hypoglycemia supervenes unless glucose feedings are provided. Fortunately, feeding the infant every 3 to 4 hours may prevent recurrence of hypoglycemia. As the interval between feedings is extended, hyperglycemia may occur immediately after feeding and persist for a few hours, followed by hypoglycemia just prior to the next feed.

Glycogen synthesis derives not only from excess glucose removed from the circulation, but perhaps from other hexoses,[5, 29, 76] such as galactose and fructose, whose major metabolism occurs in the liver. In this disease the rate of uptake of galactose and fructose appears to be more rapid than normal, which may be attributed to hepatic mass, large in relation to the rest of the body. Except for glycolysis and oxidation via the pentose cycle, these sugars can be converted only to glycogen. In addition to these other carbohydrates in the diet, an excessive supply of amino acids either from dietary sources or from endogenous protein catabolism, may contribute to the glycogen stores as a result of gluconeogenesis. The latter process may be increased in these patients secondary to the hyperadrenocortical response to the persistent hypoglycemia.

During the period of starvation and inability of the liver to sustain a normal glucose level, a variety of secondary effects occur. The hormonal response to hypoglycemia presumably includes an initial release of epinephrine, glucagon and growth hormone, and later glucocorticoid if hypoglycemia persists. Phosphorylase is activated, hepatic glycogenolysis is increased, but glucose release from the liver cannot occur except to a minor degree, i.e., hydrolysis of branch points by amylo 1,6 glucosidase results in approximately 8 per cent free glucose release. Since glycogen is multitiered, with a higher percentage of branch points in the inner tiers, more glucose is theoretically available as glycogen degradation occurs. Although no quantification of this effect has been made by *in vivo* studies as yet, this has been the explanation for the fact that hypoglycemia does not always accompany starvation and also for the minor rise in blood glucose sometimes noted with administration of glucagon or epinephrine. The breakdown of glycogen thus increases phosphorylated hexose intermediates[22] of both the glycolytic and pentose cycle. The former results in hepatic production of excessive lactic acid, which is a reversal of normal metabolism.

Normally, lactate is produced in the peripheral tissues, especially in muscle, so that venous blood from the forearm contains a higher concentration of lactate than arterial or capillary blood. It is usually removed from the circulation by the liver and either metabolized via the Krebs' cycle or converted to glucose via the gluconeogenetic pathway. Mason and Sly[38] first reported the presence of excessive lactate in the blood of patients with glycogen storage disease. In recent years, several studies have confirmed this important observation and elucidated the origin of the lactate.[27, 28]

Blood pyruvate is similarly elevated, but to a lesser degree than lactate (presumably because of the abundance of TPNH formed by pentose cycle activity).[23] Some studies indicate that extrahepatic tissues may take up and metabolize the excessive lactate. The increased intrahepatic metabolism of glucose results in overactivity of all pathways from glucose-6-phosphate so that production of DPNH and TPNH is presumably increased.[23] These key metabolites are necessary for a variety of biochemical reactions, including the conversion of pyruvate to lactate and synthesis of fatty acid, ketones, and cholesterol, which require either or both these co-factors. Thus, the reason for hepatic fat accumulation, ketone production and lactate formation may be secondary to the single defect, a failure to convert glucose-6-phosphate to glucose, as postulated by Howell et al.[23] In addition to the above secondary effects, at least one tertiary effect has been noted, that being the rise in plasma urate. This has been attributed to either an increase in purine metabolism or increased tubular reabsorption. The latter is the more likely explanation and has been related to the elevation in blood lactate which is now known to inhibit urate secretion in the renal tubule. Gout has been reported as occurring in glycogen storage disease.[20] Growth retardation, often evident, cannot be satisfactorily explained biochemically. Human growth hormone levels have been normal in isolated samples at the time of severe hypoglycemia (blood glucose < 15 mg./100 ml.) in one 4 year old patient, but additional studies are needed.

Hypoglycemia. The fact that, quite frequently, there are no symptoms of hypoglycemia in this disease deserves special attention.[29, 39] Several cases have been documented in which blood glucose levels were unmeasurable (well under 10 mg./100 ml.) for several hours yet there were no seizures or other symptoms of hypoglycemia (Fig. 30). The explanation for this phenomenon is unknown. The implication, unproven, is that the brain can, under these circumstances, metabolize a substrate or substrates other than glucose. Schulman[21] reported electroencephalographic studies in two biochemically proven cases and could perceive no differences in electrical activity whether blood glucose concentrations were high or low. Both EEGs were interpreted as normal at very low blood sugar levels. These observations may explain the varied picture of mental development noted in these patients. While the central nervous system manifestations of hypoglycemia (coma, limpness, convulsions, etc.) are not consistently evident, other symptoms attributable to hypersecretion of epinephrine are more common, like sweating, irritability and pallor. Tachypnea, hyperpnea and acidosis also may be seen at this time.

Therapy

Management is directed toward maintaining glucose homeostasis and avoiding the secondary consequences of hypoglycemia. In the most severe cases, feedings every 3 to 4 hours continuously throughout the 24-hour period are necessary. The diet must be carefully selected: a diet excessive in calories or in *any* nutrient, whether protein, fat or carbohydrate, can only result in excessive fat and glycogen accumulation. In early infancy and childhood, then, milk, fruits, and cane sugar are to be avoided since both galactose and fructose are converted to glycogen and lactic acid in the liver.[76] Therefore, the source of carbohydrates should be glucose or its polymers (dextro-maltose, starch, or glycogen). The diet may be relatively normal in protein, but low in fat and not excessive in total calories. In type I disease, the excess protein is of no benefit since increased gluconeogenesis cannot result in release of glucose from the liver, but only in the accumulation of more glycogen. Evaluation of dietary adequacy depends upon serial blood sugar, lactate, and free fatty acid analyses and urinary ketones. In addition, clinical appraisal of growth, development and hepatomegaly are important.

Persistent acidosis with depletion of buffer is to be avoided if possible. In patients with high blood lactate levels (over 60 mg./100 ml. or 6 mEq./L.), supplementary oral sodium bicarbonate is indicated in a dose of 2 to 4 mEq./kg./day. This may be given as baking soda (⅛ to ½ tsp. supplements) in a milk substitute. In the event of an intercurrent infection with its attendant hypermetabolism and starvation, signs of acidosis and ketonuria must be watched for carefully. Urine pH and acetone may be checked at home by the parents. If pH is low (less than 5.5) or ketone positive, then additional oral sodium bicarbonate is indicated. If the acidosis is severe or if oral intake is inadequate, the child should be hospitalized and intravenous fluids containing glucose, sodium bicarbonate and other appropriate electrolytes given early in the course of illness. Intravenous fluids should never contain lactate; it cannot be adequately or rapidly metabolized to provide buffer.

Many forms of hormonal therapy have been tried in this disorder. In particular, repetitive injections of aqueous glucagon, long-acting zinc glucagon, corticosteroid, androgen, Halotestin (fluoxymesterone) and thyroid have been recommended. Although these agents have produced temporary salutory effects, none has been consistently efficacious.

Prognosis

Prognosis in early infancy must be guarded because of the high susceptibility of these patients to infections and their complications. Survival beyond adolescence is said to be associated with adaptation to the disease and amelioration of symptoms.[20, 22] Prognosis may be more precise when more is known about the biochemical nature of alternate pathways of metabolism in this disorder.

Genetics

The genetic defect has been described, on the basis of family histories, to be an autosomal recessive. No simple, biochemical or physiological test has yet been devised to detect the heterozygote. See Addendum, page 158.

Case Reports

Three patients are presented in brief to illustrate the extreme variation in the clinical manifestations observed in type I G.S.D.

Case 1. M. G. (Figs. 35, 36) represents the severe manifestations of this inherited defect in metabolism. The patient suffered from severe hypoglycemia, hyperlipidemia, hepatomegaly, ketonuria, acidosis and recurrent infections requiring frequent hospitalizations for parenteral buffer therapy beginning at 46 hours of age. His male sibling died at 4 months of age of glycogen storage disease. The glucagon and galactose tolerance tests are compatible with a complete deficiency of glucose-6-phosphatase (Fig. 36).

In contrast, the two following patients had only partial enzyme deficiencies and mild disease.

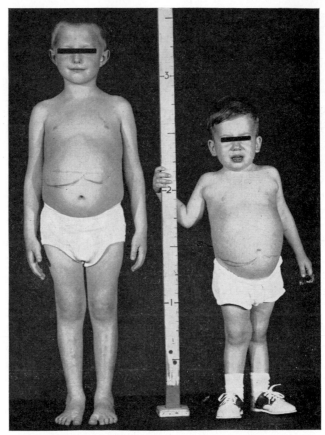

Figure 35. Type I glycogen storage disease.

	R.B.	M.G.
Age	6 10/12 years	4 years
Height	44¼ inches	33¾ inches
Weight	48 pounds	28 pounds
Hypoglycemia	0	++++
Ketonuria	0	++++
Epistaxis	++++	+

Case 2. R. B. (Figs. 35, 36) presented with progressive hepatomegaly, recurrent epistaxis, weakness and failure to thrive at 5½ years of age. Liver glucose-6-phosphatase activity was 60 μg./100 mg./hr. or about 10 per cent of normal. Glycogen structure was normal, as were the activities of amylo-1,6-glucosidase and phosphorylase (assayed by Dr. Barbara Illingworth Brown, Washington University School of Medicine). The glucagon and galactose tolerance tests reflect the partial defect (Fig. 36). This patient has done very well on Halotestin (fluoxymesterone) 2 mg./day, with an increase in strength and activity and a striking reduction in the number of nose bleeds.

Case 3. L. O. was a 6½ year white female who was apparently well until, during an upper respiratory infection, hepatomegaly was noted. Past history was unremarkable. The patient had no symptoms of hypoglycemia or acidosis, but some episodes of epistaxis were recorded. Physical examination revealed a large smooth liver (6 cm.) but not nephromegaly or splenomegaly. Laboratory

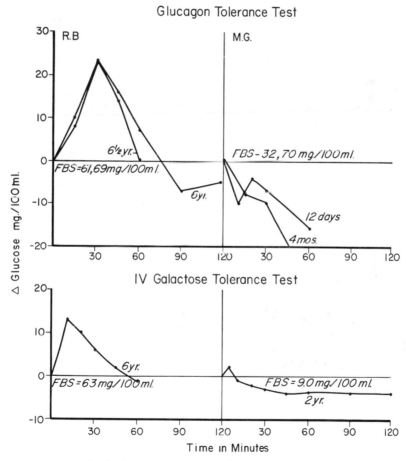

Figure 36. Blood glucose responses to glucagon and galactose in two patients with hepatorenal glycogen storage disease. The patient with 10 per cent enzyme activity showed a slight but definite increase in the level of glucose during each test, while the patient with a complete enzyme defect was unresponsive.

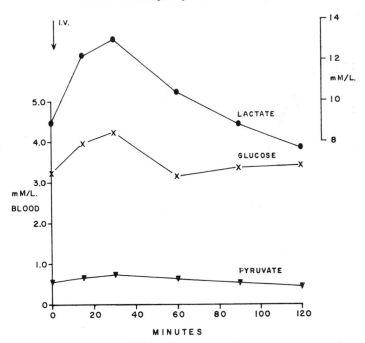

Figure 37.   Glucagon tolerance test in a patient with proved hepatorenal glycogen storage disease. Liver biopsy showed 6.6 per cent glycogen and normal phosphorylase, phosphoglucomutase and glycogen synthetase. Glucose-6-phosphatase
activity was 9 per cent of normal. There was a slight but definite rise in glucose but
a marked increase in lactate.

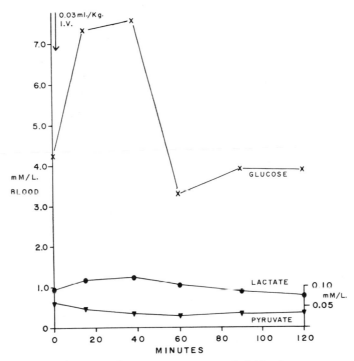

GLUCAGON RESPONSE IN NORMAL CHILD

AFTER GALACTOSE 0.5gm./Kg. I.V.

Figure 38. Glucagon tolerance test in a normal child. There was a prompt rise in the concentration of glucose, with no change in lactate or pyruvate.

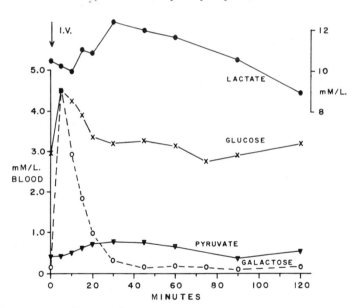

GALACTOSE TOLERANCE IN
GLYCOGEN STORAGE DISEASE
Pt. L.O. 16,7 Kg. 0.5gm./Kg. I.V.

Figure 39. Galactose tolerance in a patient with hepatorenal glycogen storage disease with some glucose-6-phosphatase activity. There was a transient increase in blood glucose, and lactate rose significantly.

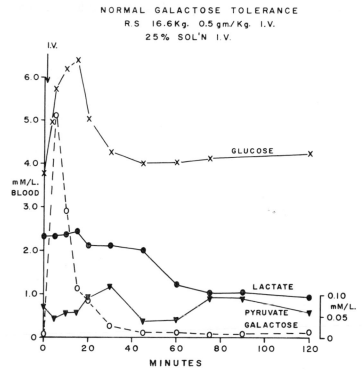

NORMAL GALACTOSE TOLERANCE
R.S   16.6 Kg.   0.5 gm./Kg.   I.V.
25% SOL'N I.V.

Figure 40. Normal galactose tolerance test in an older child presented to show contrast with Figure 39. Glucose rose significantly; lactate declined.

studies were not remarkable except for fasting blood sugar values of 63-73 mg./100 ml. and elevated blood lactates of 54-100 mg./100 ml. At laparotomy the liver was smooth and large. Glycogen content was 6.6 gm. per 100 gm.; enzyme analyses were normal for phosphorylase, phosphoglucomutase, and uridinidiphosphate pyrophosphorylase, but only 9 per cent of normal for glucose-6-phosphatase (determined by Dr. Joseph Larner). The responses to glucagon and galactose are shown in Figures 37 to 40.

The latter patients are of interest because of their minimal ability to convert galactose to glucose and because of their response to glucagon, which seems to correlate with the inadequate enzyme activities.

Summary

Hepatomegaly in a young child with a "doll-like" facies may be associated with epistaxis, hypoglycemia, ketonuria and lactic acidosis. The basic problem is inability to release glucose from the liver because of an absence of glucose-6-phosphatase activity. The diagnosis is dependent upon an adequate biochemical analysis of liver tissue taken by biopsy, but may be inferred from glucagon and galactose tolerance tests. Complications associated with plasma lipid elevations and lactic acidemia may be minimized by maintaining normoglycemia.

Debrancher, Amylo 1,6 Glucosidase Deficiency (Type III)

Although the first documented case with an abnormal glycogen structure due to an absence of the enzyme, amylo 1,6 glucosidase was studied by Illingworth and Cori[40] and reported by Forbes,[41] the original two cases described by van Creveld have been re-evaluated recently and reclassified into this group.[20, 42] The latter cases, elegantly presented, represent an experience extending over more than 30 years of careful clinical observation.

This disorder has clinical and physiological abnormalities similar to those of type I disease. In the absence of biochemical analyses of liver tissue taken by biopsy, distinction may be difficult. However, certain differences which are generally present enable the clinician to suspect this type of defect. The type III patient tends to have a milder disease and not to be so seriously affected by minor infections. While hepatomegaly and hypoglycemia are present, the latter is usually not so severe as in type I disease. In addition, lactic acidosis, an important complication of type I disease, is not found so often or as markedly in the type III defect. Ketonuria after fasting does occur, but acidosis is not a problem.

Diagnosis

The disease is often unsuspected until a protuberant abdomen and enlarged liver are found. Evaluation shows no evidence of liver dysfunction or splenomegaly. Laboratory studies may indicate nothing more than low fasting blood glucose values. Mild elevation of plasma cholesterol has been noted, but marked hyperlipemia as in type I disease is unusual. The blood sugar is not well sustained during fasting. A glucagon or epinephrine stimulation test may give variable results. When performed after a brief period of starvation (4 to 6 hours), a prompt, significant elevation of blood sugar may be found; however, when performed after a 12- to 14-hour fast, there is usually no rise in blood sugar.[43] Both the galactose and fructose tolerance tests show normal disappearance of hexose, with prompt elevation of blood glucose (glucose oxidase). These results may be used to make a presumptive diagnosis of type III disease. They suggest normal hepatic glucose-6-phosphatase activity and a store of glycogen which can be mobilized after a short fast, but is unavailable after a prolonged fast. The latter situation presumably results from an absence of debrancher, amylo 1,6 glucosidase.

The diagnosis may be further established by analysis of erythrocytes as described by Sidbury et al.,[24] or of leukocytes as described by

Williams and associates.[26] The erythrocytes may contain an excessive content of glycogen which can be isolated and characterized to be a limit dextrin. The leukocytes have been shown to have a deficiency in debrancher enzyme. Further proof of the diagnosis is obtained by analysis of muscle and liver obtained at biopsy. The studies of Illingworth[44] and Hers[16] have indicated the nature of the defect to be an absence of amylo 1,6 glucosidase which results in a multibranched glycogen with short outer chains. The techniques of biochemical identification are given in detail by these authors.

Histologically, the liver may be indistinguishable from that found in type I disease. Accumulations of fat in hepatic cells have been noted in addition to the glycogen.

Course

The course of this disease appears to be milder than that of type I as evidenced by the survival to adulthood of van Creveld's cases[20] and to adolescence in the case of Forbes'.[41] Furthermore, in the larger series of Illingworth,[32] most of the patients were alive in their teens. With adolescence, the hepatomegaly becomes less prominent and ketonuria is less severe. Growth is no longer impaired and maturation, while delayed, does occur. Although the underlying defect persists, as evidenced in erythrocyte analyses of glycogen or in epinephrine responsiveness, no adverse consequences have been reported. The two patients of van Creveld had normal motor and intellectual development, were married and had normal sons. Mental retardation does not appear to be a frequent complication.

Management

Management is directed toward maintenance of normoglycemia and prevention of progressive hepatic enlargement. Since blood sugar cannot be sustained during prolonged starvation, the long overnight fast should be avoided and a feeding taken in the middle of the night. Excessive calories from any source should also be avoided. While galactose and fructose may be converted to glucose (since glucose-6-phosphatase activity is intact), any excessive hexose would be converted to glycogen, and be stored in the liver where it would be less available and would increase the size of the liver. Protein and amino acids should be able to sustain blood glucose through gluconeogenesis since glucose-6-phosphatase activity is normal; therefore, the suggestion of Bridge and Holt[45] for a night feeding high in protein is worthwhile. Hepatic fat accumulation can best be limited by maintenance of normoglycemia.

Prognosis in this disorder is good for attaining adulthood. Van Creveld's adult patients produced normal progeny.

While the genetics of this disorder has not been clearly established, the occurrence in both sexes suggests a simple autosomal recessive inheritance. It is interesting that 8 of the 9 patients reported by van Creveld and Huijing were female.[75]

Summary

Asymptomatic hepatomegaly in childhood may be associated with hypoglycemia, which is more manifest during a period of fasting. Absence of debrancher enzyme, amylo 1,6 glucosidase, may be noted in leukocytes, while erythrocytes have an abnormal glycogen in excess quantity. Survival to adulthood with diminution in hepatic size is usual. Prolonged fasting and excessive caloric intake should be avoided.

Liver Phosphorylase Defect (Type VI)

This disease, which is similar to types I and III clinically and therefore considered a form of hepatic glycogen storage disease, was identified biochemically in 1959 by Hers.[46] He states that this may be a more common form of defect than type I, glucose-6-phosphatase deficiency.[16]

The disease has been described in siblings and has an early onset, with hepatomegaly. Fasting blood sugar values and carbohydrate tolerance are variable: low or normal blood glucose values are reported with fasting. The hyperglycemic responses to glucagon may be absent, slightly positive or normal. The blood lactic acid level is not usually elevated but ketonuria may be present. Galactose given intravenously produces a prompt elevation of blood glucose, and fructose given in the same way should produce a similar result.[47] Erythrocyte glycogen may be normal or elevated.

Biochemical Studies

Histologically, the liver is similar to that in type I, glucose-6-phosphatase defect, and has a very high glycogen content with a normal structure. Enzyme analyses have shown normal activities of glucose-6-phosphatase and amylo 1,6 glucosidase, but depressed levels of phosphorylase (as low as one-seventh normal activity).[46] It is of interest that complete absence of the enzyme has not been reported.[32] Activators of the phosphorylase system appear intact, and inhibitors of the system have not been found in the livers of these patients. Hers has emphasized the variability in this enzyme's activity in liver specimens obtained at biopsy. He cautions against overinterpretation of the biochemical data until further clarification of the factors contributing to this analytical problem. Muscle analyses in such patients have indicated normal phosphorylase activity, which is further evidence for the biogenetic differences of these enzymes.

Two groups of investigators, studying the normal individual, have demonstrated that phosphorylase activity is present in the leukocytes.[25, 48, 49] They have also reported extremely low enzyme activity levels in patients with type VI disease proven by biopsy of the liver. In addition, normal leukocyte phosphorylase levels have been found in patients with types I, II, III and V disease. Interestingly, in two family studies, low levels of leukocyte phosphorylase were found in the white cells from the mothers, who were clinically well, whereas the fathers had normal enzyme levels.[25, 48] The genetic significance of this observation is unclear, since the disease has been observed in both sexes. Activities of debrancher enzyme in the leukocyte have been shown to be normal in patients with type VI disease.[26]

The variability in responsiveness to tolerance tests (glucagon, epinephrine, galactose) in fasting hypoglycemia and in ketonuria may be due to the variations in the extent of the enzymatic defect. Even low levels of activity of this enzyme are apparently sufficient in some patients to produce adequate blood glucose elevations after administration of epinephrine or glucagon.

Course and Prognosis

The course and prognosis in this disease have not yet been adequately defined. The pattern of tissue distribution and the extent of the enzymatic defect would be important variables in comparing this entity to types I and III. Physiologically, greater similarity would be expected to the type III, glycogen debrancher defect, than to type I, glucose-6-phosphatase deficiency. In view of the prompt conversion of galactose to glucose and the site of the enzymatic defect, gluconeogenesis should be unimpaired and should be able to sustain the blood glucose. Therefore, a high protein diet with frequent feedings should be beneficial. In addition, glucocorticoids, which increase gluconeogenesis, may also be of value. It is not known to what extent the glucose formed will be released or synthesized to glycogen.

Summary

A decrease in hepatic and leukocytic phosphorylase activity has been found associated with hepatomegaly and hypoglycemia in early childhood. This entity is difficult to differentiate from the other two types of hepatic storage disease on clinical and physiological observations alone.

Critique of Hepatic Glycogen Storage Diseases

In the foregoing sections emphasis has been placed on the positive features of the three types of hepatic glycogen disease (I, III, VI). There is considerable similarity in both clinical manifestations and physiological responses, which often makes clear separation of these entities difficult, if not impossible, without enzymatic biochemical analyses. The functional tests (glucagon, epinephrine, galactose and fructose) do not always bear a direct relationship to the biochemical defect.[50] This is not to suggest that these tolerance studies are without value, but rather to emphasize the difficulty in correlating cellular biochemical events with integrated, physiologic responses.

The variation in degree of the specific enzyme defect has been pointed out; a few additional observations will be made here. Hepatocellular disease of either specific or nonspecific etiology may result in a diffuse, generalized decrease in hepatic enzymes. Multiple enzyme defects involving glucose-6-phosphatase and amylo 1,6 glucosidase have been described.[51] In addition, families in which two siblings have had distinct differences in glycogen structure or enzyme activity have been reported,[52] but Hers has criticized these observations as being inadequately defined biochemically (i.e., structural differences in glycogen are not entirely adequate to define the enzyme defect).[16] Furthermore, the genetic likelihood of having two rare defects in the same family is remote at best.

The spectrum of exceptions in this group of diseases includes documented cases in which the clinical and functional changes are found in the presence of normal enzyme activities. Further detailed physiological and biochemical studies are necessary to clarify these areas.

Lowe and Mosovich[79] have reported recently on the paradoxical effects of alcohol on carbohydrate metabolism in 4 patients with liver glycogen disease. Alcohol infusions resulted in marked decrease in lacticacidemia and increased responsiveness to glucagon. The authors suggested that alternate pathways for alcohol metabolism may be operative. These unexpected observations offer further leads to the abnormal metabolism of these patients and may be of importance therapeutically.

Frequently, the more obvious clinical manifestations are secondary to the primary disturbance. This is most obvious in type I disease when a total enzyme defect occurs. Analysis of these changes may permit a separation of the effects observed in the milder defects. Hypoglycemia, which is the major common factor in this group of diseases, affects different tissues in different ways. A systematic analysis of its effects on the central nervous system, muscle, adipose tissue and viscera is indicated in this group of patients.

GLYCOGEN DISEASE OF SKELETAL MUSCLE

Muscle Phosphorylase Deficiency (Type V), McArdle's Syndrome

This rare myopathy, first recognized in 1951,[12] is of great significance because it represents the first discovery of a genetic disease of muscle caused by the absence of a single, specific enzyme. In addition, the recently defined synthetic pathway for glycogen formation in muscle was verified in this uniquely suitable tissue.[53, 54]

Clinical Considerations

Less than a dozen cases of this condition have been reported or alluded to in the literature, and of these, 3 have been studied extensively.[12, 55, 56] The disease is characterized by a late onset. In early childhood the patient is relatively free of symptoms, although one noted muscle fatigue and inability to keep up with his playmates by 7 years of age. Generally, symptoms are absent or minimal in the first decade. During the teens, muscle fatigue, particularly with strenuous exercise, may be evident. Transient episodes of dark urine (presumably due to myoglobinuria) may occur. During early adulthood, progressive weakness of exercised muscles associated with severe cramping pain may be found. No other symptomatology has been reported. It is striking that dyspnea and tachycardia after marked exertion have been less evident than in normal controls. No muscle wasting is noted until the 4th or 5th decade, when the previous symptoms may be complicated by apathy and irregular muscle atrophy. No particular pattern of skeletal muscle loss has been noted. In another recent report, two family members were studied in whom no symptomatology was found prior to the 5th decade, at which time muscle wasting as well as muscle fatigue were observed in one patient.[57]

In addition to marked weakness and cramping pain, prolonged stiffness of the muscles is produced by moderate degrees of exercise. Physiologic contractures with localized swelling may be found over the involved muscles, which later appear putty-like in consistency as recovery with rest occurs slowly over several hours. A decrease in exercise tolerance is noted, with infection and with depression in mood. Except for muscle wasting in the older individual, no neuromuscular abnormalities are present. Hepatomegaly is also absent, and the cardiopulmonary system is not remarkable.

Laboratory Studies

Laboratory studies, including blood and urine, are singularly unrewarding, except for the rare, postexercise episode of transient myoglobinuria. Serum enzyme and carbohydrate studies are particularly unremarkable, although transient elevation of aldolase and phosphocreatine kinase has been reported. Electrolytes, including K and Ca, and concentrations of glucose, phosphate, lactate and pyruvate are normal in the resting state.

Carbohydrate tests, including glucose tolerance, glucose and insulin tolerance, epinephrine and glucagon tolerances, are all normal. The latter two tests indicate, indirectly, that liver phosphorylase is normal. Although the rise in blood glucose concentration following administration of epinephrine is as great as in normal individuals, the elevation of blood lactate and pyruvate is significantly less. Lactate production in blood incubated *in vitro* is also normal in these patients.

Physiologic Studies

McArdle[12] studied his 30 year old male patient extensively and noted particularly a failure of ischemic exercise* to produce an elevation in venous blood lactate. Normally, prolonged exercise produces a significant elevation of the lactate concentration in venous blood, and ischemic exercise, depending upon duration, similarly produces a characteristic elevation of from 25 to 30 mg./100 ml. above the basal level. McArdle postulated a defect in muscle carbohydrate metabolism with inadequate breakdown of glycogen to lactate. He did not determine the site of the defect and considered a block lower in the glycolytic schema, rather than at the level of glycogen degradation. Muscle biopsy material was not available to him at that time.

Subsequently, two similar cases were simultaneously studied and reported by Mommaerts et al.[56, 58] and Schmid and associates.[54, 55] These two groups studied their patients in detail, physiologically, pathologically and biochemically. They confirmed the original relationship between work capacity, ischemic exercise and muscle fatigue. They verified the failure of the expected rise of lactate in venous blood with exercise. Muscle activity could be sustained by the infusion of glucose or glucose and insulin, but insulin alone produced hypoglycemia without improvement in muscle exercise. Whether insulin would enhance the effects of supplemental intravenous glucose is unclear. Other substrates found to be effective in sustaining muscle activity were lactate, fructose and emulsified fat with glucose; whereas saline, glycerol and galactose were ineffective. It was of interest that fructose infusions were as and even more effective than glucose infusions.[58] Since the plasma glucose levels remained unchanged in the normal range during the fructose infusion, Pearson et al.[56] concluded that fructose was metabolized directly by muscle. Hers[16] has criticized this interpretation and suggested that hepatic conversion of fructose to pyruvate with muscle uptake of the latter is more likely. The exact mechanism of the fructose effect awaits clarification.

Biochemical Studies

Biochemical studies of biopsied muscle have indicated an absence of phosphorylase a and b, but the presence of UDPG-glycogen synthetase, phosphorylase kinase and phosphoglucomutase (although the activity of

---

* The patient squeezes a sphygmomanometer bulb once a second after the circulation of the upper arm has been occluded by a sphygmomanometer cuff at a pressure of 200 mm. Hg. The patient had (a) early onset of ischemic pain and fatigue, both of which occurred with 10 to 20 per cent of the normal amount of work, and (b) abnormal shortening of the flexor muscles following the exercise.

the latter was lower than normal).[53, 54] In another patient with the phosphorylase defect, but without muscle atrophy, normal activity of phosphorylase kinase, "phosphate-removing" (PR) enzyme, and UDPG-glycogen synthetase were found.[56] Glycogen content in muscle in the three original cases was excessive at 2.4 to 4 gm. per cent (normal less than 1 per cent wet weight); however, in three additional recently reported cases muscle glycogen was found to be at the upper limit of normal (1 to 1.1 per cent).[57, 59] The glycogen has been found to be structurally normal, indicating normal activities of "branching" enzyme. Incubation of muscle extracts with normal muscle has revealed no inhibitors, and glycolysis with lactate production proceeds normally, with hexose-phosphate intermediates below the level of glucose-1-phosphate or glucose-6-phosphate. Additional glycogen is not metabolized unless exogenous phosphorylase enzyme is added *in vitro*.

Pathology

Histological examination of muscle has indicated variable morphology; in younger individuals muscle appears normal, while in the older person with muscle atrophy, hypertrophied fibers with blebs of raised sarcolemma are found.[55, 56] The damaged fibers appear necrotic and may disappear altogether. Stains for glycogen reveal intense PAS-positive granular material, particularly under the raised sarcolemma. Histochemical studies with the method of Takeuchi have verified the absence of phosphorylase activity in muscle.

Pathogenesis

Resting muscle derives its energy mainly from oxidation of noncarbohydrate substances, although glucose uptake and degradation to lactate do occur.[60] In other words, glycogen breakdown is not an important source of energy for *resting* muscle. In contrast, *contracting* muscle has an enormous demand for high energy phosphates, which cannot be supplied adequately by substrates from the blood, even though blood flow does increase with exercise. Under these conditions, glycogenolysis and the anaerobic metabolism of glucose with lactate production are important sources of energy to sustain muscle activity. The limitation of the individual with phosphorylase myopathy to sustain muscle exercise is directly related to the inability to degrade glycogen, thus limiting the availability of hexose intermediates as a source of energy.

Differential Diagnosis

Differential diagnosis is confined to other muscular disorders, including muscular dystrophy and congenital myotonia (Thomsen's disease). McArdle dismissed the latter from further consideration because of lack of stiffness at the onset of exercise, the striking effect of ischemic exercise in provoking the pain and the stiffness, in addition to the biochemical findings.

Course

The course of the disease is variably benign; longevity does not appear to be affected. Improvement in work and exercise tolerance has been reported following either glucagon injections and glucose or fructose ingestion (30 to 45 gm. by mouth, 3 or 4 times daily).[61] Further study is needed.

Genetics

The genetics of this rare disease have been clarified in a detailed family study by Schmid and Hammaker.[62] They found 3 cases (2 proven) in a sibship of 13 individuals. Their findings suggest a single, completely recessive, rare, autosomal gene.

Summary

Myopathy due to the absence of muscle phosphorylase is a rare genetic disease manifest by intolerance to exercise in adult life. The abnormal response to ischemic exercise is characterized by a fall in venous lactate concentration. Muscle biopsy is necessary to demonstrate the biochemical defect. Other phosphorylases (liver, leukocyte, etc.) are not affected.

GENERALIZED GLYCOGEN STORAGE DISEASE

Deficiency of α-Acid Glucosidase (Acid Maltase) (Type II) (Pompe's Disease)

Although this type of glycogen storage disease was one of the first to be described in terms of pathology (by Pompe in 1932[7]), the biochemical etiology was unknown until the recent report of Hers.[18] This group of glycogen storage diseases represents a spectrum including idiopathic cardiomegaly of infancy, a neuromuscular disorder simulating amyotonia congenita, and a diffuse cardio-neuromuscular disease. It is characterized by an onset early in infancy, with a rapidly progressing deterioration to death, often within the first year of life, generally by the second year.

Pompe's original case was a 6¾ months old infant who was well until admission to the hospital with pneumonia and cyanosis.[7] The infant succumbed after a brief febrile illness of 3 days. At postmortem examination an enlarged, globular heart without valvular disease was found. On microscopic examination the hypertrophied musculature of the ventricles had a lacework appearance and contained increased glycogen as demonstrated by Best's carmine stain. Pompe also found increased glycogen in a variety of other organs, including liver, kidney, adrenal, thyroid, spleen and muscle. Van Creveld[4, 8] studied a similar case in 1934 and confirmed, by means of chemical analysis of the heart and other organs, the observation of an abnormal accumulation of glycogen. In particular he noted central nervous system involvement. Pompe originally proposed the name cardiomegalia glycogenica; however, the more generalized involvement reported later by others prompted the designation *idiopathic generalized glycogenosis.*

Di Sant'Agnese, Andersen, Mason and Bauman[9] critically reviewed this subject in 1950 and reported 2 additional cases. Their criteria for a diagnosis of glycogen storage disease of the heart were: (1) marked enlargement of the heart, (2) death within the first year of life, (3) typical "lacework" appearance of histological sections of myocardium, resulting from the massive deposition of stored material in all cardiac fibers, and (4) chemical or histochemical demonstration of glycogen as the material.

These criteria are too rigid, since cases have been reported without cardiomegaly, but with predominantly muscular involvement; also, the child may live beyond the first year of life, though this is unusual.

Clinical Considerations

Onset can be at any time within the first year of life, from the first day of life to a few months of age. In the generalized type, the clinical manifestations often include generalized muscular weakness, respiratory difficulty and progressive cardiac failure. Undernutrition due to difficult feeding, with failure to thrive and loss of subcutaneous fat, may be early manifestations. The muscles feel firm, although hypotonia may be present. Sometimes reflexes are totally absent. The heart is enlarged on percussion, but auscultation reveals no murmurs. The liver is normal or only minimally enlarged. The tongue may be large and protuberant, giving the infant the appearance of a cretin or of a baby with 21 trisomy. Progressive muscle weakness may involve the respiratory muscles, thus simulating amyotonia congenita. Cardiac enlargement progresses to failure, with dyspnea and cyanosis. Respiratory infection with fever is common and often is the precipitating terminal event.

Laboratory Studies

Laboratory studies are remarkable in that they afford no clues pointing toward an abnormality of glycogen metabolism. Routine blood and urine analyses are merely consistent with the infant's nutritional and infection status. In contrast with findings in the hepatorenal forms of glycogen disease, physiologic abnormalities in carbohydrate metabolism are not characteristic. In particular, low blood sugar, when reported, has been due to inadequate nutrition: generally, blood glucose levels are normal. Glucose tolerance tests have been normal, as have epinephrine, glucagon and galactose tolerances. Lactic acid concentration is normal and rises normally after administration of epinephrine. Ketosis, ketonuria and acidosis are not features of this disorder. Neostigmine responses and electromyography have not been helpful.

X-Ray Findings

Roentgen examination may reveal a large, globular heart which is diffusely involved and fills both sides of the thorax. Consolidation of the lungs may be present. The kidneys are not enlarged.

Cardiac Studies

The electrocardiogram is abnormal in those patients with involvement of the heart.[62] The P-R interval is short, while the QRS complex may be high. Vectorcardiograms are compatible with bilateral ventricular enlargement and have extremely large QRSs E loops with nearly normal contour and orientation in all three planes. Ehlers and associates[63] reported muscular subaortic stenosis diagnosed on clinical and hemodynamic evidence; they postulated left ventricular hypertrophy. At surgery a normal aortic valve was visualized, and no resectable, fixed obstruction was found in the ventricle. Ruttenberg et al.[64] did hemodynamic studies and angiocardiograms on 2 patients and found no evidence of subaortic stenosis. The incidence of subaortic stenosis in generalized glycogenosis is at present unknown.

Differential Diagnosis

The diagnosis, which can only be suspected from clinical evidence, depends upon pathological and biochemical studies. The patients with cardiac enlargement must be differentiated from the group of infants with primary endomyocardial disease, such as primary endocardial sclerosis, anomalous origin of a coronary artery from the pulmonary trunk, myocarditis, calcification of the coronary arteries, and idiopathic myocardial hypertrophy. Skeletal muscle involvement is a distinguishing feature. The latter must be differentiated from amyotonia congenita, a more common entity.[65] The general appearance of the infant with protuberant, large tongue and umbilical hernia may suggest Down's syndrome or cretinism.

It must be remembered that cardiomegaly can also occur in the newborn infant of the diabetic mother.

Previous biochemical studies have indicated that the glycogen content of tissues, especially the heart and skeletal muscle, are very high. The values are the highest found in any form of disease, including other types of glycogen storage disorder. The values may exceed 10 per cent by wet weight in both heart and skeletal muscle. Glycogen structure has been reported to be normal, although in the report of Krivit et al.[66] of 2 cases with the predominantly neuromuscular form, the glycogen had an increased number of branch points. In all other aspects, the diagnosis in these patients was more consistent with type II than type III or debrancher disease. Analyses of the activity of the enzymes phosphorylase and debrancher, as well as glucose-6-phosphatase, in liver have been normal. Attempts to demonstrate increased glycogen content in leukocytes, either chemically or histochemically, have given equivocal results. Erythrocyte glycogen is not elevated.[67] Acid maltase activity has been found to be low in the leukocytes of a patient with type II disease.[68]

Pathology

Tissues taken for histochemical analysis must be carefully handled, as the glycogen is highly soluble in water. The changes in cardiac, skeletal and smooth muscle are similar: a honey-combed or lacework appearance due to extensive vacuolization is characteristic. Alcoholic PAS stains reveal heavy deposits of glycogen with intensely stained, closely packed granules of different sizes. In contrast to muscle, the liver has an increased glycogen without the lacework appearance; furthermore, fat infiltration is not found, as it is in the hepatorenal type disease. Glycogen deposition granules may be found in a variety of tissues, including the central nervous system. The latter may be involved diffusely, including brain, spinal cord and peripheral nervous system, or the deposition may be localized to specific areas such as the spinal cord and the autonomic nervous system.

Pathogenesis

Although an enzymic defect has been demonstrated, the pathogenesis is not entirely clear. Lejeune, Thines-Sempoux and Hers[69] have localized α-acid glucosidase in the lysosomes in rat liver. These subcellular fractions contain a variety of enzymes, hydrolases, which are capable of breakdown and digestion of localized areas within the cell. Apparently, there is a continual breakdown and synthesis of local cell constituents. Glycogen, which is synthesized normally and usually degraded by glycogenolytic enzymes, phosphorylase and debrancher, may also be degraded locally within the lysosome cell by α-acid glucosidase to maltose and glucose. In the absence of this enzyme, other lysosomal hydrolases might destroy the enzymes which usually break down glycogen, allowing normal glycogen to accumulate in the vacuoles. In other cellular sites containing glycogen and the enzymes of synthesis and degradation, no physiologic defect in glucose metabolism is apparent. The accumulation of glycogen in localized vacuolated areas within the cell would be progressive. Ultimately, as normal cytoplasm is replaced by excessive glycogen granules, cellular function is impeded and muscle fibers are disrupted. In this respect, then, the presence of normal glycogen in excessive quantity in this disorder and the presence of an abnormal glycogen in type IV disease may have a similar effect in interfering with normal cell function. The proof of the above hypothesis must await further biochemical and physiological studies clarifying the role of lysosomes.

The disease is familial, with as many as three affected siblings having been reported in a single family. More than 50 cases of this apparently genetically determined, autosomal recessive disorder have been cited.[63]

Gutman and associates[77] have reported a 17 year old female with generalized glycogen storage disease in whom no enzyme defect was found. They determined glucose-6-phosphatase, liver and muscle phosphorylase, amylo 1,6 glucosidase, α-1,4-glucosidase and amylo 1,4-1,6 transglucosidase. Glycogen structure was normal.

Summary

Generalized glycogenosis is a progressive disorder of young infants in whom cardiac hypertrophy, skeletal muscle dysfunction, and central nervous system deterioration result in a fatal outcome in the first year of life. Abnormalities of carbohydrate physiology are not found, although excessive glycogen accumulation in a variety of tissues is characteristic. Diagnosis is established by muscle biopsy and the biochemical demonstration of an absence of α-acid glucosidase. The enzymatic defect may also be shown in the leukocyte. There is no satisfactory therapy. The role of lysosomes in the pathogenesis of this disease remains to be defined.

STORAGE OF ABNORMAL GLYCOGEN

Brancher (?) Deficiency (Amylo 1,4-1,6 glucosidase) (Type IV)

This disorder was first described by Andersen,[11] and the structure of the glycogen was characterized biochemically by Cori.[15] Only two documented cases have been reported.[11, 70] Additional presumptive cases cited by Sidbury include a detailed study by Craig[71] of a patient proven to have an abnormal mucopolysaccharide in various organs.

Both cases reported in detail had an onset of liver disease toward the end of the first year of life, with progressive abdominal enlargement, hepatomegaly and splenomegaly. Dilated superficial veins were present over the upper abdomen. Minimal icterus was present in Andersen's case.

Laboratory Findings and Diagnosis

The hemogram indicated a mild anemia. Carbohydrate studies revealed a variable fasting blood sugar level, ranging from a low of 30 mg./100 ml. to a high of 79 mg./100 ml. Oral and intravenous glucose tolerance tests were not remarkable. Response to administration of epinephrine was variable, with a delayed rise in blood glucose in both patients. In contrast, Sidbury's patient failed to show a significant elevation of blood sugar after intravenous glucagon.

The major laboratory abnormalities were in liver function tests. Cephalin flocculation, thymol turbidity, zinc turbidity, and phenol turbidity were elevated. Alkaline phosphatase was abnormal in one case. SGOT rose as high as 240 units (normal < 30), while SGPT reached levels of 114 units (normal < 30). Values for cholesterol and total lipids were not elevated. Blood lactate, pyruvate and uric acid levels were within normal limits. Serum electrolyte concentrations were not remarkable.

Initial diagnosis as determined by biopsy in both cases was glycogen storage disease with diffuse early portal cirrhosis.

Course

The two patients reported had a similar course, with progressive liver failure; Andersen's patient succumbed at 17 months of age, while Sidbury's survived until 4 years of age. The complications of portal hypertension and cirrhosis predominated. Ascites, esophageal varices with hemorrhage, jaundice and malnutrition were present. Hypoproteinemia occurred late in the course of the disease, while hypoprothrombinemia occurred early.

Pathology

At postmortem the livers were large and firm with golden yellow nodules. The spleen was large. The kidneys were enlarged, but otherwise normal on inspection. Histologically, the liver contained fibrous tissue and bile duct proliferation. Best's stain indicated the liver cells to be packed with red granules. On iodine stain, this material gave a purplish brown color instead of the usual reddish brown characteristic of glycogen. Excess polysaccharide was identified histologically in many tissues, including liver, spleen, lymph nodes, intestinal mucosa (Andersen), as well as kidneys, heart, muscle, reticuloendothelial system and nervous system (Sidbury).

Andersen noted difficulty in chemically isolating glycogen and submitted tissue to Cori for further biochemical analysis. Cori isolated the polysaccharide and characterized it as an amylopectin with abnormal inner and outer straight chains. On this basis, she postulated a deficiency of brancher enzyme. Sidbury studied a variety of enzymes in liver and muscle and noted a general depression, without absence of a specific enzyme. He isolated and characterized the polysaccharide also as an amylopectin. It is of interest that the liver did not contain an excessive content of this glycogen-like material (0.18 to 2.86 per cent) or of fat.

The diagnosis was suspected, in Sidbury's case, from an analysis of red blood cell glycogen. While the amount of material (polysaccharide) was not increased in content, the iodine spectrum* was similar to that found with amylopectin and different from that of normal glycogen.

The genetics of this disorder is unknown, although Andersen's patient had a sibling who had died earlier with a similar disorder. She suggested that familial cirrhosis in infancy may be due to this disorder.

The biochemical basis for this defect is as yet inferential and based on the structural analysis of the glycogen. The specific brancher enzyme deficiency has not been identified. The suggestion of Andersen that the polysaccharide acts as a foreign body to produce a reaction in the reticulo-endothelial system and in liver parenchymal cells has been questioned by Sidbury. How the specific enzyme defect and abnormal polysaccharide result in tissue damage remains to be elucidated.

Summary

The accumulation of an abnormal polysaccharide perhaps due to a deficiency of brancher enzyme results in pathological changes in the reticuloendothelial system. In particular, cirrhosis occurs in the liver, with progressive signs of hepatic dysfunction and, ultimately, death due to liver failure. The clinical and chemical picture cannot be distinguished from other causes of cirrhosis in infancy. Identification of the glycogen is necessary to establish the diagnosis.

GLYCOGEN DEFICIENCY DISEASE

Glycogen Synthetase Defect

This is the second clinical condition which may result from a defect in glycogen synthesis. As discussed above in the type IV disease, a brancher defect has been inferred from an abnormality in glycogen structure. In contrast, the absence of glycogen synthetase in the liver is the first exam-

* See p. 127.

ple of a defect in the synthetic pathway leading to inadequate glycogen formation.

In 1963, Lewis, Spencer-Peet and Stewart[19] reported a set of twins who were born after 38 weeks' gestation and weighed 1.9 and 1.6 kg. Both infants were found to be apneic at 46 and 40 hours, respectively, prior to the initiation of feeding at 48 hours. The first twin progressed less well than the second. Significant signs were not noted until after 7 months of age when withdrawal of the night feeding was associated with pallor and transient strabismus in both twins prior to morning feeding. Early morning convulsions occurred at 9 and 8½ months of age and were recurrent in the second twin.

When hospitalized both infants were found to be retarded. Both had decreased head circumference. Hepatosplenomegaly was not evident. Acetonuria was not found, but fasting blood sugar levels were very low (< 30 mg./100 ml.) after an overnight fast. Hypoglycemia was not precipitous in these patients, but blood sugar levels declined slowly over several hours after a meal. Epinephrine administration followed an overnight fast resulted in minimal elevation of blood sugar; glucagon had no effect. In contrast, glucagon given 3 hours after a meal produced a prompt and significant elevation of the blood glucose concentration. The administration of exogenous insulin was followed by a marked fall in blood sugar concentration which required glucose administration to restore normal levels. Plasma insulin levels, as assayed by the rat diaphragm technique, were not elevated. Catecholamine excretion in the urine was not increased during hypoglycemia.

Diagnosis

A liver biopsy taken from one twin while the patient was maintained by intravenous glucose contained 0.45 per cent glycogen and 9.8 per cent total lipid. Histologically, there was glycogen depletion and pronounced fatty change of the liver. Enzyme studies revealed undetectable glycogen synthetase activity, but normal activities of UDPG-pyrophosphorylase, phosphorylase and glucose-6-phosphatase.

Since glycogen synthetase activity has been demonstrated in the erythrocyte by Cornblath et al.,[72] this tissue might serve as a possible source for verification of the diagnosis. Erythrocytes from these patients and other family members were found to contain normal glycogen synthetase activity. This observation has been confirmed in all family members as recently reported by Spencer-Peet.[73] Thus, erythrocyte glycogen synthetase appears to be unrelated to hepatic glycogen synthetase.

Several regimens of management, including high fat diet and ephedrine, were without significant effect on morning hypoglycemia. However, the patients could be effectively managed with a late night feeding, especially if it was high in protein.

Parr, Teree and Larner[74] have reported another family in which an infant did poorly with feedings in the first days of life but then thrived until 3½ months of age. At 4 months she had a catastrophic illness following 12 hours of marked lethargy and poor feeding. She was hospitalized after a "stiffening out spell" and unresponsiveness. She had a "doll-like facies" and an enlarged liver. Initial blood sugar level was 4 mg./100 ml., although spinal fluid sugar was 40 mg./100 ml. Ketonuria and a metabolic acidosis were present. The patient initially responded to intravenous glucose but became comatose again on the third day despite treatment with intravenous fluids (glucose and electrolyte): her blood sugar levels varied from 30 to 162 mg./100 ml. She received 100 mg. of hydrocortisone daily. An abdominal viscus (stomach) perforated on the third hospital day and the patient died on the fifth day. No physiological studies were possible.

Enzyme Studies

The liver and samples of skeletal muscle of the patient of Parr et al.[74] were frozen 90 minutes after death for enzyme studies. While activities of the enzymes of the glycogen cycle were generally low, *very* low values were found for both glycogen synthetase and phosphorylase in liver. The glycogen content was also low by chemical analysis, although the patient had received intravenous glucose. The generally low enzyme values were attributed to a high fat content. No inhibitors were found by addition of the patient's liver to normal liver extract.

Pathologically, both liver and kidneys were enlarged, and yellowish orange in appearance. Histologically, there was marked distortion of normal hepatic architecture by excessive fat accumulation which compressed the nuclei of parenchymatous cells. Glycogen could not be identified histochemically. Similar vacuoles of sudanophilic material were found in the kidney tubules at the level of loops of Henle, distal convoluted and collecting ducts. Muscle histology was not remarkable. On gross examination the central nervous system was not abnormal. By microscopic examination, reactive astrocytes and increased numbers of microglia cells were present in the white matter of the cerebral convolutions.

This infant had three siblings who died in infancy with apnea and coma and central nervous system signs. One had birth trauma, another had a cyst in the brain in place of the corpus callosum. At postmortem examination, two of the infants were found to have fatty metamorphosis of the liver. There were two normal living children.

In contrast, the original family in the study of Lewis et al.[72] included two normal older siblings and one younger sibling of normal mentality, but who had hypoglycemia and reduced glucagon response after fasting. This patient received late night feedings and was asymptomatic. Reduced tolerance to oral glucose was present in all family members except the mother.

The genetic aspects of this familial disease remain to be defined.

Pathogenesis

These two studies may represent variants of the same basic defect, an absence of glycogen synthetase. The pathophysiology and the precise biochemical defect remain to be defined. How glycogen synthesis occurs in the absence of an enzyme activity is unknown. Lewis has suggested that glycogen is synthesized by the reversible phosphorylase action. Glycogen is apparently formed after meals, since there was a hyperglycemia response to glucagon at that time but not after fasting. Parr et al.[74] have considered the decreased phosphorylase activity to be secondary to a lack of glycogen substrate. Why the affected infants survived beyond the initial neonatal period is also unexplained. The failure of glycogen synthesis alone is inadequate to explain the hypoglycemia with fasting, since increased gluconeogenesis might be expected to compensate for this. Lewis reported that ACTH over a 4-day period produced a response of the adrenal cortex which prevented fasting hypoglycemia; he postulated a failure of endogenous adrenal cortical function to explain the hypoglycemia. Obviously, further studies in this area are indicated. The lack of response to epinephrine in this syndrome is obscure.

Management

The management of these patients must be individualized. Dietary control with high protein feedings appears to be effective in the mildly affected patient. When hypoglycemia is persistent and severe, then glucocorticoid therapy is indicated. It is important to recognize that there are serious complications of the latter, such as ulceration of the gastrointestinal tract (as in the patient of Parr et al.) or sepsis. Whether other forms of therapy, such as that used in idiopathic hypoglycemia, are indicated is not known.

The prognosis is unpredictable, but certainly the cases so far described have had a poor outcome.

Summary

A new familial disease characterized by hypoglycemia with starvation in early infancy has been associated with an absence of glycogen synthetase in the liver and decreased glycogen stores. Signs of hypoglycemia may be severe, including convulsions before a feeding. Diagnosis may be suspected from a failure of glucagon response after overnight fast, but requires enzyme studies of liver for its establishment.

ADDENDUM

Preliminary studies by Field et al.[81] have indicated that intestinal glucose-6-phosphatase activity was markedly deficient in two patients. Both parents of each patient had significantly decreased intestinal glucose-6-phosphatase activities consistent with the heterozygous state and a recessive type of inheritance for this disease.

REFERENCES

1. Snapper, I., and van Creveld, S.: Un cas d'hypoglycémie avec acétonémie chez un enfant. Bull. et mém. Soc. méd. hôp. Paris 52:1315, 1928.
2. von Gierke, E.: Hepato-Nephromegalia glykogenica (Glykogenspeicherkrankheit der Leber und Nieren). Beitr. path. Anat. 82:497, 1929.
3. Schönheimer, R.: Über eine eigenartige Storung des Kohlehydrat-Stoffwechsels. Hoppe-Seylers z. physiol. chem. 182:148, 1929.
4. van Creveld, S.: Glycogen disease. Medicine 18:1, 1939.
5. Mason, H. H., and Andersen, D. H.: Glycogen disease. Am. J. Dis. Child. 61:795, 1941.
6. Debré, R.: Les Polyconles. Paris, Gaston Doin & Cie., 1947.
7. Pompe, J. C.: Over idiopatische hypertrophie van het hart. Nederl. tijdschr. geneesk. 76:304, 1932 (Abstract).
8. van Creveld, S.: Investigations on glycogen disease. Arch. Dis. Child. 9:9, 1934.
9. Di Sant'Agnese, P. A., Andersen, D. H., Mason, H. H., and Bauman, W. A.: Glycogen storage disease of the heart. I. Report of two cases in siblings with chemical and pathological studies. Pediatrics 6:402, 1950.
10. Di Sant'Agnese, P. A., Andersen, D. H., and Mason, H. H.: Glycogen storage disease of the heart. II. Critical review of the literature. Pediatrics 6:607, 1950.
11. Andersen, D. H.: Studies on glycogen disease with report of a case in which the glycogen was abnormal. In Najjar, V. A. (ed.): Carbohydrate Metabolism. Johns Hopkins University Press, Baltimore, Md., 1952, p. 28.
12. McArdle, B.: Myopathy due to a defect in muscle glycogen breakdown. Clin. Sc. 10:13, 1951.
13. Stetten, D., Jr., and Stetten, M. R.: Glycogen metabolism. Physiol. Rev. 40:505, 1960.
14. Larner, J.: Genetic and hormonal control of glycogen metabolism. Fed. Proc. 19:971, 1960.
15. Cori, G. T.: Glycogen structure and enzyme deficiencies in glycogen storage disease. Harvey Lect. (1952–53) 48:145, 1954.
16. Hers, H. G.: Glycogen storage disease. In Levine, R., and Luft, R. (eds.): Advances in Metabolic Disorders. Vol. 1. New York, Academic Press, Inc., 1964, pp. 1–44.
17. Cori, G. T., and Cori, C. F.: Glucose-6-phosphatase of the liver in glycogen storage disease. J. Biol. Chem. 199:661, 1952.
18. Hers, H. G.: α-Glucosidase deficiency in generalized glycogen-storage disease (Pompe's disease). Biochem. J. 86:11, 1963.
19. Lewis, G. M., Spencer-Peet, J., and Stewart, K. M.: Infantile hypoglycemia due to inherited deficiency of glycogen synthetase in liver. Arch. Dis. Child. 38:40, 1963.
20. van Creveld, S.: The Blackader lecture, 1962: the clinical course of glycogen disease. Canad. Med. Assoc. J. 88:1, 1963.
21. Schulman, J. L., and Saturen, P.: Glycogen storage disease of the liver. I. Clinical studies during the early neonatal period. Pediatrics 14:632, 1954.

22. Brante, G., Kaijser, K., and Ockerman, P. A.: Glycogenosis type I (lack of glucose-6-phosphatase) in four siblings. Acta Paediat. (suppl.) 157:1, 1964.
23. Howell, R. R., Ashton, D. M., and Wyngaarden, J. B.: Glucose-6-phosphatase deficiency glycogen storage disease. Studies on the interrelationships of carbohydrate, lipid and purine abnormalities. Pediatrics 29:553, 1962.
24. Sidbury, J. B., Cornblath, M., Fisher, J., and House, E.: Glycogen in erythrocytes of patient with glycogen storage disease. Pediatrics 27:103, 1961.
25. Williams, H. E., and Field, J. B.: Further studies on leukocyte phosphorylase in glycogen storage disease. Metabolism 12:464, 1963.
26. Williams, H. E., Kendig, E. M., and Field, J. B.: Leukocyte debranching enzyme in glycogen storage disease. J. Clin. Invest. 42:656, 1963.
27. Sokal, J. E., Lowe, C. U., Sarcione, E. J., Mosovich, L. L., and Doray, B. H.: Studies of glycogen metabolism in liver glycogen disease (von Gierke's disease): six cases with similar metabolic abnormalities and responses to glucagon. J. Clin. Invest. 40:364, 1961.
28. Perkoff, G. T., Parker, V. J., and Hahn, R. F.: The effects of glucagon in three forms of glycogen storage disease. J. Clin. Invest. 41:1099, 1962.
29. Schwartz, R., Ashmore, J., and Renold, A. E.: Galactose tolerance in glycogen storage disease. Pediatrics 19:585, 1957.
30. Hers, H. G., and Malbrain, H.: Étude biochimique d'un cas de maladie glyco-génique. Mod. Probl. Paediat. 4:203, 1959. (Bibliothica paediatrica, fasc. 70.)
31. Field, R. A.: Glycogen deposition diseases. In Stanbury, J. B., Wyngaarden, J. B., and Fredrickson, D. S. (eds.): The Metabolic Basis for Inherited Diseases. New York, McGraw-Hill Book Co., Inc., 1960, p. 156.
32. Illingworth, B.: Glycogen storage disease. Am. J. Clin. Nutrition 9:683, 1961.
33. Larner, J.: Unpublished observations.
34. Williams, H. E., Johnson, P. L., Fenster, L. F., Laster, L., and Field, J. B.: Intestinal glucose-6-phosphatase in control subjects and relatives of a patient with glycogen storage disease. Metabolism 12:235, 1963.
35. Ockerman, P. A.: Glucose-6-phosphatase in human jejunal mucosa. Lack of activity in glycogenosis of Cori's type I. Clin. Chim. Acta 9:151, 1964.
36. Villee, C. A.: The intermediary metabolism of human fetal tissues. Cold Spring Harbor Symposium on Quantitative Biology 19:186, 1954.
37. Nemeth, A. M.: Glucose-6-phosphatase in the liver of the fetal guinea pig. J. Biol. Chem. 208:773, 1954.
38. Mason, H. H., and Sly, G. E.: Blood lactic acid in liver glycogen disease. Proc. Soc. Exper. Biol. 53:145, 1943.
39. Levine, R., and Taubenhaus, M. (eds.): Clinical conference on metabolic problems. Glycogen storage disease. Metabolism 3:173, 1954.
40. Illingworth, B., and Cori, G. T.: Structure of glycogens and amylopectins. III. Normal and abnormal human glycogen. J. Biol. Chem. 199:653, 1952.
41. Forbes, G. B.: Glycogen storage disease. J. Pediat. 42:645, 1953.
42. van Creveld, S., and Huijing, F.: Differential diagnosis of the type of glycogen disease in two adult patients with long history of glycogenosis. Metabolism 13:191, 1964.
43. Hug, G., Krill, C. E., Jr., Perrin, E. V., and Guest, G. M.: Cori's disease (amylo-1,6-glucosidase deficiency). New England J. Med. 268:113, 1963.
44. Illingworth, B., Cori, G. T., and Cori, C. F.: Amylo-1,6 glucosidase in muscle tissue in generalized glycogen storage disease. J. Biol. Chem. 218:123, 1956.
45. Bridge, E. M., and Holt, L. E., Jr.: Glycogen storage disease; observations on the pathologic physiology of two cases of the hepatic form of the disease. J. Pediat. 27:299, 1945.
46. Hers, H. G.: Études enzymatiques sur fragments hépatiques; application a la clasification des glycogénoses. Rev. int. Hepat. 9:35, 1959.
47. Lamy, M., Dubois, R., Rossier, A., Frezal, J., Loeb, H., and Blancher, G.: La glycogénose par defici. Arch. franç. pediat. 17:14, 1960.
48. Hulsmann, W. C., Oei, T. L., and van Creveld, S.: Phosphorylase activity in leukocytes from patients with glycogen storage disease. Lancet 2:581, 1961.

49. Williams, H. E., and Field, J. B.: Low leukocyte phosphorylase in hepatic phosphorylase deficient glycogen storage disease. J. Clin. Invest. 40:1841, 1961.

50. Lowe, C. U., Sokal, J. E., Sarcione, E. J., Saks, G. L., Mosovich, L. L., and Markello, J. R.: An unusual response to galactose, fructose and glucose administration in nine subjects with a syndrome of hepatic glycogenosis without hypoglycemia. Proc. Am. Ped. Soc. Abs. No. 123, p. 133, 1964. J. Pediat. 65:1061, 1964.

51. Eberlein, W. R., Illingworth, B. A., and Sidbury, J. B.: Heterogenous glycogen storage disease in siblings and favorable response to synthetic androgen administration. Am. J. Med. 23:20, 1962.

52. Calderbank, A., Kent, P. W., Lorber, J., Manners, D. J., and Wright, A.: Biochemical investigation of a case of glycogen-storage disease (von Gierke's disease). Biochem. J. 74:223, 1960.

53. Larner, J., and Villar-Palasi, C.: Enzymes in glycogen storage myopathy. Proc. Nat. Acad. Sci. 45:1234, 1959.

54. Schmid, R., Robbins, P. W., and Traut, R. R.: Glycogen synthesis in human muscle lacking phosphorylase. Proc. Nat. Acad. Sci. 45:1236, 1959.

55. Schmid, R., and Mahler, R.: Chronic progressive myopathy with myoglobinuria; demonstration of a glycogenolytic defect in the muscle. J. Clin. Invest. 38:2044, 1959.

56. Pearson, C. M., Rimer, D. G., and Mommaerts, W. F. H. M.: A metabolic myopathy due to absence of muscle phosphorylase. Am. J. Med. 30:502, 1961.

57. Engle, W. K., Eyerman, E. L., and Williams, H. E.: Late-onset type of skeletal muscle phosphorylase deficiency. New England J. Med. 268:135, 1963.

58. Mommaerts, W. F. H. M., Illingworth, B., Pearson, C. M., Guillory, R. J., and Seraydarian, K.: A functional disorder of muscle associated with the absence of phosphorylase. Proc. Nat. Acad. Sci. 45:791, 1959.

59. Mellick, R. S., Mahler, R. F., and Hughes, B. P.: McArdle's syndrome; phosphorylase-dificient myopathy. Lancet 1:1045, 1962.

60. Andres, R., Cader, G., and Zierler, K. L.: The quantitatively minor role of carbohydrate in oxidative metabolism by skeletal muscle in intact man in the basal state. Measurements of oxygen and glucose uptake and carbon dioxide and lactate production in the forearm. J. Clin. Invest. 35:671, 1956.

61. Mahler, R. F., and McArdle, B.: Specific enzyme defect in glycogen breakdown causing a myopathy. Quart. J. Med. 29:638, 1960 (Abstract).

62. Schmid, R., and Hammaker, L.: Hereditary absence of muscle phosphorylase (McArdle's syndrome). New England J. Med. 264:223, 1961.

63. Ehlers, K. H., Hagstrom, J. W., Lukas, D. S., Redo, S. F., and Engle, M. A.: Glycogen storage disease of the myocardium with obstruction to the left ventricular outflow. Circulation 25:96, 1962.

64. Ruttenberg, H. D., Steidl, R. M., Carey, L. S., and Edwards, J. E.: Glycogen-storage disease of the heart. Am. Heart J. 67:469, 1964.

65. Clement, D. H., and Godman, G. C.: Glycogen disease resembling mongolism, cretinism and amyotonia congenita. J. Pediat. 36:11, 1950.

66. Krivit, W., Polglase, W. J., Gunn, F. D., and Tyler, F. H.: Studies in disorders of muscle. IX. Glycogen storage disease primarily affecting skeletal muscle and clinically resembling amyotonia congenita. Pediatrics 12:165, 1953.

67. Kahana, D., Telem, C., Steinitz, K., and Solomon, M.: Generalized glycogenosis. J. Pediat. 65:243, 1964.

68. Huijing, F., van Creveld, S., and Losckoot, G.: Diagnosis of generalized glycogen storage disease (Pompe's disease). J. Pediat. 63:984, 1963.

69. Lejeune, N., Thines-Sempoux, D., and Hers, H. G.: Tissue fractionation studies. 16. Intracellular distribution and properties of α-glucosidases in rat liver. Biochem. J. 86:16, 1963.

70. Sidbury, J. B., Jr., Mason, J., Burns, W. B., Jr., and Ruebner, B. H.: Type IV glycogenosis. Report of a case proven by characterization of glycogen and studied at necropsy. Bull. Johns Hopkins Hosp. 111:157, 1962.

71. Craig, J. M., and Uzman, L. L.: A familial metabolic disorder with storage of an unusual polysaccharide complex. Pediatrics 22:20, 1958.

72. Cornblath, M., Steiner, D. F., Bryan, P., and King, J.: UDPG-glycogen glucosyltransferase in human erythrocytes. Fed. Proc. 23:379, 1964 (Abstract No. 1667).
73. Spencer-Peet, J.: Erythrocyte glycogen synthetase in glycogen storage deficiency resulting from the absence of this enzyme from liver. Clin. Chim. Acta 10:481, 1964.
74. Parr, J., Teree, T. M., and Larner, J.: Symptomatic hypoglycemia, visceral fatty metamorphosis and aglycogenosis in an infant lacking glycogen synthetase and phosphorylase. Pediatrics 35:770, 1965.
75. van Creveld, S., and Huijing, F.: Glycogen storage disease. Biochemical and clinical data in sixteen cases. Am. J. Med. 38:554, 1965.
76. Fernandes, J., and Van de Kamer, J. H.: Studies on the utilization of hexoses in liver glycogen disease. Pediatrics 35:470, 1965.
77. Gutman, A., Rachmilewitz, E. A., Stein, O., Eliakim, M., and Stein, Y.: Glycogen storage disease. Israel J. Med. Sc. 1:14, 1965.
78. Sutherland, E. W., Jr.: The biological role of adenosine 3',5'-phosphate. The Harvey Lect. 57:17, 1962.
79. Lowe, C. U., and Mosovitch, L. L.: The paradoxical effect of alcohol on carbohydrate metabolism in four patients with liver glycogen disease. Pediatrics 35:1005, 1965.
80. Whelan, W. J., and Cameron, M. P. (eds.): Ciba Foundation Symposium: Control of Glycogen Metabolism. Boston, Little, Brown and Co., 1964.
81. Field, J. B., Epstein, S., and Egan, T.: Studies in glycogen storage diseases. I. Intestinal glucose-6-phosphatase activity in patients with von Gierke's disease and their parents. J. Clin. Invest. 44:1240, 1965.

Chapter Eight

HEREDITARY GALACTOSE
INTOLERANCE

Hereditary galactose intolerance or galactosemia is one of the better defined genetic, molecular diseases of the biochemical era of medicine. The disease, as first described by Von Reuss[1] in 1908, was associated with failure to thrive, liver disease and galactosemia, it being assumed that the latter was related to the ingestion of milk. Nine years later, Göppert[2] observed that the ingestion of galactose itself as well as milk resulted in galactosuria. The first patient described in the English literature was reported by Mason and Turner in 1935.[3] Subsequently, scattered cases and large series of cases have been reported through 1961,[4-7] including a report of the follow-up of Mason's original case by Townsend et al. in 1951.[8] Initially, attention was focused on the clinical consequences of the diverse metabolic disturbances. These concerned (a) clinical description and course, (b) pathological findings, and (c) physiological disturbances of carbohydrate metabolism. These careful clinical investigations resulted in a plan of effective dietary therapy.

Leloir[9, 10] clarified the metabolic pathway for galactose and for galactose to glucose interconversion, thus permitting further biochemical studies of the disease. Schwarz et al.[11] later observed the accumulation of galactose-1-phosphate in red cells of affected patients, while Kalckar,[12] and Isselbacher[13] and associates proved the basic defect to be an absence of a specific enzyme, Gal-P-uridyl transferase (galactose-1-phosphate uridyl transferase). These studies resulted in new interest in the disease and the specific biochemical lesion, with emphasis on (a) chemical methods of detection, (b) biochemical genetics, and (c) specific biochemical toxicity.

While careful family histories suggested that the defect was transmitted as a recessive trait, the development of a sensitive enzymatic method for blood analysis was necessary to detect the heterozygote.[14] The disease has been shown to be a simple autosomal recessive. The gene frequency for this condition, previously considered to be 1/70,000 has been estimated most recently by Hansen to be as high as 1/18,000.[15]

CLINICAL MANIFESTATIONS

Prenatal Effects

The newborn infant with hereditary galactose intolerance shows no apparent evidences of his enzymatic defect at birth. *In utero,* the fetus may be exposed to variable amounts of lactose or galactose from the mother. The heterozygote mother may be unable to dispose of a galactose load as rapidly as a normal person can. This relative deficiency may result in increased levels of galactose reaching the fetus even under a normal dietary regimen. The presence of nuclear cataracts, which usually develop in the third fetal month and before lens development takes place, has been considered by Ritter to be a further indication of intrauterine fetal abnormalities related to galactose.[16] Additional studies concerning maternal–fetal galactose metabolism are necessary to clarify this area.

The Neonate and His Problems

At birth the affected infant is normal, both physically and developmentally. But shortly after he begins to ingest milk, he develops a characteristic course which varies only in the severity and rapidity of the clinical manifestations.[7, 17] Failure to gain weight in first few days is common, as is jaundice, which increases and persists beyond the usual period of "physiological jaundice." Subcutaneous bleeding may take place. Vomiting, diarrhea and dehydration also occur. The skin appears dry, rough, thick and scaly. The liver enlarges and is smooth, firm and nontender. If the disease is unrecognized, the course is one of progressive deterioration associated with liver disease (cirrhosis), cataracts and mental retardation. The characteristic abdominal distention is the combined result of ascites, hepatomegaly and splenomegaly. Zonular or lamellar cataracts may be seen as early as one month of age. Mental retardation does not become manifest until later in the initial year of life. Malnutrition, extreme loss of subcutaneous fat tissue and retarded growth become evident as the untreated disease progresses (Fig. 41).

In contrast to these marked abnormalities, the onset in some cases may be subtle and the disease manifested only in a failure to feed well or

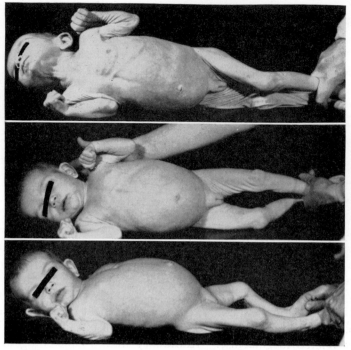

Figure 41. Infant with chronic diarrhea who was not discovered to have galactose intolerance until 5 months of age. Removal of lactose from the diet resulted in rapid improvement in nutrition.

to gain weight. In these infants, the course progresses to a more characteristic clinical picture as they take more milk formula. Mental retardation, which is the most serious consequence for untreated surviving children with this disorder, varies in severity.[18] The heterozygote does not have clinical manifestations, but the disease may be difficult to detect even in the homozygote. Hugh-Jones and associates[19] have reported a family in which a homozygous grandfather with the disease, including cataracts and hepatomegaly undetected until his sixth decade in life, was of normal intelligence.

LABORATORY DATA

Blood

Laboratory studies may show no initial effects on the erythrocytes or leukocytes; in a few instances, a normocytic, hypoplastic anemia has been described later in the course of the disease. Chemical analysis of the plasma electrolytes is not remarkable, unless extensive diarrhea and dehydration are present: under these circumstances, azotemia and metabolic acidosis are found. Liver function tests show variable results; elevations of serum bilirubin may be present. Cephalin flocculation and thymol turbidity may be abnormal, but are inconsistently so. Bromsulfophthalein dye retention tests usually show high levels if the patient is taking a diet containing galactose, but dye retention reverts to normal after the patient is fed a galactose-free diet. Total reducing substances in the blood are either normal, or elevated only postprandially. Fasting blood glucose levels as determined by yeast fermentation or with specific glucose oxidase are normal. Serum alpha amino nitrogen concentrations have not been elevated.

Urine

Abnormalities in the urine include generalized proteinuria, positive reducing substances and amino-aciduria. The sediment has not been reported to be abnormal, nor has ketonuria been reported. The reducing substances are positive to Benedict's test, Clinitest tablets or any test which measures ferric or cupric ion reduction. Specific analyses with glucose oxidase (TesTape, Clinistix, Combistix) are negative or show a trace reaction, indicating that the reducing substance is not glucose. Further identification is best made by paper chromatography as described by Partridge and Westall.[20] Other techniques for identification of the reducing sugar include the nitric acid–mucic acid test, the isolation of specific phenylosazone, and optical rotation.

Carbohydrate Tolerance Tests

Effects of both oral and intravenous administration of glucose, fructose, and galactose have been studied. The glucose and fructose are disposed of normally, and neither abnormal hyper- nor hypoglucosemia has been reported. In contrast, galactose given orally per se or as lactose (as in milk) is promptly absorbed and results in high sustained blood concentrations. Intravenous administration of galactose is characterized by a very slow rate of disappearance from the blood. In several studies, hypoglucosemia has been reported following galactose administration,[21] but, while emphasized by several reviewers,[22, 23] this has not been a consistent observation. The authors have unpublished records of intravenous galactose tolerance (0.5 gm./kg.) studies in 5 patients with hereditary galactose intolerance, not one of whom developed hypoglucosemia as determined by glucose oxidase (Figs. 42, 43). It is to be noted, however, that these patients were otherwise well and had been carefully controlled for 1 to 9 years on a galactose-limited diet. Hypoglucosemia appears to be a more

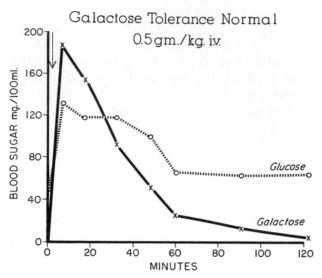

Figure 42. Rapid intravenous galactose tolerance test in a normal child. Observe the rise in blood glucose and the rapid disappearance of galactose.

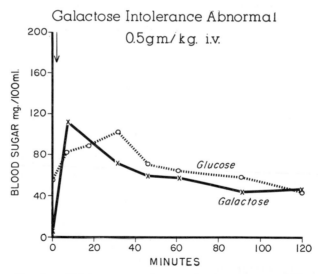

Figure 43. A rapid intravenous galactose tolerance test in a child with galactose intolerance who was controlled on a low galactose diet. Observe the slow disappearance of galactose and the rise in blood glucose. Hypoglucosemia did not occur.

significant feature in patients with chronic galactose toxicity, in whom liver disease may be present.

Roentgen Findings

After a variable period of exposure to milk, roentgen studies may show generalized osteoporosis, hepatomegaly and splenomegaly and ascites. The kidneys, visualized by intravenous pyelography, are normal.

DIAGNOSIS

A variety of diagnostic tests for this disorder have been devised and have been summarized by Kirkman.[24] These include the identification of sugar in urine, galactose tolerance tests, and specific enzyme tests on red blood cells. A variety of enzymatic techniques have been used for the erythrocytes and include: measurement of galactose-1-phosphate, UDPG consumption, and a methylene blue coupled reaction with measurement of $C^{14}O_2$ from $1-C^{14}$ galactose.[25, 26] The enzymatic methods are diagnostic and specific but may not be available in smaller laboratories. The tolerance tests are available in most laboratories, but carry a risk of central nervous system toxicity and possible hypoglucosemia.

When the diagnosis is suspected from either family history or clinical manifestations, the first examination should be a urinalysis to determine whether reducing substances are present. This determination must be done with either Benedict's solution or Clinitest tablets and *not* with glucose oxidase reagents, such as TesTape, Clinistix, Combistix, etc. If reducing substance is found in the urine and is not glucose, the removal from the diet of all lactose containing foods (milk) should result in elimination of the sugar (presumably galactose) from the urine within 24 to 72 hours.

The specific diagnosis is then established by the enzymatic methods utilizing red blood cells. In the newborn infant suspected of having this disorder because of a positive family history, the diagnosis should be made by demonstrating the absence of galactose-1-P uridyl transferase in the red blood cells before the initiation of milk feedings, and *not* upon the presence of reducing sugars in the urine.

Differential Diagnosis

Differential diagnosis in the neonate is concerned principally with mellituria and with hyperbilirubinemia associated with hepatic disease. The latter includes consideration of sepsis, cytomegalic inclusion disease, toxoplasmosis, biliary atresia, and neonatal hepatitis. The presence of minute amounts of galactose in the urine of the newborn, especially the low birth weight infant, may be a transient physiologic phenomenon[27] related to a decreased tissue uptake of galactose. (See Chapter Three.)

Later, the causes for failure of growth, diarrhea, cirrhosis, cataracts and mental retardation must be differentiated. A high index of suspicion and efforts at prompt diagnosis are essential to avoid a prolonged course with progressive deterioration and irreversible changes.

THERAPY

The management of patients with this disorder requires meticulous attention to detail. The course changes dramatically when milk sugar (lactose) is removed from the diet. Even an infant with the full blown disorder unrecognized for many months makes a remarkable response to the simple elimination of milk sugar from the diet. His appetite increases, vomiting and diarrhea subside within a few days, weight gain ensues promptly, liver function improves and jaundice subsides. Even the cataracts may disappear when he is placed on a lactose-free diet. Holzel,[17] however, has indicated that several of the low galactose formulas are not devoid of oligosaccharides containing galactose. However, Gitzelmann and Auricchio[46] have examined critically the ability of a normal and a galactosemic child to metabolize soya α-galactosides. They detected no α-galactosidase activity in the human small intestine, no rise in erythrocyte galactose-1-phosphate after raffinose ingestion, and slow absorption of galactose from the colon of the galactosemic child. They concluded that soybean formulas are generally safe for galactosemic infants, provided that they do not have diarrhea.

Although the affected children *may* reject galactose-lactose-containing foods, a *laissez faire* policy of self-selection is inadequate and may be dangerous: this is in contrast to children with hereditary fructose intolerance (Chapter Nine). In older children, avoidance of milk sugar is more difficult because many foods contain unlabeled lactose. Thus, candies and compounded foods, especially bread, sausage, frankfurters, etc., must be rigidly excluded unless the exact composition is known in detail. For the infant, several satisfactory proprietary formulas are available.[28, 29] (See Appendix I.)

GENETICS

A careful family history is essential, as in all inherited disorders. Family counseling regarding further pregnancies can be more specific if enzymatic analysis of erythrocytes from all family members is done to

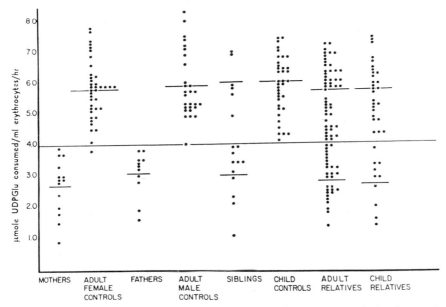

Figure 44. Erythrocyte enzyme assays in a large survey of families with hereditary galactose intolerance. Observe the difference in the distribution of values between the controls (values above 4 μmoles/ml.) and the members of families with affected children. (From Donnell et al., Pediatrics 25:572, 1960.)

define heterozygotes. Family history and oral galactose tolerance tests have been inadequate in defining the individual heterozygote, but the enzymatic tests have made possible a more precise analysis of the genetic situation. Refinement of the assay system has resulted in the detection of a definite difference in transferase levels in normal adults and in parents of galactosemic children. Kirkman[24] found 18 parents with levels below the mean for normal adults, and 13 of these were below two standard deviations. Donnell[14] studied 278 individuals, including 55 family members from 14 galactosemic families, and clearly identified the heterozygotes (Fig. 44). Hansen et al.[15] state that there may be about a 5 per cent overlap in transferase levels between the heterozygote and the normal, so that a single individual cannot be classified with absolute certainty on the basis of these tests. They recently reported on a population survey (penal prisoners, mentally retarded groups, hospitalized individuals randomly selected, and galactosemic families) from which were selected individuals with low erythrocyte enzyme levels (transferase less than 4 micromoles substrate per ml. erythrocytes per hour). Five unsuspected individuals were identified as galactosemic out of 268 in the total population (excluding members of known galactosemic families). In 3 of these the diagnosis was verified further by study of other family members. Hansen's analysis from this study suggests that the gene frequency of the homozygote is much higher than previously estimated; 1 per 18,000 instead of 1 per 70,000. There is agreement that the disorder is a simple autosomal recessive, perhaps with variable expressivity.[30, 31]

PATHOLOGY

Pathological studies indicate that the liver disease is a fatty infiltration with varying degrees of portal fibrosis resulting in a lobular pattern.[8] The hepatic cells may have a granular appearance. Infiltrates of leukocytes may be seen in the connective tissue. Bell[32] observed vacuolar changes in the epithelial cells of the proximal tubule of the kidney in one case. Crome[33] reported recently on the neuropathological findings in a child with physical and mental retardation who survived to 8 years of age. He found microencephaly with pronounced fibrous gliosis of the white matter; the cerebellum showed marked loss of Purkinje's cells and less conspicuous loss of the granular layer. All the findings were considered nonspecific and could not be differentiated from those seen in other forms of mental retardation. Cataracts are usually lamellar or zonular, although a few nuclear or anterior cortical changes in the lens have been reported.[16]

PATHOGENESIS

The metabolic pathways of lactose and galactose have been recently elucidated. Lactose, which is the disaccharide of D-galactose and D-glucose joined by an α-1,4 linkage, is normally hydrolyzed in the brush border of the small intestine by lactase (see Chapter Twelve) and the component monosaccharides are actively absorbed. Lactose itself rarely appears in blood or urine except late in pregnancy. The absorbed galactose is removed promptly and efficiently from the portal circulation by the liver where most of the sugar is metabolized. In insulin-sensitive tissues, *both* monosaccharides enter the cell by an active transport mechanism which is stero-specific. All three sugars (glucose, galactose and lactose) have reducing properties, although galactose has only 80 per cent of the reducing effect of glucose.

Normal Biochemical Sequence

The pathway of galactose metabolism has been clearly defined by Leloir and associates.[9, 10] In the cell, galactose is phosphorylated from ATP to galactose-1-phosphate by a specific galactokinase. The galactose-

1-P reacts with uridine-di-phosphoglucose (UDPG) in the presence of the specific enzyme, P-gal uridyl transferase to form uridine-di-phospho-galactose (UDPGal) and glucose-1-phosphate. UDPGal-4-epimerase with DPN is necessary for the conversion of the UDPGal to UDPG. UDPG may be metabolized by several pathways. It can react with pyrophosphate in the presence of UDPG pyrophosphorylase to form UTP and glucose-1-phosphate, or in the presence of glycogen synthetase to form glycogen. (See Chapter Seven for glycogen cycle.)

Site of Defect

In hereditary galactose intolerance, Schwarz[11] found that galactose-1-phosphate accumulated in erythrocytes, suggesting that galactokinase was active normally and that the defect was beyond the first phosphorylation step. Kalckar[12] demonstrated the defect to be an absence of the specific transferase, P-gal uridyl transferase, and with Isselbacher[13] showed that the epimerase and UDPG pyrophosphorylase were normal. The latter authors suggested that the reversibility of the epimerase reaction permitted synthesis of UDPGal under circumstances of dietary deprivation. This could account for normal galacto-lipid synthesis and central nervous system development in the absence of exogenous galactose.[13]

Mechanism of Toxicity

The mechanism of toxicity at the biochemical level is not entirely proven. The original suggestion of Mason and Turner that hypoglycemia was responsible for much of the symptomatology is untenable. The toxic effects appear to be more directly related to the accumulation of galactose-1-phosphate. Young rats fed diets high in galactose (up to 80 per cent, by weight, of total food) develop cataracts and renal disease.[34, 35] The livers, however, do not show histologic changes. Lerman[36] has shown that a tenfold rise in the concentration of galactose-1-P is found in the lens in cataracts in experimental rats. Although little information is available about the metabolism of the human lens in this disease, transferse activity was apparently absent in the lens tissue from one galactose-intolerant infant.[37] Several theories have been proposed to explain the cataracts that develop when there is galactose intolerance. One relates the changes to decreased oxidation of glucose and consequent interference with normal lens metabolism.[36] Another proposes conversion of galactose to its alcohol, dulcitol which accumulates with water to produce vacuoles in the lens.[38] The latter theory suggests that fiber rupture, secondary to the osmotic effects, precedes cataract formation.

The presence of galactose-1-P in erythrocytes impairs oxygen uptake, and tissue damage in liver, kidney and brain is apparently related to this compound, although the mechanism of action is unknown. *In vitro,* galactose-1-P has been shown to inhibit phosphoglucomutase, glucose-6-phosphatase and glucose-6-dehydrogenase, but how this might explain cellular damage is unknown.[39] It is of interest that, from a clinical standpoint, both the rate of development and rate of decline of toxicity suggest the slow accumulation of a toxic metabolite. This has been demonstrated with respect to amino-aciduria in the study of Cusworth et al.[40] They showed that a 3- to 5-day interval was necessary after initiation of a galactose diet before renal amino acid excretion increased. Similarly, removal of galactose from the diet resulted in a decrease in amino-aciduria only after a few days had passed. Although extensive liver disease might affect the plasma amino acid levels with overflow amino-aciduria, the studies of Hsia et al.[41] and of Cusworth and associates[40] indicate that the primary effect is in the renal tubule, with minimal changes in plasma amino acids. Thus, the amino-aciduria is the result of an reabsorptive alteration in the proximal tubule.

PROGNOSIS

The clinical manifestations are so highly variable that the ultimate course is unpredictable. In the undetected severe cases, death occurs in early infancy. In other untreated children, mental retardation and liver disease may be the major complications, with few surviving beyond childhood. Early diagnosis and careful dietary management can result in normal growth and development, both physically and intellectually, without serious complications[17, 18] (Fig. 45). When the diagnosis has been delayed for several months, there may be some degree of permanent mental retardation, although other signs of galactose toxicity subside with dietotherapy.

Alternate Biochemical Pathways

One vexing problem concerns the degree of completeness of the enzymatic defect. Clinical observations have suggested that the older patient becomes more tolerant of galactose. Very sensitive enzyme studies have indicated that there are low but definite levels of activity in patients with the disorder, indicating that galactose may be metabolized by some of these patients. Eisenberg and associates[42] recovered the metabolic product, menthyl glucosiduronic derivative, from a patient given radio-C^{14}-galactose. Weinberg[25] also found one patient whose leukocytes metabolized galactose to carbon dioxide. Segal et al.[43] similarly noted definite

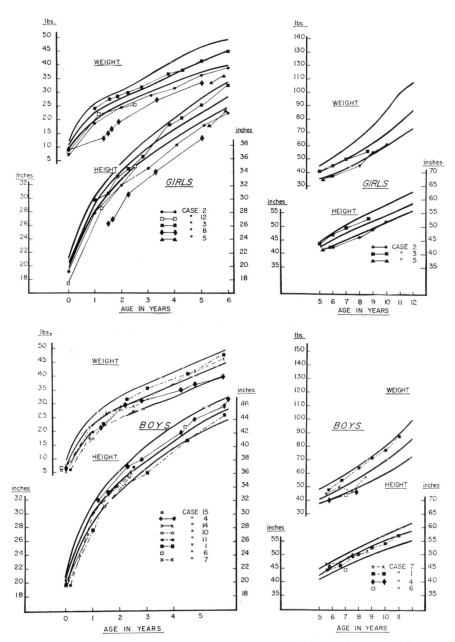

Figure 45. Growth data in children with hereditary galactose intolerance. Observe the normal growth patterns in both height and weight of children of both sexes fed galactose-restricted diets. (From Donnell et al., J. Pediat. 58:836, 1962.)

radiocarbon dioxide excretion in two patients given radioactive galactose. Ng, Bergren and Donnell[44] found three families with galactosemic children whose erythrocytes had low, but significantly detectable, transferase activity; they also recovered a small fraction of hexose intermediates beyond galactose-1-phosphate.

These data indicate, then, that a small fraction of galactose can be metabolized in certain individuals with this defect. Isselbacher[45] has identified a uridine-diphosphate galactose pyrophosphorylase in mammalian liver tissue, but not in erythrocytes. While this enzyme could bypass the known usual pathway, its existence in patients with the defect has not been proved. In lieu of an alternate pathway, there might be an incomplete block in the specific transferase. The isolation and purification of the protein enzyme will permit further studies of these problems. Whether there is a reduction in the enzyme per se, an alteration of active receptor sites, or a failure of "maturation" of enzyme activity is unknown. Other unanswered problems concern the clinical significance of the low enzyme levels found in the heterozygote, and the inadequate correlation between enzyme lack and the varied clinical manifestations in the homozygote.

SUMMARY

Hereditary galactose intolerance is an autosomal recessive defect in the specific enzyme, galactose-1-phosphate uridyl transferase. Manifestations in early infancy relate to liver disease, failure to thrive, cataracts and mental retardation. Mellituria and amino-aciduria are present. Avoidance of galactose (lactose) prevents progression of the symptoms and permits normal growth and development. Early recognition of this problem in the newborn period and meticulous dietary control are essential to minimize the toxic effects of the accumulation of galactose-1-phosphate.

REFERENCES

1. Von Reuss, A.: Zuckerausscheidung im Sauglingsalter. Wien. med. Wchnschr. 58:799, 1908.
2. Göppert, F.: Galaktosurie nach Milchzuckergabe bei angeborenem, familiärem, chronischem Leberleiden. Berl. Klin. Wchnschr. 54:473, 1917.
3. Mason, H. H., and Turner, M. E.: Chronic galactemia: report of case with studies on carbohydrates. Am. J. Dis. Child. 50:359, 1935.
4. Goldbloom, A., and Brickman, H. F.: Galactemia. J. Pediat. 28:674, 1946.
5. Donnell, G. N., and Lann, S. H.: Galactosemia. Pediatrics 7:503, 1951.
6. Komrower, G. M., Schwarz, V., Holzel, A., and Goldberg, L.: A clinical and biochemical study of galactosemia. Arch. Dis. Child. 31:254, 1956.
7. Hsia, D. Y.-Y., and Walker, F. A.: Variability in the clinical manifestations of galactosemia. J. Pediat. 59:872, 1961.

8. Townsend, E. H., Jr., Mason, H. H., and Strong, P. S.: Galactosemia and its relation to Laennec's cirrhosis; review of literature and presentation of 6 additional cases. Pediatrics 7:760, 1951.

9. Leloir, L. F.: The metabolism of hexosephosphates. In McElroy, W. D., and Glass, B. (eds.): Symposium on Phosphorus Metabolism. Vol. 1. Baltimore, Johns Hopkins University Press, 1951, p. 67.

10. Leloir, L. F.: Enzymatic transformation of uridine diphosphate glucose into a galactose derivative. Arch. Biochem. 33:186, 1951.

11. Schwarz, V., Goldberg, L., Komrower, G. M., and Holzel, A.: Some disturbances of erythrocyte metabolism in galactosemia. Biochem. J. 62:34, 1956.

12. Kalckar, H. M., Anderson, E. P., and Isselbacher, K. J.: Galactosemia, a congenital defect in a nucleotide transferase: a preliminary report. Proc. Nat. Acad. Sc. 42:49, 1956.

13. Isselbacher, K. J., Anderson, E. P., Kurahashi, K., and Kalckar, H. M.: Congenital galactosemia, a single enzymatic block in galactose metabolism. Science 123:635, 1956.

14. Donnell, G. N., Bergren, W. R., Bretthauer, R. K., and Hansen, R. G.: The enzymatic expression of heterozygosity in families of children with galactosemia. Pediatrics 25:572, 1960.

15. Hansen, R. G., Bretthauer, R. K., Mayes, J., and Nordin, J. H.: Estimation of frequency of occurrence of galactosemia in the population. Proc. Soc. Exper. Biol. & Med. 115:560, 1964.

16. Ritter, J. A., and Cannon, E. J.: Galactosemia with cataracts; report of a case, with notes on physiopathology. New England J. Med. 252:747, 1955.

17. Holzel, A.: Some aspects of galactosemia. Mod. Probl. Paediat. 4:388, 1959 (Bibliotheca Paediatrica, fasc. 70).

18. Donnell, G. N., Collado, M., and Koch, R.: Growth and development of children with galactosemia. J. Pediat. 58:836, 1961.

19. Hugh-Jones, K., Newcomb, A. L., and Hsia, D. Y.-Y.: The genetic mechanism of galactosemia. Arch. Dis. Child. 35:521, 1960.

20. Partridge, S. M., and Westall, R. G.: Filter paper partition chromatography of sugars. Biochem. J. 42:238, 1948.

21. Greenman, L.: Alterations in blood glucose following intravenous galactose. J. Biol. Chem. 183:577, 1950.

22. Mortensen, O., and Søndergaard, G.: Galactosemia (Progress in Pediatrics). Acta Paediat. 43:467, 1954.

23. Isselbacher, K. J.: Galactosemia. In Stanbury, J. B., Wyngaarden, J. B., and Fredrickson, D. S. (ed.): The Metabolic Basis of Inherited Diseases. New York, McGraw-Hill Book Co., Inc., 1960, p. 208.

24. Kirkman, H. N.: Galactosemia. Symposium on hereditary metabolic diseases. Metabolism 9:316, 1960.

25. Weinberg, A. N.: Detection of congenital galactosemia and the carrier state using galactose C14 and blood cells. Metabolism 10:728, 1961.

26. Eggermont, E., and Hers, H. G.: Une nouvelle méthode de détection de la galactosémie congénitale. Clin. Chim. Acta 7:437, 1962.

27. Haworth, J. C., and MacDonald, M. S.: Reducing sugars in the urine and blood of premature babies. Arch. Dis. Child. 32:417, 1957.

28. Holzel, A., Komrower, G. M., and Schwarz, V.: Low-lactose milk for congenital galactosaemia. Lancet 269:92, 1955 (Letter to the Editor).

29. Koch, R., Acosta, P., Ragsdale, N., and Donnell, G. N.: Nutrition in the treatment of galactosemia. J. Am. Diet A. 43:216, 1963.

30. Schwarz, V., Wells, A. R., Holzel, A., and Komrower, G. M.: A study of the genetics of galactosemia. Ann. Hum. Genet. 25:179, 1961.

31. Walker, F. A., Hsia, D. Y.-Y., Slatis, H. M., and Steinberg, A. G.: Galactosemia: a study of twenty-seven kindreds in North America. Ann. Hum. Genet. 25:287, 1962.

32. Bell, L. S., Blair, W. C., Lindsay, S., and Watson, S. J.: Lesions of galactose diabetes; pathological observations. A.M.A. Arch. Path. 49:393, 1950.

33. Crome, L.: A case of galactosaemia with the pathological and neuropathological findings. Arch. Dis. Child. 37:415, 1962.
34. Mitchell, H. S.: Cataracts in rats fed on galactose. Proc. Soc. Exper. Biol. & Med. 32:971, 1935.
35. Craig, J. M., and Maddock, C. E.: Observations on nature of galactose toxicity rats. A.M.A. Arch. Path. 55:118, 1953.
36. Lerman, S.: The lens in human and experimental galactosemia. New York J. Med. 62:785, 1962.
37. Lerman, S.: The lens in congenital galactosemia. A.M.A. Arch. Ophth. 61:88, 1959.
38. Kinoshita, J. H.: Selected topics in ophthalmic biochemistry. A.M.A. Arch. Ophth. 70:558, 1963.
39. Sidbury, J. B., Jr.: The enzymatic lesions in galactosemia. J. Clin. Invest. 36: 929, 1957 (Abstract).
40. Cusworth, D. C., Dent, C. E., and Flynn, F. V.: Amino-aciduria in galactosemia. Arch. Dis. Child. 30:150, 1955.
41. Hsia, D. Y.-Y., Hsia, H. H., Green, S., Kay, M., and Gellis, S. S.: Amino-aciduria in galactosemia. A.M.A. Am. J. Dis. Child. 88:458, 1954.
42. Eisenberg, F., Jr., Isselbacher, K. J., and Kalckar, H. M.: Studies on metabolism of carbon-14-labelled galactose in a galactosemic individual. Science 125: 116, 1957.
43. Segal, S., Blair, A., and Topper, Y. J.: Oxidation of carbon[14] labelled galactose by subjects with congenital galactosemia. Science 136:150, 1962.
44. Ng, W. G., Bergren, W. R., and Donnell, G. N.: Galactose-1-phosphate uridyl transferase activity in galactosemia. Nature 203:845, 1964.
45. Isselbacher, K. J.: Evidence for an accessory pathway of galactose metabolism in mammalian liver. Science 126:652, 1957.
46. Gitzelmann, R., and Auricchio, S.: The handling of soya α-galactosides by a normal and a galactosemic child. Pediatrics 36:231, 1965.

Chapter Nine

HEREDITARY FRUCTOSE INTOLERANCE

Hereditary fructose intolerance (HFI), an uncommon inborn error of metabolism first described in 1956,[1] is characterized by symptoms of substernal pain, nausea, vomiting, malaise, excessive sweating, tremor, confusion, coma and convulsions that follow the ingestion of foods containing fructose.[2] With the continued ingestion of fructose, cirrhosis of the liver, with fatty infiltration, proteinuria, amino-aciduria and brain damage may ensue.[3-7] Although the incidence is not known, more than 40 patients with HFI have been described in detail, many in the last few years. Froesch and associates[6] were the first to describe fully the symptoms of this condition and to find that, in the patients affected, the administration of fructose lowered the level of glucose in blood. These authors also postulated the primary defect to be the absence of fructose-1-phosphate aldolase in the liver. Subsequently, Hers and Joassin,[8] Nikkilä et al.,[9] and Froesch et al.,[2] found a marked reduction in the activity of this enzyme in the liver. That the secondary hypoglucosemia is due to an inhibition of hepatic glucose release and is not a result of insulin secretion has been shown by assays of insulin,[2, 10, 11] by a lack of a hyperglycemic response following glucagon administration,[7, 11] and by indirect measures of glucose output from the liver.[12] In the majority of families studied, an autosomal recessive mode of inheritance has been suggested.

In addition to those in England and Switzerland, patients with HFI have been reported from Germany,[13] France,[3, 4] Finland,[7] Belgium,[12] Italy[14] and the United States,[11, 15] indicating a wide distribution of this genetic defect. There are probably a number of unrecognized cases of HFI since the patients develop a strong aversion for any sweet foods, and

177

symptoms occur only after the ingestion of fructose or fructose-containing food, e.g., sucrose (table sugar) which breaks down to glucose and fructose, fruits, honey, and similar foods.

CLINICAL MANIFESTATIONS

A variety of clinical signs and symptoms have been described in patients with hereditary fructose intolerance. The manifestations depend upon age, severity of the disease, and other, still undefined, factors. In some patients gastrointestinal symptoms predominate, while others show evidences of hypoglucosemia. If fructose-containing foods are avoided, the patients remain perfectly well and free of symptoms.

Young Infants

The most severe manifestations of this syndrome may occur in the young infant who is given either sucrose (as the carbohydrate supplement to his artificial formula) or fruits or fruit juices. Breast-fed infants remain symptom free. Generally, the firstborn infant with the disease may die or may suffer more than subsequently affected siblings, who profit from the experience of the parents and the physician with the first child.

In the first few months of life, the infant may have signs of failure to thrive, prolonged vomiting, anorexia, frequent attacks of hypoglycemia, occasional unconsciousness, and convulsions.[3, 4, 12] The vomitus may be blood-stained. On examination, the infants are often cachectic, stunted in growth, and jaundiced and have hepatosplenomegaly. If fructose-containing feeds are continued, the symptoms progress and death may ensue. These infants may have elevated bilirubin levels, abnormal liver function tests, anemia, albuminuria and amino-aciduria. On biopsy, increased fibrosis and fatty infiltration of the liver have been described.[5] Hypoglucosemia is frequent, as are hyperfructosemia and fructosuria after either an oral tolerance test or ingestion of fructose in the diet. Elevations of plasma free fatty acids and lactic acid have been found as well.

Some infants may have milder signs and symptoms if only minimal amounts of fructose are offered or if their disease is less marked. Thus, the clinical syndrome of HFI in the infant may vary a great deal.

Early diagnosis of this condition is mandatory. All the clinical and all the abnormal laboratory findings appear to be reversible once fructose has been removed from the diet. The more seriously ill infants have been reported from Europe.[3, 4, 7] One explanation for this might be that, in Europe, sucrose (glucose and fructose) is used more commonly as the carbohydrate added to artificial feeding than in the United States, where syrups containing dextrins or maltose are used.

In instances in which the affected infants can reject or select foods, the majority develop a profound aversion to and distaste for anything sweet, thus protecting themselves from the toxic effects of fructose. This is particularly true in the adult in whom a chronic syndrome has never been reported, because he has learned what food to avoid.

The Older Child and Adult

In the older child and adult with HFI, fructose taken orally produces a varying response. Some patients may have severe epigastric pain, nausea, bloating, vomiting and even diarrhea, with or without the symptoms specifically associated with hypoglycemia. Others, especially adults, may have little gastrointestinal discomfort and manifest only a delayed hypoglucosemic response. Of interest is the observation that no severe gastrointestinal reactions, except for mild epigastric discomfort, have been observed following *intravenous* administration of fructose in patients with HFI. Epigastric pain has also been noted in 12 of 19 *normal* adults after 50 grams of fructose were rapidly infused intravenously within a period of 20 minutes.[16]

The patients with HFI usually have excellent teeth, with a minimal number of caries.[2, 11] This is especially evident when patients are compared to nonaffected siblings.

DIAGNOSIS

The diagnosis of HFI is dependent upon a high index of suspicion and a careful history. In the infant, the onset of vomiting, drowsiness and coma date from the introduction of fructose into the diet. In contrast to the infant with galactosemia (see Chapter Eight), the neonate with HFI remains perfectly well on breast feedings. In the older child and adult, there is a history of a marked avoidance of sweets and of symptoms only following the ingestion of fructose-containing foods.

In the symptomatic young infant, a low blood glucose, an elevated blood fructose and fructosuria following the ingestion of fructose establish the diagnosis. A complete reversal of symptoms occurs when fructose is eliminated from the diet.

Benign Fructosuria

Hereditary fructose intolerance is quite different from benign fructosuria, which is due to a deficiency of the enzyme fructokinase and also results in high levels of fructose and fructosuria.[17] In benign fructosuria the patients are perfectly well and have no clinical disease.

Laboratory Diagnosis

Intravenous Fructose Tolerance Test. In the asymptomatic individual an intravenous fructose tolerance test (0.25 gm./kg.) will produce a fall in the level of inorganic phosphorus in plasma and a prolonged hypoglucosemia; this may be overlooked if one does not use a method specific for measuring glucose alone rather than all reducing sugars (see page 36) (Fig. 46). Because of the severe and often prolonged intestinal symptoms associated with the oral test, the intravenous test is the method of choice in establishing the diagnosis.

Oral Fructose Tolerance Test. If an oral fructose tolerance test (0.5 to 1.75 gm./kg.) is done, prolonged and elevated levels of fructose, free fatty acids, lactic acid, and growth hormone may follow, with a decline in the values for glucose, inorganic phosphorus and insulin in plasma (Fig. 47).[11]

Fructosuria may be present after either tolerance test, but the amount

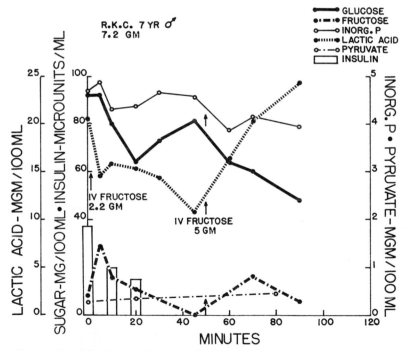

Figure 46. Intravenous fructose tolerance test in Case 1, resulting in a fall in the levels of glucose, inorganic phosphorus and insulin. Significant elevations of fructose and lactic acid levels occurred simultaneously. (From Cornblath et al., New England J. Med. *269*:1271, 1963.

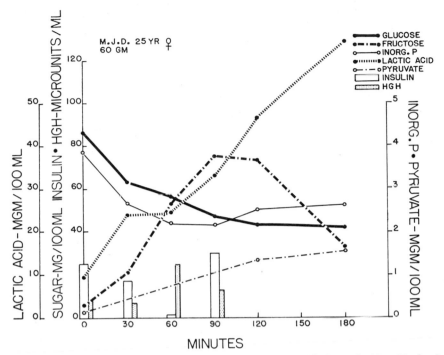

Figure 47.   Oral fructose tolerance test. (From Cornblath et al., New England J. Med. 269:1271, 1963.)

detectable in the urine does not exceed 3 to 5 per cent of the administered load.[7]

THERAPY

Therapy is simple and consists of the total elimination of fructose and all potential sources of fructose from the diet. (See Appendix I for fructose-free diet). Intravenous glucose may be given to treat the acute symptoms, which are due to hypoglucosemia, if the patient inadvertently eats or is given food containing fructose. There is no specific therapy for the intestinal manifestations. Some patients, as they become older, can tolerate small but increasing amounts of fructose.

GENETICS

Hereditary fructose intolerance occurs in both sexes and is, therefore, not sex-linked. Siblings may be affected but except for one family,[13] the parents and children of the patients have been reported as healthy. These findings support the original contention of Froesch et al.[6] that the mode of inheritance is of the autosomal recessive type. The finding of a father and son with HFI by Wolf et al.[13] and the pedigree of the 5 patients described by Cornblath et al.[11] raise some question as to whether a dominant mode of inheritance with variable penetrance may be an alternative explanation. The exact genetic analysis of affected families is impossible until methods are developed to identify the heterozygotic person or the member with incomplete expressivity.

PATHOGENESIS

Before discussing the enzymatic deficiency and its secondary consequences in HFI, a brief description of the normal metabolism of fructose seems appropriate. As illustrated in Figure 48, fructose may be phosphorylated in the liver and intestine by a specific fructokinase at the 1-position or by a nonspecific hexokinase at the 6-position. In other tissues of the body, phosphorylation of fructose occurs only at the 6-position. Glucose inhibits the phosphorylation of fructose in muscle, erythrocytes and leukocytes, but not in adipose tissue.[17] In the liver and intestine, fructose-1-phosphate (F-1-P), in the presence of F-1-P aldolase (1-phosphofructaldolase) is split into the two trioses, glyceraldehyde and dihydroxyacetone phosphate, which may enter the glycolytic cycle. On the other hand, fructose-6-phosphate may be phosphorylated again by phosphofructokinase and ATP to fructose-1-6-diphosphate (F-1-6-diP) in the pathway common to the catabolism of glucose, galactose and glycogen (Fig. 49). The F-1-6-diphosphate is split to dihydroxyacetone phosphate and glyceraldehyde phosphate by (1-6-diphosphofructaldolase). Currently, controversy exists as to whether both aldolase activities are the result of a single enzyme or of two distinct enzymes.[8, 19-21] Another prob-

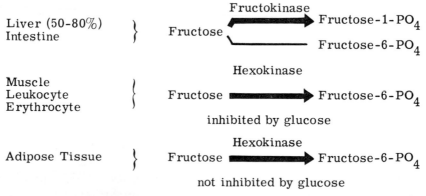

Figure 48.   Normal fructose metabolism.

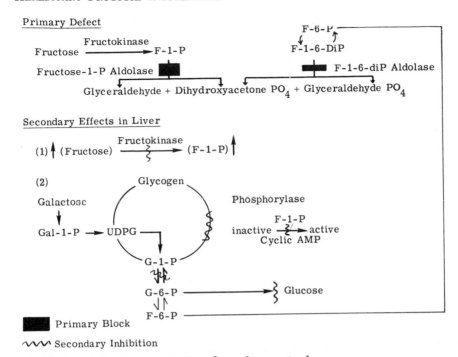

Figure 49. Hereditary fructose intolerance.

lem is that F-1-6-diP aldolase activity is diminished, but to a significantly lesser degree than that of F-1-P aldolase, in the liver of patients with HFI (Fig. 49).

All the evidence supports the concept that the primary enzymatic deficiency in hereditary fructose intolerance is a marked reduction in fructose-1-phosphate aldolase activity in hepatic parenchymal cells[2, 8, 9, 17] and also in the cells of the intestinal villi.[22] As a result of the enzyme deficiency, fructose-1-phosphate accumulates in the liver and intestine and inhibits fructokinase,[2, 6] accounting for the high blood levels of fructose seen after the ingestion of fructose. Ultimately 80 to 90 per cent of the fructose is utilized, probably in the adipose tissue.[2] The mechanism of the gastrointestinal symptoms remains obscure, although the accumulation of fructose-1-phosphate in the brush border of the small intestine may be indirectly responsible.

The exact metabolic defect responsible for the low levels of blood glucose is less evident. The data indicate that the hypoglucosemia results from a block in hepatic glucose output due to the secondary inhibition of a rate-limiting enzyme and not from an increase in the peripheral utilization of glucose due to insulin secretion. The studies that support the concept of a block in hepatic glucose output are of two kinds. First, the original investigations by Dubois et al.[12] demonstrated a decreased rate of disappearance of a dose of intravenous glucose administered after fructose in a patient with HFI. Furthermore, in a patient with HFI given C[14]-labeled glucose intravenously, the slope of the decline in the specific activity of radioactive glucose diminished significantly after fructose administration, indicating that dilution of the glucose pool by nonlabeled hepatic glucose was markedly diminished. Second, whereas the patient with HFI responds to glucagon with a significant hyperglycemia when he is either fasting or at the end of a glucose tolerance test, he does not show a hyperglycemic response to glucagon after the ingestion of fructose[2, 7, 11] (Fig. 50). The evidence against an increased utilization of glucose is the diminished disappearance rates cited above and the lack of change or actual fall in the level of insulin as measured by immunoassay after fructose.[2, 10, 11] (See Figures 46 and 47.)

The site of the secondary enzymatic block in the liver responsible for the hypoglucosemia has also been investigated. On the basis of *in vitro* studies, F-1-P was found to inhibit phosphoglucomutase.[23] However, the increase in the level of blood glucose after intravenous galactose in these patients indicates that the secondary block in glucose output by the liver is not due to the inhibition of phosphoglucomutase or glucose-6-phosphatase[11, 24] (Fig. 51). In addition, Hers[25] has reported an increase in glucose-6-phosphatase activity in livers from patients with HFI. Therefore, it would appear that the fructose-1-phosphate that accumulates as a result of the primary enzymatic deficiency inhibits glycogenolysis either at the phosphorylase or debrancher (amylo 1-6 glucosidase) reactions. Fructose-

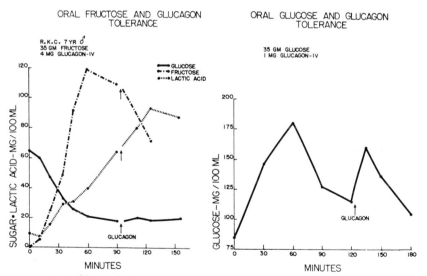

Figure 50. Test with 4 mg. of glucagon administered intravenously in Case 1, resulting in no elevation in the blood level of glucose 90 minutes after fructose given by mouth. However, 2 hours after the ingestion of glucose, 1 mg. of glucagon produced significant hyperglycemia. (From Cornblath et al., New England J. Med., 269:1271, 1963.)

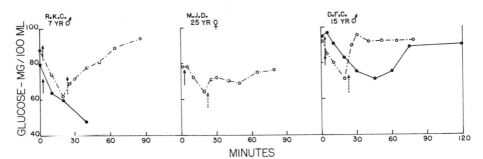

Figure 51. Intravenous administration of galactose in three patients with hereditary fructose intolerance, producing a prompt rise in the level of blood glucose previously depressed by intravenously infused fructose. The duration of the hypoglycemia was shortened after galactose administration as compared with that after fructose alone in Case 1 (R. K. C.) and Case 2 (D. F. C.). (From Cornblath et al., New England J. Med. *269*:1271, 1963.)

1-phosphate, in 3×10^{-5} molar concentrations, inhibits the activation of phosphorylase by cyclic 3′,5′ adenosine monophosphate (cyclic AMP) *in vitro*, while fructose does not.[26] It would appear that the mechanism of the hypoglycemia is a result of the accumulation of fructose-1-phosphate which, in turn, inhibits phosphorylase breakdown of glycogen in liver. Confirmation of this observation is necessary *in vivo*, with data on the quantities of fructose 1-phosphate which accumulate as well as data on phosphorylase activity in liver biopsies of patients with HFI after a fructose load.

In addition, an inhibition of gluconeogenesis could contribute to the hypoglucosemia. It has been shown *in vitro* that F-1-P does inhibit F-1-6-diphosphofructaldolase[2] and that the activity of this enzyme was reduced in some liver biopsy samples from patients with HFI.[2, 8, 9] Recently, a block in the conversion of dihydroxyacetone phosphate to glucose has been reported in patients with HFI.[24] More data are needed to evaluate whether and where the interruption in gluconeogenesis occurs and what the mechanism might be.

Since the secretion of growth hormone (HGH) occurred in normal individuals following hypoglycemia induced by the administration of insulin,[27] of particular interest was the elevation in plasma growth hormone levels which followed the induction of hypoglycemia by fructose in patients with HFI.[11] In this way it was possible to demonstrate that the secretion of growth hormone was in response to hypoglucosemia without a change in the plasma insulin concentration. The increase in the levels of free fatty acids in plasma may result from the intracellular hypoglucosemia in adipose tissue triggering lipolysis, or from elevated amounts of growth hormone and the secretion of epinephrine in response to the hypoglucosemia. The elevated levels of lactic acid found may also be due to the action of epinephrine on muscle phosphorylase. In addition, elevations in the magnesium levels in plasma have been found after fructose ingestion.[28] Thus, the patient with HFI may manifest a wide variety of metabolic aberrations if given fructose. Additional investigations of these various parameters in patients with this relatively rare congenital enzymatic defect may elucidate fundamental mechanisms in carbohydrate metabolism.

Case Reports

Case 1. R. K. C., a 7 year old boy, was referred to the University of Illinois Research and Educational Hospitals because of symptoms of hypoglycemia. A careful history revealed that he became nauseated and vomited, perspired excessively and became pale and drowsy after the ingestion of "sweets," such as candy, cake, cookies, gum and ice cream. On additional questioning it was found that similar symptoms followed the ingestion of fruits, for example, oranges, apples and grapes. These symptoms were first noticed at the age of 2 months, when orange juice was added to the diet. The patient was breast fed until the age of 6 months and then placed on a regimen of whole milk without added sugar. No difficulties were noted after the ingestion of cereals, meats and vegetables, but the ingestion of fruits repeatedly caused symptoms. Since the mother had experienced similar difficulties with two of her older children, she eliminated the foods that were not tolerated from the child's diet. Until the age of 5 years, nausea and vomiting developed immediately after the ingestion of foods containing fructose. After vomiting, the patient always requested additional food, which he thought would make him feel better. After the age of 5 years the mother noted some change in the symptoms. More pronounced pallor, excessive sweating and nausea developed before vomiting occurred. After vomiting, the patient became drowsy and fell into a deep sleep for a period of 30 to 60 minutes. On awakening, he usually felt well. A physician consulted because of the change in symptoms referred the patient to this hospital.

Intellectual development has been normal and the boy was in the second grade. On examination in the clinic there were no evident abnormalities except for height and weight: he was 109 cm. tall (less than the third percentile) and weighed 20 kg. (tenth percentile). The blood pressure was 120/60. He was admitted to the hospital for special studies because of the possibility of hereditary fructose intolerance.

Urinalysis gave negative tests for protein, sugar and acetone. The hemoglobin was 13 gm./100 ml., and the hematocrit 37 per cent. The white cell count was 5400/mm.[3], with a normal differential. The total protein was 7.4 gm./100 ml. (with an albumin of 5.2 and a globulin of 2.2 gm./100 ml.); the cholesterol, 225 mg./100 ml.; and the bilirubin, 0.29 mg./100 ml. The serum electrolytes were normal. Enzyme studies on serum revealed normal levels of glutamic oxalacetic transaminase (SGOT) and glutamic pyruvic transaminase (SGPT), lactic dehydrogenase, aldolase, isocitric dehydrogenase, phosphohexose isomerase, malic dehydrogenase, and glutamic reductase.

Thirty minutes after an oral fructose tolerance test (50 gm. per square meter of body surface area) the patient complained of abdominal pain, sleepiness and hunger. He became pale and drowsy and sweated profusely; vomiting occurred after 90 minutes. He subsequently became semicomatose but responded dramatically to glucose administered intravenously.

After the ingestion of fructose, there was a marked fall in the level of glucose from 65 to 18 mg./100 ml. and a rise in fructose from 0 to 109 mg./100 ml. and in lactate from 9.9 to 64 mg./100 ml. No significant changes in serum enzyme activities were found after the oral tolerance test. Electroencephalograms taken with the patient awake and asleep revealed no abnormalities.

Case 2. D. F. C. the 15 year old brother of Case 1, also became ill and vomited after the ingestion of fruits or other food containing fructose. The neonatal course had been normal. He was breast fed and did well until orange juice was introduced into the diet at 8 weeks of age. Orange juice repeatedly induced vomiting and was therefore discontinued by the mother. No other fruits were introduced during the first year of life. He was weaned at the age of 6 months from the breast to cow's milk without added sugar and had no difficulty. The mother subsequently noticed that he could not tolerate fruits or foods containing cane sugar and, without medical advice, she eliminated these foods from the diet. As he became older the patient avoided these foods by choice. Intellectual development was normal. He weighed 54.5 kg. (fortieth percentile) and was 163 cm. tall (twenty-fifth percentile). Sexual development was normal for his age. During the past year he had become able to tolerate small amounts of foods containing sucrose or fructose without vomiting. Laboratory studies revealed a normal blood count and the urinalysis was negative. Alkaline phosphatase, SGOT, thymol turbidity, cephalin flocculation, cholesterol and bilirubin were within normal limits.

An oral fructose tolerance test resulted in severe nausea and abdominal discomfort after 20 minutes. He perspired profusely. Symptoms were relieved by intravenous glucose. Subsequently, he again became nauseated, vomited and then slept for 4 hours. The blood glucose fell from 82 to 51 mg./100 ml., the plasma inorganic phosphorus, from 4.08 to 2.09 mg./100 ml.; the blood fructose rose from 0 to 34 mg./100 ml. and the blood lactate from 16.4 to 36.0 mg./100 ml. Intravenously administered fructose produced a marked fall in blood glucose, without symptoms (Fig. 6, D. F. C.).

Case 3. J. C., the 9 year old sister of the proband, was evaluated because of symptoms similar to those of her brothers. In her, too, symptoms developed at the age of 8 weeks when she first took orange juice. She had been breast fed until 5 months of age and then placed on whole milk. The mother noticed that she, like her older brother, did not tolerate fruits. In contrast to her younger brother, she had an intense distaste for sweets and fruits and had avoided these foods completely. Intellectual development had been excellent. She was in the fourth grade. No abnormalities were found on physical examination except for a mild degree of understature. She weighed 28.6 kg. (forty-seventh percentile) and was 127 cm. tall (tenth percentile).

Routine laboratory analyses showed a normal blood count, negative urinalysis and normal values for SGOT, cephalin flocculation, thymol turbidity, cholesterol and bilirubin. After oral administration of fructose, she developed abdominal pain, sleepiness and hunger within 30 minutes. Soon thereafter, she became pale and drowsy, sweated profusely and became semicomatose. Her blood glucose levels were below 30 mg./100 ml. at this time. She responded dramatically to intravenous glucose, although abdominal pain persisted for many hours.

Case 4. M. J. D., a 26 year old woman, was a first cousin of the proband. (She was the daughter of the proband's mother's brother.) Her story came out during a survey of the relatives of the original three patients. This patient also became ill, with nausea and vomiting, after the ingestion of foods containing sucrose or fructose. She perspired profusely and became so weak that it was necessary for her to go to bed.

She had been born prematurely, weighing 1050 gm., and was hospitalized for a period of 3 months. She was placed on an evaporated milk formula containing Dextri-Maltose, which was well tolerated. Orange juice was introduced at the age of 3½ months and immediately produced severe vomiting. Other fruits were also noted to induce vomiting and were eliminated from the diet by the mother. It was found subsequently that any food containing cane sugar caused vomiting, and these foods were eliminated from the diet.

An aversion to anything sweet, including fruits and foods containing sucrose, soon developed, and the patient had avoided these foods. She was a college graduate and worked as a chemist. Physical development had been normal, and she weighed 76 kg. and was 163 cm. tall.

Laboratory tests revealed a negative urinalysis, a cephalin flocculation of +, a thymol turbidity of 3.3 units and a cholesterol of 204 mg./100 ml. The results of the patient's oral fructose tolerance test are shown in Figure 47: she developed nausea and bloating within 20 minutes but did not vomit. After 2 hours (blood glucose was 43 mg./100 ml.), she became dyslexic and dysphonic, then sleepy and semicomatose. She responded promptly to the administration of intravenous glucose.

A male sibling of this patient had died at 11 months of age with convulsions; postmortem examination revealed cirrhosis of the liver. It is not clear from the history whether this infant had had intolerance to fructose.

Case 5. J. A. C., an 18 year old woman, also had symptoms and was discovered during the family survey. She was a distant cousin of Cases 1 to 3 on the mother's side. She became ill, with nausea and vomiting, after the ingestion of foods containing fructose. The symptoms were first seen in infancy after the introduction into the diet of orange juice. Subsequently, the mother noted that she was intolerant also to other fruits and to foods containing sucrose. These foods were eliminated from the diet, and she had a marked aversion to sweets. At the time of the survey she was in college and doing well. Physical development had been normal; she was 152 cm. tall (third percentile) and weighed 45 kg. (tenth percentile).

Analysis of her urine was negative; the alkaline phosphatase, cholesterol, SGOT, thymol turbidity, cephalin flocculation and bilirubin values were within normal limits.

Fifteen minutes after the ingestion of fructose, she complained of nausea and abdominal pain, which persisted for about 1 hour. She vomited at 1 hour, but never developed signs or symptoms of hypoglycemia. Her blood glucose was never less than 80 mg./100 ml., yet the fructose level rose to 31 mg./100 ml. and inorganic phosphorous fell from 3.96 to 2.28 mg./100 ml. In 13 controls given equal amounts of fructose, the level of fructose did not exceed 9 ± 5.3 mg./100 ml. (mean ± 1 S.D.).

Brief histories of 5 patients have been presented to illustrate the variety of clinical manifestations as well as the change in symptomatology that occurs with age. The first 3 patients had both severe gastrointestinal manifestations and hypoglucosemia, yet the oldest boy is now beginning to tolerate small quantities of fructose. Patient 4 (M. J. D.) had minimal intestinal discomfort and delayed profound hypoglycemia (Fig. 47), whereas patient 5 (J. A. C.) had abdominal symptoms but never developed hypoglucosemia.

SUMMARY

Since its recent description, a new metabolic disorder, hereditary fructose intolerance, has been shown to be relatively uncommon but of wide distribution. The defect in HFI appears to be a marked reduction in the activity of fructose-1-phosphate aldolase in the liver and intestine resulting in epigastric pain, bloating, nausea and vomiting after the ingestion of fructose, and severe hypoglucosemia with its concomitant drowsiness, coma and convulsions as a result of a secondary block in hepatic glucose output. A careful history makes the presence of this condition self-evident and simple tolerance tests confirm the diagnosis.

If unrecognized in early infancy, hereditary fructose intolerance can be responsible for severe failure to thrive, protracted vomiting, hepatosplenomegaly, stunted growth and development and, ultimately, death. Therefore, since all these complications are reversible with removal of fructose from the diet, it is critical that the diagnosis be made and therapy instituted promptly in young infants.

REFERENCES

1. Chambers, R. A., and Pratt, R. T. C.: Idiosyncrasy to fructose. Lancet 2:340, 1956.
2. Froesch, E. R., Wolf, H. P., Baitsch, H., Prader, A., and Labhart, A.: Hereditary fructose intolerance. An inborn defect of hepatic fructose-1-phosphate splitting aldolase. Am. J. Med. 34:151, 1963.
3. Jeune, M., Planson, E., Cotte, J., Bonnefoy, S., Nivelon, J. L., and Skosowsky, J.: L'intolérance héréditaire au fructose. Pédiatrie 16:605, 1961.
4. Lelong, M., Alagille, D., Gentil, C., Colin, J., Tupin, J., and Bouquier, J.: Cirrhose hépatique et tubulopathie par absence congénitale de l'aldolase hépatique. Bull. et mém. Soc. méd. hôp. Paris 113:58, 1962.
5. Lelong, M., Alagille, D., Gentil, J., Colin, J., Mercie, C., Tupin, J., and Bouquier, J.: L'intolérance héréditaire au fructose. Arch. franç. pédiat. 19:841, 1962.
6. Froesch, E. R., Prader, A., Labhart, R., Stuber, H. W., and Wolf, H. P.: Die hereditäre Fructoseintoleranz, eine bisher nicht bekannte kongenitale Stoffwechselstörung. Schweiz. med. Wchnschr. 87:1168, 1957.
7. Perheentupa, J., Pitkänen, E., Nikkilä, E. A., Somersalo, O., and Hakosalo, J.: Hereditary fructose intolerance. A clinical study of four cases. Ann. Paediat. Fenn. 8:221, 1962.
8. Hers, H. G., and Joassin, G.: Anomalie de l'aldolase hépatique dans l'intolérance au fructose. Enzymol. biol. Clin. 1:4, 1961.
9. Nikkilä, E. A., Somersalo, O., Pitkänen, E., and Perheentupa, J.: Hereditary fructose intolerance, an inborn deficiency of liver aldolase complex. Metabolism 11:727, 1962.
10. Samols, E., and Dormandy, T. L.: Insulin response to fructose and galactose. Lancet 1:478, 1963.
11. Cornblath, M., Rosenthal, I. M., Reisner, S. H., Wybregt, S. H., and Crane, R. K.: Hereditary fructose intolerance. New England J. Med. 269:1271, 1963.
12. Dubois, R., Loeb, H., Ooms, H. A., Gillet, P., Bartman, J., and Champenois, A.:

Étude d'un cas d'hypoglycémie fonctionnelle par intolérance au fructose. Helvet. paediat. Acta 16:90, 1961.

13. Wolf, H., Zschocke, D., Wedemeyer, F. W., and Hübner, W.: Angeborene hereditäre Fructose-intoleranz. Klin. Wchnschr. 37:693, 1959.

14. Corsini, F.: L'intolleranza congenita al fruttosio. Clin. pediat. (Bologna) 42:716, 1960.

15. Doherty, R. A., Williams, H. E., and Field, R. A.: Hereditary fructose intolerance. J. Pediat. 63:721, 1963 (Abstract).

16. Saxon, L., and Papper, S.: Abdominal pain occurring during the rapid administration of fructose solutions. New England J. Med. 256:132, 1957.

17. Schapira, F., Schapira, G., and Dreyfus, J. C.: La lésion enzymatique de la fructosurie bénigne. Enzymol. biol. Clin. 1:170, 1962.

18. Froesch, E. R., and Ginsberg, J. L.: Fructose metabolism of adipose tissue. 1. Comparison of fructose and glucose metabolism in epididymal adipose tissue of normal rats. J. Biol. Chem. 237:3317, 1962.

19. Kaletta-Gmünder, U., Wolf, H. P., and Leuthardt, F.: Ueber aldolasen. II. Chromatographische Trennung von 1-phosphofructaldolase und diphosphofructaldolase der Leber. Helvet. chem. Acta 40:1027, 1957.

20. Peanasky, R. J., and Lardy, H. A.: Bovine liver aldolase. I. Isolation, crystallization and some general properties. J. Biol. Chem. 233:365, 1958.

21. Dahlqvist, A., and Crane, R. K.: The influence of the method of assay on the apparent specificity of rabbit-liver aldolase. Biochim. et Biophys. Acta 85:132, 1964.

22. Froesch, E. R.: Personal communication.

23. Sidbury, J. B., Jr.: Zur Biochemie der hereditären Fructoseintoleranz. Helvet. paediat. Acta 14:317, 1959 (Letter to the Editor).

24. Gentil, C., Colin, J., Valette, A. M., Alagille, D., and Lelong, M.: Étude du métabolisme glucidique au cours de l'intolérance héréditaire au fructose. Essai d'interprétation de l'hypoglucosémie. Rev. franç. Étud. clin. biol. 9:596, 1964.

25. Hers, H. G.: Augmentation de l'activité de la glucose-6-phosphatase dans l'intolérance au fructose. Rev. int. Hépat. 12:777, 1962.

26. Sutherland, E. W., and Cornblath, M.: Unpublished observations.

27. Roth, J., Glick, S. M., Yalow, R. S., and Berson, S. A.: Hypoglycemia: a potent stimulus to secretion of growth hormone. Science 140:987, 1963.

28. Levin, B., Oberholzer, V. G., Snodgrass, G. J. A. I., Stimmler, L., and Wilmers, M. J.: Fructosaemia, an inborn error of fructose metabolism. Arch. Dis. Child. 38:220, 1963.

Hypoglycemic Syndromes in Infancy

Chapter Ten

GENERAL CONSIDERATIONS

Hypoglycemia is relatively rare beyond the neonatal period. When it occurs and persists, however, it may be a catastrophic insult to the central nervous system, particularly in infants under 6 months of age. Therefore, it is important to consider the possibility of hypoglycemia in any situation in which the signs or symptoms are compatible with an inadequate supply of glucose to the brain. If the diagnosis is established, steps must be taken at once to achieve normoglycemia.

Hypoglycemia is significant when the concentration of glucose, or true sugar, in the blood is below 40 mg./100 ml. in the infant or child whether or not clinical manifestations are present.[1] In the full-sized newborn, levels of blood glucose lower than 30 mg./100 ml. during the first 72 hours of life and less than 40 mg./100 ml. thereafter are considered abnormally low[2, 3] (see p. 45). In the low birth weight neonate, values lower than 20 mg./100 ml. are significant.[4] The hypoglycemia may be symptomatic and associated with one or more of the following clinical manifestations: listlessness, apathy, irritability, pallor, sweating, weakness, hunger, headache, visual disturbances, mental confusion, coma, convulsions, or repetitive bizarre behavior.[1, 5, 6] If signs and symptoms are of short duration, are documented by low blood sugar values, and disappear promptly with the administration of glucose, the diagnosis of symptomatic hypoglycemia is established.

INCIDENCE

The hypoglycemic syndromes in infancy are poorly defined and their incidence is virtually unknown. However, among 6000 pediatric admis-

Table 18.   Causes of Hypoglycemia
in Children

University of Gothenburg 1958-59[7]	
Epinephrine deficiency	5
Leucine sensitivity	2
Idiopathic	4
Total	11

sions within a 2-year period to a general university hospital in Sweden, Broberger and Zetterström[7] discovered 11 patients with spontaneous hypoglycemia recurring beyond the neonatal period (Table 18). Between 1950 and 1965 at the University of Minnesota, Sauds and Ulstrom[8] reviewed 100 infants and young children with spontaneous hypoglycemia (Table 19). In both series, the frequency was approximately 180 to 200 per 100,000 of hospital admissions. Although the actual incidence of this relatively rare condition is unknown, it appears to be much lower than that of transient hypoglycemia found in the neonate[9] (see p. 83).

The prolonged interval between onset of symptoms and correct diagnosis reported in most studies indicates that the possibility of symptomatic spontaneous hypoglycemia has not received proper consideration early in the course of many clinical situations. Therefore, whenever repetitive, episodic, bizarre manifestations occur at any time, whether after a fast, an acute illness, or shortly after meals, a blood sugar level should

Table 19.   Causes of Hypoglycemia in Children
1 Week to 15 Years (The University of
Minnesota 1950–1965)[8]

Idiopathic		72
1. Familial	17	
2. Leucine–sensitive	7	
3. Infant giants (two leucine sensitive)	3	
4. Transient hypoglycemia of prematurity	2	
5. Ketotic hypoglycemia	31	
6. Unclassified	12	
Glycogenoses		6
Galactosemia		4
Congential adrenal hyperplasia		4
Addison's disease		1
Cretinism		3
Islet cell adenoma (two leucine–sensitive)		2
Severe liver disease		2
Central nervous system disease (one leucine–sensitive)		4
Trisomy 13–15		1
Prediabetes		1
Total		100

be obtained at the time of symptoms. Every patient with unexplained convulsions or coma should have a blood and spinal fluid sugar determination at the time of the first episode. Only in this way can the diagnosis be established and therapy instituted early, thus avoiding the sequelae of prolonged hypoglycemia.

Age of Onset

The age of onset of proven hypoglycemia is a very important factor in probing the etiology. As shown in Figure 52, the more usual types of hypoglycemia, with onset under 6 months of age, include neonatal symptomatic, leucine sensitive, and familial. With an onset after 18 months of life, the probability is ketotic hypoglycemia; after 4 years of age, tumors of the pancreatic islet cells and functional hypoglycemia predominate. This age element is important in planning the initial diagnostic investigation of the individual patient. If the definitive diagnosis of the type of hypoglycemia is not established, then further consideration of the other types of hypoglycemia is necessary because of the overlap in the age distribution. Current concepts of carbohydrate physiology and metabolism have been utilized in devising the comprehensive differential diagnosis of spontaneous symptomatic hypoglycemia of infancy.

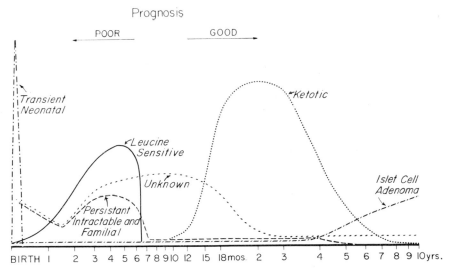

Figure 52. Schematic representation of the age distribution of the various types of idiopathic hypoglycemia. No true incidence data are available and the maxima are gross approximations. It should be noted that the age scale has been artificially manipulated for graphic presentation. The prognosis for transient neonatal hypoglycemia is unknown; however, the persistent types with onset before age 6 months incur a poor prognosis.

CLASSIFICATION

Once the diagnosis of hypoglycemia has been established, the cause of the low blood sugar level must be ascertained because the type of treatment and its efficacy depend on understanding of the pathogenesis. Previous investigators have suggested a variety of classifications of these disorders.[1, 5, 6, 10, 11]

    I. ENDOCRINE

        A. *Deficiencies*

            1. Growth hormone

            2. Thyroid

            3. Corticosteroid

                a. Congenital adrenal hyperplasia

                b. Addison's disease (atrophy or destruction)

            4. Epinephrine?

            5. Glucagon?

        B. *Excess*

            1. Insulin

                a. Infants of diabetic mothers

                b. Islet cell adenoma

                c. Hyperplasia of beta cells

                d. Prediabetes mellitus

    II. METABOLIC

        A. *Hereditary*

            1. Glycogen storage diseases (see Chapter Seven)

            2. Galactose intolerance (see Chapter Eight)

            3. Fructose intolerance (see Chapter Nine)

            4. Glycogen synthetase deficiency (see Chapter Seven)

            5. Cystinosis

        B. *Acquired*

            1. Fatty degeneration of liver

            2. Hepatitis, cirrhosis

            3. Malnutrition

                a. Kwashiorkor

                b. Low phenylalanine diet

        C. *Poisoning or Toxic*

            1. Alcohol

            2. Salicylate

            3. Oral hypoglycemic agents, e.g., tolbutamide

            4. Insulin

            5. Blighia sapidum (hypoglycin), Jamaican vomiting sickness

    III. MISCELLANEOUS

        A. *Tumors*

            1. Fibrosarcoma

N-LABSTIX for Routine Urinalysis.

TRADE MARK

Where bacteriuria is significant ---------

    2. Wilms' tumor
    3. Islet cell tumors
    4. Hepatomas
  B. *Central Nervous System*
    1. Tumors
    2. Thalamic lesions
    3. Hemorrhage
  C. *Cold Injury*
  D. *Renal Glycosuria*
IV. IDIOPATHIC
    1. Transient in neonate (see Chapter Five)
    2. Infant "giants" (Ulstrom) or *foetopathia diabetica* (see
       Chapter Five)
    3. Leucine sensitive
    4. Familial
    5. Lack of epinephrine response?
    6. Sporadic ketotic
    7. Unknown

DIAGNOSIS

Many of the possibilities listed above can be eliminated by a careful
history and physical examination. The history should detail the character
of the symptoms and signs and, equally important, the time of occurrence
in relation to meals, illness or periods of fasting. The association of manifestations with intake of a specific type of food is also pertinent, e.g., collapse following the ingestion of sweets in hereditary fructose intolerance,
or clinical manifestations following a high protein meal in leucine sensitive
hypoglycemia. A carefully taken family history that reveals convulsions,
bizarre behavior and hypoglycemia may be very significant. No positive
family history has been noted with isolated islet cell tumors, but a familial
occurrence of multiple endocrine adenomata has been reported.[12] Questions should be asked about the possible ingestion of alcohol, aspirin or
tolbutamide. A careful physical examination may reveal stigmata of the
various endocrinopathies listed. The size and texture of the liver are particularly pertinent and should be recorded.

Routine laboratory examinations must always include a complete
urinalysis, with tests for acetone and all reducing sugars (Clinitest tablet,
Benedict's solution). If the test for sugar is positive, glucose can be identified by a glucose oxidase reagent (Tes-Tape, Glucostik, Combistik, etc.);
the other sugars by chromatography. Fasting and postprandial glucose
determinations are indicated as well as serum electrolyte studies to evalu-

ate whether hypo- or, hypernatremia or hypocalcemia are contributing or causative factors in producing the central nervous system manifestations.

More specialized determinations include studies of protein bound or butanol extractable iodine and urinary or blood 17-hydroxycorticosteroids before and following ACTH stimulation. Hepatic function tests are indicated to exclude hepatocellular disease.

Special Tolerance Tests to Define Hypoglycemia and Its Cause

Because of the multiple etiologies of hypoglycemia in infancy, an individualized approach to each patient is necessary. The extent and the number of special studies depend primarily upon the age at onset, the history, and the course. For example, the infant under 6 months of age with persistent symptomatic hypoglycemia is more likely to have leucine sensitivity or familial hypoglycemia. He may be so difficult to control, with intractable low blood sugar levels, that studies of carbohydrate metabolism may be almost impossible to perform or to interpret. In contrast, a definitive relationship between a prolonged fast or illness, ketosis and hypoglycemia in an infant over a year of age, suggests ketotic hypoglycemia which can be proved directly with appropriate studies (see page 202). Since the majority of older patients have intermittent episodes, a systematic study to define the metabolic abnormality is indicated.

Because of the serious sequelae of hypoglycemia in the young infant under 6 months of age[10, 13] (Table 20), a comprehensive evaluation of these patients in the hospital is essential as soon as the diagnosis is suspected. For the older infant or child, an alternative approach is to allow the child to stay at home but with instructions to the parents to bring him to the hospital as soon as symptoms occur. Definitive determinations of blood sugar levels can then be made. A therapeutic response to intravenous glucose alone, without a confirmatory low blood or spinal fluid sugar level, is suggestive but is not definitive evidence for the diagnosis.

Preparation for Study

Proper preparation of the patient is essential for the interpretation of all metabolic studies. This includes the adjustment of the infant to the hospital environment as well as an adequate diet. A diet calculated to provide adequate calories and a high carbohydrate intake is essential. A reasonable estimate of the daily caloric needs is as follows: up to 1 year of age, at least 100 calories per kg. body weight (50 calories per pound); after 1 year of age, 1000 calories plus 100 calories for every year of age up

Table 20.   The Age of Onset of Spontaneous
Symptomatic Hypoglycemia and Neurologic
Sequelae or Mental Subnormality

		Neurologic Sequelae	
	Age of Onset	Present	Absent (%)
Haworth and Coodin[13]	< 6 mos.	18	17 (49%)
	> 6 mos.	3	20 (88%)
		I.Q.	
		< 80	> 80
Ulstrom[10]	< 6 mos.	12	3 (25%)
	7 mos.–1 year	2	6 (75%)
	1 yr.–5 yrs.	1	18 (95%)

to adolescence. The distribution of calories should be 50 per cent from carbohydrate, 15 per cent from protein and 35 per cent from fat. This provides approximately 10 gm. of carbohydrate per kg. body weight per day (5 gm./lb.). This diet must be carefully calculated and specifically ordered. Furthermore, the actual food consumption must be observed and recorded at every meal. A minimum of 3 days of preparation on a proper diet is necessary before and between carbohydrate tolerance tests.

Serial Blood Sugar Determinations

In any patient in whom the diagnosis of hypoglycemia is either proven or suspected, serial blood samples should be obtained at 4-hour intervals throughout a 24-hour period (samples are taken just before meals during waking hours) to define the magnitude of the problem. Serial blood glucose levels are of particular value in the infant under 6 months of age because of the types of hypoglycemia encountered. Hypoglycemia may occur at any time with or without symptoms, often is persistent, and follows food ingestion. The appearance of symptoms is an indication to obtain a blood sample for glucose immediately and, if possible, for plasma free fatty acids, insulin and growth hormone. Through the same needle, one can administer promptly 0.5 gm./kg. of 50 per cent (0.5 cc./lb.) glucose intravenously, followed by a continuous infusion of parenteral glucose (0.5 gm./kg./hr. or, if necessary, 1.0 gm./kg./hr.) until symptoms abate and the blood sugar becomes stabilized.

In the patient over 18 months of age, the absence of a low blood sugar during this survey does not rule out the possibility of symptomatic hypoglycemia. An additional period of observation is indicated.

The sequence of performing the diagnostic tolerance tests is determined by the presumptive specific diagnosis, which is based on the age of onset, on the clinical evaluation of the patient, and on the results of the

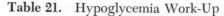

Table 21.   Hypoglycemia Work-Up

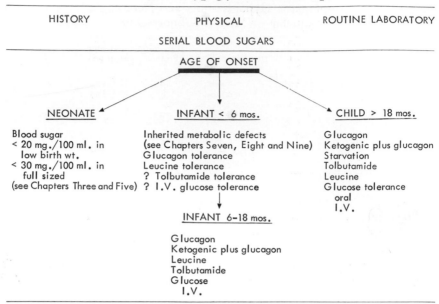

routine laboratory studies and serial blood sugars (Table 21). The technique* and interpretation of these tests follows.

Glucagon Tolerance Test (0.03 mg./kg.)[2]

Glucagon activates the hepatic phosphorylase system, resulting in glycogenolysis and the release of glucose from the liver in the presence of adequate glycogen stores and normal enzymes. After a 4- to 12-hour fast, depending upon the severity of the hypoglycemia, a control sample of blood is obtained and 0.03 mg. glucagon/kg. (*not* to exceed a total of 1 mg.) is administered intravenously or intramuscularly. Blood samples are obtained for sugar analysis at 15, 30, 45, 60, 90, and 120 minutes thereafter. A rise in blood glucose of 25 to 50 mg./100 ml. should be found normally within 15 to 45 minutes, with a return to fasting levels or below at 60 to 90 minutes. Plasma samples should be obtained for free fatty acids, insulin, and growth hormone determinations (Fig. 22, page 100).

If hyperglycemia does not occur, the test should be repeated 3 to 4 hours after a meal. If a normal hyperglycemic response is noted at this

---

* The multiple blood samples can often be obtained from a single venipuncture if an indwelling scalp vein needle (21 or 23 gauge) is left *in situ* and is filled with a sterile dilute heparin-saline solution (100 units heparin/ml.) between samples. The initial 0.3 ml. of the heparin-saline sample (it simply fills the dead space in the scalp vein set) is withdrawn into the syringe containing the dilute heparin solution and then the blood sample is withdrawn into a clean syringe. The technique is applicable in adults, children, and infants, including premature babies.

time, either glycogen storage disease, type III, or synthetase deficiency must be considered in the differential diagnosis (see Chapter Seven). A persistent lack of response to glucagon suggests von Gierke's disease (glycogen storage disease, type 1), or severe hepatocellular dysfunction.

In adults, a marked hyperglycemia followed by hypoglycemia may indicate an islet cell adenoma.[14] Such a response has been found in young infants with other forms of hypoglycemia so that this interpretation has not been found to be valid. Furthermore, the number of glucagon tests done in infants and children with islet cell tumors have been too few to evaluate.

Leucine Tolerance Test (orally 150 mg./kg.[15] or intravenously 75 mg./kg.[16])

Leucine stimulates the release of insulin from the beta cells of the pancreas. In addition, leucine may interfere with gluconeogenesis.[17]

After a short fast, 150 mg./kg. of L-leucine is given by mouth. The L-leucine can be dissolved in a dilute alkaline solution and flavored with saccharin and oil of orange or given as an iced slurry.[15] If prepared immediately prior to administration, leucine can be dissolved in CO_2 free water which has been boiled for 30 minutes.[8] In small infants, the leucine is best given through a stomach tube. A technique found to be successful is to use a Foley catheter for the stomach tube, with the outer bag inflated to occlude the esophagus and the cardiac end of the stomach.* This prevents vomiting throughout the test.

Blood samples for glucose and insulin determinations are obtained before and at 15, 30, 45, 60, 90 and 120 minutes after oral leucine or at 10-minute intervals for 1 hour after intravenous leucine.† If possible, insulin, free fatty acids and growth hormone levels should be estimated in the plasma as well.

For the diagnosis of leucine-induced hypoglycemia the fall in the blood sugar after the administration of leucine must be at least *50 per cent* of the fasting value. This usually occurs within 20 to 45 minutes, often precipitating hypoglycemic manifestations. The leucine tolerance test may be difficult to interpret if the fasting blood sugar level is less than 40 mg./100 ml. In several infants, as little as 15 to 40 mg./kg. of oral L-leucine produced a significant fall in the blood sugar level.[16, 18]

Recent studies have indicated that the administration of any one of a variety of amino acids may be associated with an elevation of plasma insulin levels and with a variable fall in blood glucose.[19] The significance of

---

* This technique was suggested by Dr. A. Drash of the Johns Hopkins Medical School.
   † L-leucine is not available as an intravenous preparation but may be made according to the technique described by Mabry, Di George and Auerbach.[16]

this observation in the pathogenesis of infantile hypoglycemia remains to be elucidated.

Ketogenic Provocative Test[20] (1200 calories/1.73 M containing 67 per cent fat)

The patient must be prepared for 3 days with a measured, calorically adequate, high carbohydrate diet as described above before the test is performed. After an overnight fast, a blood sample is obtained for sugar and plasma free fatty acids. The diet, consisting of 67 per cent fat, 16 per cent carbohydrate and 17 per cent protein,* is given in three equal parts at 8:00 A.M., 12 noon and 5:00 P.M. Water is allowed *ad libitum*. Spontaneously voided serial urines are collected and tested for acetone. Unrestricted activity is permitted. Blood sugars and plasma free fatty acids are measured every 4 hours throughout the day and night.

In the majority of children, acetonuria occurs in 8 to 12 hours. In the susceptible child this is followed by both a fall in blood sugar and clinical manifestations of hypoglycemia in another 4 to 12 hours. Since both these reactions usually occur in the early hours of the morning, the patient must be observed carefully throughout the night as well as day. At the time of the appearance of symptoms, a blood sample is obtained for sugar and free fatty acids. A glucagon tolerance test should be done at this time, if the patient's condition permits. An absent or reduced hyperglycemic response is characteristic. Symptoms should be terminated by the administration of intravenous glucose.

Tolbutamide Tolerance Test (20 mg./kg. intravenously,† not to exceed 1 gm.)

Tolbutamide facilitates the release of insulin from the beta cells of the pancreas. After an overnight fast, a sample of blood is obtained for glucose, insulin, free fatty acids and growth hormone determinations. After the injection of the intravenous tolbutamide, blood samples are obtained at 5, 10, 20, 30, 45, 60, 90 and 120 minutes for similar determinations. A normal response consists of a fall in blood glucose of 20 to 40 per cent of the fasting level within 20 to 30 minutes, with a return to within 10 per cent of the initial level by 90 to 120 minutes[21, 22] (Fig. 53).

Quantitative urine collections for catecholamines, nor- and metanephrine, and VMA (3 methoxy-4 hydroxymandelic acid) should be done for the 12 hours preceding and also during the test. Low glucose levels are associated with a two- to fivefold increase in catecholamine excretion, similar to that observed after insulin.[23, 24]

---

* 800 gm. whole milk, 285 gm. 20 per cent cream, 17 gm. Casec, 102 gm. water, 1 calorie/gm. formula.[20]

† Orinase for intravenous use.

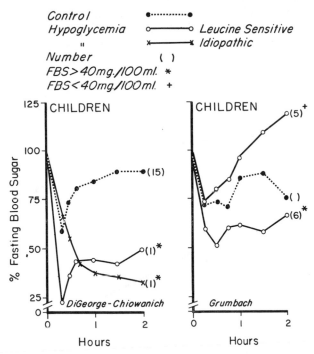

Figure 53. Intravenous tolbutamide tolerance test. Data published by Di George and Chiowanich: Diabetes, (suppl.) *11*:135, 1962, and kindly provided by M. Grumbach (personal communication).

Additional data are needed on changes of plasma insulin, growth hormone and free fatty acids after challenge with tolbutamide in hypoglycemic and control infants and children.

Insulin Sensitivity or Responsiveness (0.1 or 0.05 units/kg. intravenously)

This test is useful to define counterregulatory mechanisms in induced hypoglycemia and should be considered only in patients with fasting blood sugars in the normal range. The initial blood glucose concentration should be estimated at the bedside before administration of the insulin (Dextrostix or Dextro-test). Blood samples are obtained before and at 10, 20, 30, 45, 60, 90 and 120 minutes after the intravenous administration of crystalline or regular insulin. In addition to blood glucose or sugar values, plasma should be analyzed for concentrations of growth hormone and free fatty acids.

Normally, the blood glucose level falls to about 50 per cent of the fasting level and then returns to the control value by 60 to 90 minutes. With the fall in blood sugar, an elevation of growth hormone levels of 200 to 500 per cent of the fasting value occurs within 30 to 45 minutes.[25, 26]

Careful continuous observation of the patient, with 50 per cent glucose available in a syringe at the bedside, is essential. The interpretation of the results of this test has been difficult because in reported studies different doses of insulin as well as different routes of administration have been used.

If the possibility of increased insulin sensitivity exists, as in pituitary dwarfism, growth hormone deficiency, adrenal insufficiency, the newborn infant, etc., the dose of insulin should not exceed 0.025 to 0.05 units/kg. Rapid and profound symptomatic hypoglycemia can occur in these patients after the intravenous administration of 0.1 units of insulin/kg. In any event, a continuous infusion of saline or Ringers lactate solution should be maintained throughout *any* insulin tolerance test so that the test can be terminated promptly with 50 per cent glucose intravenously.

Quantitative urine collections for catecholamines, nor- and meta-nephrine and VMA should be done as described above in the section on tolbutamide tolerance tests (page 202).

Starvation

A prolonged fast of 24 to 36 hours with water or low caloric diet sodas *ad lib* and blood sugar determinations at 2- to 6-hour intervals has proved to be a useful technique in verifying the diagnosis of hypoglycemia in infants over a year of age. In addition to the sample of blood for sugar analysis, plasma should be obtained for free fatty acids, insulin, and growth hormone assays if possible during the fast. The appearance of symptoms at any time is an indication to obtain an immediate blood glucose determination and to terminate the fast with 0.5 gm./kg. of 50 per cent glucose intravenously, followed by a continuous infusion of parenteral glucose (0.5 gm./kg./hr. or if necessary, 1.0 gm./kg./hr.) until feedings are established. Kaye and associates[27] reported blood sugar values below 40 mg./100 ml. without symptoms after a 24-hour fast in 8 of 25 normal infants between 1 week and 6 months of age. In contrast, only 1 of 8 subjects between 7 months and 4 years of age had similar findings. In 10 normal children, ages 4 to 12 years, none had blood sugar levels lower than 40 mg./100 ml. Therefore, the interpretation of blood sugar determinations during a prolonged fast is age dependent and is difficult in infants under 6 months of age.

In addition, marked elevations in the levels of ketones in blood occurred in normal infants and children between age 36 hours and 4 years after a 24-hour fast.[27] The ketonemia was significantly less with fasting in newborn infants under 36 hours of age and in older children. In all age groups, the levels of free fatty acids were increased after starvation. Thus, the young infant responds to food deprivation both by an increase in lipolysis and by the formation of ketones.[27]

Symptomatic hypoglycemia following a prolonged fast is nonspecific and has been observed in patients with leucine sensitivity, islet cell tumor, idiopathic and ketogenic hypoglycemia.

Intravenous Glucose Tolerance Test (0.5 to 1 gm./kg., not to exceed 25 gm. as a 25 per cent solution)

The intravenous tolerance test circumvents the variability of gastro-intestinal motility and absorption; however, inadequate standardization has limited the possibility of precise interpretation in infants and children. Various doses and techniques have been used.[28-32] A recommended procedure is to administer 1 gm./kg. of glucose to infants under 2 years of age, and 0.5 gm./kg. to older infants and children to a maximal dose of 25 gm. Following a 12- to 15-hour fast, a blood specimen is obtained and the glucose solution (25 to 50 per cent) is injected rapidly intravenously in 2 to 4 minutes. Thereafter, blood samples are obtained at 5, 10, 15, 20, 30, 45, 60, 75, 90, 120, 180, 240, and 360 minutes. All samplings must be timed precisely for proper interpretation of the results. An indwelling scalp vein needle placed in a peripheral vein should be used to obtain all blood samples (see page 200). It is recommended that the glucose be administered into a different vein from the one used for blood sampling.

Several techniques for analyzing the data have been used in children and adults.[26, 32] The absolute values from 5 minutes to 60 minutes may be plotted semilogarithmically, i.e., ordinate, log glucose concentration, abscissa, time in minutes (k_t) (see Fig. 12, page 73). Alternatively, the difference between each value and the fasting blood sugar value may be plotted similarly (k_i). A straight line is usually obtained between 10 and 45 minutes and the plot must contain at least 4 points. The slope of this line is known as the glucose disappearance rate and is expressed as per cent per minute. The initial hour of the tolerance test is used to determine a single rate constant (k) (see page 10). In diabetes mellitus, this disappearance rate is slow; in hyperinsulinism, the rate is rapid.

The later portion of the tolerance test (60 to 360 minutes) is an indication of glucose homeostasis and rebound. Usually, a slight hypoglycemic dip below the control fasting level is observed at 75 to 90 minutes, with stabilization by 120 minutes. In hypoglycemic states with a rapid initial rate, a failure of maintenance of normal blood sugar is evident by a hypoglycemic phase persisting between 60 and 360 minutes. This is why the prolonged period of observation is recommended.

Von Euler and Larsson[30] in a series of 27 normal hospitalized children, plus 14 with renal glycosuria and 5 with obesity, used 0.5 gm. glucose/kg. intravenously. The rate of disappearance for total blood sugar (k_t) was 1.65 ±0.08 per cent per minute (mean ±S.E.). The obese children (weights not given) had low values of approximately 1.0 per cent/min.

Values greater than 2.5 per cent/min. were observed only in 3 of the patients with renal glycosuria.

In an extensive study of carbohydrate metabolism in infants and children, Loeb[31] administered 0.33 gm. glucose/kg. intravenously rapidly. He evaluated the influence of the duration of fasting on the glucose disappearance rate in infants 6 to 16 months of age. A slower rate (k_t) was found after a 12- to 18-hour fast (2.7 $\pm$0.11 per cent/min.), than after a 6-hour fast (3.5 $\pm$0.15 per cent/min.). This value is faster, however, than the rate of 1.74 $\pm$0.34 per cent/min. reported for adults after a 15-hour fast with the same dose. Therefore, Loeb recommended a fast of 6 hours for infants under 6 months of age, and a fast of 15 hours for older infants and children. In children ages 6 months to 10 years, a glucose disappearance rate (k_t) of 2.8 $\pm$0.55 per cent/min. was reported.

In adults, the disappearance constant derived from the absolute glucose values (k_t) is dose dependent, whereas the k_i (the disappearance rate calculated from the increase in the concentrations of blood sugar above the fasting value) is independent of the amount of glucose administered.[32] Similar analyses in children have not been made. Therefore, further studies using the intravenous glucose tolerace test require meticulous attention to detail and to the variables described.

Oral Glucose Tolerance Test[33]

Age	Dose
0–18 months	2.5 gm./kg.
1½–3 years	2.0 gm./kg.
3–12 years	1.75 gm./kg.
> 12 years	1.25 gm./kg.

The oral glucose tolerance test has been the most popular test utilized in studying infants and children with hypoglycemia. Unfortunately, the vast amount of data accumulated to date are uninterpretable because of the variability in response of each patient as a result of differences in adequacy of preparation, the stress of the procedure, the variety of doses administered in different series, the inconstancy of gastric emptying and intestinal absorption, etc. The test, if properly performed, is of value, especially in absorptive defects, e.g., cretinism, monosaccharide malabsorption and celiac disease, and in reactive functional hypoglycemia in the older child and adult if the 5-hour test is used.

After 3 days of careful preparation and an overnight fast, a blood sample is obtained for sugar, insulin, free fatty acids and growth hormone. The glucose (*not* table sugar or sucrose) is given as a 25 per cent solution, chilled and flavored to avoid nausea and vomiting.* Repeat blood samples are obtained at ½, 1, 1½, 2, 3, 4 and 5 hours.

---

* Glucola (Ames) may overcome these; however, no standards in children are available for this as yet.

A diabetic-type glucose tolerance curve with values exceeding 120 mg./100 ml. at 2 hours may be found if the patient has consumed a diet low in carbohydrate or calories (starvation diabetes).

The normal fasting values vary between 50 and 90 mg./100 ml. A flat curve may indicate failure of absorption due to a variety of causes. A diphasic curve has been observed in glycogen storage disease (type I) as well as in hepatocellular disease. In functional, alimentary or reactive hypoglycemia, the initial rise may be rapid, with a subsequent fall to hypoglycemic levels between 3 to 5 hours.

Epinephrine Tolerance Test **(0.03 mg./kg. intramuscularly, not to exceed 0.3 mg.)**

Except for investigational purposes, the epinephrine tolerance test, because of its sympathomimetic side effects, has been replaced by the glucagon tolerance test (see p. 200). Epinephrine activates the phosphorylase system in muscle, fat and liver, resulting in a rise in blood sugar and lactic acid. This hormone differs from glucagon in that it inhibits the peripheral uptake of glucose and increases glycogenolysis in muscle. Recent studies have indicated that intravenous epinephrine given with a glucose load suppresses plasma insulin levels.[34] The diagnostic importance of these specific actions has been limited to the study of the glycogen storage diseases (see Chapter Seven).

THERAPY

Parenteral Glucose

Any acute symptomatic hypoglycemic episode must be terminated as soon as possible. The prompt and rapid administration of 50 per cent glucose in water intravenously (1 to 2 ml./kg.) continued with the infusion of 10 to 15 per cent glucose (0.5 to 1.0 gm./kg./hr.) may result in rapid subsidence of symptoms. Thereafter if blood glucose levels are stabilized at normal or greater than normal levels for 6 to 12 hours, the rate and concentration of glucose administration may be reduced over a 6-hour period while feedings are resumed. A rate of 1.0 gm. of glucose/kg./hr. requires the administration of 120 cc./kg./day of 20 per cent glucose. If lower fluid or higher glucose rates are indicated, more concentrated glucose solutions are necessary.

Glucagon and/or Epinephrine

Until an intravenous infusion of glucose can be started, glucagon (0.3 mg./kg. I.V. or I.M., *not to exceed 1 mg.*) and/or epinephrine (1:1000 concentration, 0.03 mg./kg. I.M. *not to exceed 0.3 mg.*) *may* be effective emergency measures, but these hormones must be followed by parenteral glucose or oral *feedings high in carbohydrates.*

If symptoms are of short duration, the response to therapy may be dramatic and prompt. On the other hand, if hypoglycemia has persisted for 12 to 24 hours or longer, the response to treatment may be slow and therapy must be continued for several days.[11] If blood glucose cannot be stabilized within 12 to 24 hours at the rate of administration cited above, ACTH or cortisone should be added.

Intravenous hypertonic glucose must never be discontinued abruptly in these infants or after prolonged administration in any infant because of the danger of precipitating a reactive hypoglycemic episode, which can be fatal.

Specific etiologies require specific therapy, e.g., thyroid for cretinism, cortisone for Addison's disease or adrenal hyperplasia, etc.

Diet

In the large group of infants with idiopathic hypoglycemia, prolonged therapy is based on the results of the tolerance tests, the patient's age and the clinical course. Unless contraindicated on the basis of the leucine test, a normal protein, high carbohydrate diet, avoiding prolonged periods of fasting, is recommended (e.g., 5 meals a day consisting of 15 per cent protein, 30 per cent fat and 55 per cent carbohydrate).

Steroids and/or ACTH

If low levels of glucose or symptoms persist, cortisone (10 mg./kg./ day) or prednisone (2 mg./kg./day) or ACTH (4 units/kg./day) should be added to the therapeutic regimen in infants; in older children, much lower doses are often effective. In infantile persistent hypoglycemia, effective doses of ACTH have varied between 2 and 20 units ACTH per day. Serial blood sugar determinations, particularly throughout the night and early morning, are essential with changing doses of medication or diet since a low sugar level is not necessarily associated with clinical manifestations. The dose is reduced over days to weeks to the minimal amount necessary to prevent symptomatic recurrences and to maintain a normal level of blood sugar.

In the ketotic type, urine acetone tests are necessary on a daily basis but should be done more frequently if there is intercurrent illness or a period of food refusal. If acetonuria is found, a high sugar diet consisting of carbonated high caloric drinks (NOT diet drinks), hard candy, sweetened orange juice, etc., are urged. If refused, parenteral glucose may be necessary.

Other Drugs

Ephedrine sulfate has been reported to be beneficial in reducing the number of episodes of hypoglycemia in those children who fail to secrete catecholamines in the urine after hypoglycemia induced by insulin.[7] More data are needed to verify these observations.

Alloxan, which produces beta cell destruction in animals and man, has been used in a patient with intractable hypoglycemia.[35] Alloxan is toxic and difficult both to prepare and to administer. The available data are insufficient to evaluate its safety or usefulness.

Pancreatectomy

Pancreatectomy, complete or partial (80 to 90 per cent), has been necessary in severe cases of hypoglycemia as well as in patients with suspected islet cell hyperplasia or tumors. Indeed, 25 of the 58 cases reviewed by Haworth and Coodin[13] came to surgery for partial or total pancreatectomy. In 10, no benefit was produced; in 15, the infants were cured. Others have also used this method of therapy with variable results.[36-38] Previously this operation was withheld until late in the clinical course of hypoglycemia, but there is current interest in evaluating early surgical intervention in young infants under 6 months of age with intractable hypoglycemia.[39] Regardless of the patient's age, the operation should be considered only after an adequate trial with hormones and hypertonic glucose.

New Therapeutic Approaches

Recently, preliminary reports have appeared describing results with new approaches to the treatment of spontaneous recurrent hypoglycemia of infancy.

Zinc Glucagon or Glucagon-gel

Glucagon has a relatively short duration of action, lasting ½ to 1 hour. A long-acting zinc preparation has been developed and is available as an experimental drug. In one patient who undoubtedly had hypoglycemia, the type of which was not characterized, Kushner, Lemli and Smith[40] reported that zinc glucagon before meals helped to maintain blood glucose at higher levels than without the hormone. The follow-up was short and the value of this therapy remains to be elucidated. Reactive hypoglycemia has been reported following the use of another long-acting glucagon, glucagon-gel.[41]

Diazoxide

It was noticed that Diazoxide, a benzothiadiazine agent used in hypertension, produced hyperglycemia and a diabetic type glucose tolerance curve in some hypertensive adults.[42] Then Drash and Wolff[43] found that Diazoxide in a dose of 12 mg./kg./day significantly elevated the blood sugar in a 4 year old patient who had previously had a partial pancreatectomy and was leucine sensitive. We studied another patient with leucine sensitive hypoglycemia, in whom Diazoxide resulted in higher fasting blood sugar levels. In addition, after 6 months of therapy, he was no longer sensitive to leucine. This agent is an experimental drug and requires further evaluation.

Growth Hormone

Several preliminary reports have suggested that human growth hormone has been useful in controlling the blood sugar level in infants with hypoglycemia and a failure to grow.[44, 45] Growth hormone had no effect in the patient who responded to Diazoxide reported by Drash and Wolff.[43] Nadler et al.[45] demonstrated a dramatic effect of human growth hormone (1 mg. 3 times a week) in a 1 year old infant who had hypoglycemia and growth failure. We have observed a similar infant who is receiving growth hormone currently. The role of growth hormone deficiency in hypoglycemia in infancy is an intriguing one and remains to be clarified.

SIGNIFICANCE

Prolonged or recurrent hypoglycemia can produce brain damage in both experimental animals and man. In man, both exogenous insulin and islet cell adenomas have been found to be etiologic factors. Yet the question remains whether, in symptomatic hypoglycemia, the hypoglycemia is responsible for or secondary to defects in the central nervous system. Once brain damage has occurred, it is not unusual to see central nervous system manifestations, e.g., epilepsy, when blood glucose is at a normal level.[1, 46, 47] On the other hand, low blood sugar values have been reported either associated with or as a result of primary or brain stem pathology, and this fact should be considered in the differential diagnosis (supra vide) of the hypoglycemia. A more puzzling aspect is the exact relation between low levels of blood glucose and clinical manifestations. A patient may have severe signs and symptoms, with a blood sugar of 40 mg./100 ml. on one occasion and no symptoms with a value of 20 mg./100 ml. on another. Another enigma is that a rapidly falling blood sugar can produce similar symptoms at high or normal levels of blood glucose in the diabetic patient. Much remains to be learned about glucose and oxygen extraction and utilization by the brain and about cerebral blood flow and function. With profound hypoglycemia (glucose less than 30 mg./100 ml.), oxygen consumption of the brain is diminished without dramatic changes in blood flow.[48, 49] Recently, with less severe hypoglycemia, an increase in oxygen consumption in normal adults has been reported following insulin administration.[50] Whether the human brain *in vivo* can utilize structural protein, lipoprotein, glycogen, cerebrosides, etc., for energy in the absence of glucose, as demonstrated in the isolated perfused cat brain by Geiger,[51] remains to be elucidated.

Cerebral function and metabolism, especially during the first months of life, have not been adequately studied. The brain appears to have an increased vulnerability to hypoglycemia during the first months of life.[10, 13] In 58 patients with spontaneous idiopathic hypoglycemia reviewed by Haworth and Coodin,[13] onset was before 6 months of age in 35 and 51 per cent had permanent neurologic sequelae. In 23 patients whose symptomatic hypoglycemia occurred after 6 months of age, only 3 (12 per cent) later showed brain damage (Table 20). In reviewing 46 patients with idiopathic hypoglycemia followed at the University of Minnesota for 11 years (26 of these patients have been included in the literature review cited above of Haworth and Coodin[13]), Ulstrom[10] reported similar results (Table 20). In part, this may reflect more severe disease in the younger infant as well as difficulty in interpreting symptoms and diagnosing the hypoglycemia early in its course before the age of 6 months. On the other hand, although inordinate delays do occur before the diagnosis is made and therapy begun in patients over 6 months of age, brain damage in the older children is apparently less severe.

REFERENCES

1. Hartmann, A. F., and Jaudon, J. C.: Hypoglycemia. J. Pediat. *11*:1, 1937.
2. Cornblath, M., Ganzon, A. F., Nicolopoulos, D., Baens, G. S., Hollander, R. J., Gordon, M. H., and Gordon, H. H.: Studies of carbohydrate metabolism in the newborn infant. III. Some factors influencing the capillary blood sugar and the response to glucagon during the first hours of life. Pediatrics *27*: 378, 1961.
3. Cornblath, M., and Reisner, S. H.: Blood glucose in the neonate and its clinical significance. New England J. Med. *273*:278, 1965.
4. Baens, G. S., Lundeen, E., and Cornblath, M.: Studies of carbohydrate metabolism in the newborn infant. VI. Levels of glucose in blood in premature infants. Pediatrics *31*:580, 1963.
5. McQuarrie, I.: Idiopathic spontaneously occurring hypoglycemia in infants. A.M.A. Am. J. Dis. Child. *87*:399, 1954.
6. Conn, J. W., and Seltzer, H. S.: Spontaneous hypoglycemia. Am. J. Med. *19*: 460, 1955.
7. Broberger, O., and Zetterström, R.: Hypoglycemia with an inability to increase

the epinephrine secretion in insulin-induced hypoglycemia. J. Pediat. *59*: 215, 1961.

8. Sauls, H. S., Jr., and Ulstrom, R. A.: Hypoglycemia. *In* Kelly, V. C. (ed.): Brennemann's Practice of Pediatrics. Vol. 1. Hagerstown, Md., W. F. Prior Co., 1966, chapter 40.

9. Wybregt, S. H., Reisner, S. H., Patel, R. K., Nellhaus, G., and Cornblath, M.: The incidence of neonatal hypoglycemia in a nursery for premature infants. J. Pediat. *64*:796, 1964.

10. Ulstrom, R. A.: Idiopathic spontaneous hypoglycemia. *In* Linneweh, F. (ed.): Erbliche Stoffwechselkrankheiten. Berlin, Urban and Schwarzenberg, 1962, p. 225.

11. Hartmann, A. F., Woltmann, H. J., and Holowach, J.: Recognition and investigation of hypoglycemia. J. Pediat. *58*:864, 1961.

12. Underdahl, L. O., Woolner, L. B., and Black, B. M.: Multiple endocrine adenomas: report of 8 cases in which the parathyroids, pituitary and pancreatic islets were involved. J. Clin. Endocrinol. *13*:20, 1953.

13. Haworth, J., and Coodin, F. J.: Idiopathic spontaneous hypoglycemia in children. Report of seven cases and review of the literature. Pediatrics *25*:748, 1960.

14. Marrack, D., Marks, V., and Rose, F. C.: A leucine-sensitive insulin-secreting tumour. Lancet *2*:1329, 1960.

15. Cochrane, W. A., Payne, W. W., Simpkiss, M. J., and Woolf, L. I.: Familial hypoglycemia precipitated by amino acids. J. Clin. Invest. *35*:411, 1956.

16. Mabry, C. C., Di George, A. M., and Auerbach, V. H.: Leucine-induced hypoglycemia. J. Pediat. *57*:526, 1960.

17. Reaven, G., and Greenberg, R. E.: Experimental leucine-induced hypoglycemia in mice. I. Clinical observations and diagnostic considerations. Metabolism *14*:625, 1965.

18. Rosenthal, I. M., Metz, R., and Pirani, C.: Congenital leucine-sensitive hypoglycemia; association with hyperplasia of beta cells of the islets of Langerhans. Am. J. Dis. Child. *107*:343, 1964.

19. Floyd, J. C., Jr., Fajans, S. S., Knopf, R. F., Rull, J., and Conn, J. W.: Postprandial aminoacidemia and insulin secretion, a physiologic relationship. J. Lab. Clin. Med. *64*:858, 1964 (Abstract No. 38).

20. Colle, E., and Ulstrom, R. A.: Ketotic hypoglycemia. J. Pediat. *64*:632, 1964.

21. Grumbach, M.: Personal communication.

22. Di George, A. M., and Chiowanich, P.: The intravenous tolbutamide response test in infants and children. Diabetes *11*(Suppl.):135, 1962.

23. Personal observations.

24. Greenberg, R. E., Lind, J., and Von Euler, U. S.: Effect of posture and insulin hypoglycemia on catecholamine excretion in the newborn. Acta Paediat. *49*:780, 1960.

25. Roth, J., Glick, S. M., Yalow, R. S., and Berson, S. A.: Hypoglycemia: a potent stimulus to secretion of growth hormone. Science *140*:987, 1963.

26. Cornblath, M., Parker, M. L., Reisner, S. H., Forbes, A. E., and Daughaday, W. H.: Secretion and metabolism of growth hormone in premature and full term infants. J. Clin. Endocrinol. *25*:209, 1965.

27. Kaye, R., Davidson, M. H., Williams, M. L., Kumagai, M., and Picou, D. M.: The response of blood glucose, ketones, and plasma nonesterified fatty acids to fasting and epinephrine injection in infants and children. J. Pediat. *59*:836, 1961.

28. Bowie, M. D., Mulligan, P. B., and Schwartz, R.: Intravenous glucose tolerance in the normal newborn infant; the effects of a double dose of glucose and insulin. Pediatrics *31*:590, 1963.

29. Cornblath, M., Wybregt, S. H., and Baens, G. S.: Studies of carbohydrate metabolism in the newborn infant. VII. Tests of carbohydrate tolerance in premature infants. Pediatrics *32*:1007, 1963.

30. Von Euler, U. S., and Larsson, Y.: Glucose tolerance tests in children: a methodological study. Scand. J. Clin. & Lab. Invest. *14* (Suppl. 64):62, 1962.

31. Loeb, H.: Contribution a l'étude du métabolisme énergétigue de l'enfant. Editions Arscia, 1962, p. 1. (Thése, Université Libre de Bruxelles.)
32. Amatuzio, D. S., Stutzman, F. L., Vanderbilt, M. J., and Nesbit, S.: Interpretation of the rapid intravenous glucose tolerance test in normal individuals and in mild diabetes melitus. J. Clin. Invest. 32:428, 1953.
33. Bridge, E. M., and Mulholland, W. M.: Intermediate carbohydrate metabolism. In Brennemann's Practice of Pediatrics. Vol. 3. Hagerstown, Md., W. F. Prior Co., 1957, chapter 24.
34. Porte, D., Jr., Graber, A., Kuzuza, T., and Williams, R. H.: Epinephrine inhibition of insulin release. J. Clin. Invest. 44:1087, 1965 (Abstract).
35. Talbot, N. B., Crawford, J. D., and Bailey, C. C.: Use of mesoxalyl urea (alloxan) in treatment of an infant with convulsions due to idiopathic hypoglycemia. Pediatrics 1:337, 1948.
36. Gross, R. E.: The Surgery of Infancy and Childhood. Philadelphia, W. B. Saunders Co., 1953, p. 547 ff.
37. Traisman, H. S., Steiner, M. M., and Ziering, W.: Spontaneous hypoglycemia treated by partial pancreatectomy. Ann. Surg. 156:743, 1962.
38. McFarland, J. O., Gillett, F. S., and Zwemer, R. J.: Total pancreatectomy for hyperinsulinism in infants. Surgery 57:313, 1965.
39. Kaye, R.: Personal communication.
40. Kushner, R. S., Lemli, L., and Smith, D. W.: Zinc glucagon in the management of idiopathic hypoglycemia. J. Pediat. 63:1111, 1963.
41. Frasier, S. D., Smith, F. G., Jr., and Nash, A.: The use of glucagon-gel in idiopathic spontaneous hypoglycemia of infancy. Pediatrics 35:120, 1965.
42. Wolff, F. W., and Parmeley, W. W.: Aetiological factors in benzothiadiazine hyperglycaemia. Lancet 2:69, 1963.
43. Drash, A., and Wolff, F.: Drug therapy in leucine-sensitive hypoglycemia. Metabolism 13:487, 1964.
44. Soyka, L. F., Molliver, M., and Crawford, J. D.: Idiopathic hypoglycaemia of infancy treated with human growth hormone. Lancet 1:1015, 1964.
45. Nadler, H. L., Neumann, L. L., and Gershberg, H.: Hypoglycemia, growth retardation and probable isolated growth hormone deficiency in a one year old child. J. Pediat. 63:977, 1963.
46. Darrow, D. C.: Mental deterioration associated with convulsions and hypoglycemia. A.M.A. Am. J. Dis. Child. 51:575, 1936.
47. Etheridge, J. E., Jr., and Millichap, J. G.: Hypoglycemia and seizures in childhood. Neurol. 14:397, 1964.
48. Kety, S. S., Woodford, R. B., Harmel, M. H., Freyhan, F. A., Appel, K. E., and Schmidt, C. F.: Cerebral blood flow and metabolism in schizophrenia: effects of barbiturate semi-narcosis, insulin coma, and electroshock. Am. J. Psychiat. 104:765, 1948.
49. Himwich, H. E.: Brain Metabolism and Cerebral Disorders. Baltimore, the Williams & Wilkins Co., 1951.
50. Eisenberg, S., and Seltzer, H. S.: The cerebral metabolic effects of acutely induced hypoglycemia in human subjects. Metabolism 11:1162, 1962.
51. Geiger, A.: Correlation of brain metabolism and function by the use of a brain perfusion method in situ. Physiol. Rev. 38:1, 1958.

Chapter Eleven

SPECIFIC HYPOGLYCEMIC SYNDROMES

In the previous section consideration has been given to the age of onset, the establishment of the occurrence of hypoglycemia and the general approach to diagnosis and management. If a specific etiology or pathogenesis can be defined, then a specific approach to therapy is possible. The purpose of this section is to describe well defined hypoglycemic syndromes.

ENDOCRINE DEFICIENCIES

Cretinism, Addison's disease, adrenal hyperplasia, and deficiencies of growth hormone and glucagon have been responsible for symptomatic hypoglycemia in rare instances.[1-4] Because of recent advances in the immunoassay of hormones, in the understanding of some of their metabolic controls, and in their availability for therapy, only a discussion of possible isolated growth hormone and glucagon deficiencies will be presented.

Growth Hormone

The classical demonstration by Houssay of the amelioration of diabetes mellitus in the dog following hypophysectomy first established the importance of the pituitary gland in carbohydrate regulation. The pituitary dwarf has been known to be susceptible to hypoglycemia. Brasel

214

et al.[105] measured fasting blood sugars in 41 patients with idiopathic hypopituitarism; of these, 12 (27 per cent) were hypoglycemic, with values lower than 50 mg./100 ml. Furthermore, 30 per cent of the patients were unusually sensitive to insulin. Because of the multiple primary and secondary endocrine deficiencies in panhypopituitarism, the specific role of growth hormone could not be delineated previously. But in recent years the isolation of the specific pituitary proteins, including human growth hormone, has led to the clarification of the role of this hormone in carbohydrate metabolism.[5-7]

The recent demonstration that growth hormone levels as estimated in plasma by immunoassay change dynamically in response to variations in blood glucose concentrations has suggested that growth hormone may be important in carbohydrate homeostasis.[6-8] Hypoglycemia induced either by insulin in normal individuals[6] or by fructose in a patient with hereditary fructose intolerance resulted in an immediate and significant rise in the level of plasma growth hormone. A similar response has been noted in normal neonates during the first days of life.[8] When hyperglycemia was produced by intravenous or oral glucose in normal children and adults, a fall in plasma growth hormone concentrations occurred.[6-8] Further studies of infants with hypoglycemia and of their ability to secrete growth hormone are needed.

Nadler et al.[9] have reported one patient with a possible isolated growth hormone deficiency and hypoglycemia. This 13 month old male failed to gain weight or grow, was poorly developed and had a generalized seizure lasting 30 minutes shortly after awakening. A blood sugar level of 18 mg./100 ml. was found. The infant had been born at term spontaneously to a 33 year old mother who had had diabetes mellitus for 20 years and was taking 30 units of NPH insulin daily. The mother was hospitalized during the sixth month of pregnancy because of diabetic acidosis. The infant weighed 5 pounds and was 17 inches long at birth. The neonatal period was not remarkable.

On admission, he weighed 11 pounds, 14 ounces, and his height was 18 inches; head circumference, 16 inches; chest circumference, 14.6 inches; and upper body–lower segment ratio, 1.4/1.0. His blood pressure was 110/60 mm. Hg, and his pulse 120 per minute. The only positive findings on physical examination were frontal bossing of the skull, with deep-set eyes and two skin tags near the right ear. The genitals were very small; the penis was 1.2 cm. long, the scrotum was tiny and the testes were not palpable.

All routine laboratory examinations including urinalysis and studies of electrolytes, urinary amino acids, serology and liver function were within normal limits. The electroencephalogram was normal. Normal endocrine function was evidenced by the level of PBI in plasma, 17-ketosteroid and 17-hydroxycorticosteroid urinary excretion and the response to ACTH stimulation and methopyrapone (SU-4885). The sex chromatin pattern was negative and the chromosomal analysis normal.

The only abnormality found was a significant reduction in growth hormone-like activity in plasma as estimated by serum-sulfation factor assay. The value obtained was similar to that found in hypopituitary dwarfs.

Studies of carbohydrate metabolism revealed: (1) a rapid fall to hypoglycemic levels in blood sugar after an oral glucose tolerance test; (2) a significant decline in blood sugar after oral leucine administration and (3) a marked hypoglycemia and a convulsion following intravenous administration of tolbutamide (20 mg./kg.).

Administration of human growth hormone (HGH) in a dose of 3 mg./day promptly induced a rise in fasting blood sugar levels and, after one week, prevented the marked hypoglycemic response to tolbutamide. The dose of HGH was reduced to 1 mg. three times a week and, after another week, the glucose and leucine tolerance tests were normal. HGH was administered for 3 months, during which time the infant grew 7 inches and gained 1 pound 6 ounces. The testes became palpable. At 2 years of age (when he had not received HGH for 8 months) the carbohydrate tolerance tests were again abnormal, but no mention was made in the report of further attacks of hypoglycemic convulsions.

The patient presented a complex problem. The influence of maternal diabetes on his course is undefined. The carbohydrate studies reported are compatible with hyperinsulinism. Unfortunately, plasma insulin levels are not reported. Furthermore, the response to growth hormone may not necessarily indicate a specific deficiency because hypoglycemia of diverse etiology has been controlled with this hormone.[10, 11]

Wilber and Odell[106] have described a 7 year old male dwarf with severe recurrent hypoglycemia which began at 1 year of age. He had normal tests of liver, adrenal and thyroid function, but a retarded bone age. Carbohydrate studies revealed fasting hypoglycemia (30 to 40 mg./100 ml.), sensitivity to insulin, a normal response to epinephrine and glucagon and no leucine sensitivity. Plasma human growth hormone levels by radioimmunoassay were < 1.0 mμg./ml. and did not rise after induced or reactive hypoglycemia. In addition, plasma insulin levels were low or normal at the time of hypoglycemia. Treatment with human growth hormone produced a dramatic reversal of the carbohydrate abnormalities. This patient fulfills all the current criteria for isolated growth hormone deficiency.

Glucagon Deficiency

In 1950 McQuarrie et al.[12] reported a brother and a sister with spontaneous hypoglycemia, both of whom had a diminished number of alpha cells in the islets of Langerhans in the pancreas. This observation has been questioned because of the staining techniques used for the islet cells and because a hypoglycemic cousin of these siblings had normal alpha cells in his pancreas. Thus, the role—or rather the absence—of glucagon in the pathogenesis of spontaneous hypoglycemia remains to be defined.

Recently, a deficiency of alpha cells, particularly in relation to the number of beta cells, has again been considered as a cause of hypoglycemia. Grollman, McCaleb and White[13] described 3 patients, one a 13 month old male admitted with coma and convulsions, who died within 20 hours; another, a 7 year old male with a fasting hypoglycemia of unknown duration, and a third, a 40 year old housewife who also had fasting hypoglycemia. The latter two patients had glucose tolerance and tolbutamide tests compatible with the diagnosis of "organic hyperinsulinism," and underwent partial pancreatectomy. No islet cell tumor was found in either of these patients. In representative areas of 5μ-sections of tissue taken from 6 control adults the average number of alpha cells was 397; and beta cells, 1633, or a ratio of 24.3 $\pm$ 6.0 per cent. In the 13 month old infant, there were 12 alpha cells to 1802 beta cells (ratio of 0.7 per cent); in the 7 year old boy, 405 alpha cells to 3689 beta cells (ratio of 9.9 per cent); and in the 40 year old housewife, 156 alpha to 2032 beta cells (7.7 per cent). Whether these patients had an absolute increase in beta cells or a deficiency in alpha cells is difficult to determine. The 13 month old infant had a CO_2 of 4.2 mM./L. and a potassium of 6.2 mEq./L., responded poorly to 40 gm. of glucose and epinephrine, had carpopedal spasms and died within 20 hours of admission. This bizarre clinical picture may have been due to poisoning, sepsis, or other conditions which may have had a destructive effect on the alpha cells. Unfortunately, the case reports and the descriptions of the techniques of the cell counts are too brief and inadequate to determine the type of hypoglycemia present or the significance of the ratios reported.

Determinations of plasma levels of glucagon and insulin as well as the extractable glucagon content of the excised pancreas might clarify these puzzling microscopic observations.

The application of the sensitive radio-immunoassay technique for estimating glucagon in plasma developed by Unger et al.[14] should result in further information about levels of this hormone in all types of hypoglycemia. The availability of zinc glucagon, which has a prolonged hyperglycemic activity, should provide additional impetus for such studies.

ENDOCRINE EXCESS

Either functioning islet cell adenoma or hyperplasia can produce an excess of insulin and hypoglycemia.

Islet Cell Adenoma in Childhood

Although rare in infancy and childhood, islet cell adenoma must be considered in every patient with hypoglycemia because surgical removal results in a prompt and permanent cure. To date, at least 30 proven cases of islet cell tumors in children younger than 15 years of age have been reported in detail or alluded to in the literature.[15-22] Boley et al.[16] have critically and carefully analyzed in detail the reports of 17 infants and children with functioning pancreatic adenomas up to 1960. Two additional patients were added by François et al.[18] and one by Hartmann et al.[17] The pertinent findings in these 20 patients as well as the results of recent diagnostic tests, including assays of plasma insulin, are reviewed.

There was no sex predilection; there were 11 males and 9 females. The family histories were negative for episodes suggestive of hypoglycemia. The most significant finding appears to be the age of onset. Although there has been one authenticated case of islet cell adenoma in a newborn infant,[18] one in a 19 month old infant[17] and two questionable adenomata in infants less than 1 year of age,[16] the other 16 patients did not have symptoms until 4 years of age or older (Fig. 54). Not included among these 20 patients are two infants discussed by Crigler.[19] These babies had the onset of symptoms in early infancy and had islet cell tumors removed at 4 and 14 months of age, respectively.

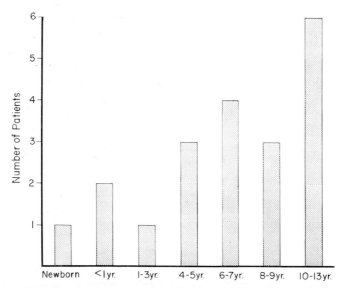

Figure 54.   Age incidence of islet cell adenoma. (Adapted from Boley et al., Surgery, *48*:592, 1960; Hartmann et al., J. Pediat., *56*:211, 1960; François et al., J. Pediat., *60*:721, 1962.)

Age at Onset of Symptoms

Islet cell adenoma occurs late in childhood (Fig. 54), in contrast to idiopathic hypoglycemia which occurs before 2 years of age in 90 per cent of the cases, and in contrast to leucine sensitive hypoglycemia, cretinism, hyperplasia of islets, and inborn errors of metabolism, all of which have a peak incidence the first days to months of life. This observation "represents the most important diagnostic criterion of pancreatic adenoma."[16] However, it should be remembered that ketogenic hypoglycemia also has a peak incidence after the second year of life.

Clinical Manifestations

Convulsions occurred in all of these children, with periods of unconsciousness, behavioral changes and sweating being common. Other central nervous system manifestations included weakness, speech changes, ataxia and mental deterioration. In 75 per cent of the patients, attacks could be precipitated by fasting or exercise. There is no characteristic time of occurrence.

Physical findings were not diagnostic or unique. If the patient was examined during a hypoglycemic attack, the neurologic findings were variable. Several children had persistent neurologic signs, ranging from transitory paraplegia to bilateral pyramidal signs. A number of the children were overweight, probably because of the medical treatment of the hypoglycemia plus the hyperinsulinism.

Delay in Diagnosis

The duration of symptoms prior to operation or death varied from less than 6 months in 6 patients, 1 to 2 years in 11, to over 2 years in 3. In one patient reported by Fonkalsrud et al.,[21] symptoms were of 10 years' duration before removal of an islet cell adenoma at age 17 years.

The diagnosis was made by finding a gross tumor at operation in 14 children and at autopsy in 3. In 3 of the cases, a microscopic examination of the pancreas was necessary to establish the diagnosis.

Laboratory Tests

The only significant laboratory findings were low blood sugar levels during hypoglycemic attacks, 7 patients having levels lower than 20 mg./100 ml., 7 between 20 and 30 mg./100 ml. and all lower than 50 mg./100 ml. Spinal fluid sugar levels were low in 5 of 6 instances. Although low levels of glucose are intermittent rather than persistent, a prolonged fast (over 24 hours) will almost invariably induce a level of glucose below 50 mg./100 ml. in these patients.

The glucose, glucagon and insulin tolerance tests have not been diagnostic. Resistance to insulin may occur but has not been consistent, and it is important to remember that the insulin sensitivity test may be dangerous, producing profound severe hypoglycemia.

Tests of adrenal, thyroid and hepatic function have been within normal limits.

The electroencephalogram has been reported in 9 children. In 7, the EEG was abnormal, and in three of these the tracing was consistent with the diagnosis of epilepsy. This again emphasizes the need for obtaining blood for the determination of glucose, calcium, phosphorous and urea nitrogen as part of the diagnostic evaluation of every child at the time of a convulsion or other peculiar neurologic manifestations.

Therapy

Medical Therapy. Medical therapy was attempted in 75 per cent of these children because of the difficulty in diagnosing islet cell tumor in the young. Dietary therapy, either with or without ACTH and steroids, was used and produced temporary remissions. In view of the periodicity of the hypoglycemic episodes, the real effect of medical management is difficult to evaluate. At best, improvement is temporary, the blood sugar values erratic, and recurrences inevitable.

Surgical Therapy. In 13 of the 20 children, a gross tumor was found and excised. Three had partial to subtotal resections of the pancreas with a solitary microscopic tumor found in 2 and multiple adenomata in 1, the latter at autopsy. A solitary adenoma was found in one newborn at autopsy and multiple adenomata (2 and 3) in two other children. Seven tumors were in the head, 5 in the body, 6 in the tail and 1 in the uncinate process of the pancreas. In adults, aberrant sites for islet cell adenomata have been described fairly frequently.[23] The tumor may vary in size from microscopic to that of "a lentil" or "a walnut" since unfortunately, the size was often given in comparative terms. The majority of the tumors were estimated to be between 1 and 2.0 cm. in diameter.

A precise and authoritative description and illustrations of an islet cell tumor studied by light and electron microscopic techniques is presented by Dr. Paul Lacy[24] on the patient described by Hartmann et al.[17]; in addition, he discusses the ultrastructure of the beta cell.

Results

No operative deaths occurred and only one child[18] became diabetic and required insulin indefinitely. Transient hyperglycemia occurred in 5 patients and one of these received insulin for 28 days. Nine children operated upon are completely well; 7 have either permanent neurologic sequelae or major personality and behavior problems. In view of the inordinate delay between the onset of symptoms and definitive care, the results are not unexpected and again emphasize the need for early diagnosis.

Specific Diagnostic Tests

In adults, a number of parameters have been found useful and fairly specific in the preoperative diagnosis of a functioning islet cell tumor.[20, 25–29] These include:

1. Plasma insulin levels
   a. with fasting
   b. after tolbutamide
   c. after leucine
   d. after glucose
   e. after glucagon
2. Tolbutamide tolerance test (see Fig. 55)
3. Leucine tolerance test

If the patients were fasting, and if sufficient random samples were obtained, Floyd et al.,[20] Samols[26] and Berson and Yalow[27] found elevated levels of plasma insulin in the majority of patients. Samols and Marks[28] and Floyd et al.[20] have found high insulin levels in portal blood and normal levels in peripheral blood. These findings suggest that excessive insulin was produced by the tumor and removed by the liver. The hypoglycemia was thought to be the result of inhibition of hepatic glucose

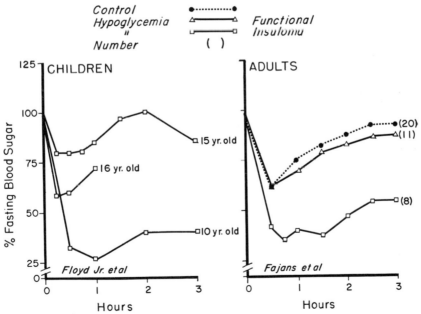

Figure 55.   Tolbutamide tolerance tests in three children with proved islet cell adenoma[20] as compared to tests in adults with tumors and functional hypoglycemia.[25]

output by the excess insulin. This may account for normal or low levels of peripheral plasma insulin in the presence of clinical and biochemical hypoglycemia.

Specifically, high plasma insulin levels, occurring between 5 and 20 minutes following intravenous administration of tolbutamide, may prove to be a valuable extension of the tolbutamide tolerance test reported by Fajans et al.[25] Unfortunately, this test has not been so specific in infants and children as in adults (see Fig. 55). False positive tests are not uncommon in the young infant with idiopathic hypoglycemia (Fig. 53, p. 203). In 3 children with islet cell tumors, ages 10 to 16 years, only one showed a positive tolbutamide test and a significant elevation in her plasma insulin, although the initial fasting insulin level was high.[20] A moderate rise in insulin occurred in the 16 year old female patient. More studies are needed in infants and children before the value and validity of the insulin levels during a tolbutamide tolerance test can be evaluated in this age group.

Almost all the infants with idiopathic hypoglycemia and leucine sensitivity have an onset of symptoms before 6 months of age (see page 231). Therefore, in children in whom symptoms and hypoglycemia first appear after 2 years of age, the elevation of plasma insulin after leucine may prove to be of diagnostic value for islet cell adenoma. Definitive studies with this test in all age groups with hypoglycemia will be necessary to clarify the role of this diagnostic procedure.

The glucose tolerance tests, with or without insulin assay, have not been helpful in either adults or children.

Summary

Hypoglycemia beginning in a child over the age of 3 may be caused by a functioning islet cell tumor. At any age, recurrent hypoglycemia resistent to medical therapy may be due to a tumor. To date no specific tolerance test or hormone assay is specific in making this diagnosis in children. Failure of medical management and elevated levels of plasma insulin, if present either with fasting or after tolbutamide, may suggest the diagnosis and indicate surgical exploration.

Islet Cell Hyperplasia

Diffuse islet cell hyperplasia in the pancreas has been observed frequently at autopsy in infants of diabetic mothers,[1, 30] in infants with severe erythroblastosis fetalis,[31] and occasionally at surgery in infants with recurrent spontaneous hypoglycemia.[32, 33] Although a number of infants with hypoglycemia have been reported with this microscopic finding, its significance remains obscure. Insulin extraction studies in the excised pancreas have not been done in recurrent spontaneous hypoglycemia nor have plasma insulin levels been assayed either in peripheral blood or in portal blood at the time of surgery. In 6 of 8 patients reported to have hypertrophy of islets, partial resection of the pancreas (65 to 80 per cent) has been curative; whereas in 17 patients with normal islet cells, only 9 were helped by partial pancreatectomy.[32]

The clinical manifestations and laboratory findings that have been reported do not distinguish hypoglycemia due to islet cell hyperplasia from idiopathic hypoglycemia with microscopically normal beta cells. Perhaps in the near future the assay of plasma for insulin and glucagon content with fasting and during various carbohydrate tolerance tests will provide data to enable one to distinguish hypoglycemia due to islet cell hypertrophy from other types of hypoglycemia.

METABOLIC DEFECTS

Metabolic causes of hypoglycemia include those due to inborn errors of metabolism (see Chapters Seven, Eight and Nine), acquired liver disease or malnutrition and poisoning.

Inherited Metabolic Defects

Glycogen storage disease (types I, III and VI), galactose intolerance, fructose intolerance, and glycogen synthetase deficiency have been discussed in detail elsewhere in the monograph. Bickel[34] has reported that hypoglycemia may occur in patients with *cystinosis*: neither the mechanism of the low blood sugar level nor the clinical significance of this observation is yet understood. These patients have also had reactions of collapse, shock, and even death during oral glucose tolerance tests: the explanation of these phenomena is obscure, but hypokalemia has been suggested as an important factor.[34]

Acquired Metabolic Defects

The liver is the major source of glucose during fasting and must be able to provide glucose to the circulation by both glycogenolysis and gluconeogenesis. Therefore, any extensive liver disease which interferes with the storage or breakdown of glycogen or the conversion of precursor amino acids, lactate, pyruvate, fructose, galactose, and glycerol to glucose may result in hypoglycemia.

Hypoglycemia has been associated with acute hepatitis, cirrhosis, severe protein malnutrition, restrictive diets and acute fatty infiltration of the liver. In all of these conditions, it is important to recognize the hypoglycemia because: (1) some of the clinical manifestations may be due to the low blood sugar level; and (2) the symptoms and the hypoglycemia are amenable to therapy.

Recurrent spontaneous attacks of symptomatic hypoglycemia are not usual in any of these clinical diseases; therefore, only brief descriptions of these entities with references to the literature are presented.

Malnutrition

Kwashiorkor.   Kahn and Wayburne[35] found severe hypoglycemia in 16 children with the nonmarasmic type of kwashiorkor. These children had a history of a relatively short period of starvation: the clinical observations were twitching of the face and limbs in 4, coma in 5, drowsiness in 6 and irritability in 1. Physical examination revealed an enlarged liver in 60 per cent and an acute nutritional dermatosis in 75 per cent. Bilirubin levels exceeded 1.5 mg./100 ml. in 5 children in whom measurements were made. Blood sugar values were lower than 20 mg./100 ml. in 14 patients and lower than 30 mg./100 ml. in 2. Only 3 infants survived even with intravenous glucose therapy. At autopsy, "advanced fatty change of the liver" was described.

Subsequent reports[36] have verified these findings of Kahn and Wayburne.

Low Phenylalanine Diet.   Dodge et al.[37] described severe hypoglycemia presenting with seizures and coma in 2 phenylketonuric children after a brief period of starvation. One child recovered, the other died. At postmortem examination, there was marked fatty infiltration in the liver and severe hypoglycemic encephalopathy. The authors reported that both children were in a state of severe undernutrition as a result of refusal to take adequate amounts of the unpalatable diet. This complication can be avoided by more careful attention to good nutritional intake in these patients.

Poisoning

Acute Alcohol Toxicity

Acute alcohol ingestion is a relatively rare cause of hypoglycemia in infancy and childhood, but has been reported within the past 5 years in the American literature by Cummins.[38] Other reports from Uruguay and France have recently been cited.[39, 40] Cummins described two cases as follows:

Case 1. A 6 year old Negro male, who was previously well, ingested an unknown quantity of gin at 7:00 p.m. The patient was not observed between 7:00 p.m. and 2:00 a.m. At 2:00 a.m. convulsions were first noted and they continued until hospitalization at 4:00 a.m. On admission, the blood pressure was 115/70; pulse, 140/min. The boy was unresponsive, with constant clonic seizures. He had a Cheyne-Stokes type of respiration and pin-point pupils unreactive to light.

Chemical studies indicated a blood alcohol concentration of 20 mg./100 ml., a CO_2 of 20.5 mM./L., chloride 83.9 mEq./L., a blood sugar level of 15 mg./100 ml. (Folin-Wu), and a cerebrospinal fluid sugar level of 10 mg./100 ml.

At 8:00 a.m. he received intravenous fluids, including 50 per cent glucose and Sodium Amytal. His course was progressive (death occurred 27 hours after admission), although blood glucose levels were maintained between 100 and 200 mg./100 ml. Histologically, glycogen was demonstrated in the liver.

Case 2. A 3 year old previously well Negro female ingested, in the morning, 20 ml. or less of cologne, which contained 85 per cent denatured alcohol, small amounts of aromatic substances and methyl alcohol. She was found comatose at 6:00 a.m. She smelled of perfume. On physical examination she had a systolic blood pressure of 76 mm. Hg and a pulse rate of 92/minute. Her pupils were small, and tendon reflexes were somewhat depressed. Chemical studies of the blood were as follows: CO_2 of 9.1 mM./L.; chloride, 86.3 mEq./L.; calcium, 10.6 mg./100 ml.; and blood sugar, 22.1 mg./100 ml. (Folin-Wu). First, the child had gastric lavage. Four hours after hospitalization she had a seizure which was treated with intravenous calcium, sodium lactate and glucose. The convulsions ceased after administration of glucose, and the patient was responsive after 30 minutes. She recovered.

The relationship between alcohol ingestion and hypoglycemia in alcoholic adults has received recent attention. Two groups[39, 40] have made extensive metabolic studies of these patients. Neither liver damage per se nor "toxic effects" of alcohol as judged by changes in plasma enzymes (SGOT, SGPT) is an important factor. There is agreement that starvation and glycogen depletion are necessary predisposing factors in the adult. Hypoglycemia has been produced in normal adults after a 2- to 3-day period of fasting followed by alcohol administration. During this hypoglycemic state, there was no elevation in the blood sugar following administration of glucagon. On the other hand, alcohol per se does not inhibit the hyperglycemia produced by glucagon in the nonfasted individual.

Alcohol does not increase the peripheral utilization of glucose during the hypoglycemic phase, and plasma free fatty acids increase. Furthermore, plasma insulin levels, by immunoassay, do not increase. The hypoglycemia appears to be due to decreased hepatic output of glucose. Fructose conversion to glucose does not appear to be impaired. However, glucagon elicited a lesser hyperglycemic response, after 2 days of starvation and the administration of both alcohol and fructose, than it did in the absence of alcohol. These observations have been investigated in rat and rabbit liver slices in which decreased glycogen synthesis was observed after alcohol perfusion or ingestion.[39]

The exact mechanism of alcohol-induced hypoglycemia in the adult man is still undefined. Individual alcohol sensitivity appears to be a factor. More importantly, prolonged starvation with an associated liver glycogen depletion, requiring an increased rate of gluconeogenesis, appears to be a necessary predisposing condition. Hyperinsulinism and increased peripheral utilization are not factors in producing this hypoglycemia.

How these data apply to the well child who ingests ethyl alcohol acutely is unclear. The first case of Cummins suggests that glycogen depletion and starvation are not necessary factors. A more direct effect of alcohol on the intermediary metabolism in the liver is likely.

This preventable form of hypoglycemia must be diagnosed early and treated promptly with intravenous glucose.

Salicylate Toxicity

The syndrome of salicylate intoxication in young children and infants is characterized by a variety of metabolic effects, of which hyperpyrexia, respiratory alkalosis and, later, metabolic acidosis are characteristic. Intermediary metabolism is markedly disturbed, with production of many endogenous organic acids.[41] More commonly, the diverse effects on glucose metabolism result in hyperglycemia and glycosuria. In a survey of 49 patients with acute salicylate intoxication, Segar and Holliday[42] noted normal or elevated blood sugar levels in 14 patients in whom initial levels had been taken. Their experience is consistent with most other reports, even though hypoglycemia *has* been reported in salicylate intoxication.[43]

More recently, Mortimer and Lepow[44] reported 4 infants of ages 3 to 6 months in whom varicella was associated with hypoglycemia and a fatal outcome. A low level of sugar was found in the blood or cerebrospinal fluid in 3 patients; the fourth died on arrival at the hospital and had no demonstrable reducing substance in spinal fluid. Although salicylate measurements were not made, the authors noted that 3 of the patients had received large amounts of salicylate for a period of several days preceding admission. They postulated that starvation and infection decreased glycogen stores, and that salicylate interfered with glucose synthesis (i.e., gluconeogenesis) so that the increased metabolic requirements of infection in the young infant could not be met. The varicella was not considered to be the primary etiologic factor other than as a stimulus for salicylate administration.

Cotton and Fahlberg[45] have reported 2 infants of ages 10 months and 2 years in whom excessive salicylate ingestion was associated with hypoglycemia (blood sugar unmeasurable) and symptoms. One patient responded promptly to intravenous glucose, while the other improved more slowly. Both recovered without neurologic deficits. Limbeck et al.[46] have reported 3 infants under the age of 22 months with hypoglycemia following salicylate ingestion. In one of these patients, hypoglycemia was induced by a small dose of aspirin and was not associated with an increased level of plasma insulin.

The effects of salicylate on carbohydrate metabolism in man remain inadequately defined. Of interest is the antidiabetic activity of acetylsalicylate in adults.[47, 48] This drug is able to reduce hyperglycemia, glycosuria and ketonuria in adult diabetics, yet it has no effect in normal controls. Although salicylates in *in vivo* animal studies and *in vitro* tissue studies have produced an uncoupling of oxidative phosphorylation, this biochemical effect is inadequate to explain the diverse effects of these drugs on blood glucose levels and glucose metabolism in man.[49] It is important that an awareness of this possible etiology of hypoglycemia be considered in young infants. Additional studies of the mechanisms involved are needed.

Therapy should include the administration of glucose as well as methods to remove the excess salicylate.

Tolbutamide or Oral Hypoglycemic Agents

Tolbutamide has been responsible for severe and protracted hypoglycemia in susceptible adults.[50] With the widespread use of oral hypoglycemic agents, a careful history to determine the possibility of poisoning due to these agents should be included in any child presenting with acute hypoglycemia.

Exogenous Insulin

Hypoglycemia may be the result of excessive insulin administration, especially in patients with diabetes mellitus. A famous British homicide was solved when insulin was extracted from the victim's tissues.

Jamaican Vomiting Sickness

This serious disease of acute onset is limited to Jamaican natives. As early as 1916, Scott suspected poisoning with unripe ackees (*Blighia sapida*) (cited in reference 51). However, since the fruit was a common food for the population, it was difficult to incriminate. Characteristically, the disease occurs sporadically in family outbreaks during the colder winter months when food is scarce in the peasant population. The onset is dramatic and sudden, with severe vomiting, rapid prostration, tachycardia and hypotension. There is no temperature elevation or diarrhea. Following a latent period of a few hours, drowsiness, twitching, convulsions and coma with death may occur within 12 hours. Some individuals may have symptoms other than vomiting and progress to a fatal outcome, while others may recover. The disorder is most common in children aged 3 to 10 years who are in subnutritional, vitamin-deficient states.

In 1954 Jelliffe and Stuart[51] reported a 6 year old boy who was well at 6:00 A.M., unconscious at 7:00 A.M., in deep coma by 2:00 P.M. and dead by 9:30 P.M. When first hospitalized at 2:00 P.M., his blood sugar was 19 mg./100 ml. and adrenaline produced no blood sugar elevation within 15 minutes. Although normal and then hyperglycemic levels of sugar were produced with intravenous glucose, the progressive fatal course was unaltered. A liver biopsy showed fatty change and a low glycogen content (0.7 gm./100 gm.). No pathologic changes in the central nervous system were reported.

More recently, several groups have isolated toxic substances from the unripe fruit, ackee. Two ninhydrin positive substances, called hypoglycin A and B, have been found to be potent hypoglycemic agents.[52] Hypoglycin A produced rapid depletion of liver glycogen without histologic effects on alpha or beta cells of the pancreas. The mechanisms of action of these hypoglycemic substances have not been established.

In another study[53] hypoglycin was found to be a $C_7H_{11}NO_2$ with alpha-amino and carboxyl groups. It increased liver lipids and inhibited oxidative phosphorylation by liver mitochondria. Its action was different from insulin in that it decreased glycogen deposition in the rat diaphragm. Species susceptibility is variable. Thus, the cat and the dog are not susceptible, while the rabbit and the monkey are.[54] The emetic action has been separated from the hypoglycemic effect. Fatty metamorphosis of the liver occurs even in animals that do not develop hypoglycemia. Possible mechanisms include decreased gluconeogenesis and increased lipogenesis. Further studies are needed to define the exact biochemical sequences to explain these findings.

This disease is preventable and should be considered in the category of disorders caused by exogenous, ingested toxins. Education of the Jamaican population and improvement in economic and nutritional status should result in its abolition.

Miscellaneous Causes of Hypoglycemia

Tumors. In addition to tumors of the islet cells of the pancreas (*supra vide*), a variety of extrapancreatic neoplasms have been held responsible for hypoglycemic symptoms.[26, 55–60, 107] Although most of the patients have been adults with large tumors of mesenchymal and epithelial origin,[26, 55–59, 107] a 5 year old boy with a highly malignant Wilms' tumor infiltrating the colon, pancreas, and retroperitoneal structures was reported recently as having associated recurrent episodes of hypoglycemia.[60] Following excision of the tumor and a relatively small portion of the pancreas, the hypoglycemia was cured. No follow-up of this patient was presented and no studies of the mechanism of the hypoglycemia were performed.

In adults, several explanations of the low blood sugars have been considered. These include (1) an increased production of insulin-like material by the tumor, (2) the formation of an insulin stimulating material, (3) a substance to inhibit insulin degradation, and finally (4) an increased utilization of glucose by the tumor, per se.[26, 55-60] That the low blood sugar levels were caused by the tumor was shown by the fact that the hypoglycemia disappeared when the tumor was removed, only to return with recurrence of the malignancy.

The possibility of hypoglycemia should be considered in pediatric patients with tumors and symptoms of low blood glucose, although the association between these phenomena appears to be rare in infancy.

Central Nervous System. The association of central nervous system damage, including infection or injury, with hyperglycemia has been well documented in experimental animals and man since the classical experiments of Claude Bernard verified by MacLeod.[61] However, the etiologic role of central nervous system defects or disease in producing *hypo*glycemia is less well defined. Several investigators have suggested this relationship,[62 64] but their observations were given a variety of interpretations and have not been substantiated. Recently, Etheridge and Millichap[65] have again suggested that "neurologic disease was primary and may have been responsible for both the hypoglycemia and seizures in 10 (50 per cent) of 20 patients with cryptogenic hypoglycemia. . . ." The patients reported represent a heterogeneous group, and while the association is difficult to establish on the basis of clinical observations alone, an onset in early infancy with severe anatomic defects in the brain is highly suggestive. However, one of their patients with a central nervous system defect was subsequently studied by Sauls and Ulstrom[96] and was found to have multiple endocrine deficiencies as the cause of the hypoglycemia. Ultimate verification of the hypothesis that the brain damage is primary and responsible for the low blood sugar will depend upon reproducing this phenomenon in experimental animals with specific lesions.

Hypoglycemia Associated with Neonatal Cold Injury. Neonatal cold injury occurs in infants after prolonged exposure to a cold environment, which results in rectal temperatures below 90°F. The clinical manifestations of the infant with cold injury have been classically described by Mann and Elliott.[66] During the first week or two of life, there is increasing apathy and refusal to eat. The cry becomes "feeble" and may be described as a "whimper or a whine." The body is cold to the touch, and edema of the extremities or eyelids may be present. Hemorrhagic manifestations and diminishing renal function have been a less constant feature.

On physical examination, the rectal temperature is well below 90°F. and a low-reading thermometer (80 to 110°F.) must be used. "Although apparently conscious, the child lies motionless. The facial expression is serene and does not suggest ill health." The skin is very cold and the face, hands and feet may be very red in appearance. Pitting edema may be quite extensive. "Local hardening" may be present or develop on rewarming and is a poor prognostic sign. During recovery, tremors and convulsions can occur as a result of hypoglycemia.

In a report of 14 infants with neonatal cold injury these authors indicated that the "only important biochemical abnormality" found was a marked hypoglycemia in 4 of the 6 infants in whom blood sugar values were measured.[66] These values ranged from 10 mg./100 ml. or less to 46 mg./100 ml. Subsequently, Bower, Jones and Weeks[67] reported 70 newborns with cold injury. They reported blood urea levels of 90 mg./100 ml. or over in 5 infants with body temperature below 89°F., whereas values below 50 mg./100 ml. were present in 3 with temperature over 89°F. High phosphorus and potassium levels were found in 2 infants. No mention was made of blood glucose values. Arneil and Kerr[68] described 110 infants with rectal temperatures of 90°F. or less during the prolonged severe winter of 1961–1962 in Glasgow. No electrolyte or blood glucose determinations were included in this report.

Treatment consists of slowly rewarming the infant, feeding, and preventing infection. Intravenous or intragastric glucose solutions and antibiotics are indicated. Cortisone may be contraindicated because of the susceptibility of these infants to infection. Barbiturates should be avoided because of their prolonged action in hypothermic patients. Oxygen appears to be of little value for these babies.

Eight of the 14 infants died within 7 to 100 hours of admission. The striking finding at autopsy was massive pulmonary hemorrhage. Mild ascites (5 to 15 ml.) was present in all. Occasionally, evidences of infection were present.[66]

Most of the patients reported to date have been from the British Isles. Dutch investigators described a similar syndrome in the 1930's and 40's,[69, 70] as did Nassau[71] from Israel in an article entitled "Cold injury in a subtropical climate." Obviously, prevention is the most important aspect of this syndrome and Mann and Elliott condemn the "popular British belief that some mystic quality of health resides in a stream of cold air through an open window."

Idiopathic Hypoglycemia

The transient and persistent types of neonatal hypoglycemia have been described elsewhere (see Chapter Five).

Leucine-Induced Hypoglycemia

In 1956 Cochrane, Payne, Simpkiss and Woolf[72] reported that the essential amino acid leucine could produce a marked fall in the blood sugar level in certain hypoglycemic infants in whom the number of convulsions had increased on a high protein, low carbohydrate diet. Subsequently, more than 30 infants with idiopathic spontaneous hypoglycemia have been found to be sensitive to leucine.[17, 73–86] Although exact estimates of the incidence of leucine-induced hypoglycemia are unknown, it has been estimated that about one-third of all infants with idiopathic hypoglycemia are leucine sensitive. Some of the patients demonstrate hypoglycemia after the ingestion of isoleucine as well, and all who were tested by Mabry et al. did so after oral alpha-keto-isocaproic acid.[87] The importance of this subgroup of spontaneous hypoglycemia lies in the fact that the approach to therapy and the study of the pathogenesis of the entity are unique.

Characteristically, the onset of leucine-induced hypoglycemia occurs early in the first year of life: 23 of 24[17, 73–86] patients had an onset at or before 6 months of age. This is in contradistinction to the later onset of ketogenic hypoglycemia and islet cell adenomas. In the leucine-sensitive group there was often an inordinate delay in making the correct diagnosis, and the incidence of subsequent mental retardation and neurologic deficits was high (over 66 per cent).

Clinical Manifestations

Clinical manifestations in infants with leucine-induced hypoglycemia can appear as early as the day of birth[76] or as late as 8 months of age,[75] but the onset in the vast majority occurred between 1 and 6 months of age. Males predominated in a ratio of 1.5:1.0.[17, 73–83] Classically, symptoms and signs occurred shortly after a high protein meal and varied in severity from pallor and weakness to major convulsions. Prolonged fasting also induced hypoglycemia, which may have resulted from the accumulation of endogenous leucine. Ocular abnormalities, especially alternating esotropia and squint, were often observed. The interval between onset of hypoglycemic episodes and diagnosis of leucine-induced hypoglycemia varied between 3 weeks and 3½ years.

Laboratory Findings

The only positive laboratory finding at the time of symptoms is a low level of sugar in blood or in cerebrospinal fluid. Neither acetone nor reducing substances have been reported in the urine. The cerebrospinal fluid sugar has been particularly low (less than 15 mg./100 ml.) and may be diagnostic of hypoglycemia.

Tests of Carbohydrate Tolerance

The leucine tolerance test is diagnostic. After administration of oral (150 mg./kg.) or intravenous (75 mg./kg.) leucine, the blood sugar level

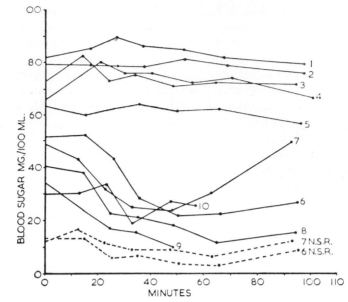

Figure 56. Blood sugar (– – – – –) of the four patients with hypoglycemia (Curves 6 through 10) and of five normal individuals (Curves 1 through 5) after being fed L-leucine. (From Cochrane et al., J. Clin. Invest., 35:411, 1956.)

decreases to at least *50 per cent* of the fasting level within 20 to 45 minutes[72, 76] (Fig. 56). The plasma level of insulin rises significantly as the blood sugar level falls.[76, 77, 83] Often the usual clinical manifestations of hypoglycemia are precipitated by the test and respond promptly to parenteral glucose or epinephrine.[72, 74–77] One syringe filled with 50 per cent glucose and one with glucagon should be at the bedside when this test is performed. If there is even a possibility that intravenous fluids may be needed, an intravenous infusion of saline should be started before the administration of leucine and continued throughout the test.

Hypoglycemia may be precipitated by a prolonged fast in these infants. The glucose tolerance test contributes little to the diagnosis and the glucagon and epinephrine tolerance tests are usually normal.

Therapy

As in all acute hypoglycemic episodes, the immediate treatment is to supply glucose for the brain by administering either epinephrine or glucagon, or oral or parenteral glucose.

The long term therapy in leucine-induced hypoglycemia is to provide a diet which contains minimal amounts of leucine, yet is adequate for growth (see Appendix I). This is essentially a low protein diet and has been described by Roth and Segal.[88] In addition, high carbohydrate feedings are provided 20 to 30 minutes after meals, upon arising, and at bedtime as originally suggested by Cochrane et al.[72] Others have used corticotropin or cortisone as well as extra carbohydrate feedings, with variable success.[73, 76] The protein catabolic effect of adrenal steroids may theoretically produce endogenous levels of leucine which could trigger hypoglycemia, depending upon the patient's sensitivity.

Gomez et al.[79] have recommended the use of sodium glutamate (10 gm./day added as "Accént") in these patients. The basis for this therapy was that glutamate produced a striking improvement in the electroencephalogram during leucine-induced hypoglycemia, without affecting the blood glucose level. The patient was reported to show marked improvement with the added glutamate over a 7-month period of observation. Additional information is needed before any conclusions are justified.

Diazoxide, one of the benzothiadiazine nondiuretic, antihypertensive drugs, has also been useful in the treatment of leucine-induced hypoglycemia.[82] However, additional data and follow-up are necessary before this drug can be recommended. In one of our patients, leucine sensitivity disappeared after 5 months of treatment with Diazoxide (12 mg./kg./day).

Clinical Course and Prognosis

The clinical manifestations tend to vary in severity; with repeated leucine-induced hypoglycemic episodes, both mental and physical deterioration ensue.[72–86] Often, the initial symptoms are mild and then increase in severity. The hypoglycemia seems to subside in some of the children and tends to improve spontaneously by 4 to 6 years of age.[74]

The prognosis for life appears good, with only an occasional infant death.[83] Whether some of the crib or cot deaths during the first 6 months of life may be related to leucine-induced hypoglycemia bears investigation. The outlook for mental and neurologic normality is poor. Over two-thirds of the children with this type of hypoglycemia are mentally retarded. The onset in early infancy, the long delay in establishing the correct diagnosis and the therapeutic problems in maintaining normoglycemia all may contribute to these results. What the outcome will be with early diagnosis and effective treatment remains to be determined.

Pathogenesis and Pathology

Although neither the etiology nor the molecular defect are known, it would appear that the hypoglycemia following leucine ingestion is the result of insulin secretion.[75, 76, 83] That the glucose response is an exaggeration of that seen in normal children and adults has been shown by Di George, et al.[89] and Becker et al.[90] Leucine can also produce hypoglycemia in about 50 per cent of patients with functioning islet cell adenomas.[77, 91, 92] An increased sensitivity to leucine can be produced in normal adults by administration of chlorpropamide or lente insulin.[90, 93]

It has not been possible to determine any block or deviation in leucine metabolism in these patients. A number of amino acids have also been administered to these children without producing hypoglycemia.[87] Some of the patients show hypoglycemia after isoleucine, although the significance of this finding remains obscure.

Gomez et al.[79] and Gentz and associates[80] suggest that leucine has a direct effect on the central nervous system in addition to inducing hypoglycemia. This hypothesis is based on observing evidences of central nervous system excitation in the absence of hypoglycemia[80] and the return to normal of the EEG in the presence of hypoglycemia after administration of glutamate.[79] Both occurrences may have been related to factors other than the presence of leucine. However, these authors present an intriguing additional possible role for leucine in the production of mental subnormality in the sensitive patients.

In 3 of 4 patients, hyperplasia of the beta cells of the islets of Langerhans has been observed at operation or post mortem.[77, 83] Whether the hyperplasia is the result of or the reason for the leucine sensitivity remains to be elucidated.

Genetics

Although the first patients described were a family consisting of a father and two daughters,[72] additional family studies are not convincing. The criteria for leucine sensitivity in one reported family were very vague.[81] The exact mode of inheritance is obscure. Sporadic cases seem to outnumber by far the patients from single families.

Summary

Leucine-induced hypoglycemia has an onset before 6 months of age and occurs following a meal high in protein or after a prolonged fast. The management of the patients has been difficult. A low leucine diet, steroids, and carbohydrate feeding 20 to 30 minutes after meals have been recommended. To date, the prognosis has been poor in that over 66 per cent of the patients are mentally retarded.

The hypoglycemia probably results from insulin secretion induced by leucine.

Ketotic Hypoglycemia

Although it was first recognized by Ross and Josephs[94] in 1924, the combination of convulsions, hypoglycemia and acetonuria received relatively little attention until the recent report by Colle and Ulstrom.[95]

Initially included in the syndrome of cyclic vomiting, which has diverse etiologies, ketotic hypoglycemia has been characterized by "a relatively late onset, long periods of good health between episodes and ease of control of symptoms with diet alone."[95] Clinical manifestations occur in the early morning following prolonged food deprivation such as missing dinner or in association with illness.

While it is probably the most common cause of hypoglycemia in young childhood, the exact incidence of ketotic hypoglycemia is not known. Thirty cases were diagnosed in a 15-year period in Minneapolis.[96] Many other cases are known to this group and to the authors. With the report of the provocative test utilizing a low calorie ketogenic diet, the diagnosis of this type of hypoglycemia should be made more frequently and with more certainty. Within the past years, at least 5 children have been classified in this group at the Research and Educational Hospitals, University of Illinois College of Medicine, including one boy who was a "Russell" dwarf (see page 237).

Clinical Manifestations

Ketotic hypoglycemia has been reported predominantly in males (22 males to 8 females). The history has often revealed a low birth weight, 23 of 30 being under 2500 grams, and the presenting height and weight of the affected children were more than 1 S.D. below the mean in many (24/30).[96] A diminished quantity of subcutaneous fat has been noted. The discrepancy in weight (underweight) was greater relatively than that in height. One patient had Turner's syndrome. In 4 of 30 cases, the hypoglycemic child was a twin and always the smaller of the two. Four of the 30 patients had cataracts of the crystalline lens. The age of onset varied between 14 months and 5½ years (mean age of 27 months) and attacks invariably occurred between 6 and 10:00 A.M. All the children had symptoms related to the central nervous system, ranging from apathy and listlessness to coma and convulsions. The clinical manifestations were transient and cleared spontaneously or with the ingestion of food. If hospitalized, all were cured by the administration of glucose. Hypoglycemic episodes recurred at intervals of a few months to a year or more.

Laboratory Findings

At the time of the appearance of symptoms, the blood sugar level was lower than 40 mg./100 ml. and the urine was strongly positive for acetone. No other characteristic laboratory findings have been described. All the patients had normal blood sugar levels of 60 to 85 mg./100 ml. after an overnight fast of 12 to 14 hours.

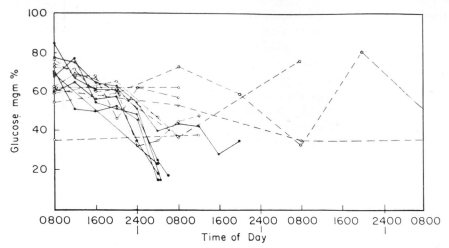

Figure 57. Response of blood sugar levels to ketogenic diet. The solid lines represent the values for the children with sporadic hypoglycemia and the dotted lines, the values for the control children who were under 4 years of age. (From Colle and Ulstrom, J. Pediat., *64*:632, 1964.)

Tolerance Tests of Carbohydrate Metabolism

The diagnosis is based on the hypoglycemic response to a ketogenic provocative test (see Fig. 57). The patient is given a high carbohydrate diet (50 per cent total calories) for 3 to 5 days. After an overnight fast, the low calorie ketogenic diet is given. All infants develop acetonuria within 8 to 12 hours, but in the susceptible child, clinical manifestations and marked hypoglycemia occur after another 4 to 12 hours (Fig. 57). A striking elevation in free fatty acids in plasma is present. At the time of hypoglycemia, a diminished to absent hyperglycemic response to glucagon is typical. In contrast, the glucagon tolerance test is normal after the usual 12-hour fast.

The other tolerance tests are not helpful. The patients are not leucine sensitive. In one patient (see Fig. 58), no increased sensitivity to insulin was found. Tolbutamide tolerance tests are essentially normal.[96] As in most instances of hypoglycemia in infancy, neither the oral nor the intra venous glucose tolerance tests are helpful.

Therapy

In the acute episode, either oral or parenteral glucose produces a prompt clearing of clinical manifestations.

In order to prevent recurrences, the parents are instructed to distribute the caloric intake over the waking hours, including a bedtime snack. Potato chips and other sources of fat should be excluded from this snack, and a high fat intake should be carefully avoided. In addition, the child's urine must be checked for acetone at bedtime and on arising, as well as during any illness. If the urine is positive for acetone, a high carbohydrate intake is encouraged until the acetone has disappeared. This diet includes hard candy, sweetened orange juice, cola drinks (NOT diet drinks), etc. If the patient is vomiting, parenteral glucose is necessary and will prevent the onset of symptomatic hypoglycemia.

Clinical Course and Prognosis

The episodes may be widely spaced or may recur regularly at monthly intervals. The patients studied have had normal or near normal intelligence. The attacks of hypoglycemia tend to become less frequent and to disappear after 4 to 7 years of age.

Pathogenesis

Colle and Ulstrom[95] have postulated several possible mechanisms to explain the hypoglycemia including (1) failure of gluconeogenesis, (2) failure to reverse the glycolytic pathway, (3) an inability to utilize free fatty acids by muscle and fat tissue, and/or (4) failure to adapt to starvation by decreasing glucose oxidation by peripheral tissue. In support of the concept that gluconeogenesis is deficient, they found that cortisone given prior to the ketogenic diet prevented hypoglycemia. In another patient on a high protein intake before the test diet, the hyperglycemic response to glucagon at the time of ketonuria was increased.

Additional possibilities have been provided by the observations of Madison et al.[97] in the dog. The administration of β-hydroxybutyrate and acetoacetate stimulated insulin secretion which, in turn, inhibited the release of glucose from the liver and prevented uncontrolled lipolysis and fatal ketoacidosis. These authors suggest that the ketones must have a controlling influence on further ketone and FFA production and also inhibit glucose utilization in the peripheral tissues. Any break in this regulative mechanism may result in hypoglycemia.

Experiments to define the cause and pathogenesis of ketogenic hypoglycemia remain to be done.

Case Reports

Case 1. R. E. "Russell" dwarf.[51] This 4 year old boy weighed 3 lb. 3 oz. (1450 gm.) at birth. The pregnancy had gone full term, but the mother was told that the placenta was one-half normal size. Pregnancy and delivery were normal. The neonatal course was uneventful and the infant was discharged after 9 weeks of hospitalization weighing 5 lb. 9 oz. (2500 gm.). The head circumference was 35.5 cm. and chest circumference 30 cm.

The mother was 29 years old, 5 ft. 7 in. tall and weighed 130 lbs. The father was 31 years old, 6 ft. 1 in. tall and weighed 195 lbs. There was one

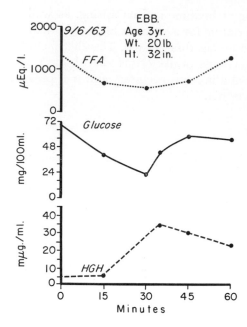

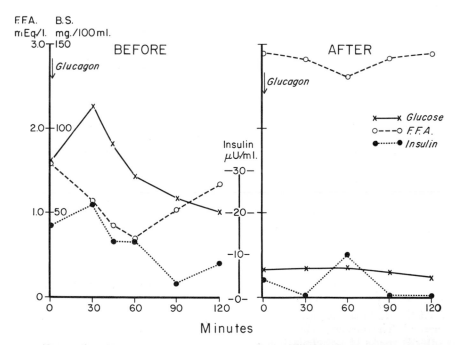

Figure 58. Insulin tolerance test in a "Russell" dwarf. Regular insulin (0.1 U./kg.) was administered intravenously at time 0. This is a normal response to insulin and the patient remained asymptomatic. FFA, free fatty acids; HGH, human growth hormone levels in plasma.

Figure 59. Ketogenic hypoglycemia in a "Russell" dwarf. Glucagon (30 μg./ kg.) was administered intravenously before and after ketogenic-provocative diet. The latter test was performed when the patient had a positive urinary acetone test and was listless and lethargic as well as hypoglycemic.

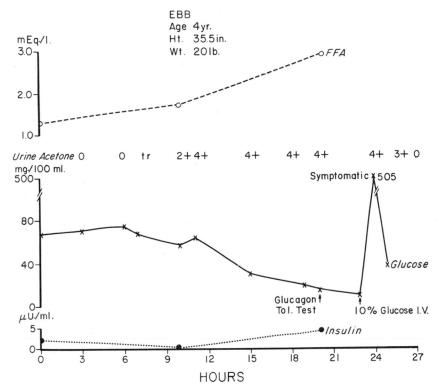

Figure 60. The effect of a 24-hour ketogenic diet in a "Russell" dwarf on the levels of blood glucose, free fatty acids (FFA) and plasma insulin and urinary acetone.

brother of age 5½ who was 4 ft. tall and weighed 50 lbs., and who had weighed 8 lb. at birth. A younger sister weighed 7½ lb. at term birth.

The patient sat at 12 months and walked at 18 months. At 18, 24 and 36 months of age, he weighed 12, 16, and 20 lb., respectively. His head always appeared large in proportion to the rest of his body.

He was relatively well until 2½ years of age, at which time he had a generalized seizure associated with fever. Since that time he has had 6 to 8 seizures, some of them associated with fever. On almost all occasions, the urine has been positive for acetone at the time of the convulsion.

He was admitted to Research and Educational Hospitals at age 3 years. At that time his head was 46 cm. in circumference, his height, 32 inches (81 cm.), and his weight 20 lb. (9.0 kg.). His palate was high arched. His chest was pigeon-like; his fifth finger was short and curved. The complete blood count and urinalysis were normal. His bone age was compatible with that of a 2 year old. An EEG was done and was abnormal, with slowing in all areas, maximal in the left frontal region. An insulin tolerance test was normal, with growth hormone levels rising from 5 to 35 mµg./ml. (Fig. 58).

He was readmitted at the age of 3 years, 10 months, at which time a pneumoencephalogram was performed and interpreted to be normal. A PBI was 7.2 µg./100 ml. His head circumference was 46.5 cm.; chest circumference, 46 cm., height 35.5 in. (90 cm.) and weight 20 lb. (9.0 kg.).

He was readmitted at 4½ years and had normal fasting blood sugar and glucagon tolerance tests (Fig. 59). After 3 days of a high carbohydrate diet, a ketogenic diet was started, and he was found to have acetonuria after 11 hours, at which time the blood sugar and glucagon tolerance tests were normal (Fig. 60). At 20 hours after the initiation of the ketogenic diet, he had severe symptomatic hypoglycemia and a depressed glucagon tolerance (Fig. 59). He responded promptly to intravenous glucose (Fig. 60).

After diagnosis was established, this patient had acetonuria on several occasions, but it responded to high carbohydrate feedings. He had not had another seizure after 5 months of follow-up observation.

Case 2. K. R. (R. & E. #56-07-12). When first seen at the Michael Reese Hospital, the patient was a 1205 gm. Negro female, born to a 15 year old primigravida mother on July 19, 1962, after 35 weeks gestation (< tenth percentile). The prenatal course was normal. Labor lasted 5½ hours and the delivery was uncomplicated. The infant breathed and cried spontaneously. Her head circumference was 28 cm., her chest circumference, 24 cm. The remainder of the examination was normal. At 36 hours of age the infant became jittery and at 45 hours of age, had a convulsion. The concentration of blood glucose at that time was undetectable. The patient was treated with 10 per cent glucose intravenously. On the third day of life ACTH (2 units twice daily) was begun. She remained listless and lethargic and a repeat blood glucose value was 13 mg./100 ml. Fifty per cent glucose (2 cc./kg.) was given intravenously but after 5 hours the blood glucose level was still only 23 mg./100 ml.

On the fourth day of life a glucagon tolerance test was done, with the following results: the fasting blood glucose was 27 mg./100 ml.; at 30 minutes, 87 mg./100 ml.; at 60 minutes, 142 mg./100 ml.; at 90 minutes, 51 mg./100 ml., and at 120 minutes, 50 mg./100 ml. The infant continued to be jittery, but was more active. On the fifth day an intravenous glucose tolerance test (1 gm./kg.) was performed with the patient still being fed with intravenous fluids. The test showed a fasting blood glucose level of 37 mg./100 ml.; at 5 minutes, 255 mg./100 ml.; at 10 minutes, 183 mg./100 ml., at 20 minutes, 179 mg./100 ml.; at 30 minutes, 122 mg./100 ml., at 45 minutes, 98 mg./100 ml.; at 60 minutes, 62 mg./100 ml., at 90 minutes, 37 mg./100 ml. and at 120 minutes, 25 mg./100 ml. A significantly increased disappearance rate (k_t) of 2.7 per cent/min. was calculated.

ACTH therapy was discontinued on the twelfth day of life. The following day, the blood glucose values were 17 and 16 mg./100 ml., and administration of ACTH was reinstituted. A leucine tolerance test 2 days later showed a fasting blood glucose of 116 mg./100 ml.; 15 minutes, 120 mg./100 ml.; 30 minutes, 73 mg./100 ml.; 45 minutes, 59 mg./100 ml.; 60 minutes, 60 mg./100 ml. and at 120 minutes, 56 mg./100 ml. Because of the possibility of leucine sensitivity, a repeat leucine tolerance test was done at 20 days of age. The fasting blood glucose was 103 mg./100 ml.; 15 minutes, 99 mg./100 ml.; 30 minutes, 92 mg./100 ml.; 45 minutes, 101 mg./100 ml.; 60 minutes, 113 mg./100 ml.; and 90 minutes, 92 mg./100 ml. This was a normal response. Following this test, ACTH was reduced to 2 units once daily and discontinued on the twenty-fifth day of life. The infant's subsequent hospital course was uneventful and she was discharged to the premature clinic for follow-up.

The patient was readmitted to Michael Reese Hospital at 9 months of age because of lethargy. At that time the blood glucose level was 25 mg./100 ml. and acetonuria was noted. A repeat leucine tolerance test was normal. The mother described numerous occasions on which the patient would awaken in

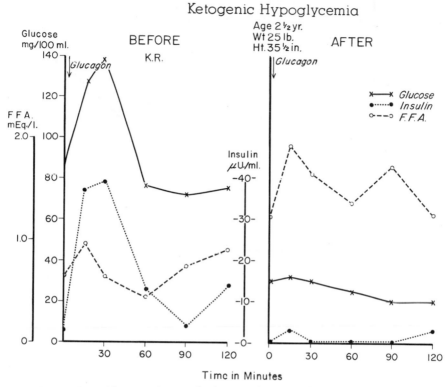

Figure 61. Glucagon (30 μg./kg.) was administered intravenously before and after a ketogenic-provocative diet. The after-test was performed when the patient was listless, lethargic and hypoglycemic and had marked acetonuria.

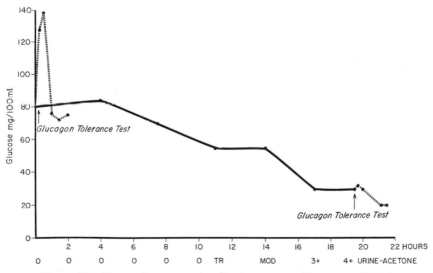

Figure 62. Ketogenic-provocative diet in a susceptible patient (K.R.).

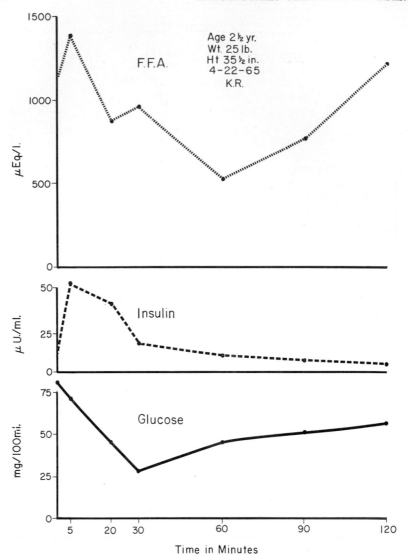

Figure 63. An intravenous tolbutamide tolerance test (20 mg./kg.) in a patient with ketotic hypoglycemia.

the mornings with listlessness and fatigue. She always seemed to improve after taking orange juice or sweetened fluids.

    She was first seen at Research and Educational Hospitals at 2½ years of age after a 24-hour period of weakness and lethargy which the mother had not been able to control in the usual manner. Physical examination revealed a slightly lethargic, uncooperative 2½ year old child whose weight was 25 lb. (tenth percentile) and height 35½ in. (twenty-fifth percentile). The examination was otherwise normal. The initial sample of urine showed a 2+ acetonuria, though repeat urinalyses throughout the day were negative for acetone.

Laboratory data included a hemoglobin of 11.2 gm./100 ml., a white blood count of 7600/mm.³, a carbon dioxide combining power of 24 mM./L., a fasting blood glucose of 84 mg./100 ml., a blood urea nitrogen of 10 mg./100 ml. and normal electrolytes. Her control cortisol levels in plasma were normal (7 μg./100 ml.) and rose to 57.2 μg./100 ml. after ACTH stimulation.

A control glucagon tolerance test was done (Fig. 61), and a provocative ketogenic test was also performed (Fig. 62). The patient became ketotic at 11 hours and the blood glucose level fell from 80 mg./100 ml. to 30 mg./100 ml. after 17 hours, at which time a repeat glucagon tolerance test was done (Fig. 61). At this time the patient was lethargic, but responded promptly to parenteral glucose.

A subsequent intravenous glucose tolerance test revealed the following results: a fasting blood glucose of 94 mg./100 ml.; at 5 minutes, 250 mg./100 ml.; at 10 minutes, 233 mg./100 ml.; at 20 minutes, 166 mg./100 ml.; at 30 minutes, 121 mg./100 ml.; at 45 minutes, 82 mg./100 ml.; at 60 minutes, 74 mg./100 ml.; at 75 minutes, 75 mg./100 ml.; at 90 minutes, 79 mg./100 ml.; at 120 minutes, 79 mg./100 ml. A k_t of 3.0 per cent/min. was calculated.

A tolbutamide test was also done and was somewhat abnormal (Fig. 63).

Following these tests the child was discharged to be followed in the Metabolic Clinic. The mother was instructed to test the child's urine each morning and evening for acetone. If the urine is acetone positive, the child is to be given orange juice or sweetened drinks. To date there have been no recurrences of the child's hypoglycemic episodes.

The case is presented because of the unusual course of an infant with transient symptomatic neonatal hypoglycemia who subsequently had recurrences between 8 and 30 months of age. At this time, she has ketotic hypoglycemia. Six other young children who had neonatal hypoglycemia were given a ketogenic provocative diet between 18 and 30 months of age and did not develop hypoglycemia.

Lack of Epinephrine Response to Induced Hypoglycemia

Von Euler and Luft[98] reported that hypoglycemia induced by insulin administration increased the urinary excretion of adrenaline and noradrenaline in normal adults. Broberger, Jungner and Zetterström[99] observed 3 patients with "idiopathic hypoglycemia" who did not develop tachycardia, an elevation in blood pressure, or other sympathomimetic signs at the time of hypoglycemic symptoms. In the same year, Kinsbourne and Woolf[100] reported an infant with similar symptoms. The former investigators subsequently found that 5 of 11 hypoglycemic children did not have an adrenomedullary response to insulin-induced hypoglycemia;[101] they also described an insulin tolerance test and the collection of urine for determination of catecholamine that they used to make this diagnosis.

After an overnight fast, a standard insulin tolerance test (see page 203) is performed at 9:00 A.M., with blood sampling for 3 hours. In addition, pulse rate and blood pressure are measured at 10-minute intervals. The bladder is emptied with a catheter at 6:00 A.M., and all the urine is collected for 3 hours as a control period prior to the administration of

insulin for adrenaline and noradrenaline determinations. Urine is then collected throughout the tolerance test for similar analyses. Normally, a
three- to fivefold increase in catecholamine excretion occurs.

In our clinics, voided urine is collected for 12 hours preceding the
test and for 4 to 6 hours thereafter. Furthermore, a number of the metabolites in addition to epinephrine and norepinephrine are measured, including VMA, metanephrine and normetanephrine (see page 202).

There have been questions raised about the explanation for the failure to increase catecholamine excretion in these patients. Broberger et
al.[101] postulated that the failure of response is due to primary adrenomedullary failure which, in turn, is responsible for the hypoglycemia.
Brunjes et al.[102] studied 8 children with hypoglycemia, 7 of whom failed
to show an increase in urinary epinephrine after insulin administration.
They postulate a primary defect in innervation of the adrenal medulla,
either in the hypothalamus or in the autonomic nervous system. On the
other hand, Goldfien et al.[103] have found that the sympathetic response
can be suppressed by prolonged insulin coma. They also comment on the
rarity of spontaneous hypoglycemia in adrenalectomized patients adequately treated with corticosteroids. Thus, this phenomenon may be a
secondary one and a consequence rather than a cause of hypoglycemia.

Irrespective of pathogenesis, the suggestion of Broberger et al.[101] for
use of ephedrine sulfate (10 mg. daily) may be a useful adjunct in the
therapy of sporadic spontaneous hypoglycemia of infancy. Further observations are indicated.

Interestingly, 11 of 16 reported cases were male.[100–102] Eleven of 15
patients weighed under 2500 gm. at birth. There is a remarkable similarity
between these infants and those with symptomatic neonatal hypoglycemia
(see Chapter Five) and ketotic hypoglycemia (see page 235).

Cases with Unknown Etiology

Even after the most careful diagnostic work-up, a significant number
of infants with recurrent spontaneous symptomatic hypoglycemia remain
in the group of unknown etiology or pathogenesis. These include the
familial type, the so-called "infant giants," neonates with intractable persistent hypoglycemia, and those with the sporadic spontaneously occurring
hypoglycemia of infancy.

The Familial Type. Although McQuarrie[2] emphasized the familial
nature of idiopathic spontaneously occurring hypoglycemia in infants,
there have been only 6[72, 81] well-documented families reported. Of these,
4 families with affected children were in the original McQuarrie report.[2]
In one family, the two sisters and the father were leucine sensitive.[72] In
the other 5 families, the cause and pathogenesis of the hypoglycemia are
not clear.

The intractable persistent hypoglycemia starting in the neonatal period has been discussed in the differential diagnosis of transient symptomatic neonatal hypoglycemia (see Chapter Five).

Idiopathic Spontaneous Hypoglycemia. This type of hypoglycemia is characterized by an early age of onset, a prolonged course, and responsiveness to steroids or ACTH. These infants are not leucine sensitive and do not fulfill the criteria for ketotic hypoglycemia. The hypoglycemic episodes can occur at any time, usually in the early morning. The clinical manifestations are not distinctive but often include convulsions. The initial episode can be diagnosed from the low glucose level in the cerebrospinal fluid, which persists into the post ictal state, at which time the blood glucose may have returned to normal. While ocular manifestations are commonly associated with the acute hypoglycemic attack, abnormalities of the eyes have only recently been emphasized and include congenital glaucoma, exotropia, estropia, congenital cataracts, etc.[104]

These infants have been described in detail by Hartmann and Jaudon,[1] McQuarrie,[2] and Ulstrom.[4] Haworth and Coodin[32] reported 7 patients of their own and reviewed 51 additional cases from the literature through 1959. Although some of these patients may well have been classified in the leucine-sensitive or ketotic groups of idiopathic hypoglycemia, the majority appear to be of the unknown type. In 60 per cent, the age of onset was under 6 months. Dietary treatment was usually of no value. Many infants responded to steroid or ACTH therapy, yet 40 per cent (25 of 58) required pancreatectomy for control. Of the latter, the operation was curative in 15 instances.

In this review,[32] the pancreas was examined histologically in 29 cases, with evidence of hypertrophy and hyperplasia of the islet cells in 9. Whether this observation reflects the primary cause of the low sugar, or the secondary effects of intensive therapy remains to be elucidated. With the availability of plasma insulin assays, the answer to this problem may be forthcoming.

Significant neurologic sequelae have been found in over half of the patients who had onset of disease under 6 months of age. In contrast, of infants in whom the onset was later, 88 per cent were normal.

The diagnostic work-up and therapy, including steroids and pancreatectomy, for this group of infants with idiopathic hypoglycemia of unknown type has been presented in detail in the previous chapter (see pages 197 to 210).

SUMMARY

The various types of hypoglycemia in infants and children have been presented. Although much has been learned in recent years about the pathogenesis and physiological mechanisms in disorders of carbohydrate metabolism, this group of conditions remains puzzling. Emphasis has been placed on the age of onset, clinical course and the use of newer diagnostic techniques, including carefully controlled carbohydrate tolerance tests and plasma hormone assays. This approach should result in more effective therapy earlier in the course of the hypoglycemia.

The high incidence of neurologic defects, especially in infants with early onset, strongly emphasizes the necessity for prompt diagnosis and therapy.

REFERENCES

1. Hartmann, A. F., and Jaudon, J. C.: Hypoglycemia. J. Pediat. 11:1, 1937.
2. McQuarrie, I.: Idiopathic spontaneously occurring hypoglycemia in infants. A.M.A. J. Amer. Dis. Child. 87:399, 1954.
3. Conn, J. W., and Seltzer, H. S.: Spontaneous hypoglycemia. Amer. J. Med. 19:460, 1955.
4. Ulstrom, R. A.: Idiopathic spontaneous hypoglycemia. In Linneweh, F. (ed.): Erblishe Stoffwechselkrankheiten. Berlin, Urban and Schwarzenberg, 1962, p. 225.
5. Raben, M. S.: Growth hormone. New England J. Med. 226:31; 82, 1962.
6. Roth, J., Glick, S. M., Yalow, R. S., and Berson, S. A.: Hypoglycemia: a potent stimulus to secretion of growth hormone. Science 140:987, 1963.
7. Hunter, W. M., and Greenwood, F. C.: Studies on the secretion of human-pituitary-growth hormone. Brit. M. J. 1:804, 1964.
8. Cornblath, M., Parker, M. L., Reisner, S. H., Forbes, A. E., and Daughaday, W. H.: Secretion and metabolism of growth hormone in premature and full term infants. J. Clin. Endocrinol. 25:209, 1965.
9. Nadler, H. L., Neumann, L. L., and Gershberg, H.: Hypoglycemia, growth retardation and probable isolated growth hormone deficiency in a one-year old child. J. Pediat. 63:977, 1963.
10. Mahon, W. A., Mitchell, M. L., Steinke, J., and Raben, M. S.: Effect of human growth hormone on hypoglycemic states. New England J. Med. 267:1179, 1962.
11. Soyka, L. F., Molliver, M., and Crawford, J. D.: Idiopathic hypoglycaemia of infancy treated with human growth hormone. Lancet 1:1015, 1964.
12. McQuarrie, I., Bell, E. T., Zimmermann, B., and Wright, W. S.: Deficiency of alpha cells of pancreas as possible etiological factor in familial hypoglycemosis. Fed. Proc. 9:337, 1950 (Abstract).
13. Grollman, A., McCaleb, W. E., and White, F. N.: Glucagon deficiency as a cause of hypoglycemia. Metabolism 13:686, 1964.
14. Unger, R. H., Eisentraut, A. M., McCall, M. S., and Madison, L. L.: Glucagon antibodies and an immunoassay for glucagon. J. Clin. Invest. 40:1280, 1961.
15. Howard, J. M., Moss, N. H., and Rhoads, J. E.: Collective review; hyperinsulinism and islet cell tumors of the pancreas with 398 recorded tumors. Internat. Abstr. Surg. 90:417, 1950.
16. Boley, S. J., Lin, J., and Schiffmann, A.: Functioning pancreatic adenomas in infants and children. Surgery 48:592, 1960.
17. Hartmann, A. F., Sr., Wohltmann, H. J., Holowach, J., and Caldwell, B. M.: Studies in hypoglycemia. J. Pediat. 56:211, 1960.
18. François, R., Pradon, M., Sherrer, M., and Uglienco, A. R.: Hypoglycemia due to pancreatic islet cell adenoma. J. Pediat. 60:721, 1962.
19. Crigler, J. F., Jr.: [Discussion of Cabot case at the Weekly Clinicopathological

Exercises of Massachusetts General Hospital.] New England J. Med. *266*: 1272, 1962.

20. Floyd, J. C., Jr., Fajans, S. S., Knopf, R. F., and Conn, J. W.: Plasma insulin in organic hyperinsulinism; comparative effects of tolbutamide, leucine, and glucose. J. Clin. Endocrinol. *24*:747, 1964.
21. Fonkalsrud, E. W., Dilley, R. B., and Longmire, W. P., Jr.: Insulin secreting tumors of the pancreas. Ann. Surg. *159*:730, 1964.
22. Rogers, F. A.: Islet cell tumors of the pancreas and hyperinsulinism. Am. J. Surg. *99*:268, 1960.
23. Crain, E. L., Jr., and Thorn, G. W.: Functioning pancreatic islet cell adenomas; a review of the literature and presentation of two new differential tests. Medicine *28*:427, 1949.
24. Lacy, P. E.: Electron microscopy of the beta cell of the pancreas. Am. J. Med. *31*:851, 1961.
25. Fajans, S. S., Schneider, J. M., Schteingart, D. E., and Conn, J. W.: The diagnostic value of sodium tolbutamide in hypoglycemic states. J. Clin. Endocrinol. *21*:371, 1961.
26. Samols, E.: Hypoglycaemia in neoplasia. Postgrad. M. J. *39*:634, 1963.
27. Berson, S. A., and Yalow, R. S.: Immunoassay of plasma insulin. Ciba Foundation Colloquia on Endocrinology *14*:182, 1962.
28. Samols, E., and Marks, V.: Insulin assay in insulinomas. Brit. M. J. *1*:507, 1963.
29. Marks, V.: The investigation of hypoglycaemia. *In* Pyke, D. A. (ed.): Disorders of Carbohydrate Metabolism. Philadelphia, J. B. Lippincott, 1962, p. 229.
30. Potter, E. L.: Pathology of the Fetus and the Newborn. 2nd ed. Chicago, Year Book Medical Publishers, 1961, pp. 334, 338.
31. Gerrard, J. W.: Kernicterus. Brain *75*:526, 1952.
32. Haworth, J. C., and Coodin, F. J.: Idiopathic spontaneous hypoglycemia in children: report of seven cases and review of the literature. Pediatrics *25*:748, 1960.
33. Douglas, D. M.: Spontaneous hyperinsulinism due to benign hyperplasia of islet cells. Arch. Dis. Child. *34*:171, 1959.
34. Bickel, H., Smallwood, W. C., Smellie, J. M., Baar, H. S., and Hickmans, E. M.: Cystine storage disease with aminoaciduria and dwarfism (Lignac-Fanconi disease). Acta Paediat. *42*(Suppl. 00):1, 1952.
35. Kahn, E., and Wayburne, S.: Hypoglycaemia in patients suffering from advanced protein malnutrition (kwashiorkor): Proc. Nutr. Soc. South. Africa *1*:21, 1960.
36. Slone, D., Taitz, L. S., and Gilchrist, G. S.: Aspects of carbohydrate metabolism in kwashiorkor; with special reference to spontaneous hypoglycemia. Brit. M. J. *1*:32, 1961.
37. Dodge, P. R., Mancall, E. L., Crawford, J. D., Knapp, J., and Paine, R. S.: Hypoglycemia complicating treatment of phenylketonuria with a phenylalanine-deficient diet. New England J. Med. *260*:1104, 1959.
38. Cummins, L. H.: Hypoglycemia and convulsions in children following alcohol ingestion. J. Pediat. *58*:23, 1961.
39. Field, J. B., Williams, H. E., and Mortimore, G. E.: Studies on the mechanisms of ethanol-induced hypoglycemia. J. Clin. Invest. *42*:497, 1963.
40. Freinkel, N., Singer, D. L., Arky, R. A., Bleicher, S. J., Anderson, J. B., and Silbert, C. K.: Alcohol hypoglycemia. I. Carbohydrate metabolism of patients with clinical alcohol hypoglycemia and the experimental reproduction of the syndrome with pure ethanol. J. Clin. Invest. *42*:1112, 1963.
41. Schwartz, R., Landy, G., Taller, D., and Thein, M. A.: Organic acid excretion in salicylate intoxication. J. Pediat. *66*:658, 1965.
42. Segar, W. E., and Holliday, M. A.: Physiologic abnormalities of salicylate intoxication. New England J. Med. *259*:1191, 1958.
43. Barnett, H. L., Powers, J. R., Benward, J. H., and Hartmann, A. F.: Salicylate intoxication in infants and children. J. Pediat. *21*:214, 1942.
44. Mortimer, E. A., and Lepow, M. L.: Varicella with hypoglycemia possibly due to salicylates. Am. J. Dis. Child. *103*:583, 1962.

45. Cotton, E. K., and Fahlberg, V. J.: Hypoglycemia with salicylate poisoning. Amer. J. Dis. Child. *108*:171, 1964.
46. Limbeck, G. A., Ruvalcaba, R. H. A., Samols, E., and Kelley, V. C.: Salicylates and hypoglycemia. Am. J. Dis. Child. *109*:165, 1965.
47. Reid, J., MacDougall, A. S., and Andrews, M. M.: Aspirin and diabetes mellitus. Brit. M. J. *2*:1071, 1957.
48. Hecht, A., and Goldner, M. G.: Reappraisal of the hypoglycemic action of acetylsalicylate. Metabolism *8*:418, 1959.
49. Segal, S., Blair, A., and Weinberg, A.: In vitro effects of salicylate on carbohydrate metabolism. Metabolism *9*:1033, 1960.
50. Cushman, P., Jr., Dubois, J. J., Dwyer, E., and Izzo, J. L.: Protracted tolbutamide hypoglycemia. Am. J. Med. *35*:196, 1963.
51. Jelliffe, D. B., and Stuart, K. L.: Acute toxic hypoglycemia in the vomiting sickness of Jamaica. Brit. M. J. *1*:75, 1954.
52. Leppla, W., and von Holt, C.: Blutzuckersenkende Peptide aus Blighia sapida. Naunyn-Schmiedeberg's Arch. exp. Path. Pharmak. *228*:166, 1956.
53. De Ropp, R. S., van Meter, J. C., and de Ronzo, E. C.: The structure and biological activities of hypoglycin. J. Am. Chem. Soc. *80*:1004, 1958 (Letter to the Editor).
54. Chen, K. K., Anderson, R. C., McCowen, M. C., and Harris, P. N.: Pharmacologic action of hypoglycin A and B. J. Pharmacol. & Exper. Ther. *121*:272, 1957.
55. August, J. T., and Hiatt, H. H.: Severe hypoglycemia secondary to a nonpancreatic fibrosarcoma with insulin activity. New England J. Med. *258*:17, 1958.
56. Sellman, J. C., Perkoff, G. T., Null, F. C., Kimmel, J. R., and Tyler, F. H.: Hypoglycemia associated with massive intra-abdominal mesothelial-cell sarcoma. New England J. Med. *260*:847, 1959.
57. Lowbeer, L.: Hypoglycemia-producing extrapancreatic neoplasms; a review. Am. J. Clin. Path. *35*:233, 1961.
58. Perkoff, G. T., and Simons, E. L.: Hypoglycemia in a patient with a fibrous tumor. A.M.A. Arch. Intern. Med. *112*:589, 1963.
59. Field, J. B., Keen, H., Johnson, P., and Herring, B.: Insulinlike activity of nonpancreatic tumors associated with hypoglycemia. J. Clin. Endocrinol. *23*:1229, 1963.
60. Loutfi, A. H., Mehrez, I., Shahbender, S., and Abdine, F. H.: Hypoglycaemia with Wilms' tumour. Arch. Dis. Child. *39*:197, 1964.
61. MacLeod, J. J. R.: Control of carbohydrate metabolism. (Herter lectures) Johns Hopk. Hosp. Bull. *54*:79, 1934.
62. Rathery, F., Dérot, M., and Sterne, J.: Hypoglycémie dans deux cas d'hémorrhagie méningée sousarachnoidienne. Bull. et Mém. Soc. Méd. hôp. Paris *47*:1578, 1931.
63. Darrow, D. C.: Mental deterioration associated with convulsions and hypoglycemia. Am. J. Dis. Child. *51*:575, 1936.
64. Meakins, J. C.: Hypoglycemia following encephalitis. Ann. Intern. Med. *13*:1830, 1940.
65. Etheridge, J. E., Jr., and Millichap, J. G.: Hypoglycemia and seizures in childhood. Neurol. *14*:397, 1964.
66. Mann, T. P., and Elliott, R. I. K.: Neonatal cold injury due to accidental exposure to cold. Lancet *1*:229, 1957.
67. Bower, B. D., Jones, L. F., and Weeks, M. M.: Cold injury in the newborn. Brit. M. J. *1*:303, 1960.
68. Arneil, G. C., and Kerr, M. M.: Severe hypothermia in Glasgow infants in winter. Lancet *2*:756, 1963.
69. Munk, J.: Hypothermia and edema in nurslings. Maandschr. kindergeneesk. *6*:12, 1936.
70. Veldkamp, A. L.: Extremely low temperatures in nurslings. Nederl. tijdschr. geneesk. *90*:209, 1946.
71. Nassau, E.: Kälteschäden im subtropischen Klima. Ann. paediat. *171*:167, 1948.

72. Cochrane, W. A., Payne, W. W., Simpkiss, M. J., and Woolf, L. I.: Familial hypoglycemia precipitated by amino acids. J. Clin. Invest. 35:411, 1956.
73. Cochrane, W.: Idiopathic infantile hypoglycemia and leucine sensitivity. Metabolism 9:386, 1960.
74. Cochrane, W. A.: Studies in the relationship of amino acids to infantile hypoglycemia. A.M.A. Am. J. Dis. Child. 99:476, 1960.
75. Grumbach, M. M., and Kaplan, S. L.: Amino acid and alpha-keto acid-induced hyperinsulinism in the leucine-sensitive type of infantile and childhood hypoglycemia. J. Pediat. 57:346, 1960.
76. Mabry, C. C., Di George, A. M., and Auerbach, V. H.: Leucine-induced hypoglycemia. I. Clinical observations and diagnostic considerations. J. Pediat. 57:526, 1960.
77. Di George, A. M., and Auerbach, V. H.: Leucine-induced hypoglycemia. A review and speculations. Am. J. Med. Sc. 240:792, 1960.
78. Sauls, H. S., Jr.: Personal communication.
79. Gomez, M. R., Gotham, J. E., and Meyer, J. S.: Effect of sodium glutamate on leucine-induced hypoglycemia: clinical and electroencephalographic study. Pediatrics 28:935, 1961.
80. Gentz, J., Lehmann, O., and Zetterström, R.: Studies on leucine-induced hypoglycemia. Acta Paediat. 51:169, 1962.
81. Dekaban, A., Field, J. B., and Stevens, H.: Familial idiopathic hypoglycemia. Arch. Neurol. 7:529, 1962.
82. Drash, A., and Wolff, F.: Drug therapy in leucine-sensitive hypoglycemia. Metabolism 13:487, 1964.
83. Rosenthal, I. M., Metz, R., and Pirani, C.: Congenital leucine sensitive hypoglycemia. A.M.A. Am. J. Dis. Child. 107:343, 1964.
84. Hartmann, V. W., and Schrier, K.: Leucinempfindliche Hypoglykamie. Mschr. Kinderheilk. 109:507, 1961.
85. Chaptal, J., Jean, R., Dossa, D., Guilliaumot, R., and Morel, G.: Étude clinique et biologique d'un nourrisson atteint d'hypoglycemie récurrente par sensibilité a la leucine. Arch. franç. Pédiat. 18:405, 1961.
86. Haddad, H. M., Roberts, W. C., Pronove, P., and Bartter, F. C.: Leucine-induced hypoglycemia. New England J. Med. 267:1057, 1962.
87. Mabry, C. C., Di George, A. M., and Auerbach, V. H.: Leucine-induced hypoglycemia. II. Studies concerning other amino acids and leucine metabolites. J. Pediat. 57:539, 1960.
88. Roth, H., and Segal, S.: Dietary management of leucine-sensitive hypoglycemia. Pediatrics 34:831, 1964.
89. Di George, A. M., Auerbach, V. H., and Mabry, C. C.: Leucine-induced hypoglycemia. III. The blood glucose depressant action of leucine in normal individuals. J. Pediat. 63:295, 1963.
90. Becker, F. O., Clark, J., and Schwartz, T. B.: L-leucine sensitivity and glucose tolerance in normal subjects. J. Clin. Endocrinol. 24:554, 1964.
91. Flanagan, G. C., Schwartz, T. B., and Ryan, W. G.: Studies on patients with islet cell tumor including the phenomenon of leucine induced accentuation of hypoglycemia. J. Clin. Endocrinol. 21:401, 1961.
92. Marrach, D., Marks, V., and Rose, F. C.: A leucine sensitive insulin-secreting tumour. Lancet 2:1329, 1960.
93. Fajans, S. S., Knopf, R. F., Floyd, J. C., Jr., Power, L., and Conn, J. W.: The experimental induction in man of sensitivity to leucine hypoglycemia. J. Clin. Invest. 42:216, 1963.
94. Ross, S. G., and Josephs, H. W.: Observations on the metabolism of recurrent vomiting. Amer. J. Dis. Child. 28:447, 1924.
95. Colle, E., and Ulstrom, R. A.: Ketotic hypoglycemia. J. Pediat. 64:632, 1964.
96. Sauls, H. S., Jr., and Ulstrom, R. A.: Hypoglycemia. In Kelly, V. C. (ed.): Brenneman's Practice of Pediatrics. Hagerstown, Md., W. F. Prior Co., 1965.
97. Madison, L. L., Mebane, D., Unger, R. H., and Lochner, A.: The hypoglycemic action of ketones. II. Evidence for a stimulatory feedback of ketones on the pancreatic beta cells. J. Clin. Invest. 43:408, 1964.

98. Von Euler, U. S., and Luft, R.: The effect of insulin on urinary excretion of adrenalin and noradrenalin; studies in ten healthy subjects and in six cases of acromegaly. Metabolism 1:528, 1952.
99. Broberger, O., Jungner, I., and Zetterström, R.: Studies in spontaneous hypoglycemia in childhood. Failure to increase the epinephrine secretion in insulin-induced hypoglycemia. J. Pediat. 55:713, 1959.
100. Kinsbourne, M., and Woolf, L. I.: Idiopathic infantile hypoglycaemia. Arch. Dis. Child. 34:166, 1959.
101. Broberger, O., and Zetterström, R.: Hypoglycemia with an inability to increase the epinephrine secretion in insulin-induced hypoglycemia. J. Pediat. 59:215, 1961.
102. Brunjes, S., Hodgman, J., Nowack, J., and Johns, V. J.: Adrenal medullary function in idiopathic spontaneous hypoglycemia of infancy and childhood. Am. J. Med. 34:168, 1963.
103. Goldfien, A., Moore, R., Zileli, S., Havens, L. L., Boling, L., and Thorn, G. W.: Plasma epinephrine and norepinephrine levels during insulin-induced hypoglycemia in man. J. Clin. Endocrinol. 21:296, 1961.
104. Scheie, H. G., Rubenstein, R. A., and Albert, D. M.: Congenital glaucoma and other ocular abnormalities with idiopathic infantile hypoglycemia. J. Pediat. Ophthal. 1:45, 1964.
105. Brasel, J. A., Wright, J. C., Wilkins, L., and Blizzard, R. M.: An evaluation of seventy-five patients with hypopituitarism beginning in childhood. Am. J. Med. 38:484, 1965.
106. Wilber, J. F., and Odell, W. D.: Hypoglycemia and dwarfism associated with the isolated deficiency of growth hormone. Metabolism 14:590, 1965.
107. Bower, B. F., and Gordan, G. S.: Hormonal effects of nonendocrine tumors. Ann. Rev. Med. 16:83, 1965.

Sugar
Malabsorption
Syndromes

Chapter Twelve

DISORDERS OF CARBOHYDRATE ABSORPTION AND DIGESTION

In the first two decades of this century pediatricians recognized that some infants fail to tolerate complex sugars, especially after acute diarrhea. Thus, high protein feedings and formulas containing either simple sugars or no sugar at all were advocated for the treatment of diarrhea by Finkelstein and Meyer,[1] Grulee[2] and Howland.[3] In 1921 Howland described the various intolerances to carbohydrates, including the congenital type, the temporary intolerance following acute diarrhea, and the prolonged type associated with chronic diarrhea.[3] Although these classical clinical observations were important, it was necessary to learn a great deal more about carbohydrate absorption and metabolism before a rational interpretation was possible.

With the elucidation of the physiology and biochemistry of intestinal digestion and absorption of mono-, di- and polysaccharides in the past decade both in America[4, 5] and Europe,[6-11] a renewed interest was stimulated in the role of sugar in the fermentative, chronic diarrheas. In 1958 Durand[6] described a 13 month old girl, the daughter of consanguineous parents, with a failure to thrive, severe chronic diarrhea, renal acidosis, lactosuria and an intolerance to lactose. Holzel and co-workers, in 1959, described two patients with a marked intolerance to lactose and with a syndrome compatible with the congenital absence of lactase.[7] Following these reports many infants with chronic fermentative diarrhea, irritability, abdominal distention, failure to gain and grow have been reported with a wide variety of defects in the ability to digest and absorb sugar. More

253

than 75 patients, including infants, children and adults, have been reported to have the disaccharide malabsorption syndrome and at least 5, an inability to absorb glucose or galactose (see reviews[12-14]).

A rational approach to the diagnosis and therapy of the carbohydrate malabsorption syndromes is now possible because of better understanding of their pathogenesis. The exact incidence of the various clinical syndromes is unknown, but the large number of patients reported within a relatively short period of time indicates that these disorders may be relatively common.

PHYSIOLOGY AND BIOCHEMISTRY OF CARBOHYDRATE DIGESTION AND ABSORPTION

With the ingestion of his very first milk feedings, the newborn infant is abruptly presented with complex carbohydrates to absorb and digest. If breast fed, he will receive milk containing a high lactose content (7 per cent), which accounts for 40 to 45 per cent of his total caloric intake. During the first weeks of life, he may ingest as much as 8 to 9 gm. of lactose per feeding or 50 to 60 gm. per day. Cow's milk, on the other hand, contains less lactose (5 per cent), is diluted and is usually supplemented with dextrins, maltose or sucrose. Thus, he will receive less lactose, but other complex sugars. When solid foods become a major source of calories, carbohydrates compose approximately 50 to 70 per cent of the normal daily caloric intake in America. However, the source of carbohydrate is

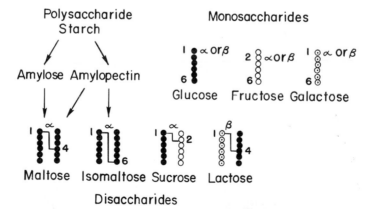

Figure 64. Mechanisms of digestion and absorption of carbohydrates. (Adapted from Prader, Auricchio and Semenza, from Bickel, H. in Mschr. Kinderheilk., *112:*177, 1964.)

different and is primarily starch and, to a lesser extent, other polysaccharides, disaccharides, and monosaccharides in older individuals.

Normal Digestion and Absorption

The various carbohydrates provided in the diet are absorbed and digested by specific mechanisms.[4, 5] Salivary alpha amylase begins the digestion of polysaccharides (starch, glycogen, dextrins) by degradation to oligosaccharides and the disaccharides. Pancreatic alpha amylase completes the digestion of oligosaccharides to disaccharides. Approximately 90 to 95 per cent of the polysaccharide is digested to maltose (alpha 1-4 linkage) and only 4 to 6 per cent, to isomaltose (alpha 1-6 linkage) (Fig. 64). The dietary disaccharides (milk sugar or lactose and table sugar or sucrose) arrive intact in the small intestine. The principal enzyme activity has been localized by electron microscopy[16] and by chemical[4] and immunofluorescent[18] techniques to the brush border (microvilli) of the mucosal cells. This brush border is regenerated every 24 to 36 hours from cells growing up from the intervillous crypts, indicating a rapid turnover of these cells and their enzymatic complex. All of the disaccharides are

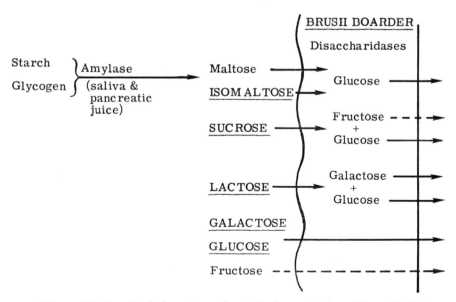

Figure 65. Intestinal absorption of carbohydrates. (Adapted from Dahlqvist. *In* Durand, P. (ed.): *Disorders due to Intestinal Defective Carbohydrate Digestion and Absorption.* Grune & Stratton, New York, 1964.)

absorbed into the brush border, where specific disaccharidases (Fig. 65) hydrolyze them into their component monosaccharides.

Galactose and glucose, whether derived from the hydrolysis of disaccharides or from the diet, are actively absorbed from the brush border or intestinal lumen. The transport or carrier mechanism is sodium dependent,[19] and the energy is ultimately provided by the sodium pump (Fig. 66). Thus, these sugars are absorbed against concentration gradients, in contrast to fructose which appears to diffuse passively or to be absorbed via a different mechanism. D-Xylose, which is absorbed by facilitative diffusion,[17] but is not metabolized in the body, has been used to estimate general absorptive capacity of the small intestine.[20]

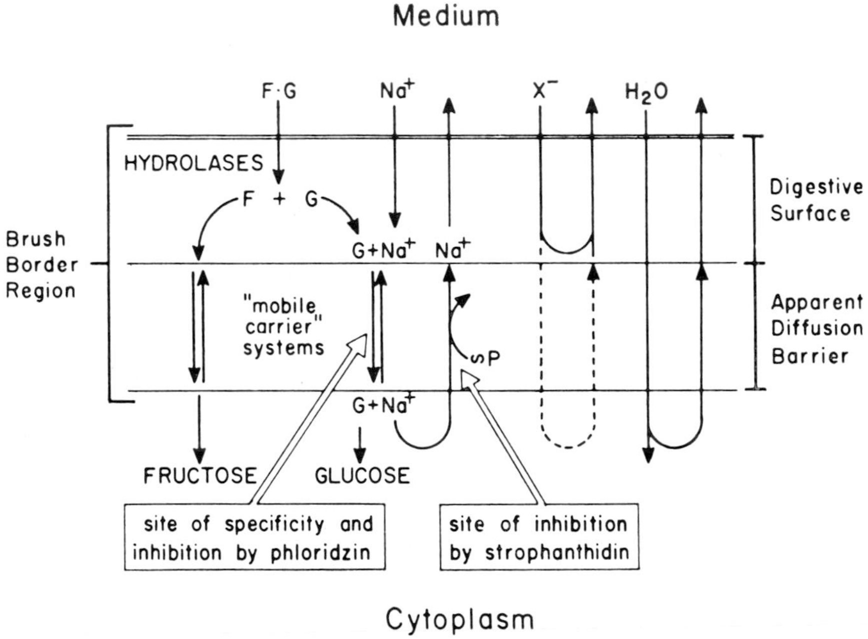

Figure 66. Schematic representation of the characteristics of disaccharide and phosphate ester hydrolysis and of the active transport of sugars in the small intestine. F.G. = sucrose. (From Crane, Fed. Proc., 21:891, 1962.)

In man, the disaccharidases were found in the particulate fractions of homogenates of the small intestinal mucosa and required solubilization for separation and identification. The enzymes were solubilized by Auricchio, Dahlqvist and Semenza[21] using papain. The individual enzymes have been characterized and separated by heat inactivation[10] and by gel filtration chromatography on sephedex G-200.[11] Two nomenclatures have been used to designate the various enzymatic activities assayed in intestinal biopsies (Table 22). The specific enzymes sucrase and isomaltase which

Table 22.   Disaccharidase Enzymes in Brush
Border of Small Intestinal Mucosa

Classification		Substrates	Products
Zürich[11]	Lund[10]		
ALPHA GLUCOSIDASES			
Maltase 1	III	Maltose	Glucose
Maltase 2	II		Glucose
Maltase 3 ⎫ Maltase 4 ⎭	Ib		
Maltase 5	Ia		
Sucrase 1 (Maltase 3)	Sucrase (Ib)	Sucrose	Glucose Fructose
Sucrase 2 (Maltase 4)			
Isomaltase (Maltase 5)	Isomaltase (Ia)	Isomaltose	Glucose Glucose
BETA GLUCOSIDASE			
Lactase 1	Lactase	Lactose	Glucose
Lactase 2			Galactose

hydrolyze sucrose and isomaltose, respectively, also split maltose. Thus, there appear to be either 4 or 5 enzymes which hydrolyze maltose, some of which are specific maltases. The lactase hydrolyzes lactose to glucose and galactose.

Embryological Development of Intestinal Glucosidases

Auricchio et al.[22] measured the intestinal glucosidase activities in 5 embryos, 25 fetuses, and in prematures and full term infants and found that all the alpha glucosidase activities (maltase, sucrase, and isomaltase) were present at 3 months' gestation in the embryo. Maximum specific activities were attained by 6 to 7 months' gestation, at which time they were equivalent to those in the adult. Lactase developed somewhat later and did not reach maximum specific activities until the end of normal gestation. The activity of lactase in the brush border in premature infants who have survived beyond 24 hours was greater than that in premature infants dying before 24 hours. This increased activity was not related to feedings. Mucosal amylase activity was present at 3 months' gestation, although its distribution throughout the small intestine was irregular and showed considerable variation. In contrast, the alpha and beta glucosidases showed maximal activities throughout the entire small intestine except for slightly less activity in the duodenum and terminal ileum.

Although the newborn infant has enzyme activities relatively equivalent to those of the adult, the quantity of disaccharide which can be digested and absorbed is limited by the total enzyme activity which is, in turn, a function of the size and length of the intestine. Auricchio et al.,[22] using their data from the fetus, have estimated the amount of disaccharide that could be hydrolyzed by the entire small intestinal mucosa in the fetus and newborn at maximal enzyme activities per 24 hours. Although these calculations are speculative, they indicate that the amounts of lactose ingested per feeding by the breast-fed baby may exceed his ability to digest the sugar. Prader and Auricchio[13] suggest that this phenomenon may account, in part, for the low pH, and high lactic acid content of the stools of breast-fed infants. On the other hand, infants drinking diluted cow's milk with other disaccharide supplements may have firm stools of neutral pH. The total amount of stool excreted by the artificially fed infant is approximately 40 to 50 gm./day as compared to 20 to 30 gm./day in the normal breast-fed infant.[23]

The pattern of development of the disaccharidases in the newborn human fetus and infant is quite different from that reported in newborn pigs,[24] and fetal rabbits and rats.[25] In the latter animals, lactase activity is very high at birth and falls off in adult life,[25] whereas sucrase activity does not appear until the time of weaning.[26] Species differences are quite distinctive in the development and activity of the individual disaccharidase enzymes as evidenced by the complete lack of lactase and sucrase activity in the small intestinal mucosa of two species of sea lion pups (*Zalophus californianus* and *Eumetopias jubata*).[27] The lack of lactase is of no significance to the pup because sea lion milk contains no lactose.

In summary, all of the ingested carbohydrate is absorbed within the mucosa of the small intestine, where the disaccharides are hydrolyzed to their component monosaccharides and absorbed. Thus, little or no sugar reaches the terminal ileum or colon under normal circumstances. If excessive amounts of sugar are ingested, the disaccharides may reach the large intestine where bacteria ferment them to lactic, acetic and other organic acids; this may produce diarrhea and acid stools. In addition, an osmotic diarrhea may result from the presence of the undigested sugars in the intestinal lumen.[9, 13, 23]

CLINICAL SYNDROMES[12, 13, 23]

If the dietary carbohydrates are not digested completely and absorbed, the patient may manifest the following characteristic symptom complex:

1. Fermentative diarrhea with the pH of the fresh stool less than 5.5 (nitrazine paper).
2. Watery stringy stools with an acid odor, containing increased lactic and other organic acids as well as the nonabsorbed sugar.
3. Abdominal distention, irritability and failure to thrive.
4. Mellituria may or may not be present.
5. Severe symptoms following the ingestion of the specific carbohydrate which is not tolerated.
6. Recovery with the removal of the offending sugar.

Thus, a careful and detailed history and a well-planned elimination dietary trial suggest and support the diagnosis.

A history of chronic diarrhea dating from shortly after birth is highly suggestive of lactose malabsorption, whereas delay of onset until the time of ingestion of starches or sucrose points to a sucrose–isomaltose malabsorption syndrome. The persistence of diarrhea after an acute episode is characteristic of the acquired disaccharide intolerance as described by Sunshine and Kretchmer.[28] In older children and adults with the acquired lactase deficiency,[29, 30] ingestion of milk may produce bloating, dyspepsia and abdominal discomfort rather than diarrhea.

The definitive diagnosis of a disaccharide or monosaccharide malabsorption syndrome depends upon laboratory confirmation of the clinical impression. Many investigators have emphasized the need for rigid control in performing and interpreting the results of oral carbohydrate tolerance tests to assess intestinal absorption. Weijers and Van de Kamer[31] and Prader et al.[8] critically define the clinical and laboratory conditions for making the diagnosis. Subsequent case reports indicate that many have not rigidly adhered to their criteria.

First and foremost, the diarrhea must be controlled before any tolerance tests are done to define the enzyme defect. This is accomplished by removing all disaccharides from the diet and replacing them with simple sugars (monosaccharides).

Weijers and Van de Kamer[31] have detailed the procedure to prepare the patient and to perform the tolerance test properly. They consider the following points to be of practical importance:

"Concerning the supply of sugars to the blood:

a) The loading has always to be done with the same quantity of carbohydrates per kg. body weight or per m² of body surface. Further the concentration of the carbohydrate solution has always to be the same, i.e., 10%.

b) The carbohydrates have to be given in a watery solution. Further, to prevent a disturbing influence by spasm of the pylorus, a loading test cannot be done when the patient is excited. . . .

"Concerning the removal of sugars from the blood:

a) To be sure that the liver is filled up with glycogen to the normal level, some days before starting the test the patient is given daily 20 to 50 g glucose—according to his age—given daily in addition to his normal diet.

b) To prevent inconstant combustion of glucose in the tissues the patient must lie down during the whole test. . . .

"The loading test is performed as follows.

"The patient is given in the fasting condition—2 g of the carbohydrate under test per kg. body weight—maximally 50 g—in a 10% aqueous solution. Next the reducing power of the blood is determined at time 0, ½, 1, 1½, 2 and 2½ hours. . . ."

The sugar analysis should include both total sugar (e.g., Somogyi) and glucose (glucose oxidase). The glucose oxidase method will measure the blood glucose, whereas the difference between the two sugar methods will indicate how much of the fructose, galactose, or lactose has been absorbed. An elevation in blood sugar of at least 50 mg./100 ml. is expected in the normal subject, but the elevation should be less than 20 mg./100 ml. in a patient with an absorptive defect.[8, 31]

Stool specimens should be collected during and following the test, and the pH, lactic acid and sugar content determined as described by these authors.[8, 31] Urine specimens should be collected during the tolerance tests and analyzed for reducing substances which, if present, should be identified chromatographically. The reasons why some patients show mellituria, whereas others do not are not clear at the moment.

After the diarrhea from the initial test subsides, the component monosaccharides should be administered in the same manner: a normal elevation of blood sugar indicates that an intrinsic absorptive defect is not present. An additional tolerance test involves the administration of the disaccharide with its specific enzyme and, again, a normal elevation in blood sugar should occur with this disease.

The definitive diagnosis of the enzyme deficiency depends upon a peroral biopsy of the jejunal mucosa. This procedure has been done in a number of infants and children, without significant morbidity in the hands of experienced investigators. The biopsy specimen should be examined histologically as well as analyzed enzymatically. In primary disaccharidase deficiency, the histologic pattern of the mucosa is usually intact and preserved, whereas in enzyme deficiencies secondary to other intestinal diseases, the mucosa may be flattened, denuded or show evidence of inflammation. The micro methods for the analyses of the individual enzyme activities have been carefully worked out and described by Dahlqvist[32] and by Auricchio et al.[33] A significant reduction in the enzyme activity verifies the diagnosis.

Monosaccharide Malabsorption Syndrome

Lindquist and Meeuwisse[34] reported a female infant with chronic diarrhea born to second cousins. She was breast fed, developed frequent loose stools on the fourth day of life, and lost weight rapidly. She became severely dehydrated but improved on parenteral fluid therapy. This child was found to have an intolerance to the simple monosaccharides, glucose and galactose, although a lactose malabsorption was first suspected. Inter-

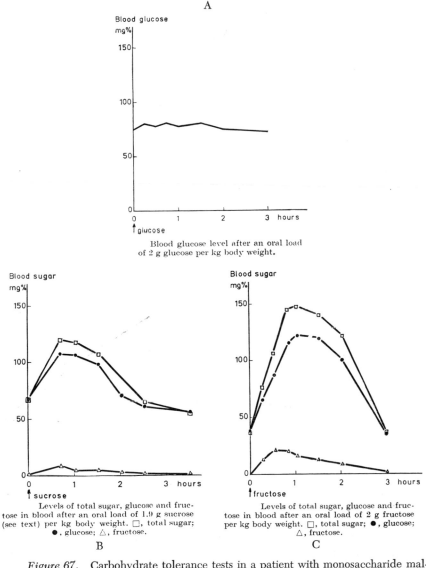

A

Blood glucose level after an oral load of 2 g glucose per kg body weight.

Levels of total sugar, glucose and fructose in blood after an oral load of 1.9 g sucrose (see text) per kg body weight. □, total sugar; ●, glucose; △, fructose.

B

Levels of total sugar, glucose and fructose in blood after an oral load of 2 g fructose per kg body weight. □, total sugar; ●, glucose; △, fructose.

C

Figure 67. Carbohydrate tolerance tests in a patient with monosaccharide malabsorption syndrome. (From Lindquist and Meeuwisse, Acta Pediat., *51*:674, 1962.)

mittent glucosuria was observed in this infant. Improvement was noted on a low carbohydrate intake. On a formula, in which the only carbohydrate was fructose, the patient thrived; sugar disappeared from the feces and urine. Diarrhea disappeared and the quantity of stool returned to normal values.

Specific oral tolerance tests of carbohydrate absorption were performed. There was no rise in the blood sugar after the ingestion of glucose (Fig. 67, A), galactose or lactose, and diarrhea persisted, with acid stools containing the ingested sugar. Following the oral administration of sucrose, there was a moderate rise in the blood glucose values (Fig. 67, B). After fructose alone, the rise in blood glucose was striking (Fig. 67, C). There was no diarrhea and no fructose in the stool following this tolerance test. These results indicate that this patient had a primary defect in the absorption of glucose and galactose but not in the absorption of fructose. This was not a disaccharidase deficiency because the fructose from sucrose was available for absorption, and lactose was split to glucose and galactose. There was no defect in the conversion of fructose to glucose (Fig. 67, C).

Two similar patients with the monosaccharide malabsorption syndrome were reported from France in 1962 by Laplane et al.[47] Subsequently, one infant from Australia[48] and two from the United States[49, 50] have been studied. An intestinal biopsy revealed normal histology and disaccharidase activities.[48]

Therapy is a diet in which the only carbohydrate is fructose. Thus, a formula without lactose, glucose, galactose or sucrose is made from protein hydrolysate, corn oil and fructose.[47-50] The diarrhea often subsides completely within 12 to 24 hours after therapy is begun.

This type of patient may make important contributions to our knowledge of the physiology and biochemistry of hexose absorption. The fact that glucose and galactose are not absorbed to the same extent as fructose suggests that the absorption of fructose is not the result of simple passive diffusion.

Disaccharide Malabsorption Syndromes

Congenital Malabsorption of Sucrose and Isomaltose

Many patients have been described who have an inability to digest sucrose, as demonstrated either by loading tests or by direct assay of the disaccharidase activity in an intestinal biopsy.[13-15, 33] Although first described by Weijers et al.[9] as a simple sucrose malabsorption, it is now apparent that these patients have a deficiency in isomaltose absorption as well. Most of the patients are young children, although 5 adults have been reported.[13] There does not appear to be any sex predilection. Being congenital in nature, the disorder is present at birth and becomes manifest when sucrose or dextrins or starch are added to the infants' diet. Dextrins and starch are poorly tolerated because of their isomaltose content after degradation. If breast fed, the infant remains well as long as breast milk is his only source of carbohydrate. Chronic diarrhea, irritability, failure to grow and gain weight follow the introduction of sucrose or isomaltose into the diet. Amelioration of symptoms occurs when the offending disaccharides are removed. These infants usually tolerate lactose well.

The symptoms are more pronounced in younger infants and children and less severe in older children and adults. Symptoms vary a great deal, depending upon the amount of ingested disaccharide, the degree of enzyme deficiency, and other ill-defined factors. With increasing age, it would appear that many of the children are able to tolerate starches and perhaps even some sucrose, although this is not certain. A few patients have also had a mild maltose malabsorption as determined by a loading test;[9, 35] one patient is reported to have a lactose malabsorption as well.[36] The latter patient also showed steatorrhea. D-Xylose absorption may or may not be normal in these patients. Both the abnormality of D-xylose absorption and steatorrhea disappear as soon as a diet free of sucrose and isomaltose is instituted. The activity of the pancreatic enzymes in the intestinal lumen has been found to be normal. In some patients sucrosuria occurs.

A complete absence of sucrase activity and a severe deficiency of isomaltase activity has been found in assaying the jejunal or small intestinal biopsies.[13-15, 33, 45] As would be expected from the previous discussion, maltase activity is also sharply reduced. Lactase activity is normal.

The occurrence of this enzyme deficiency in affected siblings and in offspring of consanguineous parents indicates that this condition is inherited. The mode of inheritance, however, is not clearly defined since it has not been possible to detect the heterozygotic carrier. Studies of disaccharidase activity in intestinal biopsy from parents of affected children may provide this answer in the future.

A deficiency of more than one enzyme in an inherited metabolic disorder is unusual ("one gene, one enzyme"). Three possibilities to explain this phenomenon have been suggested by Prader and Auricchio: a mutation may have affected (1) a regulator gene, thus inhibiting the synthesis of several enzymes or (2) a structural gene affecting a polypeptide chain common to several enzymes or (3) different active centers of the same enzyme molecule which contain the various disaccharidase activities. Launiala et al.[35] suggest that only one enzyme deficiency is involved and that the various alpha glucosidase activities are affected differently by heat. Further studies may well elucidate the mechanism of this interesting enzymatic enigma.

Case Report[37] *(Table 23)*

A 21 month old Caucasian female child was first seen in the pediatric clinic on November 30, 1961, because of chronic diarrhea. The diarrhea had begun early in infancy and had persisted despite numerous therapeutic measures. The child had not been breast fed. The mother could not recall the nature of the formula but did remember that solid foods were introduced into the diet at an early age. At the time of the first clinic visit the child was having an average of 5 watery stools per day. Despite the chronic diarrhea, growth and development proceeded along normal lines. A variety of changes in formula had resulted in no improvement. Various hypoallergenic diets had also failed to alleviate the chronic diarrhea.

The child's mother and father were in good health. Neither gave a history of diarrhea in childhood. There was no history of allergy in the family. The patient has 2 brothers, who were 6 and 4 years of age, in good health.

The patient was admitted for study at the Research and Educational Hospitals of the University of Illinois College of Medicine on March 6, 1962, at the age of 24 months. She weighed 28 pounds and was 35 inches tall. No abnormalities were found on physical examination. On a general ward diet she was observed to have diarrhea as described by her mother.

The hemoglobin was 12.6 gm./100 ml. The white blood cell count was 6900 mm.[3] with 47 segs., 46 lymphocytes and 7 monocytes. Serum protein was 6.4 gm./100 ml. with gamma globulin 12 per cent, beta 14.5 per cent, $alpha_2$ 12.6 per cent, $alpha_1$ 3.5 per cent, and albumin 55.2 per cent. Sweat chloride was 10 mEq./L. Fasting blood glucose, serum calcium and serum phosphorus were normal. The CO_2 content was normal. Upper and lower GI studies by x-ray examination were negative. Stool cultures were negative for pathogenic organisms. There were no ova or parasites present in the stools. Stool pH was 4.5 while the child was on a general diet.

The child was placed on a diet free of sucrose and of starch. The diarrhea was promptly alleviated. The stools became well formed, and only one stool was passed each day. The stool pH rose to 7.5.

The tolerance tests showed no elevation in blood sugar after sucrose, but a normal hyperglycemia after glucose, fructose and maltose (Table 23).

Table 23. Sugar Absorption—Oral
Tolerance Tests

Sugar (Dose)				Hours			
	0	1/2	1	2	2-1/2	3	4
			Blood Sugar mg./100 ml.				
Glucose (25 Gm.)	63	92	101	122	121	117	-
Fructose (25 Gm.)	66	79	102	105	102	83	76
Sucrose (25 Gm.)	75	79	74	73	-	71	71
Maltose (25 Gm.)	94	192	197	140	-	86	74

Patient:
  Female, white,
  24 mos.
  wt. 12.7 kg.

Stool: General diet, pH-4.5;
on sucrose-free diet, pH-7.5.
After sucrose tolerance test,
pH-5.0. Diarrhea recurred
only following sucrose ingestion.

This patient has subsequently done well on a sucrose-free and starch-poor diet (see Appendix I).

Congenital Malabsorption of Lactose (without Lactosuria)

Congenital malabsorption of lactose, as first described by Holzel et al.,[7] is, in contrast to sucrose malabsorption, characterized by fermentative diarrhea and a failure to thrive beginning during the first days of life. Clinical manifestations are particularly severe if the infant is breast fed. One patient with congenital lactose malabsorption also had mucoviscidosis[38] and another showed a marked retardation of growth and development at 14 years of age.[39] Lactosuria does not appear to occur in the congenital lactose malabsorption syndrome.

Intestinal biopsies have been obtained for enzyme analysis in patients with this syndrome.[33, 38] The lactase activity was markedly diminished but not absent, whereas normal values of alpha glucosidase activities were found. This condition is probably also inherited since affected siblings and relatives have been reported. The mode of inheritance is unknown.

Case Report (Durand[40])

"A 10 month old boy was admitted to G. Gaslini Hospital because of persistent tendency to develop diarrhoea.

"The boy was the 5th child of healthy parents. The first and the second, born prematurely, died at the age of 3 months and the second at 4 weeks, respectively. The course of their illness was similar to that of the patient. The boy weighed 2600 g, he was breast-fed at first but during the first few days of life the number of motions varied from 4 to 8 in 24 hours. The body weight was stationary in spite of adequate food intake. On feeding with Arobon and Elonac mixture, diarrhoea disappeared, but recommenced as soon as the patient was breast-fed in spite of various therapeutic measures.

"During successive periods, the patient was given a 50 per cent milk formula and acid milk mixtures, but none of the dietary regimens improved his condition; he produced normal stools only on a milk-free mixture and the baby's weight increased, though rather slowly.

"On admission he was a dystrophic baby weighing 5900 g. The failure to gain, followed by a slow increase in weight associated with a diet of starch or cereal, suggested that lactose might not be hydrolysed in the intestine.

"The results of examinations of the frothy, bulky faeces, containing very finely distributed mucus, showed a pH of 4, 5.5 and a high content of lactose (by stool chromatography) and lactic acid (40-50 mg per g dry faeces). Xylose tests were 25 and 38%.

"The fat excretion was normal. Carbohydrate tolerance curves showed no rise in blood sugar on peroral administration of lactose (2 g per kg/body weight on a first test and 3 g/kg on second and a third test; Fig. 68) and the unhydrolysed disaccharide has been demonstrated in watery stools. At no time reducing substances were found in the urine.

"When an absorption test was carried out with a glucose-galactose mix-

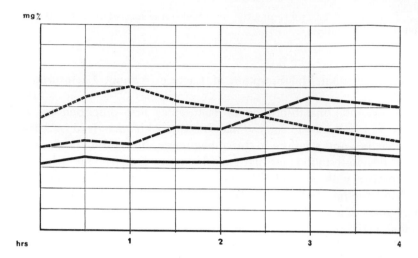

Blood sugars levels after oral load of 2 g/kg body weight of lactose
on the first (——) and 3 g/kg body weight lactose on the second
(— — —) and the third (----).

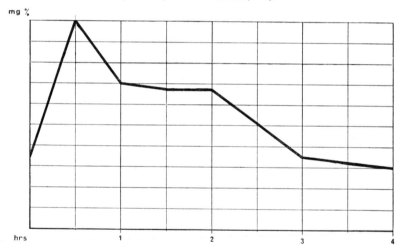

Levels of total sugars after an oral dose of a mixture of 1 g
glucose + 1 g galactose per kg body weight.

Figure 68. Carbohydrate tolerance tests in a patient with congenital lactose
malabsorption syndrome. (From Durand, *Disorders due to Intestinal Defective Carbohydrate Digestion and Absorption.* Grune & Stratton, New York, 1964.)

ture the response was normal (Fig. 68). After sucrose and also maltose loading
normally rising curves were determined."

Lactose Intolerance with Lactosuria

In 1958 Durand[6] described the first case of lactose intolerance with
lactosuria in a 13 month old girl who was weak, poorly nourished, failed

to thrive, and suffered from chronic diarrhea resistant to therapy. From birth, this infant was fed breast milk and had symptoms of vomiting, diarrhea and abdominal pain. When studied at 13 months, she was markedly malnourished, showed a profound lactosuria, renal acidosis and intermittent proteinuria. On a lactose-free diet, she improved temporarily, but died at 15 months of age. Postmortem examination revealed atrophic enteritis as well as hepatic and adrenal atrophy and degeneration of the convoluted tubules. Durand considered this case to represent a deficiency of intestinal lactase, with the urinary findings secondary to an osmotic nephrosis as a result of the lactose absorbed.

Since 1958, 9 additional cases having similar clinical manifestations have been reported and reviewed by Durand.[40] There was no significant sex difference, and the onset was within the first days of life. All the infants showed a failure to thrive and the majority, severe diarrhea and lactosuria. Only 6 children had lactose absorption tests and the results are confusing: some had a marked rise in the level of blood sugar, whereas others had only a minimal rise.

In addition to lactosuria, several patients showed renal acidosis and aminoaciduria as well as hemorrhages and pyloric stenosis. Familial incidence was noted in the histories of 2 infants, consanguinity of the parents in one, and consanguinity of the great grandparents in another. Of the infants reported, about half died, indicating the need for early recognition and therapy in these neonates. The removal of lactose from the diet or the addition of other carbohydrates with a minimal lactose intake produced improvement immediately. Some patients showed severe clinical manifestations following the ingestion of even minimal amounts of lactose. This has suggested to Holzel et al.[41] that lactose may be as toxic in these infants as gluten is in celiac disease. The precise pathogenesis and etiology of this important confusing syndrome remains unknown.

An infant with a clinical course indistinguishable from those reported above has been investigated at the Cleveland Metropolitan General Hospital by McCann, Gold and Schwartz.[42] This infant had severe vomiting, diarrhea, dehydration and lactosuria as well as other disacchariduria; proteinuria was also observed. An extensive evaluation indicated that this infant was sensitive to milk protein, but absorbed and digested lactose without difficulty. Therefore, sensitivity to milk protein must be considered in the differential diagnosis. Sick infants would also respond well to non-milk substitutes, e.g., soy-bean milk and Nutramigen.

Acquired Lactase Deficiency in the Adult

Disaccharidase activities have been studied in intestinal tissue obtained either at operation or by peroral biopsy in adults. A significant number of adults have been found with lactase deficiency and a variable intolerance to milk.[29, 30] Many had been classified as having a milk allergy. These patients often reported that milk caused dyspepsia or diarrhea, especially if ingested in large amounts. This observation is important when one does genetic studies in the parents of infants and children with lactose malabsorption syndrome. Since a number of adults may have acquired lactase deficiency, one must be cautious in interpreting results of tolerance tests with reference to the mode of inheritance or genetics of this condition.

Secondary Disaccharidase Deficiency

Weijers and Van de Kamer[31] have indicated a number of conditions which have been associated with mono-, di- and polysaccharide malabsorption syndromes. These include the lack of absorption secondary to infectious diarrhea; a reduction in the intestinal surface, as with surgical resection, shunts and atrophy of the villi; and increased intestinal parasites. In addition, secondary disaccharide malabsorption syndromes have been described by Sunshine and Kretchmer[28] in 6 infants following diarrhea in early infancy. In these babies, the diarrhea persisted beyond a month's duration and all had a low pH of the fresh stool (less than 5.5). Two infants were intolerant to lactose, 3 to lactose and sucrose, and 1 to sucrose alone. All showed a flat tolerance curve after ingestion of the disaccharide and a normal elevation in the blood glucose after the component monosaccharides were administered. In all the deficiency was transient and all were normal within 1 to 12 months. Reports of reduced disaccharidase activity have also been noted in malnutrition, kwashiorkor,[43] cystic fibrosis,[38] celiac disease[44] and giardiasis.[40] Although the absorption and digestion of all of the disaccharides may be involved in these conditions, lactose malabsorption frequently dominates. The recovery from the underlying intestinal disorder is necessary before the intolerance for the disaccharide subsides. This may be a slow process.

SUMMARY

A persistent fermentative diarrhea with watery stringy sour stools should always alert the physician to determine the pH (Nitrazine paper) of the fresh stool and to consider the possibility of a sugar malabsorption syndrome. It should be emphasized that the diagnosis of the various disaccharide or monosaccharide malabsorption syndromes must be made carefully and meticulously. A high index of suspicion, careful preparation of the patient, the proper carbohydrate tolerance tests and the response to an elimination diet are all necessary to make a definitive diagnosis. Peroral biopsy of the intestinal mucosa permits direct confirmation of the diagnosis. These malabsorption syndromes may be congenital or primary and acquired or secondary to a variety of underlying conditions.

REFERENCES

1. Finkelstein, H., and Meyer, L. F.: Zur Technik und Indikation der Ernahrung mit Eiweissmilch. München. med. Wchnschr. 58:340, 1911.
2. Grulee, C. G.: The use and abuse of carbohydrates in infant feeding. J. Lancet (Minneapolis) 32:141, 1912.
3. Howland, J.: Prolonged intolerance to carbohydrates. Tr. Amer. Pediat. Soc. 33: 11, 1921.
4. Crane, R. K.: Intestinal absorption of sugars. Physiol. Rev. 40:789, 1960.
5. Quastel, J. H.: Intestinal absorption of sugars and amino acids. Amer. J. Clin. Nutr. 8:137, 1960.
6. Durand, P.: Lactosuria idiopathica in una paziente con diarrea cronica ed acidosi. Minerva pediat. 10:706, 1958.
7. Holzel, A., Schwarz, V., and Sutcliffe, K. W.: Defective lactose absorption causing malnutrition in infancy. Lancet 1:1126, 1959.
8. Prader, A., Auricchio, S., and Mürset, G.: Durchfall infolge hereditaren Mangels an intestinaler Saccharaseaktivitat (Saccharoseintoleranz). Schweiz. med. Wchnschr. 91:465, 1961.
9. Weijers, H. A., Van de Kamer, J. H., Dicke, W. K., and Ijsseling, J.: Diarrhoea caused by deficiency of sugar-splitting enzymes. I. Acta Paediat. 50:55, 1961.
10. Dahlqvist, A.: Specificity of human intestinal disaccharides and implications for hereditary disaccharide intolerance. J. Clin. Invest. 41:463, 1962.
11. Semenza, G., and Auricchio, S.: Chromatographic separation of human intestinal disaccaridases. Biochim. et Biophys. Acta 65:172, 1962.
    Semenza, G., Auricchio, S., and Rubino, A.: Multiplicity of human intestinal disaccharidases. I. Chromatographic separation of maltases and of two lactases. Biochim. et Biophys. Acta 96:487, 1965.
    Auricchio, S., Semenza, G., and Rubino, A.: Multiplicity of human intestinal disaccharidases. II. Characterisation of the individual maltases. Biochim. et Biophys. Acta 96:498, 1965.
12. Durand, P. (ed.): Disorders due to Intestinal Defective Carbohydrate Digestion and Absorption. New York, Grune & Stratton, 1964.
13. Prader, A., and Auricchio, S.: Defects of intestinal disaccharide absorption. Ann. Rev. Med. 16:345, 1965.
14. Littman, A., and Hammond, J. B.: Progress in gastroenterology: Diarrhea in adults caused by deficiency in intestinal disaccharidases. Gastroenterology 48:237, 1965.
15. Anderson, C. M., Messer, M., Townley, R. R. W., Freeman, M., and Robinson, M. J.: Intestinal isomaltase deficiency in patients with hereditary sucrose and starch intolerance. Lancet 2:556, 1962.
16. Miller, D., and Crane, R. K.: The digestive function of the epithelium of the small intestine. II. Localization of disaccharide hydrolysis in the isolated brush border portion of the intestinal epithelial cells. Biochim. et Biophys. Acta 52:293, 1961.
17. Alvarado, F.: D-Xylose, a substrate for the process of sugar active transport by the small intestine. Experientia 20:302, 1964.
18. Doell, R., Rosen, G., and Kretchmer, N.: An immunochemical study of the development of intestinal invertase. J. Pediat. 65:1118, 1964 (Abstract).
19. Crane, R. K.: Hypothesis for mechanisms of intestinal active transport of sugars. Fed. Proc. 21:891, 1962.
20. Oestreicher, R., Richterich, R., and Rossi, E.: The diagnostic value of the xylose-tolerance test in children. Germ. med. Mth. 9:236, 1964.
21. Auricchio, S., Dahlqvist, A., and Semenza, G.: Solubilization of the human intestinal disaccharidases. Biochim. et Biophys. Acta 73:582, 1963.
22. Auricchio, S., Rubino, A., and Mürset, G.: Intestinal glycosidase activities in the human embryo, foetus and newborn. Pediatrics 35:944, 1965.
23. Weijers, H. A., and Van de Kamer, J. H.: Aetiology and diagnosis of fermentative diarrhoeas. Acta Paediat. 52:329, 1963.

24. Dahlqvist, A.: Intestinal carbohydrases of a newborn pig. Nature (Lond.) *190*:31, 1961.

25. Doell, R. G., and Kretchmer, N.: Studies of small intestine during development. I. Distribution and activity of β-galactosidase. Biochim. et Biophys. Acta *62*:353, 1962.

26. Doell, R. G., and Kretchmer, N.: Intestinal invertase: precocious development after injection of hydrocortisone. Science *143*:42, 1964.

27. Sunshine, P., and Kretchmer, N.: Intestinal disaccharidases: absence in two species of sea lions. Science *144*:850, 1964.

28. Sunshine, P., and Kretchmer, N.: Studies of small intestine during development. III. Infantile diarrhea associated with intolerance to disaccharides. Pediatrics *34*:38, 1964.

29. Auricchio, S., Rubino, A., Landolt, M., Semenza, G., and Prader, A.: Isolated intestinal lactase deficiency in the adult. Lancet *2*:324, 1963.

30. Dahlqvist, A., Hammond, J. B., Crane, R. K., Dunphy, J. V., and Littman, A.: Intestinal lactase deficiency and lactose intolerance in adults. Gastroenterology *45*:488, 1963.

31. Weijers, H. A., and Van de Kamer, J. H.: Fermentative diarrhoeas, *In* Durand, P., (ed.): Disorders due to Intestinal Defective Carbohydrate Digestion and Absorption. New York, Grune & Stratton, 1964, p. 57.

32. Dahlqvist, A.: Method for assay of intestinal disaccharidases. Analyt. Biochem. *7*:18, 1964.

33. Auricchio, S., Rubino, A., Prader, A., Rey, J., Jos, J., Frezal, J., and Davidson, M.: Intestinal glycosidase activities in congenital malabsorption of disaccharides. J. Pediat. *66*:555, 1965.

34. Lindquist, B., and Meeuwisse, G. W.: Chronic diarrhoea caused by monosaccharide malabsorption. Acta Paediat. *51*:674, 1962.

35. Launiala, K., Perheentupa, J., Visakorpi, J., and Hallman, N.: Disaccharidases of intestinal mucosa in a patient with sucrose intolerance. Pediatrics *34*:615, 1964.

36. Lifshitz, F., and Holman, G. H.: Disaccharidase deficiencies with steatorrhea. J. Pediat. *64*:33, 1964.

37. Rosenthal, I., Cornblath, M., and Crane, R. K.: Congenital intolerance to sucrose and starch presumably caused by hereditary deficiency of specific enzymes in the brush border membrane of the small intestine. J. Lab. & Clin. Med. *60*:1012, 1962 (Abstract No. 103).

38. Cozzetto, F. J.: Intestinal lactase deficiency in a patient with cystic fibrosis. Pediatrics *32*:228, 1963.

39. Sobel, E. H., Davidson, M., Kugler, M. M., Zuppinger, K. A., Hsu, L. Y-F., and Prader, A.: Growth retardation associated with intestinal lactase deficiency. J. Pediat. *63*:731, 1963 (Abstract No. 63).

40. Durand, P.: Lactose intolerance. *In* Durand, P. (ed.): Disorders due to Intestinal Defective Carbohydrate Digestion and Absorption. New York, Grune and Stratton, 1964, p. 105.

41. Holzel, A., Mereu, T., and Thomson, M. L.: Severe lactose intolerance in infancy. Lancet *2*:1346, 1962.

42. McCann, M. M., Gold, E., and Schwartz, R.: Disacchariduria in an infant with milk sensitivity (in preparation).

43. Bowie, M. D., Brinkman, G. L., and Hansen, J. D.: Diarrhoea in protein-calorie malnutrition. Lancet *2*:550, 1963.

44. Plotkin, G. R., and Isselbacher, K. J.: Secondary disaccharidase deficiency in adult celiac disease (nontropical sprue) and other malabsorption states. New England J. Med. *271*:1033, 1964.

45. Semenza, G., Auricchio, S., Rubino, A., Prader, A., and Welsh, J. D.: Lack of some intestinal maltases in a human disease transmitted by a single genetic factor. Biochim. et Biophys. Acta (in press).

46. Prader, A., Auricchio, S., and Semenza, G.: Die hereditäre saccharose- und isomaltose-malabsorption. Mschr. Kinderheilk. *112*:177, 1964.

47. Laplane, R., Polonovski, C., Etienne, M., Debray, P., Lods, J. C., and Pissarro, B.:

L'intolérance aux sucrés a transfert intestinal actie. Ses rapports avec l'intolérance au lactose et le syndrome coeliaque. Arch. Franç. Pédiat. *19*: 895, 1962.

48. Anderson, C. M., Kerry, K. R., and Townley, R. R. W.: An inborn defect of intestinal absorption of certain monosaccharides. Arch. Dis. Child. *40*:1, 1965.
49. Marks, J. F., Fordtran, J., and Norton, J. B.: (To be published).
50. Liu, H. Y., and Tsao, M. U.: A.M.A. Amer. J. Dis. Child. (To be published).
51. Snow, R., Sachs, M. O., and Cornblath, M.: Ketotic hypoglycemia in a Russell dwarf. J. Pediat. (In press.)

Diets for Disorders of Carbohydrate Metabolism*

* Prepared by Miss Bernita A. Youngs, Chief Nutritionist, Maternity and Infant Care Project, Chicago Board of Health; Formerly, Clinic Dietitian, Research and Educational Hospitals, University of Illinois College of Medicine.

GALACTOSE-FREE DIET

Type of Food	Food to Include	Food to Omit
Milk and milk products	None. Nutramigen to be used in place of milk.	All milk of any kind: skim, dried, evaporated, condensed. Cheeses. Ice cream, sherbets. Any food containing milk or milk products.
Meat, fish, fowl	Beef, chicken, turkey, fish, lamb, veal, pork, ham.	Creamed or breaded meat, fish, or fowl. Luncheon meats, hot dogs, liver sausage. Meats containing milk or milk products. Organ meats such as liver, pancreas, brain.
Eggs	All.	None.
Vegetables	Artichokes, asparagus, beets, green beans, wax beans, broccoli, cauliflower, celery, corn, chard, cucumber, eggplant, kale, lettuce, greens, okra, onions, parsley, parsnips, pumpkin, rutabagas, spinach, squash, tomatoes.	Sugar beets, peas, lima beans, soybeans, legumes. Creamed, breaded, or buttered vegetables. Any vegetables in which lactose has been added during processing.
Potatoes and substitutes	White potatoes, sweet potatoes, macaroni, noodles, spaghetti, rice.	Any creamed, breaded, or buttered; mashed. French fried potatoes and instant potatoes if lactose or milk has been added during processing.
Breads and cereals	Any that do not contain milk or milk products.	Prepared mixes such as muffins, biscuits, waffles, pancakes; some dry cereals; instant cream of wheat. (Read labels CAREFULLY.) Dry cereals with added skim milk powder or lactose. Breads and rolls made with milk. Crackers.
Fats	Oils, shortenings, dressings that do not contain milk or milk products. Bacon.	Margarine, butter, cream, cream cheese. Dressings containing milk or milk products.
Soups	Clear soups, vegetable soups that do not contain peas or lima beans. Consommes.	Cream soups, chowders, commercially prepared soups that contain lactose.
Desserts	Water and fruit ices, jello, angel food cake, homemade cakes, pies, cookies from allowed ingredients.	Commercial cakes and cookies and mixes. Custard, puddings, ice cream made with milk. Anything containing chocolate.
Fruits	All fresh, canned, or frozen that are not processed with lactose.	Any canned or frozen that are processed with lactose.
Miscellaneous	Nuts, peanut butter, popcorn (unbuttered), pure sugar candy, jelly or marmalade, sugar, Karo, carob powder, chewing gum, olives.	Gravy, white sauce, chocolate, cocoa, toffee, peppermints, butterscotch, caramels, molasses candies, instant coffee, powdered soft drinks, monosodium glutamate, some spice blends.

Labels should be read carefully and any products that contain milk, lactose, casein, whey, dry milk solids or curds should be omitted.

Lactate, lactic acid, lactalbumin and calcium compounds do not contain lactose.

SUCROSE- AND FRUCTOSE-FREE DIET

Food	Amount	Foods to Use	Foods to Avoid
Milk	Any.	Any.	None.
Meat, fish, poultry, cheese	Any.	Beef, veal, lamb, pork chicken, turkey, fish, cheese.	Ham, bacon, lunch meats, and any other meats in which sugar is used in processing.
Eggs	Any.	Any.	None.
Vegetables	Any.	Asparagus, cabbage, cauli-flower, celery, green beans, green peppers, lettuce, spinach, wax beans.	All other vegetables.
Potato or substitute	Any.	White potatoes, macaroni, noodles, spaghetti, rice.	Sweet potatoes.
Fruits	None.	None.	All fruits and fruit juices.
Bread	None.	No bread. Soda crackers, saltines.	Any bread. Other crackers.
Cereal	Any.	Cooked or ready-to-eat cereals (except sugar-coated cereals).	Sugar-coated cereals.
Fat	Any.	Butter, margarine, oil, home-made mayonnaise or French dressing made without sugar.	Mayonnaise, salad dressings made with sugar.
Desserts	Any.	Dietetic jello, dietetic ice cream, dietetic puddings.	All desserts containing sugar, such as cake, pie, cookies, candy, puddings, jello, ice cream, sherbet and others. Any desserts containing honey, fruit or fruit juice.
Miscellaneous	Any.	Vegetable juices (no tomato). Coffee, tea. Salt, pepper and other condiments. Broth, soups from allowed vegetables. Sugar substitute. Dietetic beverages.	Catsup, chili sauce and other sauces containing sugar. Car-bonated beverages. Sugar, honey, maple syrup, jam, jellies, pre-serves.

Labels of all canned, packaged or processed foods should be checked to be sure that sugar or fruit is not used.

LEUCINE-RESTRICTED DIET*

Food	Amount	Foods to Use	Foods to Avoid
Milk	Only as indicated.	Special leucine-poor formula.	All milk—whole, skim, evaporated, condensed, dried, buttermilk. Milk products such as cheese. Foods prepared with milk such as ice cream.
Eggs	None.	None.	Eggs or foods prepared with eggs.
Meat, fish, poultry or cheese	Only as indicated.	Beef, veal, lamb, pork, liver, chicken, turkey.	Any other meat or poultry, sausage, lunch meat, other meat products, except as allowed on individual meal plan. Cheese, fish.
Vegetables	As desired.	Fresh, frozen, canned or juice. Asparagus, green beans, beets, cabbage, carrots, cucumbers, eggplant, onions, pumpkin, squash, tomatoes.	Peas, lima beans, kidney beans, soybeans, lentils, any other vegetables not listed to use. Vegetables prepared with cream sauce or breaded.
Potato or substitute	Only as indicated.	White potato, sweet potato.	Rice, noodles, spaghetti, macaroni.
Fruits	As desired.	Fresh, canned, frozen or juice. Any fruit.	Dried fruits.
Bread	Only as indicated.	White bread.	Any other bread such as whole wheat, rye, special breads, crackers, cornbread, biscuits, etc.
Cereal	Only as indicated.	Cornflakes, cream of rice, pablum rice, shredded wheat.	Any other cereal.
Fats	As desired.	Butter, margarine.	
Desserts	As desired.	Cakes and cookies made without egg, milk or nuts. Sherbet made without milk. Gelatin.	Cakes, cookies, pies, puddings, ice cream. Any desserts made with milk, eggs or nuts.
Miscellaneous	As desired.	Carbonated beverages, jams, jelly, preserves. Sugar (glucose or sucrose).	Nuts.

The foods should be arranged into a meal plan in a way that the prescribed amount of protein will be spaced to avoid an excess of leucine at one time, which would precipitate hypoglycemia. Three meals a day with a prescribed amount of sugar given upon rising, 20 to 30 minutes after breakfast, lunch, and supper and before sleep are necessary. Foods should be given in measured amounts to meet the calculated requirements for the individual child.

*Adapted from Roth, H., and Segal, S.: Dietary management of leucine-sensitive hypoglycemia. Pediatrics 34:831, 1964.

SUCROSE- AND STARCH-FREE DIET

Foods	Foods to Use	Foods to Avoid
Milk	Any.	Milk drinks with sugar. Condensed milk.
Meat or substitute	Beef, pork, veal, lamb, poultry, prepared in any way. Cheese.	Lunch meats, bread dressings.
Eggs	Prepared any way.	None.
Vegetables	Asparagus Eggplant Green beans Kale Wax beans Kohlrabi Broccoli Lettuce Brussels sprouts Mushrooms Cabbage Okra Cauliflower Peppers Celery Parsley Chard Spinach Collards Tomato Cucumbers Watercress	Any other vegetable not listed to use.
Fruits	Any—fresh, dried, canned or frozen—without sugar. Fruit juices—unsweetened.	Sweetened fruits. Sweetened fruit juices. Check labels on can—use only those which say unsweetened or no sugar added.
Breads and cereals	None.	Bread of any kind, crackers, flour, pancakes, waffles, cornbread, biscuits, muffins, bread crumbs, rolls.
Potato or substitute	None.	White potatoes, sweet potatoes, rice, noodles, spaghetti, potato chips, macaroni.
Fats	Any.	Any with flour or sugar added, such as salad dressing.
Miscellaneous	Tea, salt, pepper, herbs, spices, vanilla, lemon, unflavored gelatin, broth, unsweetened pickles.	Carbonated beverages, cornstarch. Any foods with flour or sugar added. Pretzels, popcorn.
Sweets and desserts	Honey, glucose.	White sugar, brown sugar, powdered sugar, candy, jam, jelly, syrup, gum, cake, cookies, pies, jello, doughnuts, marmalade, preserves, ice cream, sherbet, puddings.

Carbohydrate
Content of Foods*

* From Hardinge, M. G., Swarner, J. B., and Crooks, H., J. Am. Dietet. A., 46:198, 1965.

More Common Carbohydrates in Foods per 100 Gm.
Edible Portion

FOOD	Fructose	Glucose	REDUCING SUGARS*	Lactose	Maltose	Sucrose	Cellulose	Dextrins	Hemicellulose	Pectin	Pentosans	Starch
	MONOSACCHARIDES			DISACCHARIDES			POLYSACCHARIDES					
	gm.	*gm.*	*gm.*	*gm.*	*gm.*	*gm.*	*gm.*	*gm.*	*gm.*	*gm.*	*gm.*	*gm.*
Fruits												
Agave juice	17.0		19.0	†								
Apple	5.0	1.7	8.3			3.1	0.4		0.7	0.6		0.6
Apple juice			8.0			4.2						
Apricots	0.4	1.9				5.5	0.8		1.2	1.0		
Banana												
Yellow green			5.0			5.1						8.8
Yellow			8.4			8.9						1.0
Flecked	3.5	4.5				11.9						1.2
Powder			32.6			33.2		9.6				7.8
Blackberries	2.9	3.2				0.2						
Blueberry juice, commercial			9.6			0.2						
Boysenberries			5.3			1.1				0.3		
Breadfruit												
Hawaiian			1.8			7.7						
Samoan			4.9			9.7						
Cherries												
Eating	7.2	4.7	12.5			0.1				0.3		
Cooking	6.1	5.5	11.6			0.1						
Cranberries	0.7	2.7				0.1						
Currants												
Black	3.7	2.4				0.6						
Red	1.9	2.3				0.2						
White	2.6	3.0										
Dates												
Invert sugar, seedling type	23.9	24.9				0.3						
Deglet Noor			16.2			45.4						3.0
Egyptian			35.8			48.5						
Figs, Kadota												
Fresh	8.2	9.6				0.9						0.1
Dried	30.9	42.0				0.1						0.3
Gooseberries	4.1	4.4				0.7						
Grapes												
Black	7.3	8.2										
Concord	4.3	4.8	9.5			0.2						
Malaga			22.2			0.2						
White	8.0	8.1										
Grapefruit	1.2	2.0				2.9					1.3	
Guava			4.4			1.9						
Lemon												
Edible portion			1.3			0.2				3.0	0.7	
Whole	1.4	1.4				0.4						
Juice	0.9	0.5				0.1						
Peel			3.4			0.1						
Loganberries	1.3	1.9				0.2						
Loquat												
Champagne			12.0			0.8						
Thales			9.0			0.9						
Mango			3.4			11.6						0.3
Melon												
Cantaloupe	0.9	1.2	2.3			4.4				0.3		
Cassaba,												
Vine ripened			2.8			6.2						
Picked green			3.2			3.9						
Honeydew												
Vine ripened			3.3			7.4						
Picked green			3.6			3.3						
Yellow	1.5	2.1				1.4						
Mulberries	3.6	4.4										
Orange												
Valencia (Calif.)	2.3	2.4	4.7			4.2						
Composite values	1.8	2.5	5.0			4.6	0.3		0.3	1.3	0.3	
Juice												
Fresh	2.4	2.4	5.1			4.7						
Frozen, reconstituted			4.6			3.2						

FOOD	MONO-SACCHARIDES		REDUC-ING SUGARS*	DISACCHARIDES			POLYSACCHARIDES					
	Fructose	Glucose		Lactose	Maltose	Sucrose	Cellulose	Dextrins	Hemi-Cellulose	Pectin	Pentosans	Starch
FRUITS, continued												
	gm.	gm.	gm.	gm.	gm.	gm.	gm.	gm.	gm.	gm.	gm.	gm.
Palmyra palm, tender kernel	1.5	3.2				0.4						
Papaw (*Asimina triloba*) (North America)			5.9			2.7						
Papaya (*Carica papaya*) (tropics)			9.0			0.5						
Pashion fruit juice	3.6	3.6				3.8						1.8
Peaches	1.6	1.5	3.1			6.6	0.7			0.7		
Pears												
Anjou			7.6			1.9				0.7		
Bartlett	5.0	2.5	8.0			1.5				0.6		
Bosc	6.5	2.6				1.7				0.6		
Persimmon			17.7									
Pineapple												
Ripened on plant	1.4	2.3	4.2			7.9						
Picked green			1.3			2.4						
Plums												
Damson	3.4	5.2	8.4			1.0						
Green Gage	4.0	5.5				2.9						
Italian prunes			4.6			5.4				0.9		
Sweet	2.9	4.5	7.4			4.4		0.5		1.0	0.1	
Sour	1.3	3.5				1.5				1.0		
Pomegranate			12.0			0.6						
Prunes, uncooked	15.0	30.0	47.0			2.0	2.8		10.7	0.9	2.0	0.7
Raisins, Thompson seedless			70.0							1.0		
Raspberries	2.4	2.3	5.0			1.0				0.8		
Sapote	3.8	4.2		0.7								
Strawberries												
Ripe	2.3	2.6				1.4						
Medium ripe			3.8			0.3						
Tangerine			4.8			9.0						
Tomatoes	1.2	1.6	3.4				0.2		0.3	0.3		
Canned			3.0			0.3						
Seedless pulp			6.5			0.4	0.4			0.5		
Watermelon												
Flesh red and firm, ripe			3.8			4.0				0.1		
Red, mealy, overripe			3.0			4.9				0.1		
Vegetables												
Asparagus, raw			1.2						0.3			
Bamboo shoots			0.5			0.2	1.2					
Beans												
Lima												
Canned						1.4						
Fresh						1.4						
Snap, fresh			1.7			0.5	0.5	0.3	1.0	0.5	1.2	2.0
Beets, sugar						12.9	0.9		0.8			
Broccoli							0.9		0.9		0.9	1.3
Brussel Sprouts							1.1		1.5			
Cabbage, raw			3.4			0.3	0.8		1.0			
Carrots, raw			5.8			1.7	1.0		1.7	0.9		
Cauliflower		2.8				0.3	0.7		0.6			
Celery												
Fresh			0.3			0.3						
Hearts			1.7			0.2						
Corn												
Fresh		0.5				0.3	0.6	0.1	0.9		1.3	14.5
Bran									77.1		4.0	
Cucumber			2.5			0.1						
Eggplant			2.1			0.6			0.5			
Lettuce			1.4			0.2	0.4		0.6			
Licorice root		1.4				3.2						22.0
Mushrooms, fresh			0.1				0.9		0.7			2.5
Onions, raw			5.4			2.9			0.3	0.6		
Parsnips, fresh						3.5						7.0
Peas, green						5.5	1.1		2.2			4.1

FOOD	MONO-SACCHARIDES		REDUC-ING SUGARS*	DISACCHARIDES			POLYSACCHARIDES					
	Fructose	Glucose		Lactose	Maltose	Sucrose	Cellulose	Dextrins	Hemi-Cellulose	Pectin	Pentosans	Starch
VEGETABLES, continued												
	gm.	gm.	gm.	gm.	gm.	gm.	gm.	gm.	gm.	gm.	gm.	gm.
Potatoes, white	0.1	0.1	0.8			0.1	0.4		0.3			17.0
Pumpkin			2.2			0.6			0.5			0.1
Radishes			3.1			0.3			0.3	0.4		
Rutabagas		5.0				1.3					0.8	
Spinach			0.2				0.4		0.8			
Squash												
Butternut	0.2	0.1				0.4						2.6
Blue Hubbard	1.2	1.1				0.4	0.7					4.8
Golden Crookneck			2.8			1.0						
Sweet potato												
Raw	0.3	0.4	0.8	1.6		4.1	0.6		1.4	2.2		16.5
Baked			14.5			7.2						4.0
Mature Dry Legumes												
Beans												
Mung												
Black gram						1.6						
Green gram						1.8						
Navy							3.1	3.7	6.4		8.2	35.2
Soy			1.6			7.2	2.6	1.4	6.6		4.0	1.9
Cow pea						1.5	5.4		4.8			
Garbanzo (chick peas)						2.4						
Garden pea (*Pisum sativum*)‡						6.7		5.0				38.0
Horse gram (*Dolichos biplorus*)						2.7						
Lentils						2.1			5.1			28.5
Pigeon pea (red gram)						1.6						
Soybean												
Flour						6.8						
Meal						6.8						
Milk and Milk Products												
Buttermilk												
Dry				39.9								
Fluid, genuine and cultured				5.0								
Casein		0.1		4.9								
Ice cream (14.5% cream)				3.6		16.6						
Milk												
Ass				6.0								
Cow				4.9								
Dried												
Skim				52.0								
Whole				38.1								
Fluid												
Skim				5.0								
Whole				4.9								
Sweetened, condensed				14.1		43.5						
Ewe				4.9								
Goat				4.7								
Human												
Colostrum				5.3								
Mature				6.9								
Whey				4.9								
Yogurt				3.8								
Nuts and Nut Products												
Almonds, blanched			0.2			2.3					2.1	
Chestnuts			2.2			3.6					1.2	18.0
Virginia			1.2			8.1		0.3			2.8	18.6
French			3.3			3.6					2.5	33.1
Coconut milk, ripe						2.6						
Copra meal, dried	1.2	1.2				14.3	15.6	0.6			2.2	0.9
Macadamia nut			0.3			5.5						

FOOD	MONOSACCHARIDES		REDUCING SUGARS*	DISACCHARIDES			POLYSACCHARIDES					
	Fructose	Glucose		Lactose	Maltose	Sucrose	Cellulose	Dextrins	Hemicellulose	Pectin	Pentosans	Starch
Nuts and Nut Products, continued												
	gm.	gm.	gm.	gm.	gm.	gm.	gm.	gm.	gm.	gm.	gm.	gm.
Peanuts			0.2			4.5	2.4	2.5	3.8			4.0
Peanut butter			0.9									5.9
Pecans						1.1					0.2	
Cereals and Cereal Products												
Barley												
Grain, hulled							2.6		6.0		8.5	62.0
Flour						3.1					1.2	69.0
Corn, yellow						4.5			4.9		6.2	62.0
Flaxseed						1.8			5.2			
Millet grain									0.9		6.5	56.0
Oats, hulled											6.4	56.4
Rice												
Bran			1.4			10.6	11.4		7.0		7.4	
Brown, raw			0.1			0.8		2.1			2.1	69.7
Polished, raw		2.0	trace#			0.4	0.3	0.9			1.8	72.9
Polish			0.7								3.8	
Rye												
Grain						3.8			5.6		6.8	57.0
Flour											4.1	71.4
Sorghum grain											2.5	70.2
Soya-wheat (cereal)											3.3	46.4
Wheat												
Germ, defatted						8.3					6.2	
Grain			2.0			1.5	2.0	2.5	5.8		6.6	59.0
Flour, patent			2.0		0.1	0.2		5.5			2.1	68.8
Spices and Condiments												
Allspice (pimenta)			18.0			3.0						
Cassia			23.3									
Cinnamon			19.3									
Cloves			9.0									2.7
Nutmeg			17.2									14.6
Pepper, black			38.6									34.2
Sirups and Other Sweets												
Corn sirup		21.2				26.4		34.7				
High conversion		33.0				23.0		19.0				
Medium conversion		26.0				21.0		23.0				
Corn sugar		87.5				3.5		0.5				
Chocolate, sweet dry						56.4						
Golden sirup			37.5			31.0						
Honey	40.5	34.2				1.9		1.5				
Invert sugar			74.0			6.0						
Jellies, pectin						40-65						
Royal jelly	11.3	9.8				0.9						
Jellies, starch						25-60						7=12
Maple sirup			1.5			62.9						
Milk chocolate				8.1		43.0						
Molasses	8.0	8.8				53.6						
Blackstrap	6.8	6.8	26.9			36.9						
Sorghum sirup			27.0			36.0						
Miscellaneous												
Beer			1.5					2.8			0.3	
Cacao beans, raw, Arriba	0.6	0.5	1.1			1.9						
Carob bean												
Pod			11.2			23.2				1.4		
Pod and seeds			11.1			19.4						
Soy sauce	0.9											

*Mainly monosaccharides plus the disaccharides, maltose and lactose.
†Blanks indicate lack of acceptable data.
‡Also known as Alaska pea, field pea, and common pea.
#Trace = less than 0.05 gm.

Index

Note: *Italicized* page numbers refer to illustrations.